Growth and Institutions in African Development

Recent years have seen a sustained research effort exploring the African development experience. The extant literature has offered a large set of explanations as to why the African development record has lagged behind that of other regions of the developing world. This new volume brings international contributors together to focus on the role of growth and institutions.

First, it provides brief evidence on the growth and institutional records, as well as on development outcomes, during the post-independence period. Second, it targets certain growth determinants, including industrial embeddedness, innovation, exchange rate regimes and environmental quality. Third, it sheds light on the dynamics and distribution of growth, and on growth-enhancing sectors of the economy. Finally, it investigates several issues of institutional development, as well as institutions generating development outcomes.

Though focused on these two key areas, the coverage strives to achieve a comprehensive analysis of how Africa's development may have been enhanced or undermined and to offer lessons for the future. This volume is essential reading for all scholars of development economics and development studies.

Augustin K. Fosu is Professor of Economics at the University of Ghana, Ghana, and Extraordinary Professor at the Faculty of Economic and Management Sciences, University of Pretoria, South Africa. He is also Research Associate, Centre for the Study of African Economies (CSAE), University of Oxford, UK, and was Deputy Director of UN University-WIDER, Finland (2006–2013).

Routledge studies in development economics

For a full list of titles in this series, please visit www.routledge.com.

'This volume throws new light on the factors that have contributed to the relatively inclusive growth pattern presently prevailing in Africa. The resurgence of growth in the last fifteen years, following a long period of stagnation, appears to be linked to major improvements in governance and economic freedom. In particular, the role of institutions is crucial to the current growth and development phase. A contribution of this book is to provide specific examples of successful developmental institutions in different African countries.'

Erik Thorbecke, Professor of Economics at Cornell University,
College of Human Ecology, USA.

'This volume contributes to a much better and broader understanding of growth and development in Africa. It gives a key role to institutions, but also pays attention to bottlenecks – such as lack of absorptive capacity and innovation and to issues as health and poverty.'

Rick van der Ploeg, Professor of Economics
at the University of Oxford, UK.

Growth and Institutions in African Development

Edited by
Augustin K. Fosu

A study prepared by the United Nations University World
Institute for Development Economics – UNU-WIDER

Routledge
Taylor & Francis Group

LONDON AND NEW YORK

First published 2015 by Routledge

2 Park Square, Milton Park, Abingdon, Oxfordshire OX14 4RN
52 Vanderbilt Avenue, New York, NY 10017

Routledge is an imprint of the Taylor & Francis Group, an informa business

First issued in paperback 2018

British Library Cataloguing in Publication Data
A catalogue record for this book is available from the British Library

Library of Congress Cataloging in Publication Data
  Growth and institutions in African development / [edited by]
  Augustin K. Fosu.
    pages cm
  Includes bibliographical references and index.
  1. Economic development–Africa. 2. Institution building–Africa.
  3. Africa–Economic conditions. 4. Africa–Social conditions.
  I. Fosu, Augustin Kwasi.
  HC800.G764 2015
  338.96–dc23   2014040037

ISBN: 978-1-138-81677-0 (hbk)
ISBN: 978-0-367-10972-1 (pbk)

Typeset in Times New Roman
by Sunrise Setting Ltd, Paignton, UK

United Nations University World Institute for Development Economics Research (UNU-WIDER) was established by the United Nations University as its first research and training centre and started work in Helsinki, Finland, in 1985. The purpose of the institute is to undertake applied research and policy analysis on structural changes affecting developing and transitional economies, to provide a forum for the advocacy of policies leading to robust, equitable, and environmentally sustainable growth, and to promote capacity strengthening and training in the field of economic and social policy-making. Its work is carried out by staff researchers and visiting scholars in Helsinki and via networks of collaborating scholars and institutions around the world.

UNU-WIDER
Katajanokanlaituri 6 B, 00160 Helsinki, Finland
www.wider.unu.edu

Contents

Figures

Tables

Contributors

Julius A. Agbor is a Research Fellow at the Department of Economics, Stellenbosch University, South Africa. He was formerly a Research Fellow at the Africa Growth Initiative at the Brookings Institution, Washington DC.

Jorge Arbache is a Professor of Economics at the University of Brasilia. From 2010–2014 he was Senior Economic Advisor to the President of the Brazilian Development Bank (BNDES). Prior to that he was Senior Economist in the World Bank's Office of the Chief Economist, Africa Region, where he led many editions of the Africa Development Indicators.

Sonia Bhalotra is Professor of Economics at the University of Essex and was previously Professor of Economics at the University of Bristol. She obtained an MPhil and PhD from the University of Oxford and a BSc (Hons) from the University of Delhi. She is a member of the Council of the European Society of Population Economics, the International Review Panel of the Danish Council for Independent Research, the Advisory Board (inaugural member) of Academics Stand Against Poverty (Yale) and the British Academy Area Panel for South Asia.

Alassane Drabo is a researcher at the Foundation for Studies and Research on International Development at the University of Auvergne. He has a Bachelor's degree from the University of Ouagadougou, Burkina Faso, as well as a Master's degree and a PhD in economics from the Centre for Studies and Research on International Development, University of Auvergne.

Marguerite Duponchel is a country economist for the International Growth Centre in Uganda. Previously, she worked for the World Bank's Research Development Group, for the University of Witwatersrand in South Africa, for UNDP and for UNHCR. She holds a PhD in economics from the University of Paris 1 Pantheon-Sorbonne.

Augustin K. Fosu is Professor, Institute of Statistical, Social and Economic Research (ISSER) at the University of Ghana, Ghana; Extraordinary Professor, Faculty of Economic and Management Sciences, University of Pretoria, South Africa; and Research Associate, Centre for the Study of African Economies, University of Oxford, UK. He was previously Deputy Director at UNU-WIDER, Helsinki, Finland.

Rosalia de la Cruz Gitau is an attorney and currently works for the United Nations Office for the Co-ordination of Humanitarian Affairs in Senegal. She was a Human Rights Fellow for the Center for Human Rights and Global Justice at the Liberian Truth and Reconciliation Commission in Monrovia, Liberia, in 2007. She received her Juris Doctor degree from New York University School of Law and her Master's in public policy from the London School of Economics and Political Science.

Thierry Kangoye is an economist at the Development Research Department of the African Development Bank. He graduated from the Clermont School of Economics at the University of Auvergne (France), from where he received a PhD in development economics.

Abdelrasaq Na-Allah is Head of the Department of Economics and Development Studies at the Federal University, Dutsin-Ma, Nigeria. He is also an Associate of the Institute for Economics Research on Innovation, Tshwane University of Technology Pretoria, South Africa.

Eric Kehinde Ogunleye is an open-economy macroeconomist affiliated with the African Development Bank Nigeria Country Office. He was a Special Assistant to the President of Nigeria on international trade and finance, and previously worked with the African Centre for Economic Transformation in Ghana. He holds a Bachelor's degree in economics from the University of Calabar and a PhD in Economics from the University of Ibadan.

Mawussé K.N. Okey is Assistant Professor of Economics at University of Lomé, Togo, and a researcher at the Center for Research and Training in Economics and Management (CERFEG).

Steve Onyeiwu is a Professor of Economics at Allegheny College, Meadville, USA. He received his PhD from the University of Connecticut, and has taught at Wesleyan University, Rensselaer Polytechnic Institute, Trinity College and the University of Port Harcourt, Nigeria.

Kesseven Padachi is an Associate Professor at the University of Technology, Mauritius. He holds a PhD in small business finance and he has recently been appointed as Chapter Secretary–Finance for the Mauritius Chapter of the Organization for Social Science Research in Eastern and Southern Africa.

John Page is a Senior Fellow in the Global Economy and Development Program at the Brookings Institution in Washington DC, and a non-resident Senior Fellow of the World Institute for Development Economics Research (UNU-WIDER). He is the author of several books and numerous published papers in the field of economic development.

Mahvash Saeed Qureshi is a Senior Economist in the Research Department of the International Monetary Fund, Washington DC, USA. She holds an MPhil and PhD in economics from Trinity College, University of Cambridge, UK.

Sawkut Rojid is a trade economist with the World Bank in Mauritius and has worked extensively in the sub-Saharan Africa region. He has published a number of academic and policy research papers and contributed to a number of books.

Boopen Seetanah is an Associate Professor at the University of Mauritius and is also the Co-Chair of the WTO Chair Programme in Mauritius. He is a consultant to a number of domestic and international organizations in the field of tourism, trade, development and financial economics.

Fiona Tregenna is a Professor in the Department of Economics and Econometrics at the University of Johannesburg. She holds a PhD in economics from the University of Cambridge and a Master's degree in economics from the University of Massachusetts (Amherst).

Charalambos G. Tsangarides is a Senior Economist in the Research Department at the International Monetary Fund, Washington DC, USA. He holds graduate degrees from the American University and George Washington University, Washington DC, and from Johns Hopkins University, Baltimore, USA.

Marcela Umaña-Aponte holds a PhD in economics and an MSc in economics and econometrics from the University of Bristol. She has been Senior Economic Adviser of the Colombian Government and has worked as international consultant on a range of fields such as impact evaluation, social networks and responsible finance.

Foreword

Existing research on Africa has produced a seemingly endless list of reasons why Africa's growth and poverty reduction records have lagged behind that of other regions of the developing world. These much-cited explanations more often than not include: conflicts, inadequate levels and poor use of foreign aid, bad policy environments, poorly performing institutions, limited export supply response capacities, a lack of physical infrastructure, poor political leadership and corruption, a lack of fiscal discipline, low levels of human capital, drought and other adverse climatic problems, brain drain, ineffective structural adjustment programmes, limited membership in international networks, and inadequate levels of foreign direct investment.

To take an in-depth examination of the compounded situation, UNU-WIDER launched a multidisciplinary research project entitled 'African Development: Myths and Realities', to focus on a subset of these explanations in an attempt to distil myths and realities in the light of current knowledge. This book is a major component of the research output, focusing on two related subject areas – growth and institutions.

I heartily thank Augustin Kwasi Fosu – the UNU-WIDER focal point, who brought together a select research team to undertake the various studies within their respective areas of academic expertise – for co-ordinating the research work and editing this comprehensive collection of studies for our further education on a multifaceted subject.

Finn Tarp, Director
UNU-WIDER, Helsinki
August 2014

Acknowledgements

I am extremely grateful to the entire UNU-WIDER staff for their excellent support towards the successful execution of the project, 'African Development: Myths and Realities', from which the current book emanates. Lisa Winkler, the project assistant, was indispensable in the project implementation. I would like to additionally thank her, as well as Lesley Ellen, for the careful editing of the book chapters. As the publishing assistant, Lorraine Telfer-Taivainen diligently oversaw the review and publication process; I am most grateful for her invaluable assistance.

I would like to also gratefully acknowledge the comprehensive reviews of several anonymous referees, which significantly improved the manuscript's quality. In addition, I am grateful for the opportunity to complete my book chapter while at the Africa Tax Institute, the Faculty of Economic and Management Sciences, at the University of Pretoria, South Africa.

I am indebted to the former UNU-WIDER director, Tony Shorrocks – under whose leadership the project was conceived and implemented – for his valuable advice and guidance. Finally, I wish to express my sincere gratitude to the current UNU-WIDER director, Finn Tarp, for his understanding and forbearance at the editing and publishing stage.

Augustin K. Fosu
Accra, August, 2014

1 Growth and institutions in African development

Augustin K. Fosu

Introduction

More is known about the African development experience than ever before, due mainly to the sustained research effort over many years. The extant literature has offered a large set of explanations of why African growth and development generally appears to have historically lagged behind that of other regions of the developing world (Sachs and Warner 1997; Collier and Gunning 1999; Azam *et al.* 2002; Ndulu *et al.* 2008a, 2008b). These explanations include: conflicts; inadequate levels and poor use of foreign aid; bad policy environments; poorly performing institutions; limited export supply response capacities; a lack of physical infrastructure; poor political leadership and corruption; a lack of fiscal discipline; low levels of human capital; drought and other adverse climatic problems; brain and talent drains; ineffective structural adjustment programs; limited membership in international networks; and inadequate levels of foreign direct investment. The United Nations University World Institute for Development Economic Research (UNU-WIDER) project 'African Development: Myths and Realities' has sought to focus on a subset of these explanations, in an attempt to distil 'myths' and 'realities' in the light of current knowledge. The present volume focuses on two related subject areas: growth and institutions.

In this chapter, I first present evidence on how African countries as a whole have performed on growth and institutions during post-independence. Next is information on trends in development outcomes in the region. Finally, I present an overview of the chapters covered in the current book. The coverage of the book strives to provide a comprehensive analysis of how Africa's development may have been enhanced or undermined, with specific reference to growth and institutions. By so doing, the book is able to draw important lessons for the future.

Growth, institutions and development outcomes

Growth

It is now well accepted that economic growth is a critical element for development. For example, growth has been the main engine for poverty reduction globally

(Dollar and Kraay 2002; Fosu 2011). This finding is corroborated for African economies also (Fosu 2014). Furthermore, growth is found to provide the major explanation for improvements in human development in African countries (Fosu 2002, 2004). Thus there is a need for re-emphasizing economic growth in the African region, consistent with the general extant literature.

There is solid evidence of growth resurgence in African countries, especially since the mid-1990s. As Figure 1.1 shows, the gross domestic product (GDP) growth of sub-Saharan Africa (SSA)[1] has resurged and trended upwards since the dismal performance in the 19080s and early 1990s. Furthermore, since 2002 Africa's growth has exceeded the world's, which must happen if the region is to catch up with the rest of the world (ROW).

On a per capita basis, however, the recent economic growth resurgence does not appear as impressive (Figure 1.2), bringing into focus the need to limit population growth to more reasonable levels. We could, of course, await the more natural demographic transition as incomes grow, but that process may take much too long. Besides, unless productivity continues to rise sustainably in the region, via increased adoption of technology for instance, this transition may be quite far off, and any economic catch-up could be much delayed.

As in ROW, Africa's growth unfortunately turned substantially downward during the recent economic crisis of 2008–2009: 'SSA's GDP growth fell by over 60 per cent between 2007 and 2009' (Fosu 2013a: 1102). However, along with ROW, the region has recovered reasonably well. Indeed, Africa has demonstrated resilience relative to ROW during this crisis and better than any other time during post-independence. Such resilience is attributed in significant part to improvements in governance and/or institutions (Fosu 2013a). Continued attention must, therefore, also be paid to institutions going forward.

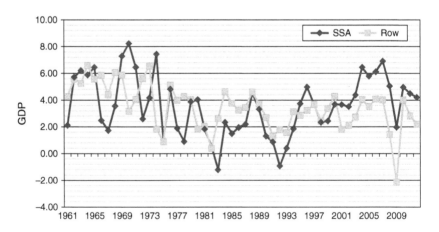

Figure 1.1 Gross domestic product (GDP) percentage annual growth for sub-Saharan Africa (SSA) compared with the rest of the world (ROW) 1961–2012

Source: Based on World Bank 2013a.

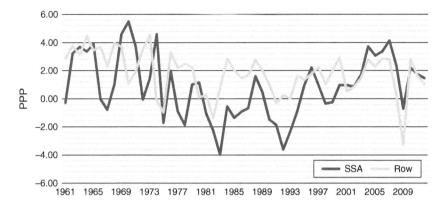

Figure 1.2 Per capita gross domestic product annual growth for sub-Saharan Africa (SSA) compared with the rest of the world (ROW) 1961–2012

Source: Based on World Bank 2013a.

Institutions

The role of institutions in development has become increasingly prominent in the literature. For example, the Washington Consensus that formed the basis for economic reforms in many African countries is often faulted for not having incorporated institutional reforms. This criticism led to subsequent modifications, resulting in the 'second-generation' reforms. Rodrik (2006, Table 1) for instance proposed the 'augmented Washington Consensus' to prominently include institutional measures. In his seminal work, North (1990) showed the dynamic importance of institutions in economic performance. Indeed, the new institutional economics (NIE) projects the supremacy of institutions over most impediments to development (Rodrik *et al.* 2004; Acemoglu *et al.* 2005; see Haggard *et al.* 2008 for an extensive review). Consistent with the NIE, Bates *et al.* (2013) find that recent institutional development in Africa has significantly contributed to the improved performance of African economies.

And, in a major research project undertaken by the African Economic Research Consortium (AERC), institutions receive considerable attention in explaining the growth performance of African economies. It attributes in large part the poor growth in the 1980s and early 1990s to weak institutions, and conversely the growth resurgence more recently to improved institutions (Ndulu *et al.* 2008a, 2008b).

For example, economic freedom (EF) as a measure of economic governance has improved appreciably (Figure 1.3), from a value of 4.5 in 1980 to 6.2 in 2010 (range: 0–10),[2] with positive implications for economic growth (Haan and Sturm 2000). As an indicator of political governance, the index of electoral competitiveness (IEC) has risen considerably (Figure 1.4), from 3.3 in 1980 to 5.9 in 2010 (range: 1–7). Unlike EF, however, the IEC gap with ROW seems to have virtually

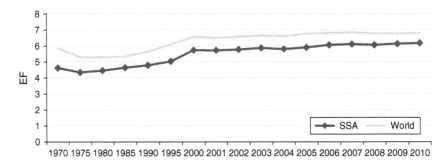

Figure 1.3 Comparison between economic freedom (EF) in sub-Saharan Africa (SSA) and the rest of the world (ROW) 1975–2010

Source: Based on Gwartney *et al*. 2012.

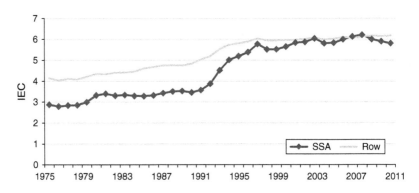

Figure 1.4 Index of electoral competitiveness (IEC)

Source: Based on World Bank (2013c).

closed. At a sufficiently high level of IEC, furthermore, a country could be viewed as having attained growth-enhancing 'advanced-level democracy'[3] (Fosu 2008).

Similarly, the degree of constraint on the executive branch of government (XCONST)[4] has increased steadily more recently (Figure 1.5). XCONST began to accelerate in SSA around 1990; the gap with ROW had narrowed substantially by 2000, although it remains significant and little changed since then. Indeed, the gap in 2012 was the same as that in 1975, when the data was first available. At 0.9, that constitutes the narrowest gap over the entire period of 1975–2012, however. The widest gap occurred in 1989, which was double that in 2012. Thus it is worth emphasizing that Africa has indeed made considerable progress on executive constraint since the late 1980s.

But why is XCONST important as an institutional variable? According to Fosu (2013b), XCONST can accentuate the likelihood of a 'syndrome-free' (SF) regime,[5] independently or by mitigating the potentially pernicious effect of ethnicity.

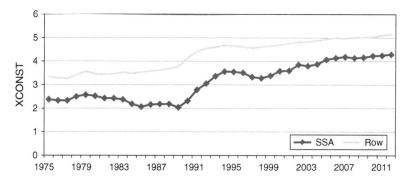

Figure 1.5 Executive constraint (XCONST)

Source: Based on Polity IV Project (2013).

Further, SF is necessary for sustaining growth and is 'virtually a sufficient condition for avoiding short-run growth collapses' (Fosu and O'Connell 2006: 31). Moreover, growth collapses have historically reduced Africa's annual per capita GDP growth by about 1 percentage point (Arbache and Page 2007). This amount is not paltry, given that the growth averaged 0.5 per cent for African economies during 1960–2000, and the growth gap with ROW was roughly 1 percentage point (Fosu 2010d). Thus avoiding growth collapses is quite crucial, and XCONST appears to constitute an important antidote in that regard. Hence, improving political governance by raising XCONST should accentuate SSA's growth sustainability.

The evidence then supports the view that institutions have improved in Africa in recent periods. Furthermore, the improvement appears to have supported increased growth. But has that growth also been transformed to improved development outcomes? I take up this issue next.

Development outcomes

Consistent with the above growth evidence, per capita purchasing power parity (PPP)-adjusted GDP stagnated during the 1980s and early 1990s, but has risen considerably since then (Figure 1.6). Indeed, GDP per capita rose by nearly 60 per cent, from 1,192 PPP-adjusted 2005 international dollars (PPP$) in 1996 to PPP$1,884 in 2012.

Furthermore, human development appears to have accelerated between 2000 and 2010, compared with the previous decade (Figure 1.7). The human development index rose by 0.063 between 2000 and 2010, 3.5 times its rise between 1990 and 2000. Nonetheless, the 2012 value is still a little below the medium human development value of 0.500.

In addition, poverty has been diminishing in SSA since the mid-1990s (Figure 1.8). This evidence suggests that the growth resurgence has been generally inclusive, though better progress on poverty is called for. Decomposing the

Figure 1.6 Sub-Saharan Africa's (SSA) mean per capita GDP (PPP) (constant: 2005 US$) 1960–2012

Source: World Bank 2013a.

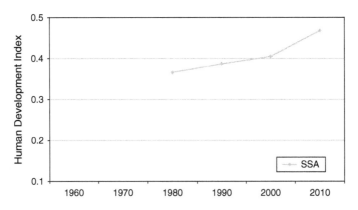

Figure 1.7 Sub-Saharan Africa's (SSA) Human Development Index 1980–2010

Source: Based on UNDP 2013.

poverty reduction into growth and inequality changes, Fosu (2014) finds, furthermore, that income growth is responsible for the lion's share of the progress, consistent with the global evidence (Dollar and Kraay 2002). Unfortunately, the responsiveness of poverty to growth or changes in inequality tends to be small in SSA compared with that of ROW (Fosu 2009, 2010c), suggesting that even greater efforts are required for progress on poverty. One of the impediments is the relatively high level of inequality (Fosu 2010a, 2010b); another, the low level of income (Fosu 2014).

Meeting the challenge of improving development outcomes, then, would probably entail the need to pay greater attention to the initial level of poverty itself (Ravallion 2012). That might in turn require certain social-protection programs

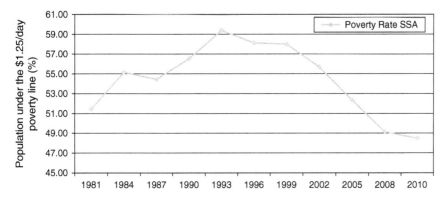

Figure 1.8 Sub-Saharan Africa's (SSA) poverty picture, headcount ratio (per cent) ($1.25)
1981–2010

Source: Based on World Bank 2013b.

that could reduce inequality while raising the level of income of the poor
(Thorbecke 2013). In the final analysis, therefore, the roles of growth and institutions cannot be minimized if the efforts in this regard are to be successful.

Overview

The book's coverage comprises two main subject areas, with each area further
divided into two parts:

1 Growth:

    (i) growth determinants: industrial embeddedness, innovation, exchange-rate
        regimes and environmental quality; and
    (ii) sectors, dynamics and distribution of growth.

2 Institutions:

    (i) institutional development; and
    (ii) institutions and development outcomes.

Growth

*Growth determinants: industrial embeddedness, innovation,
exchange rate regimes and environmental quality*

DETERMINANTS OF INDUSTRIAL EMBEDDEDNESS

By enhancing the interconnectedness of manufacturing, 'industrial embeddedness' –
the extent of manufacturing establishments' linkage with local sources of input

supply – constitutes a crucial determinant of long-term growth. Using detailed data on manufacturing firms in Lesotho, Na-Allah (this volume) uncovers that the inability of local producers to fill large orders was the main rationale for limited embeddedness. This inability can be traced to the limited availability of domestic suppliers and their inadequate competence to fill large orders, as well as to their relatively weak international competitiveness. Thus significant attention should be accorded to improving such supply-side factors, in order to enhance the backward linkage to manufacturing.

DOES THE LACK OF INNOVATION AND ABSORPTIVE CAPACITY RETARD ECONOMIC GROWTH?

Historically, manufacturing has constituted the main pillar of economic transformation, diversifying many economies and fostering sustained growth and development. In today's knowledge-based economies, however, innovation involving new technologies and absorptive capacity is likely to be particularly consequential for growth. Indeed, certain scholars strongly argue that capability development was crucial for the economic development of East Asian countries such as South Korea (Lee 2013).

With the share of information and communication technology (ICT) goods in imports as a measure of innovation and absorptive capacity, Onyeiwu (this volume) finds that countries with higher levels of ICT tend to grow faster. This finding probably reflects the ability of ICT to improve resource utilization (absorptive capacity) and to raise total factor productivity. The result provides further justification for African countries, in particular, to strive to further improve their attractiveness to ICT technology.

EXCHANGE-RATE REGIMES AND TRADE

African economies have come a long way from the period of domestic currency overvaluation, which was such a huge culprit for the dismal growth record (Sachs and Warner 1997). A key element of the economic reforms pursued by many of these countries since the 1980s is foreign-exchange liberalization, which eliminated currency controls and resulted in floating exchange-rate systems. While such foreign-exchange flexibility helps to prevent overvaluation, it nonetheless introduces volatility that can adversely affect trade, with adverse implications for growth.

Yet, the empirical investigation by Qureshi and Tsangarides (this volume) finds that a fixed exchange-rate regime significantly promotes bilateral trade. They attribute this finding to the ability of such a regime to minimize exchange-rate volatility and to reduce transaction costs. The authors further observe that if some flexibility is required, then pegging the currency to a foreign currency, relative to maintaining a fully flexible exchange-rate regime, would be trade-enhancing. The caution here, however, is that returning to fixed exchange rates might revert to overvaluation of the domestic currency that historically proved so deleterious to African economies (Sachs and Warner 1997). Furthermore, even a peg could also lead to overvaluation, as was the case with the CFA franc zone, hampering growth of these economies and requiring a major devaluation in 1994 (Fosu 2012: 192). An appropriate conclusion here, then, is that while a fixed exchange-rate regime, or a peg, might improve bilateral trade by removing volatility, one must balance this potential benefit against the increased downside risk of currency overvaluation with adverse economic growth consequences.

INTERRELATIONSHIP BETWEEN HEALTH, ENVIRONMENTAL QUALITY
AND ECONOMIC ACTIVITY

The pervasive view in the literature is that there is a trade-off between economic growth and the environment, especially for developing economies. For example, rapid growth may require the use of the cheapest input, such as coal, which is among the least environment-friendly fuels. Developing countries, therefore, tend to be on the increasing portion of the income–environmental-degradation Kuznets inverted-U curve. For this reason, these countries are usually reluctant to accept environmental regulations.

Taking health into account in a simultaneous model involving panel data on some 117 developed and developing countries, however, Drabo (this volume) uncovers no such trade-off. Instead, the study finds that *higher* levels of environmental quality are associated with *higher* GDP growth levels. The main rationale for this finding is that environmental degradation tends to lower the quality of health, which in turn reduces economic growth. Thus, African countries should be particularly mindful of the environmental impact of their development actions, especially as related to the health of their citizenry.

Growth sectors, dynamics and distribution

EMERGING EVIDENCE ON THE RELATIVE IMPORTANCE OF SECTORAL
SOURCES OF GROWTH

What is the leading sector in African economies? Historically, agriculture has been so identified. Ogunleye (this volume), however, finds that since the 1980s service has become the leading sector in SSA. This result occurs in large part because this sector has seen a significant shift in employment towards the upper end, led by the telecommunications subsector, thanks in large part to major developments in ICT. Hence, while agriculture remains important (indeed, Ogunleye places this sector as second in importance), efforts must be directed toward facilitating the operation of especially the high-valued segment of the service sector. In particular, and consistent with Onyeiwu (this volume), the subsector's high potential to raise productivity across all sectors of the economy implies that ICT should be accorded a disproportionately significant priority.

TOURISM AND ECONOMIC GROWTH

Tourism is among the key subsectors contributing to the rise of service as a leading sector in Africa (Ogunleye, this volume). Seetanah *et al.* (this volume) specifically explore the extent to which tourism affects economic growth, based on a 1990–2006 panel of 40 African countries. They find that the sector significantly promotes economic growth and that the relationship is reinforcing, since growth conversely raises tourism. The fundamental causes of tourism, in turn, include private investment, openness and human capital. Thus strategically investing in tourism, by providing significant attention to these fundamental factors, should yield growth dividends for many African countries.

HUNTING FOR LEOPARDS: LONG-TERM COUNTRY INCOME DYNAMICS IN AFRICA

Conducting country-level dynamics of long-term growth is crucial if we are to understand the upward mobility of African economies from low towards middle-income status. How does the growth trajectory differ among African countries? In particular, which countries have transitioned into 'leopards', the regional equivalent of the Asian 'tigers'? And, what can we learn from these countries? Arbache and Page (this volume) provide some answers. Among their findings are:

- Growth has been low and quite volatile across Africa; however, this finding is not restricted to any specific economic or geographic attributes.
- Growth has accelerated since the mid-1990s, with an increasing number of countries experiencing more frequent growth accelerations.
- There is some evidence of incipient convergence of growth rates, but not of incomes; the latter finding indicates significant country-level inertia.
- Indeed, the cross-country distribution of income is becoming less equal; although the poor countries have been growing faster more recently, the rich countries are growing even faster, with the consequence that income clubs by country are becoming increasingly distinct.
- Only a small number of countries seem to be emerging as possible leopards, but there is uncertainty about their durability, and most of these are resource-rich economies.

HALVING POVERTY IN SOUTH AFRICA: GROWTH AND DISTRIBUTIONAL ASPECT

Achieving the United Nations 2000 millennium development goals (MDGs) has been a preoccupation of many African countries. The most important MDG is arguably MDG1: halving poverty by 2015, from its level in 1990. Might economic growth alone achieve this goal? As the extant literature amply demonstrates, the role of inequality in reducing poverty cannot be underestimated, though the impact differs considerably across regions globally (Fosu, 2010c). Furthermore, South Africa is among the most unequal countries in Africa, suggesting that the poverty-decreasing effect of growth might be minimal (Fosu, 2009, 2010a, 2010b, 2010c, 2014). Nonetheless, using the $2.00 poverty line, Tregenna (this volume) finds that achieving MDG1 is feasible for South Africa, provided the country maintains moderate growth rates and a slight pro-poor improvement in income distribution.

As many African countries are off track in their quest to meet MDG1, the South African case study is instructive, despite the fact that the country's much higher average income might facilitate its ability to meet MDG1 (Fosu 2014). Indeed, South Africa reduced the $1.25 headcount poverty rate from 24.3 per cent in 1993 to 13.8 per cent in 2008, despite the rise of its Gini coefficient from 59.3 per cent to 63.1 per cent over the same period (World Bank 2013b). Thus, the country has virtually achieved MDG1, notwithstanding South Africa's relatively large and increasing levels of inequality. This evidence then seems to bolster the view that growth, relative to income distribution, should constitute the primary policy instrument for poverty reduction (Dollar and Kraay 2002), and even more so for African economies generally, notwithstanding country-specific fixed effects (Fosu 2009). For a higher poverty line, though, it appears from the Tregenna evidence that growth inclusiveness is crucial for further significant progress on poverty in South Africa.

Institutions

Institutional development

OUTFITS: NARROWLY TAILORED LAWS THAT HARM INSTEAD OF HELP

Telecommunications represents an expanding and potentially dynamic sector, with significant positive implications for economic growth and employment creation across the African continent. In particular, the legal framework for attracting foreign investment is crucial in terms of maximizing the expected benefits for a given African economy. A particularly important aspect is the set of laws governing the operation of telecommunications.

Gitau (this volume) provides a case study of Liberia's telecommunications to demonstrate how the laws governing the sector's operation may have been detrimental to local actors. For example, these laws have tended to: (1) delegitimize the informal economy and, thus, hurt the country's development goals; (2) preserve rather than reduce the monopolistic tendencies of Liberia's telecommunications sector; and (3) harbour provisions that avail unnecessary discretion in the application of laws that can be abused to the detriment of domestic agents. As heretofore observed, providing an attractive environment for ICTs constitutes an important policy imperative. Nonetheless, consistent with Gitau's findings, caution must be exercised by the institutional reformers, in order to avoid these potential pitfalls in their quest to draft laws governing the sector.

DOES FOREIGN AID PROMOTE DEMOCRACY?

Much of the literature has focused on the impact of aid on growth. There has not been as much evidence, however, on the role of aid in institutional development. Kangoye (this volume) explores this issue by analysing the impact of external aid on the quality of institutions, which are crucial for sustaining growth.

Kangoye uncovers that aid flows can improve democratization by dampening the potential adverse effects of external shocks. This finding has significant implications for African countries, which often experience terms of trade (TOT) shocks. The negative TOT shocks have, furthermore, been found to contribute substantially to economic growth collapses (Arbache and Page 2007), which could derail the process of democratization. Thus, by smoothing out such shocks, external aid can virtuously enhance the success of the democratic dispensation recently embarked on in many African countries.

WHO IS THE ALIEN? XENOPHOBIA AND POST-APARTHEID SOUTH AFRICA

'Most international migration from SSA nations is destined for other SSA countries (intra-SSA migration)' (Naudé 2010: 334), with migrants in search of political and/or economic betterment. Developing appropriate institutions to cope with migration would, therefore, constitute a worthwhile undertaking. South Africa presents an interesting case study of the potential conflict that may occur and the need to develop institutions to obviate the risk of such occurrence.

Recently the country has become a theatre of conflict between the locals and 'outsiders' (foreigners), in the form of widespread violence against the latter group. As pan-African integration proceeds, it is important to explore this conflict phenomenon, by identifying the characteristics of the victims and factors behind the violence. Duponchel (this volume) does just that, based on 2009 household data from the Johannesburg inner city and from the township of Alexandria.

The study finds that foreigners indeed face a higher likelihood of being victimized on the basis of xenophobia. It finds further that those foreigners living in the relatively poor and high unemployment areas face a higher likelihood of attack. These findings cannot be unique to South Africa, though, as migratory conflicts abound across the continent (Naudé 2010). They suggest, therefore, the need to develop immigration institutions that take into account the realities of the labour market in the receiving country.

Institutions and development outcomes

HOW DOES COLONIAL ORIGIN MATTER FOR ECONOMIC PERFORMANCE IN SSA?

Recent literature suggests that colonial origins have important implications for the current patterns of growth and development. For example, Acemoglu and Robinson (2001) attribute much of the current economic performance of African economies to institutions, which were in turn shaped by colonial origins.

Agbor (this volume) explores the issue of the channel by which colonial origin has influenced economic performance. The author finds that it is not so much the initial conditions at independence, which the extant literature seems to emphasize, but more so the legacy of education that appears to have led Anglophone countries to economically outperform their Francophone counterparts. An important implication of this finding is that the educational systems of both groups of countries should be examined in order to distil their productivity-enhancing attributes. Future educational policies in African countries could then be more appropriately informed.

INSTITUTIONAL REFORMS, PRIVATE SECTOR AND ECONOMIC GROWTH

Institutional reforms undertaken recently by many African countries were meant to improve the business environment for private sector development. Have these reforms succeeded? Okey (this volume) uses the indicators on the difficulty of doing business and on economic freedom. He finds that the reforms have indeed increased private investment, foreign direct investment and domestic credit to the private sector, with positive implications for economic growth. These findings are in concert with findings by Bates *et al.* (2013), who observe that recent institutional reforms have improved both agriculture and the general economy.

WOMEN'S LABOUR SUPPLY AND HOUSEHOLD INSURANCE

Increasing attention, over recent years, has been accorded to the importance of gender equality, especially in the areas of education, health and employment opportunities, in improving growth and development in the developing world (Blackden 1999; Klasen 2000; Morrison *et al.* 2007). In particular, gender equality measured by the female-to-male ratio of human development indices enhances women's decision making and improves children's health and educational achievement. It also enhances women's access to markets and employment opportunities, which, in turn, accentuates income growth and poverty reduction in the long run (Morrison *et al.* 2007).

Complementary to the existing literature, Bhalotra and Umana-Aponte (this volume) find that economic recessions are associated with increases in African women's unemployment and self-employment relative to paid employment, leading to a decline in their incomes. They further uncover that women who own agricultural land are immune to the business cycle. It appears, therefore, that women's land ownership could provide a key income-smoothing mechanism. In many African countries, moreover, women are disenfranchised in this regard. Hence, improving such land ownership could have beneficial institutional outcomes, not only by enhancing equity, but also by insuring against volatility in women's incomes, thus improving overall social welfare.

Conclusion

The present volume has focused on two crucial aspects of African development: growth and institutions. It presents substantial evidence that improves our understanding of Africa's development from both historical and current perspectives, and paves the way forward in terms of optimal policies for the future. We have noted, first, that African countries generally retrogressed on both growth and institutions during the earlier part of post-independence. That period also coincided with the cold-war era when minimal attention was paid to institutions. Government was generally the dominant player in resource allocation, while the private sector was virtually suppressed. Paradoxically, the focus on rapid growth and structural transformation through the public sector actually resulted in poor long-term growth and development outcomes.

The more recent post-mid-1990s period has, however, witnessed improved growth, institutions and development outcomes. Such improvements may be attributable to the various economic and political reforms that took place during this period, reforms that were probably facilitated by the end of the cold war.

The following conclusions stand out from the book's coverage:

- If African countries are to achieve structural transformation, industrial embeddedness must be improved considerably, which in turn calls for paying significant attention to local supply-side factors that increase their ability to fill large orders.
- ICT plays a critical role in today's knowledge-intensive world, via enhancing innovation and absorptive capacity. Indeed, service has been emerging as a leading sector, thanks primarily to ICT. Thus African countries must strive to achieve increasing levels of ICT. As institutional reformers draft laws governing the sector, however, they must be cognizant of several pitfalls, in order to ensure that maximum benefits are derived by the citizenry.
- Exchange-rate regimes matter. Floating exchange rates recently adopted by many African countries have served to mitigate the risk of overvaluation of their respective domestic currencies and to help revive their heretofore moribund economies. Yet, such flexible regimes might retard bilateral trade via their tendency to increase exchange-rate volatility, as uncovered in this volume. Thus, in the final analysis, one must balance a floating exchange-rate regime's ability to prevent overvaluation against its tendency to limit bilateral trade due to increased volatility.
- The usual view is that developing countries need to pay more attention to growth than to the accompanying environmental impact. The potential negative impact on health and its adverse implication for growth and development, as uncovered in the present volume, suggests, however, that these countries should indeed be mindful of the environmental impact of their development actions.
- Only a small number of countries seem to be emerging as possible leopards, but there is uncertainty about their durability, and most of these are resource-rich countries. Hence, a particularly critical challenge facing African countries is how to transform their respective resource economies in order to significantly increase the likelihood that the current favourable growth record will endure into the longer term.
- Both growth and its distribution matter for poverty reduction, with growth appearing to be on average the most important instrument. The South African evidence is consistent with this global finding. Nonetheless, the relative importance of growth versus distribution appears to be country specific, and appropriate policies must take into account such idiosyncratic country characteristics to ensure that growth is inclusive.
- Can external aid improve institutional quality in Africa? The answer appears to be in the affirmative. By smoothing out external shocks, aid can help to enhance the likelihood of success of the democratic dispensation embarked on in many African countries.

- Intra-Africa migration has been a dominant feature on the continent. The South African case of conflict between immigrants and the local citizens portrays the need to develop institutions to obviate such conflicts and to render migration an important safety valve for mitigating the suffering of a large number of the African population.
- Recent economic reforms have served to increase private investment, foreign direct investment and domestic credit to the private sector, with positive implications for economic growth. Yet, reforms of the educational system have lagged behind for many African countries. Studying colonial origins might help in this regard, as they are observed herein to influence economic performance via education. Thus educational systems of both Anglophone and Francophone countries should be examined in order to distil their respective productivity-enhancing attributes. Future educational policies could then be more appropriately informed.
- Many African countries have land ownership systems, usually traditionally based, that tend to disadvantage women. Evidence presented in the current volume shows that agricultural land ownership by women tends to insure against shocks and to reduce uncertainties associated with their incomes. Therefore, institutional reforms that improve such land ownership for women would not only be good from an equity perspective, but they could also raise overall social welfare by reducing such uncertainties.

Notes

1 In this chapter, 'sub-Saharan Africa (SSA)' is used synonymously with 'Africa'.
2 However, the improvement seems to follow a similar pattern as ROW's, with the gap relative to ROW not closing appreciably.
3 Fosu (2008) estimates the threshold for this regime as the index of electoral competitiveness in excess of 4.4 (range: 0.0–7.0).
4 XCONST measures the degree of constraint on the executive branch of government, and it takes on values of 0–7, where 7 is for 'strict rules for governance', 1 means 'no one regulates the authority', 0 signifies 'perfect incoherence', and so on (for details, see Fosu 2013b).
5 'Syndrome-free regime' means a 'combination of political stability with reasonably market-friendly policies' (Fosu and O'Connell 2006: 54).

References

Acemoglu, D. and J. Robinson (2001). 'The Colonial Origins of Comparative Development: An Empirical Investigation'. *American Economic Review*, 91(5): 1369–401.

Acemoglu, D., J. Johnson and J. Robinson (2005). 'Institutions as a Fundamental Cause of Long-run Growth'. In P. Alghion and S. Durlauf (eds), *Handbook of Economic Growth*, Vol. 1A, Chapter 6. Amsterdam: Elsevier.

Arbache, J.S. and J. Page (2007). 'More Growth or Fewer Collapses? An Investigation of the Growth Challenges of Sub-Saharan African Countries'. World Bank Policy Working Paper No. 4384. Washington, DC: World Bank.

Azam, J.-P., A. Fosu and N. Ndungu (2002). 'Explaining Slow Growth in Africa'. *African Development Review*, 14(2): 177–220.

Bates, R.H., S.A. Block, G. Fayad and A. Hoeffler (2013). 'The New Institutionalism and Africa'. *Journal of African Economies*, 22(4): 499–522.

Blackden, C.M. (1999). *Gender, Growth, and Poverty Reduction*. Washington, DC: World Bank. Available at: https://openknowledge.worldbank.org/handle/10986/9873 (accessed: 2014). License: CC BY 3.0 Unported.

Collier, P. and J.W. Gunning (1999). 'Why has Africa Grown Slowly?'. *Journal of Economic Perspectives*, 13(3): 3–22.

Dollar, D. and A. Kraay (2002). 'Growth is Good for the Poor'. *Journal of Economic Growth*, 7(3): 195–225.

Fosu, A.K. (2002). 'Transforming Growth to Human Development in Sub-Saharan Africa: The Role of Elite Political Instability'. *Oxford Development Studies*, 30(1): 9–19.

Fosu, A.K. (2004). 'Mapping Growth into Economic Development: Has Elite Political Instability Mattered in Sub-Saharan Africa?'. *American Journal of Economics and Sociology*, 63(5): 137–56.

Fosu, A.K. (2008). 'Democracy and Growth in Africa: Implications of Increasing Electoral Competitiveness'. *Economics Letters*, 100: 442–44.

Fosu, A.K. (2009). 'Inequality and the Impact of Growth on Poverty: Comparative Evidence for Sub-Saharan Africa'. *Journal of Development Studies*, 45(5): 726–45.

Fosu, A.K. (2010a). 'Does Inequality Constrain Poverty Reduction Programs? Evidence from Africa'. *Journal of Policy Modelling*, 32(6): 818–27.

Fosu, A.K. (2010b). 'The Effect of Income Distribution on the Ability of Growth to Reduce Poverty: Evidence from Rural and Urban African Economies'. *American Journal of Economics and Sociology*, 69(3): 1034–53.

Fosu, A.K. (2010c). 'Inequality, Income, and Poverty: Comparative Global Evidence'. *Social Science Quarterly*, 91(5): 1432–46.

Fosu, A.K. (2010d). 'Africa's Economic Future: Learning from the Past'. *CESifo Forum*, 11(1): 62–71.

Fosu, A.K. (2011). 'Growth, Inequality and Poverty Reduction in Developing Countries: Recent Global Evidence'. CSAE Working Paper WPS/2011-07. Oxford: Centre for the Study of African Economies.

Fosu, A.K. (2012). 'The African Economic Growth Record, and the Roles of Policy Syndromes and Governance'. In A. Noman, K. Botchwey, H. Stein and J. Stiglitz (eds), *Good Growth and Governance in Africa: Rethinking Development Strategies*: 175–218. Oxford: Oxford University Press.

Fosu, A.K. (2013a). 'Impact of the Global Financial and Economic Crisis on Development: Whither Africa?'. *Journal of International Development*, 25(8): 1085–104.

Fosu, A.K. (2013b). 'African Economic Growth: Productivity, Policy Syndromes and the Importance of Institutions'. *Journal of African Economies*, 22(4): 523–51.

Fosu, A.K. (2014). 'Growth, Inequality, and Poverty in Sub-Saharan Africa: Recent Progress in a Global Context'. *Oxford Development Studies*, in press.

Fosu, A.K. and S.A. O'Connell (2006). 'Explaining African Economic Growth: The Role of Anti-growth Syndromes'. In F. Bourguignon and B. Pleskovic (eds), *Annual Bank Conference on Development Economics*: 31–66. Washington, DC: World Bank.

Gwartney, J.D., J.C. Hall and R. Lawson (2012). 'Economic Freedom of the World: 2012 Annual Report'. Vancouver, BC: The Fraser Institute.

Haan, J. and J.-E. Sturm (2000). 'On the Relationship between Economic Freedom and Economic Growth'. *European Journal of Political Economy*, 16(2): 215–41.

Haggard, S., A. MacIntyre and L. Tiede (2008). 'The Rule of Law and Economic Development'. *Annual Review of Political Science*, 11: 205–34. Available at: http://polisci.annualreviews.org (accessed: 2014).

Klasen, S. (2000). 'Does Gender Inequality Reduce Growth and Development? Evidence from Cross-Country Regressions'. Collaborative Research Center 386, Discussion Paper 212. Munich: Collaborative Research Center 386.

Lee, K. (2013). 'How Can Korea be a Role Model for Catch-up Development? A "Capability-Based View"'. In A.K. Fosu (ed.), *Achieving Development Success: Strategies and Lessons from the Developing World*. Oxford: Oxford University Press.

Morrison, A., D. Raju and N. Sinha (2007). 'Gender Equality, Poverty and Economic Growth'. Policy Research Working Paper 4349. Washington, DC: World Bank.

Naudé, W. (2010). 'The Determinants of Migration from Sub-Saharan African Countries'. *Journal of African Economies*, 19(3): 330–56.

Ndulu, B., S. O'Connell, R. Bates, P. Collier and C. Soludo (eds) (2008a). *The Political Economy of Economic Growth in Africa 1960–2000*, Vol. 1. Cambridge: Cambridge University Press.

Ndulu, B., S. O'Connell, J.-P. Azam, R.H. Bates, A.K. Fosu, J.W. Gunning and D. Njinkeu (eds) (2008b). *The Political Economy of Economic Growth in Africa 1960–2000*, Vol. 2. Cambridge: Cambridge University Press.

North, D.C. (1990). *Institutions, Institutional Change, and Economic Performance*. New York: Cambridge University Press.

Polity IV Project (2013). *Political Regime Characteristics and Transitions*. http://www.systemicpeace.org/polity/polity4.htm (accessed: 2014).

Ravallion, M. (2012). 'Why Don't We See Poverty Convergence?'. *American Economic Review*, 102(1): 504–23.

Rodrik, D. (2006). 'Goodbye Washington Consensus, Hello Washington Confusion? A Review of the World Bank's Economic Growth in the 1990s: Learning from a Decade of Reform'. *Journal of Economic Literature*, XLIV, December.

Rodrik, D., A. Subramanian and A. Trebbi (2004). 'Institutions Rule: The Primacy of Institutions over Geography and Integration in Economic Development'. *Journal of Economic Growth*, 9(2): 131–65.

Sachs, J.D. and A.M. Warner (1997). 'Sources of Slow Growth in African Economies'. *Journal of African Economies*, 6: 335–76.

Thorbecke, E. (2013). 'The Interrelationship Linking Growth, Inequality and Poverty in Sub-Saharan Africa'. *Journal of African Economies*, 22(1): 115–48.

United Nations Development Programme (UNDP) (2013). *Human Development Report 2011/2012*, New York: UNDP.

World Bank (2013a). *World Development Indicators Online*. Washington, DC: World Bank.

World Bank (2013b). *POVCALNET*. Washington, DC: World Bank.

World Bank (2013c). *Database of Political Institutions*. Washington, DC: World Bank.

2 Determinants of industrial embeddedness

Evidence from manufacturing firms in an African economy

Abdelrasaq Na-Allah

Introduction

The centrality of the phenomenon of industrial embeddedness to the prospect of economic development in territorialized locations is an issue around which some recent strands of theories of globalization converge. One analytical posture with lineage to the global-value chain theory suggests that industrial upgrading at the national level requires a move from simple assembly of imported inputs to more integrated forms of production involving greater use of both forward and backward linkages (Gereffi 1999). Another intriguing paradigm, as revealed in contributions to the emerging works on global production networks, emphasizes the importance of local business linkage as a determinant of value retention or value capture. As claimed by its authors, this is what is needed to make gains from participation in the current system of global production and trade networking sustainable in the long-run (Coe *et al.* 2004). All these are echoes of past sentiments previously expressed in the writings of many notable scholars of regional development, which include, among others, Dicken *et al.* (1994), Amin and Thrift (1994), and Conti (1997). In their various demonstrations, suggestions to the effect that strong regional embeddedness of industrial activities is important for significant positive-growth spillovers have either been made or implied.

In policy circles also, it is apparent that many of the current frameworks reflect concerns about the need to strengthen regional linkages. Within the realm of efforts to support economic growth in the least developed countries (LDCs) for instance, the cumulation provisions in some of the trade-related development assistance programmes of the more affluent northern donors are designed to encourage local linkages.[1] At a more specific continental Africa level, a recently adopted framework by the African Union, entitled the African Productive Capacity Initiative, seeks to promote sustainable industrial development in the region through, among others, the strengthening of production interdependencies within the continent.[2] Running parallel with all these are various programmes at sub-regional and sovereign national levels with strategic mandates to foster industrial embeddedness in their respective local economies.

But perhaps a more emphatic demonstration of the importance of industrial embeddedness to the Africans is found in the recent export crisis that afflicted their garment sector shortly after the Agreement on Textile and Clothing (ATC) came to an end in December 2004.[3] Having left in its wake a trail of negative consequences – not least of which is the closure and subsequent relocation of garment factories to other regions of the world – the issue of enclave practices of firms and what to do to make them develop strong local commitment became topical (Na-Allah and Muchie 2010).

Despite these realities, relatively little is known about what determines industrial embeddedness in a sub-Saharan African (SSA) context. Although extant research documents some important stylized facts, it is surprising that their relevance has so far been confined to studies of developed and some non-SSA developing economies. For a survey of these works, see UNCTAD (2001) and, for more recent studies, see Crone and Watts (2003) and Williams (2005). Some exceptions to this are, however, the linkage-related works of Kirsten and Rogerson (2002) and Barnes and Kaplinsky (2000), both of which focused on South Africa, as well as that of Arimah (2001), whose research examined the determinants of linkages between formal and informal enterprises in Nigeria.

Besides the fact that the different analytical paradigms adopted for these works differ from the one adopted here, it is also important to point out that South Africa and, to some extent, Nigeria that were the empirical subjects of the abovementioned investigations, qualify only as outliers and not as suitable proxies for a typical SSA economy. This is because some of the key defining attributes of a truly representative economy from the subcontinent, such as small market size and landlockedness, are not generally associable with these two economies. Yet, these are attributes which, when their potential implications for embeddedness behaviour of firms are considered alongside those of other incumbents such as agricultural dependence and poor socio-economic environment, a useful perspective to the debate may be uncovered.

For instance, in the current literature on the determinants of linkages, emphasis appears to be more on the demand-related factors, whereas it is likely that, for reasons just mentioned, supply-related factors may be more relevant in a SSA context. We can legitimize this expectation on a number of grounds: (i) the attribute of agricultural dependence would almost certainly restrict supplier availability to the incumbent sector; (ii) small market size can hardly support the large number of firms needed to make demands for inputs significant and local investment in their production attractive; and (iii) by virtue of being embedded in a landlocked and inefficient socio-economic environment, it is not unlikely that relative competitiveness of domestic suppliers would be compromised.

Against this background, this chapter contributes to the debate by conceptually fine-tuning the supply-side argument and empirically situating the investigation within the context of a 'typical' SSA economy. The small landlocked country of Lesotho, which in my opinion accurately embraces our implied definition of an African economy, has been chosen for the study. Consequently data from the World Bank investment climate survey that was completed for the country's private sector enterprises in 2004 is used to specify and estimate an ordered probit model for establishments in the sample. In accordance with my expectations, results reveal that no other factor than local supply potentials is more important in explaining the incidence of industrial embeddedness in the country.

The rest of the chapter is organized as follows. The first section provides a brief review of the theoretical and empirical foundation for the various factors that are considered to be important in the analysis of the determinants of embeddedness formation. This is followed by a description of the data, methodology and presentation of results. The chapter ends with the Conclusion.

Industrial embeddedness: key explanatory variables

Early interests in the industrial embeddedness issue, as demonstrated in works by regional scientists such as Hirschman (1958) and Perloff *et al.* (1960), were inspired by a desire to maximize the full development potentials of industrialization. However, studies that have evolved within the last decade or so have primarily been driven by the pressures of globalization (Ohmae 1995; Yeung 1998) that some analysts fear are leading to an increasing level of enclave behaviour by multinational subsidiaries (Turok 1993). A major preoccupation of this literature therefore lies with understanding the set of required conditions for integrating or 'tying' a focal firm to the region of its operation.

Conceptually, industrial embeddedness can be viewed as the creation of a continuous inter-firm relationship between a focal firm and others in a region.[4] To the extent that the former becomes dependent on supply of its inputs and related services, or sales of its output on the latter, the 'tying to the region' requirement for local integration or linkage formation is assumed satisfied. From this broad conceptualization it is possible to identify two basic manifestations of the embeddedness phenomenon. The first one concerns the kind of dependence that is conferred by virtue of a focal firm's reliance on other firms for sales of its output (forward integration). When such dependence is of the type that places a firm at the mercy of others for supplies of input materials, the second form is revealed. In this study our concern is with this latter manifestation, which is commonly referred to in the literature as 'backward integration'.

The literature emerging from this strand of research has over the years advanced various explanations for the degree of backward linkages that are assumed by enterprises within their host economies. Such explanations can be thought of as essentially describing various aspects of demand- and supply-side attributes.

Demand-side attributes

Linkage potentials are related to certain demand attributes of firms. These attributes may be defined by such important factors as industrial affiliation, size, ownership, network, age, market condition and degree of autonomy.

It is possible to identify two basic criteria for distinguishing between firms of different industrial affiliations. These are differences with respect to both complexity of production technology and product-demand characteristics (Crone and

Watts 2003). Linkages are usually low in the high-tech sector, because capacities to produce complex inputs that are demanded by firms in the sector are not widely distributed. Perhaps the empirical reality that foreign affiliates in the garment industry, with relatively sophisticated input needs, display a low level of regional linkages in a survey of Costa Rica, the Dominican Republic and Morocco is a confirmation of this hypothesis (UNCTAD 2000). On the other hand it is likely that low-tech industries with relatively uncomplicated input requirements will find their demand easily met by local suppliers and will thus exhibit high levels of regional sourcing. This may well be the case with the finding that the food processing industry tends to be strong on local linkage formation, since its input needs mainly come in the form of unsophisticated basic agricultural produce (UNCTAD 2001).

Classifying industries by product-demand characteristics reveals a differentiation between demand for standardized and unstandardized products. Standardized inputs can easily be procured from far distances, as suppliers already know in advance what is required in terms of product specifications and other details. Firms in such industries will therefore exhibit a low linkage profile. However, industries requiring specialized (unstandardized) inputs have reasons to source locally because of the degree of close monitoring required to produce such products. In a study of the determinants of regional sourcing by multinational manufacturing firms in the UK, Crone and Watts (2003) raised and confirmed this hypothesis by showing that firms producing customer-specific products with unstandardized input requirements had a significantly higher level of regional linkage than firms producing standardized products.

The size of the buying plant is another demand-related factor that has been discussed in the literature. Because of the potential large-order requirements of large firms and the possibility that local suppliers may not possess the needed capacity to meet such high demand, it is reasoned that large-scale manufacturers will show greater inclination for out-of-region sourcing. Empirical support for this hypothesis is available in a number of studies. For instance, Barkley and McNamara (1994) find that larger operations are associated with relatively lower domestic-input purchases in the US states of Georgia and South Carolina. Gorg and Ruane (2001) also report similar findings for the Irish electronic sector.

One of the most widely acknowledged factors in conceptual and empirical treatments of industrial linkages is the impact that firm ownership exerts on demand preference for local input. Distinguishing between foreign and indigenous ownership, claims have been made that firms in the former group are not likely to be locally oriented as much as those in the latter. One intuitive justification for this line of reasoning is the fair chance that exists for indigenous enterprises to have better knowledge of the local supply market, which makes patronage relatively less risky. Although Barkley and McNamara's (1994) work falls short of finding support for this proposition, more recent attempts document evidence in line with predictions of the theory (Tóth 2000; UNCTAD 2000). A related hypothesis along this line of ownership issue is the suggestion that nationality of firms plays a role in determining sourcing preferences. Japanese firms have especially been the main target of this kind of analysis. Because of their inclination to maintain close inter-firm networks, it has been pointed out that subsidiaries of Japanese *keiretsu*[5] tend to exhibit weak linkages with their host economies (Rawlinson and Wells 1993). In recent studies, the focus has moved to wider Asia, with contributions from Na-Allah and Muchie confirming that Asian investments in SSA garment manufacturing have yielded little linkage spillover (Na-Allah and Muchie 2010). However, the study of Chesnais *et al.* (2000) of firms operating in Europe found that non-European firms are likely to be more Eurocentric in their sourcing behaviour than their European counterparts (ibid.).

Closely linked with geographical identity is the geographical spread factor. Some firms belong in conglomerates with extensive operations that are spread across many countries. Because such membership facilitates access to information on global sourcing practices, demand preferences of these firms will, in comparison with others without such networks, probably be biased in favour of global sourcing. Therefore, the prediction is that network membership will negatively affect the degree of local embeddedness.

Furthermore, the notion that demand preference for local input is positively related to age of the buying plant is supported by two principal arguments. One, the learning curve hypothesis advanced by O'Farrell and O'Loughlin (1981) postulates that the kind of confidence and trust in the capacity of local suppliers needed by multinational subsidiaries to engage in local patronage often takes time to build. Therefore, the longer a firm stays in a region the higher the chances for linkage development. Two, differences in the degree of local sourcing between old and new firms may also reflect the possibility of inertia. Older firms may be reluctant to change from old, established and possibly regional sourcing habits, while their younger counterparts may be more disposed to the global dimension that recent sourcing trends have taken (Phelps 1997). Most studies that relate age to degree of local embeddedness have generally confirmed its theoretical prediction (Handfield and Krause 1999; Gorg and Ruane 2001).

Demand preference can also be shaped by market condition facing a firm as well as the strategy of an organization. Firms in highly competitive markets where price sensitivity is an attribute are generally perceived as having preferential disposition for global sourcing where the best price deal can be struck (Laurisden 2004). On the other hand, if an organization adopts a decentralized strategy that places a significant amount of power and autonomy in the hands of its subsidiaries it is very likely that such a subsidiary plant will buy more from the locals than their counterparts with centralized strategy (Zanfei 2000).

Supply-side attributes

As a usual suspect in most analyses of constraints to regional economic development, it is not surprising that the question of capacity to supply has come to feature in the industrial embeddedness literature. What is surprising, however, is the realization that it has received little attention in empirical studies (Crone and

Watts 2003) and can arguably be described as the least investigated factor. In line with its analytical orientation, authors who have modelled this variable as a function of linkage behaviour have generally predicted, just as the converse is also the case, that firms in regions with robust supply potentials will literally exhibit stronger regional ties than their counterparts in a relatively poor supply environment. Of obvious interest, however, is the crucial task of defining the attributes of a good supply environment.

A useful way of approaching this issue is to recognize that while availability of domestic suppliers of input materials will necessarily constitute an incontrovertible credential it is not sufficient unless such availability can be expressed in terms of relative competitiveness with suppliers in other locations. In other words, arguing from the supply-side perspective, we will expect the extent of a firm's local linkage to be shaped not only by the fact of strong local presence of input suppliers, but also by that of their relative competitiveness with others elsewhere.

One can fathom from recent contributions to research that the phenomenon of regional presence with respect to availability of domestic suppliers with sufficient capacity to meet both quantity and quality requirements of buying firms can be explained by two key regional attributes: size and industrial identity of the region in question. The theory that regional size, as may be revealed in national economic size, matters for supplier presence is premised on the logic that in large economies where concentration of multitudes of both large and small manufacturing firms is an attribute, the demand for industrial input materials will be significant enough to make investment in the upstream operations attractive. Conversely, small-sized economies such as SSA economies can, by virtue of their inherent inability to support large numbers of plants in their regions, be judged as less likely to succeed in generating the kind of input demand volume needed to enable suppliers to flourish. For their potentials to facilitate the emergence of domestic suppliers, local linkage possibilities will be brighter for large economies than for small ones. Twomey and Tomkins (1996) confirm this hypothesis for the UK, while a related focus on Japanese plants in the USA by Reid (1995) finds no such evidence.

Related to the above idea of size factor is the structural identity of an economy. Some economies can be so profoundly attached to a single or few interrelated sectors that one can understandably equate the identity of such sectors with national economic and/or industrial identity. While this may not necessarily be a feature to be observed with a typical, relatively diversified Western economy, it rears its head sufficiently well in SSA to merit special attention. For instance, it is a common knowledge that many of the continental economies are described as unsophisticated simply because their structural profiles are so significantly skewed in favour of the dominance of agricultural and low-tech light-manufacturing activities.

As a variable influencing the incidence of supplier presence, we might expect that, since the sector(s) with commanding presence will show higher demand for input than others with inferior status, its input/supply market is also more likely to be well developed. Put in a different way, this argument implies that it is hardly likely for us to find sufficient suppliers of, say, high-tech rather than low-tech industrial input in regions dominated by low-skilled and uncomplicated economic activities.

The revealed identity of SSA economies, to which reference was made earlier, thus implies that firms belonging to sectors such as food and beverages and other light-manufacturing will have little problem sourcing their input locally, as suppliers will readily come in handy. For the related reason that the performance of high-tech industrial activities, such as those typical of engineering and biotechniques is very negligible in many of these countries, its input market will also be correspondingly underdeveloped and few (if any) of its suppliers will be available. This argument will lead us to expect linkage development prospects to be brighter for firms in industries with an established regional presence. An early study by Barkley and McNamara (1994), mentioned previously, illustrates the importance of a well-developed supply base to the prospects for linkage formation. Their work shows that manufacturers in industries with a highly developed input market display stronger local ties than their counterparts.

Even if suppliers are sufficiently available in a locality, there is definitely no guarantee that its resident firms will engage in any significant patronizing behaviour. This is because the criterion of market competitiveness that relates cost and quality of domestically produced items to those of extra-regional locations still has to be met. Past research has probably taken it for granted that for many industries firms are regionally confined in terms of their sourcing scope. Approaches of this sort can be understood within the context that, in the recent past, the performance of the whole range of value-adding activities required to transform an idea into a finished product was essentially confined within national boundaries. But with the advent of globalization, where production sharing across boundaries is an essential attribute, it is increasingly becoming easier for firms to jettison uncompetitive local suppliers for the friendlier global markets.

Data, methodology and results

Data environment

Data for the study is a cross-section one that comes from a survey of manufacturing establishments in Lesotho. Lesotho was chosen because it exhibits many of the attributes of a typical economy from the sub-region. For instance, like some of its regional neighbours it is, according to the United Nations classification, a LDC. Its per capita income of US$550 in 2004 mirrors that of the SSA average of US$611. The negative implication that this has for market demand is further strengthened by a population figure that stood at less than 2 million in 2004.[6]

Again, like many of its SSA neighbours economic competitiveness is haunted by a landlocked geography that makes it share all of its border areas with South Africa. Further compounding the problem is the absence of key environmental efficiency drivers such as strong economic, social and institutional infrastructures. Based on the 2007 Global Competitiveness Index Report (GCIR), Figure 2.1

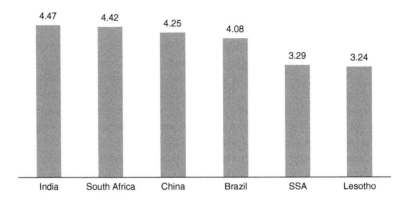

Figure 2.1 Index of the relative competitiveness of Lesotho's economy compared
with economies of other countries

Source: Based on the World Economic Forum (2007) Global Competitiveness Index Report.

shows that Lesotho's competitiveness performance indicator of 3.24, which some-
how mimics that of the SSA mean of 3.29, is worse off than those of China, India,
Brazil and even South Africa.[7]

Lesotho's dependence on agriculture is also typical of an average SSA country.
At the time of independence in 1966, the share of agriculture in gross domestic
product (GDP) was 45 per cent (Maile 2001). Although, according to the Word
Bank (World Bank 2003), this dependence has been declining ever since, the
primary sector (predominantly agriculture and livestock) still accounted for
about 20 per cent of GDP between 1990 and 1999 (Hassan and Ojo 2002). This
attribute in a way defines the kind of manufacturing activities that the economy
is able to support.

However, in the context of manufacturing, which is the sector of interest to
this research, Lesotho presents a further attraction in the sense that it is among
the continent's 'best performers' in this area. Its share of manufacturing production in GDP was approximately 18 per cent in 2002. This figure is far higher
than the entire SSA average of 11.25 per cent during the same period and places
it among the 'top ten' in the World Bank country performance report (World
Bank 2010).

The cross-section survey to which our data refers takes 2002 as a reference
year and was obtained from the database of the World Bank-coordinated
Investment Climate Assessment exercise conducted and completed for about
75 manufacturing establishments in Lesotho around the end of 2004. The small
sample size, which was carefully drawn to provide adequate representation of the
broader population, is itself a reflection of the broader economic size of the country. After initial editing we were left with only 69 firms to work with. The main
characteristics of the sample are summarized in Table 2.1.

Table 2.1 Characteristics of a sample of Lesotho's manufacturing establishments

Sector	(%)	Ownership	(%)	Size	(%)	Market orientation	(%)
Food and beverages	28	African	50.7	Micro (1–9 employees)	31.9	Very large (500 and above)	18.8
Garment and footwear	50	Asian	34.8	Small (10–99 employees)	29.0	Exporter (export ≥ 5% of sales)	62.3
Other manufacturing	22	European	14.5	Large (100–499 employees)	20.3	Non-exporter	37.7

Source: Author's calculation from the World Bank Enterprise Survey database (2004).

Variable definition

Being an exercise that was principally motivated by a need to have better understanding of conditions in the local investment climate and how they are affecting firm performances, the survey questionnaire addressed a number of wide-ranging issues. We were able to extract some key variables of interest from the resulting database for employment in the analysis that was undertaken. A background discussion on these variables together with how they have been measured follows next.

Industrial sector

An important feature of the manufacturing sector in Lesotho is that it is relatively unsophisticated and for the most part allied with the primary sector. The incidence of these attributes cannot be divorced from the country's relative backwardness and its history of dependence on agriculture as previously suggested. It is quite obvious from Table 2.1 that not only are the high-tech sectors completely unrepresented in the data, the dominance of light manufacturing is also evidently shown. Accounting for approximately 50 per cent of the total number of firms in the sample, the industrial identity of this economy seems to be revealed in low-tech garment (including leather and footwear) manufacturing activities.

Four dummy variables were generated to capture the influence of sector in the empirical specification: fb, gt, lf and om for food and beverages, garment, footwear and leather, and other manufacturing, respectively. For each of the four variables, a value of 1 is assigned for positive observations and 0 otherwise. Based on discussions in the previous, we know that food and beverages belong to the low-tech category of manufacturing, with relatively uncomplicated input requirements. This led us to expect a positive sign for its variable. However, with respect to garment (gt), the probable direction of its sign cannot be foretold. On one hand, by virtue of having a relatively complicated input requirement in textiles as argued earlier, Lesotho may not have the right supply capacity. On the other hand, having its industrial identity revealed in garment and related light-manufacturing activities may confer on it good supply potentials in inputs that

Table 2.2 Level of local supplier patronage and foreign presence by sector

Sector	Local supplier patronage (%)	Foreign presence (%)
Food and beverages	42.8	12.5
Garment	18.8	74
Footwear and leather	1.7	66
Other manufacturing	30.8	40
Mean (all sectors)	23.5	48.3

Source: Author's calculation from the World Bank Enterprise Survey database (2004).

feed into the production of these items. Positive signs can be expected for the remaining variables (*lf* and *om*), because they generally belong to the low-tech category of manufacturing.[8]

Embeddedness

Embeddedness is captured by the degree of backward integration that firms assume within the local economy. In other words, it is the extent of manufacturing establishments' linkage formation with domestic suppliers of input. Consistent with the popular approach in the literature, this variable, which serves as the explained variable in the model, is measured as a percentage of a firm's material inputs and supplies procurement in 2002 that came from domestic sources (Reid 1995; Williams 2005). With domestic sources being defined as purchases made from manufacturers, distributors or foreign-owned firms in Lesotho, responses vary between 0 and 100 per cent.

Revelations from Table 2.2 show that the component of input purchases from local suppliers is, for all sectors, generally low (less than one-quarter). This may not be unexpected in a small and relatively unsophisticated economy. As further revealed in the table, firms in the food and beverages sector are more patronizing of domestic suppliers than their counterparts in the garment and footwear and leather sectors. This may reflect a combination of factors: one, that suppliers to firms in the garment and leather sector may not come in handy as suppliers to firms in food and beverages, for the simple reason that input requirements of the latter are not as technically complex as requirements of the former; two, the garment and leather sector in Lesotho is largely export-oriented, and stringent requirements for high standards may also compel firms to seek high-quality input which may not be available locally. Discussion on how the embeddedness variable was introduced into the model is provided in a later part of this section.

Foreign ownership

An important assumption in the literature on foreign direct investment (FDI) is that the decision to engage in off-shore production is generally driven by *resource* or *market-seeking* motive. A firm would be interested in direct investment in a foreign land only if such investment would afford it access either to badly needed resources or a substantially large market. This assumption is well echoed in a recent United National Development Programme (UNDP) report on 'needs assessment to attract Asian FDI into Africa'. Two of the key areas identified as commanding great potential for attracting such investments have strong resource and market-related attributes: the first is the extractive sector while the second is export-oriented manufacturing (United Nations 2007).

In the case of Lesotho, the latter motive appears to be the case. A sectoral analysis of distribution of foreign ownership, as given in Table 2.2, shows that the two sectors that command more than 50 per cent foreign presence (garment and leather) are technically the sectors with substantial market potentials.[9]

In defining foreign ownership, variable distinctions are made between African, European and Asian firms. We use ownership by the Africans as our proxy for local firms and ownership by Europeans and Asians as two different dimensions of foreign firms. While we recognize that the local ownership variable can be better represented, as it is often the case, by firms owned and controlled by nationals of the focal economy (in this case Lesotho), our leverage is constrained by limitations of the data. The classification of firms' nationalities in the data only reveals a differentiation between firms of African, Asian and European stocks, with the Lesotho subgroup impliedly subsumed within the larger African group. This inability to break down results by nationalities is, according to the World Bank, an inevitable consequence of dealing with a poor, small economy where relatively few numbers of firms are available for observation.

In any case, we have good reason to be confident that our choice of African investors as substitute for local investors would not present a serious misclassification problem. This is because the South Africans who share the closest geographical proximity with the small landlocked economy of Lesotho are the only significant non-native African investors in the country. Proximity of this sort, as we all know, enhances interaction and collaboration, which promotes good knowledge of one another. If, as argued earlier, knowledge of the local economy is the issue in the distinction between foreigners and locals, then the South Africans could, for the above reason, qualify to be described as 'locals' in Lesotho.

For econometric purposes, a value of 1 is assigned for the event of observing positive outcome for African ownership; otherwise, 0. The exercise is repeated for each remaining ownership status (European and Asian). Expectation of a negative association of European ownership status with embeddedness behaviour is justifiable on the grounds that foreign firms are not generally patronizing of local suppliers. Furthermore, aside from their foreign status, negative linkage behaviours of Asian entities can also be explained by nationality factor, as argued above, in Industrial embeddedness: key explanatory variables.

Supply-capacity deficits

The suggestion from our discussions in Industrial embeddedness that regional supply potential is a country- rather than firm-level phenomenon raises important questions on the feasibility of modelling this variable in a single-country focus like this one. From an empirical analytical point of view, it seems more meaningful to introduce the influence of the regional supplier presence or their competitiveness in a cross-country regression framework, where differences across countries can easily be revealed.

In the context of a single-country analysis, however, Hoare (1985) made an insightful contribution that makes it possible for us to get around this problem. The scholar had argued that, in determining the level of local patronage, firm managers' perceptions of the availability and competitiveness of domestic suppliers can be taken to be just as important as the reality itself (ibid.). It follows from this viewpoint that if we can figure out the kind of judgements that Lesotho firm managers have on the availability and competitiveness of local suppliers we should have a fairly good proxy for modelling the influence of supply capacity in our empirical equation.

Fortunately, data available for analysis allows for some leverage in this regard. One of the survey questions had particularly addressed the issue by requiring respondents to identify, from a list of factors, some of the key obstacles that prevent them from patronizing local suppliers. Three of the listed factors which allow some extrapolations to be made on respondents' perceptions are:

- There are no local suppliers.
- Local suppliers do not have sufficient capacity to meet orders.
- The quality of local supplies is inadequate.

These perceptions, as ranked by respondents from various sectors and different sizes, are reported in Table 2.3. From column 2 in the table, it is observed that all firms from various sectors, regardless of size, believed unavailability of local suppliers is the most important obstacle. This, no doubt, is the main supply-side

Table 2.3 Ranking of constraints to local input procurement by sector and size of firms

Sector and size	1st	2nd
Sector		
Food and beverages	A[a]	C[c]
Garment; footwear and leather	A	B[b]
Other manufacturing	A	C
Size		
Large firm (employment ≥ 100)	A	B
Small firm (employment ≤ 100)	A	C

Source: Author's calculation from the World Bank Enterprise Survey database (2004).

Notes
a A, there are no local suppliers.
b B, local suppliers do not have sufficient capacity to meet orders.
c C, competitiveness of local suppliers in terms of cost and quality is inadequate.

issue facing the manufacturing sector in the country and quite consistent with earlier theoretical argument that supplier availability in a small economy may be a serious issue.

As further revealed in column 3, the view that domestic firms lack sufficient capacity to meet orders is rated second and shared jointly by respondents from both large firms and the garment and footwear and leather sectors. This coincidence is not accidental: nearly two-thirds of all firms with up to 100 employees or more come from the garment, and footwear and leather sectors. Besides this, the rest of our respondents (small firms with less than 100 employees and sectoral affiliations with food and beverages, and other manufacturing) rated poor competitiveness of local suppliers as their second major problem.

The technique adopted to model the impact of this variable places respondents, who identified any of these factors as an explanation for being unfavourably disposed to local sourcing, in the category of those who have a poor impression of the country's supply potentials. In this respect, observations with positive outcomes are assigned the value of 1, while others are captured by 0 values. Local sourcing by the former group of respondents (that is, observations with positive values), if it ever took place at all, would at best be minimal. We are thus inclined to expect the association between this variable and local embeddedness to be negative.

Size and age

To capture the influence of size, four dummy variables that discretely classify firms into micro, small, large and very large plants were generated. A microenterprise (*mcsz*) has in its payroll between 1 and 9 employees, while the range for a small-sized enterprise (*ssz*) is given as 10–99 workers. The staff strength of a large organization (*lsz*) falls within the band of 100 and 499. If the total number of workforce exceeds 500, then such a firm is considered to be of very large size (*xlsz*). Consistent with our earlier arguments, the large size variable is expected to be negatively associated with linkage levels.

The determination of a firm's age (*age*) is a straightforward issue. It is accomplished simply by defining a benchmark of 5 years below which firms are considered unqualified to be classified as old and are captured by the value of 0. It therefore follows that old establishments are those that, in 2002, had spent up to 5 years or more in operation. This variable, which is assigned the value of 1, is, unlike size, expected to be positively associated with domestic sourcing. The choice of 5 years as our benchmark is not without precedent. Williams (2005) used a similar value in his analysis of supplier linkages of foreign-owned manufacturing firms in the UK.

Network membership

Finally, the last variable that was introduced involved proxies for the incidence of belonging to a conglomerate group. We were able to model the influence of this

Table 2.4 Descriptions of variables and expected signs

Variable	Description	Expected sign
fb	Food and beverage sector	Positive
gt	Garment sector	Unknown
fl	Footwear and leather sector	Positive
om	Other manufacturing sector	Positive
eur	European ownership	Negative
asia	Asian ownership	Negative
scd	Supply capacity deficits	Negative
ssz	Small size	Positive
size (lsz; xlsz)		Negative
age	Firm age (older firms)	Positive
ntw	Network membership	Negative

Source: Author's compilation.

factor by utilizing respondents' answers to a question which required them to state whether their firms had operations in other countries. Organizations with affirmative answers are classified as being members of a network group and are given the value of 1; otherwise, 0. The coefficient of this explanatory variable is anticipated to show up with a negative sign.

Table 2.4 presents the expected signs of all the explanatory variables introduced in the estimation.

Estimation technique

The discrete nature of the dependent variable (embeddedness) requires that we think through the appropriate econometric technique to use. Obviously because of its discontinuity the standard least squares technique is ruled out of favour. One option is to treat responses in terms of binary choice that indicates linkage or no linkage. But this will not capture the degree of embeddedness which is more meaningful in an analysis of this type (Williams 2005). Another option is to view responses as ordered, since it is possible to distribute the percentage share of local content of input procurement into ordered categories. While this will definitely eliminate the usefulness of a technique such as multiple discriminant analysis, it will make the choice of ordered probit model quite appropriate.

The ordered probit method models ordered response data in terms of an underlying latent variable such that:

$$\ddot{y}^*_i = x_i\beta + u_i \tag{2.1}$$

where $i = 1 \dots n$, β and x_i are vectors of unknown parameters and variables believed to possess explanatory powers, respectively; u_i is a stochastic error term that follows a normal distribution, while $\ddot{y}^*_i$ is the unobserved dependent variable, which is related to the observed dependent variable $\ddot{y}_i$ as follows:

$$y_i = \begin{matrix} 1 & \text{if } y^*_i < \acute{\alpha}1 \\ 2 & \text{if } \acute{\alpha}1 < y^*_i < \acute{\alpha}2 \\ 3 & \text{if } \acute{\alpha}2 < y^*_i < \acute{\alpha}1 \\ . \\ . \\ . \\ J & \text{if } \alpha J - 1 <= y^*_i \end{matrix} \qquad (2.2)$$

The model recognizes a natural ordering in the values of the dependent variables such that the threshold parameter $\alpha1 < \alpha2 < \alpha3 \ldots < \alpha J - 1$. If we denote the probability of a particular observed outcome being associated with yi by Pr $(y_i = j)$, we have the following expression:

$$Pr(y_i = j) = Pr(\alpha j - 1 < y^*_i < \alpha j) = \Phi(\alpha j - x_i \beta) \\ - \Phi(\alpha j - 1 - x_i \beta), \quad j = 1, 2, 3, \ldots J \qquad (2.3)$$

where $\Phi(\cdot)$ defines the cumulative distribution function. A maximum likelihood estimation technique is used to estimate the model after transforming it into log-likelihood function as follows:

$$LogL = \sum \ln\left[Pr(ji)\right] = \sum \ln\left[\Phi(\alpha\, ji - xi\beta) - \Phi(\alpha\, ji - 1 - xi\beta)\right] \qquad (2.4)$$

Maximization in Equation 2.4 is carried out with respect to threshold parameters $\alpha1, \alpha2, \alpha3 \ldots \alpha J - 1$, as well as elements of β.

To ensure that outcomes are not context specific, two versions of banding for the explained variable were considered. The first calibrated the percentage of input usage that are of domestic sources into four discrete ordered-choice categories that take on a range of values between 0 (no linkage) and 3 (high linkage) as follows:

Model 1

$$embd = \begin{matrix} 0 & \text{if } y_i = 0\% \text{ (no linkage)} \\ 1 & \text{if } 0 < y_i \le 33\% \text{ (low linkage level)} \\ 2 & \text{if } 33\% < y_i \le 66\% \text{ (moderate linkage level)} \\ 3 & \text{if } 66\% < y_i \le 100\% \text{ (high linkage level)} \end{matrix} \qquad (2.5)$$

The second has the following five-ordered classification:

Model 2

$$embd = \begin{matrix} 0 & \text{if } y_i = 0\% \text{ (no linkage)} \\ 1 & \text{if } 0 < y_i \le 25\% \text{ (low linkage level)} \\ 2 & \text{if } 25\% < y_i \le 50\% \text{ (moderate linkage level)} \\ 3 & \text{if } 50\% < y_i \le 75\% \text{ (high linkage level)} \\ 4 & \text{if } 75\% < y_i \le 100\% \text{ (very high linkage level)} \end{matrix} \qquad (2.6)$$

where *embd* is the extent of local embeddedness that we measured as a percentage of material input procurement in 2002 which originated from domestic sources. Consequently, the estimated model is given by:

$$embd = g(ssz, lsz, xlsz, fb, gt, fl, eur, asia, age, scd, ntw) \qquad (2.7)$$

where *embd* is as defined above; *ssz*, *lsz* and *xls* are all size dummies that stand for small, large and very large sizes, respectively. Sectoral dummies are also introduced as *fb*, *gt* and *fl*; *eur* stands for European ownership, just as *asia* represents the incidence of firms belonging to Asians; and g is a function. Proxy for being an 'old' business is *age*. Both supply-capacity deficits and network membership are given by *scd* and *ntw*, respectively. In order to avoid collinearity, both micro size (*mcz*) and other manufacturing (*omm*) variables were dropped from the estimation.

Results

Adopting a general-to-specific method of model selection, Table 2.5 presents results for two different specifications of Model 1 (model A and model B).[10] Model A is the more general form, with all explanatory variables included; while model B represents results for the most parsimonious equation. Regression outputs for this best-fitting version are reported in columns 4 and 5 under model B. Both the Bayesian information criterion (BIC) and Akaike's information criterion (AIC) suggest that model B is an improved specification over model A.

Table 2.5 Ordered probit regression results for the embeddedness equation

Variable	Model A		Model B	
	Coefficient	P>|z|	Coefficient	P>|z|
ssz	0.41	0.34	0.52	0.21
lsz	−1.48	0.01	−1.42	0.02
xlsz	−0.82	0.15	−0.98	0.08
fb	0.98	0.06	1.10	0.02
gt	1.41	0.03	1.39	0.02
fl	−0.44	0.65	–	–
asia	−1.27	0.05	−1.25	0.06
eur	−0.52	0.44	−0.76	0.19
age	0.04	0.08	0.04	0.04
scd	−0.98	0.01	−0.98	0.01
ntw	−0.50	0.34	–	–
Observations	n = 64		n = 64	
Log likelihood	−43.242165		−43.75384	
BIC[a]	−121.460		−128.754	
AIC[b]	1.789		1.742	

Source: Author's calculations.

Notes
a Bayesian information criterion.
b Akaike's information criterion.

Table 2.6 Marginal effects for estimated model

	Linkage 0 (no linkage)	Linkage 1 (low linkage)	Linkage 2 (moderate linkage)	Linkage 3 (high linkage)
lsz	0.42	−0.24	−0.02	−0.16
xlsz	0.33	−0.18	−0.02	−0.14
age	−0.02	0.01	0.00	0.01
asia	0.40	−0.22	−0.02	−0.17
scd	0.36	−0.16	−0.02	−0.17
fb	−0.42	0.12	0.02	0.28
gt	−0.51	0.18	0.03	0.30

Source: Author's calculations.

In analysing the result, the focus is therefore on Model B. With the exception of *ssz* and *eur*, all variables retained in this model are statistically significant. The results generally confirm the conventional wisdom in the literature that large-size, Asian ownership nationality and regional scd exert negative influences on local input procurement, while affiliation with the food and beverages sector as well as a firm's age confer positive impacts. The observed positive association between the garment sector variable and the dependent variable is also not totally unexpected.

An examination of marginal effects of the significant variables on predicted probabilities reported in Table 2.6 sheds further light on all these. The table shows that large-size establishments with 100–499 employees have about 16 per cent lower probability of being strong on embeddedness (linkage 3) than micro enterprises (1–9 employees). Also in contrast with recent evidence from Europe, as in Williams (2005), that there is no support for the claim that embeddedness is related to nationality of owners, our finding here reveals that there is indeed a negative association between Asian ownership status and patronage of local suppliers in Africa. Evidence contained in the table shows that Asian presence reduced the probability of high linkage formation by 17 per cent. Furthermore, the poor supply potential variable (*scd*) is seen to have diminished the prospects of having *linkage 3* also by 17 per cent in 2002.

With respect to the positive influences, we can confirm that sectoral affiliations with food and beverages as well as garment increased the probability of linkage at the highest level by 28 per cent and 30 per cent, respectively. But for older firms the probability of such linkage formation associates with just a marginal increase of 1 per cent.

Conclusion and policy recommendation

This chapter examines the phenomenon of industrial embeddedness in the context of SSA manufacturing firms. While much of the extant analysis in this area has typically been concerned with non-SSA economies, our departure from the literature is both relevant and necessary. It is relevant because countries in the

subcontinent present a unique set of economic attributes with potentially significant implications for linkage behaviour. The necessity of the exercise is also justified on the grounds that some recent policy initiatives, as well as real world
practical events, made serious debate on the issue inevitable.

On the basis of identified attributes, the small, landlocked country of Lesotho
was chosen as proxy for a typical SSA economy. Of course, to the extent that
there are a few countries in the subcontinent whose economic characteristics
depart from some of our qualifying criteria, a legitimate objection can be raised
against the quality of representation that our choice affords. We acknowledge
this as an important limitation and call for further research to improve on this
shortcoming.

Estimates from a model of embeddedness, specified for a sample of manufacturing firms in the small landlocked economy, generally confirm conventional
wisdom in the literature. Large firm size, poor supply potentials and Asian ownership status manifest in significant negative supplier linkage spillover. Positive
linkage effects are, however, associated with variables that proxy for plant age
and two sectoral identities: garment, and food and beverages.

But what is probably more important is to unravel the puzzle presented by these
findings. It seems reasonable to conclude that our expectation of the centrality of
supply-side factors to the prospects of industrial embeddedness in SSA manufacturing has been borne out by the evidence. For instance, besides the negative
contribution of poor supply-potential variable, the finding that large-sized establishments are unfavourably disposed to local sourcing is traceable to the inability
of local suppliers in a typical small African economy to fill large orders.

Also, despite the complex nature of the input needs of the garment sector, the
positive coefficient associated with the sector may be picking up the favourable
supply potentials conferred by the country's revealed industrial identity in that
sector. Moreover, in an economy with a history of substantial dependence on
agriculture, the positive linkage associated with the food and beverages sector
may not be divorced from the existence of a robust local resource base. In crafting linkage-related policies in Africa, therefore, it is important that concerns
shift to fostering the development of a strong local supply base.

Notes

1 Two prominent recent examples of these initiatives with focus on Africa are the
US 'African Growth and Opportunity Act' Programme that was passed into law in
May 2000 and the EU 'Everything but Arms' Scheme which came into existence
in March 2001. These schemes have various forms of in-built linkage related cumulation provisions.

2 http://74.125.95.104/u/UAAU?q=cache:qY9g0whPdPUJ:www.africa-union.org/root/
AU/Conferences/2007/september/TI/cami/doc/Doc.%252014.doc+apci&hl=en&ct=clnk&
cd=1&ie=UTF-8 (accessed: 3 December 2010).

3 During the ATC tenure, African garment exports enjoyed privileged access to some
industrialized countries' internal markets partly because quota restrictions on similar
exports of some other countries such as China were in force.

4 Regional inter-firm relationship could refer to either inter-firm collaboration at the
level of cluster area within a country or at a much wider country or national level. In

our present case, since the objective is to understand the determinants of inter-firm linkages regardless of whether this takes place countrywide or within a specific regional cluster, we adopt the wider concept and define regional collaboration as linkages between firms that are observed at the entire national level.

5 *Keiretsu* is a Japanese term for a conglomerate headed by a major Japanese bank or one consisting of companies with a common supply chain linking wholesalers and retailers.

6 See World Bank (2004) 'Environment at a Glance 2004 Lesotho'. Available at: http://siteresources.worldbank.org/INTEEI/Data/20857101/Lesotho.pdf (accessed 2 August 2008).

7 The Global Competitiveness Index Report is a product of the World Economic Forum's attempt to capture and reveal the competitive potentials of countries. For each country, the report measures and rates the level of development of a number of factors considered to be drivers of national productivity and general economic competitiveness. Factors considered in this 2007 exercise include: institutions, infrastructure, macroeconomy, health and primary education, higher education and training, market efficiency (goods, labour, financial), technological readiness, business sophistication and innovation. See http://www.weforum.org/en/initiatives/gcp/Global%20Competitiveness%20Report/index.htm (accessed: 3 December 2010).

8 The World Bank defines 'other manufacturing' as firms in varieties of other light-manufacturing sub-sectors, which include construction materials and printing.

9 Lesotho's trade agreements with the West give its outputs from these sectors preferential access to the larger internal markets of the latter.

10 In results not reported here, we tested the sensitivity of the estimates to changes in width banding for the explained variable by estimating Model 2 and found that there is practically no difference in the regression outputs of the two models.

References

Amin, A. and N. Thrift (1994). 'Living in the Global'. In A. Amin and N. Thrift (eds), *Globalisation, Institutions and Regional Development in Europe*. Oxford: Oxford University Press.

Arimah, B.C. (2001). 'Nature and Determinants of Linkages between Informal and Formal Sector Enterprises in Nigeria'. *African Development Review*, 13(1):114–44.

Barkley, D.L. and K.T. McNamara (1994). 'Local Input Linkages: A Comparison of Foreign-Owned and Domestic-Manufacturers in Georgia and South Carolina'. *Regional Studies*, 28: 725–37.

Barnes, J. and R. Kaplinksy (2000). 'Globalisation and the Death of the Local Firms: The Automobile Components Sector in South Africa'. *Regional Studies*, 34(9): 797–812.

Chesnais, F., G. Ietto-Gillies and R. Simonette (eds) (2000). *European Integration and Global Corporate Strategies*. London: Routledge.

Coe, N.M., M. Hess, H.W. Yeungt, P. Dicken and J. Henderson (2004). '"Globalising" Regional Development: A Global Production Networks Perspective'. *Transactions of the Institute of British Geographers*, 29(4): 468–84.

Conti, S. (1997). 'Interdependent and Uneven Development: A Systemic View of the Global–Local Dialectic'. *International Geographical Union Bulletin*, 47: 195–204.

Crone, M. and H.D. Watts (2003). 'The Determinants of Regional Sourcing by Multinational Manufacturing Firms: Evidence from Yorkshire and Humberside, UK'. *European Planning Studies*, 11(6): 717–37.

Dicken, P., F. Mats and M. Andres (1994). 'The Local Embeddedness of Transnational Corporation'. In A. Amin and N. Thrift (eds), *Globalisation, Institutions and Regional Development in Europe*. Oxford: Oxford University Press.

Gereffi, G. (1999). 'International Trade and Industrial Upgrading in the Apparel Commodity Chain'. *Journal of International Economics*, 48: 37–70.

Gorg, H. and F. Ruane (2001). 'Multinational Companies and Linkages: Panel Data Evidence for the Irish Electronic Sector'. *International Journal of the Economics of Business*, 8: 1–18.

Handfield, R.B. and D.R. Krause (1999). 'Think Globally, Source Locally'. *Supply Chain Management Review*, 35(1): 36–46.

Hassan, F.M.A. and O. Ojo (2002). *Lesotho: Development in a Challenging Environment*. Abidjan: The African Development Bank.

Hirschman, A.O. (1958). *The Strategy of Economic Development*. New Haven, CO: Yale University Press.

Hoare, A.G. (1985). 'Industrial Linkages Studies'. In M. Pacione (ed.), *Progress in Industrial Geography*. London: Croom Helm.

Kirsten, M. and M. Rogerson (2002). 'Tourism, Business Linkages and Small Enterprise Development in South Africa'. *Development Southern Africa*, 19(1): 29–59.

Laurisden, L.S. (2004). 'Foreign Direct Investment, Linkage Formation and Supplier Development in Thailand during the 1990s: The Role of State Governance'. *The European Journal of Development Research*, 16(3): 561–86.

Maile, N. (2001). Forestry Outlook Studies in Africa: Lesotho. Available at: ftp://ftp.fao.org/docrep/fao/004/AB589E/AB589E00.pdf (accessed: 3 December 2010).

Na-Allah, A. and M. Muchie (2010). 'Industrial Upgrading in Sub-Saharan Africa: The Competitive Impact of China on Supplier Linkage Development Potentials of Resident Asian Entrepreneurs'. *International Journal of Technological Learning Innovation and Development*, 3(3): 272–92.

O'Farrell, P.N. and B. O'Loughlin (1981). 'New Industry Input Linkages in Ireland: An Econometric Analysis'. *Environment and Planning A*, 13: 285–308.

Ohmae, K. (1995). *The End of the Nation State: The Rise of the Regional Economies*. London: Harper Collins.

Perloff, H.S., E.S. Dunne, E.E. Lamparde and R.F. Muth (1960). *Regions, Resources, and Economic Growth*. Baltimore: John Hopkins Press.

Phelps, N.A. (1997). *Multinationals and European Integration: Trade, Investment and Regional Development*. London: Jessica Kingsley and Regional Studies Association.

Rawlinson, M. and P. Wells (1993). 'Japanese Globalisation and the European Automobile Industry'. *Tijdschrift voor Economische en Sociale Geografie*, 84(5): 349–61.

Reid, N. (1995). 'Just-in-time Inventory Control and the Economic Integration of Japanese-owned Manufacturing Plants with the Country, State and National Economies of the United States'. *Regional Studies*, 29: 345–56.

Tóth, I.J. (2000). 'Outstanding Expectations, more Balanced Growth: The Business Situation and Perspectives of the Hungarian Largest Exporting Manufacturing Firms in January 2000'. Business Cycles Research Papers 1/2000. Budapest: TÁRKI Research Institute.

Turok, I. (1993). 'Inward Investments and Local Linkages: How deeply Embedded is Silicon Glen?' *Regional Studies*, 27: 401–17.

Twomey, J. and J.M. Tomkins (1996). 'Supply Potentials in the Region of Great Britain'. *Regional Studies*, 30(8): 783–90.

UNCTAD (2000). *The Competitiveness Challenge: Transnational Corporations and Industrial Restructuring in Developing Countries*, New York and Geneva: United Nations.

UNCTAD (2001). *World Investment Report: Promoting Linkages*. New York and Geneva: United Nations.

United Nations (2007). Asian Foreign Direct Investment in Africa: Towards a New Era of Cooperation among Developing Countries. New York and Geneva: United Nations. Available at: <http://unctad.org/en/Docs/iteiia20071_en.pdf> (accessed: 23 July 2014)

Williams, D. (2005). 'Supplier Linkages of Foreign-owned Manufacturing Firms in the UK: The Influence of Entry Mode, Subsidiary Autonomy and Nationality'. *European Planning Studies*, 13(1): 73–91.

World Economic Forum (2007). 'The Global Competitiveness Index Report'. Available at: http://www.weforum.org/en/initiatives/gcp/Global%20Competitiveness%20Report/index.htm (accessed: 2 August 2008).

World Bank (2003). 'Lesotho: Integrated Framework Diagnostic Trade Integration Study'. Available at: http://www.integratedframework.org> (accessed: 3 December 2010).

World Bank (2004). 'Lesotho: An Assessment of Investment Climate'. Washington, DC: World Bank, CD-Rom.

World Bank (2010). Africa Development Indicators. Available at: http://data.worldbank.org/data-catalog/africa-development-indicators (accessed:)

Yeung, H.W.C. (1998). 'Capital, State and Space: Contesting the Borderless World'. *Transactions of the Institute of the British Geographers*, 23: 291–310.

Zanfei, A. (2000). 'Transnational Firms and the Changing Organisation of Innovative Activities'. *Cambridge Journal of Economics*, 24: 515–42.

3 Does lack of innovation and absorptive capacity retard economic growth in Africa?

Steve Onyeiwu

Introduction

Is it a myth or reality that Africa's economic growth is influenced by absorptive capacity (AC) and innovative capability (IC)?[1] Should ineffective science and technology (S&T) policy be considered part of the 'policy syndromes' (Collier and Gunning 1999; Fosu 2009) that are widely believed to affect Africa's growth record? This chapter discusses the ICs and ACs of African countries and uses cross-country regressions to explore whether they have played significant roles in inter-country variations in the region's growth performance.

Africa's growth performance has been attributed to various factors, none of which, surprisingly, include innovation and technology.[2] In explaining inter-country variations in African economic growth, as well as the episodic nature of that growth, analysts often focus on stylized variables such as private investment (Devarajan *et al.* 2003), savings and interest rates (Oshikoya 1992), proximity to the tropics (Sachs and Warner 1999), openness of the economy (Hoeffler 2002) and governance (Fosu 2009). Yet, historically, technological change has been the most important source of productivity growth (Scherer 1984). As Moore (1983: 212–213) also points out:

> concern with technological progress as a source of economic growth in the developing world has taken second place in the literature to concern with choice of technology at the level of the firm, and the possibilities of substitution among factors, particularly the substitution of labour for capital.

The role of innovation and technological change has been underplayed by the literature on Africa's economic growth despite evidence from endogenous growth theorists (Romer 1986) and the experiences of the newly industrialized countries (NICs) that technological change does influence economic growth (Amsden 1989).

The non-recognition (at least explicitly) of the potential role of innovation and technology in Africa's growth performance may be attributed to a number of factors. First, innovation and technology are inherently difficult to model, and analysts find it more convenient to regard them as residuals in growth equations or as part of the so-called Africa dummy. Second, data on Africa's S&T infra-structure are very spotty, making empirical analysis a very daunting task. Third, many analysts who work on Africa's growth performance have limited knowledge of the literature on 'national systems of innovation' and are therefore more prone to regarding technology as exogenous to African economies.[3]

This chapter is premised on the notion that, difficult as it may seem, we need to begin to investigate the interconnections between AC, technological innova-tion and Africa's growth performance. Such an attempt has the potential to yield policy insights that might be foreclosed under the current approach of analysing Africa's growth performance in terms mainly of stylized variables. For instance, the salience of innovation and AC would imply that African governments should consider using industrial policy to spur growth by correcting distortions, exter-nalities and other failures in technology and factor markets. It also would mean that the state should facilitate growth by playing a more active role in skill and human resource development. Perhaps more importantly, it would imply that more attention should be paid to brain drain from Africa, which has recently generated debates amongst analysts and policy makers in Africa (Easterly and Nyarko 2008).

The chapter is structured as follows. After the Introduction, the next section reviews the state of scientific and technological development in sub-Saharan Africa (SSA). The section entitled 'Should we be concerned about Africa's weak technological capabilities?' discusses the debate on the salience of IC and AC for growth. The penultimate section uses cross-country regressions to identify some of the determinants of inter-country variations in Africa's economic growth, and the final section consists of the chapter's conclusions and policy recommendations.

How weak is Africa's IC and AC, and does it really matter for the region's growth performance?

A logical starting point for investigating the relationship between technology and growth in Africa is to ascertain the level of technological development of the region. A review of several indicators of S&T supports the widely held notion that Africa has weak IC and AC relative to other developing regions. Table 3.1 shows that Africa's share of world expenditure on research and development (R&D) was a paltry 0.5 per cent in 2001, compared with 15.6 per cent for devel-oping countries as a group, 27.9 per cent for Asia and 3.1 per cent for Latin America and the Caribbean. Africa's expenditure on R&D as a percentage of gross domestic product (GDP) has not only been the lowest in the world, but also been declining over time. In 1990, it was 0.6 per cent, and by 1997 it had plum-meted to just 0.3 per cent.[4]

Table 3.1 shows that African countries spent an average of US$6 per person (PPP$) in 2001 on R&D (the lowest in the world), compared with US$20 for developing countries, US$46 for Asia and US$34 for Latin America and the Caribbean. The table also reveals that Africa accounted for just 1 per cent of researchers in the world; again the lowest. The region's unimpressive scientific

Table 3.1 Regional science and technology indicators

Regions/countries	GERD* as percentage of world GERD	GERD as percentage of GDP	GERD per inhabitant (PPP$)	Researchers as percentage of world total	Researchers per million inhabitants	GERD per researcher (thousands of PPP$)
Developing countries	15.6	0.6	20	28.4	347	57.9
Developed countries	84.4	2.2	377	71.6	3,033	124.2
Asia	27.9	1.3	46	34.5	537	85.1
Latin America & the Caribbean	3.1	0.5	34	6.7	715	48.2
SSA (excluding Arab States)	0.5	0.3	6	1.0	113	49.1
Arab States (in Africa)	0.2	0.2	7	1.5	489	14.9
Arab States (in Asia)	0.1	0.2	11	0.1	52	211.4
Arab States (All)	0.4	0.2	8	1.6	356	23.6
China	3.9	0.6	17	10.6	454	38.3
India	2.0	0.7	11	2.8	151	75.8

Source: Computed from UNESCO statistics (UNESCO Institute of Statistics 2001: 7).

Note: *GERD, gross domestic expenditure on research and development.

Table 3.2 Technology output, absorptive capacity and economic growth for selected African countries (2005)

Country	R&D as percentage of GDP*	Researchers per million inhabitants*	Economic growth in 2005 (%)**	Economic growth in 2006 (%)**	Mean economic growth (2005–2006) (%)***
Algeria	0.1	170	5	2	3.5
Botswana	0.4	–	5	3	4.0
Burkina Faso	0.2	22	6	6	6.0
Cameroon	–	26	2	3	2.5
Cape Verde	–	127	7	11	9.0
Dem. Republic of Congo	0.5	–	6	5	5.5
Cote d'Ivoire	–	68	1	1	1.0
Egypt	0.2	–	4	7	5.5
Ethiopia	0.2	20	12	11	11.5
Gambia	–	28	5	7	6.0
Lesotho	0.1	10	3	7	5.0
Madagascar	0.2	43	5	5	5.0
Mauritius	0.4	–	5	4	4.5
Morocco	0.7	–	3	8	5.5
Mozambique	0.5	–	8	9	8.5
Niger	–	8	7	5	6.0
Senegal	0.1	–	6	2	4.0
Seychelles	0.4	157	1	5	3.0
South Africa	0.9	361	5	5	5.0
Sudan	0.3	–	6	11	8.5
Tunisia	1.0	1,450	4	6	5.0
Uganda	0.2		6	11	8.5
Zambia	0.0	52	5	6	5.5
India	0.7	111	9	10	9.5
China	1.4	926	10	12	11.0
Ireland	1.3	2,882	6	6	6.0
South Korea	3.2	4,162	4	5	4.5

Sources: *UNESCO statistical database http://data.uis.unesco.org/; **World Development Indicators http://data.worldbank.org/data-catalog/world-development-indicators; and ***author's calculations.

and technological performance is more disappointing when the S&T indicators are disaggregated into various countries, as shown in Table 3.2. As the table shows, most African countries spend less than 0.5 per cent of GDP on R&D, compared with 1.4 per cent in China and 3.2 per cent in South Korea.

Although African countries spend more on their researchers than some developing regions, the region has had the lowest volume of scientific and technical publications. In 2001, for instance, SSA spent US$49,000 per researcher, compared with Latin America at US$48,000 and China at US$38,000 (see Table 3.1). However, Table 3.3 shows that other regions have had higher scientific and technical publication levels than Africa. Between 2000 and 2005, the number of scientific and technical publications in Africa grew by just 6 per cent, compared with 119 per cent for East Asia and the Pacific, 36 per cent for Latin America and

Table 3.3 Regional distribution of number of scientific and technical publications (2000–2005)

Region	2000	2001	2002	2003	2004	2005	Mean 2000–2005	Growth rate 2000–2005 (%)
East Asia & Pacific	20,116	22,818	25,101	30,812	37,075	44,064	29,998	119
LAC	14,786	15,776	17,126	17,889	19,361	20,045	17,497	36
MENA	3,689	4,017	4,379	5,154	5,551	6,243	4,839	69
South Asia	10,796	11,334	12,262	13,162	14,086	15,429	12,845	42
SSA	3,355	3,279	3,438	3,331	3,517	3,563	3,413	6
ROW	629,230	628,047	637,041	660,304	687,174	708,086	658,314	13

Source: Based on World Development Indicators database.

Notes: LAC, Latin America and the Caribbean; MENA, Middle East and North Africa; SSA, sub-Saharan Africa; ROW, rest of the world.

the Caribbean, 69 per cent for the Middle East and North Africa and 43 per cent for South Asia. According to data gathered from the UNESCO website, Africa's share of world scientific publications was 1.4 per cent in 1990 and 2000, respectively, compared with 1.7 per cent for Latin America in 1990 and 3.2 per cent in 2000. Asia's researchers accounted for 14.5 per cent of world scientific publications in 1990 and 21.1 per cent in 2000.[5]

The technological output of African countries, as measured by the number of US patents granted to firms in these countries, also lags behind those of other developing countries (see Table 3.4). Patent data show that, with the exception of South Africa, Kenya and Nigeria, most African countries received virtually no patents between 2000 and 2008.[6] This is in stark contrast to countries like South Korea, China, India and Brazil which received thousands of patents within this period. Even when one controls for the relatively small size of African countries, their technological output has been grossly marginal.

There are variations, however, in the levels of IC and AC amongst African countries. Top R&D spenders, according to Table 3.2, include Tunisia (1.0 per cent), South Africa (0.9 per cent) and Morocco (0.7 per cent). In terms of the number of researchers per million inhabitants, the leading countries are Tunisia (1,450), South Africa (361), Algeria (170), Seychelles (157) and Cape Verde (127). Tunisia and South Africa are thus the two leading countries in Africa with regard

Table 3.4 Number of US patents granted to selected African and other developing countries (2000–2008)

Country	2000	2001	2002	2003	2004	2005	2006	2007	2008	Total
Benin	0	0	0	0	0	0	0	1	0	1
Cameroon	0	0	0	0	0	0	0	1	0	1
Cote d'Ivoire	0	0	0	0	1	0	0	0	0	1
Gabon	0	0	0	0	0	0	0	1	0	1
Ghana	0	0	0	0	0	0	0	1	0	1
Kenya	3	4	1	10	16	10	3	1	4	62
Mauritius	0	0	0	0	0	0	0	0	1	1
Namibia	1	0	0	0	0	0	0	0	1	2
Nigeria	2	1	4	4	1	0	0	1	1	14
South Africa	125	137	123	131	115	108	127	116	124	1106
Uganda	0	1	1	0	0	0	0	0	0	2
Costa Rica	8	12	8	10	10	13	26	17	13	117
Dominican Republic	5	0	1	0	0	2	2	2	3	15
India	131	180	267	356	376	403	506	578	672	3469
Indonesia	14	10	15	12	23	23	16	15	19	147
Brazil	113	125	112	180	161	98	148	118	133	1188
China (excluding Hong Kong)	161	265	390	424	597	565	970	1235	1874	6481
South Korea	3472	3763	4009	4132	4671	4591	6509	7264	8731	47142

Source: Based on US Patent office statistical database.

to expenditure on R&D and the number of scientists. Notice, also, from Table 3.3 that these countries achieved respectable levels of economic growth during the 2005–2006 period, suggesting that there could be a correlation between AC and growth. South Africa, Kenya and Nigeria stand out amongst other African countries with regard to the number of patents (see Table 3.4).

Two critical questions need to be addressed regarding the disappointing technological performance of most African countries. First, to what extent has the poor S&T infrastructure of African countries affected their growth performance? Does the variation in the levels of technological development of African countries explain inter-country variations in the region's economic growth? The opinion is divided on these questions, as the following section shows.

Should we be concerned about Africa's weak technological capabilities?

The previous section has shown that Africa has weak technological capabilities, but the extent to which this weakness has affected the region's growth performance is unclear. A review of the literature suggests that there are two broad perspectives on this question.

Arguments in support of IC and AC for growth in Africa

Analysts who believe that weak AC and lack of IC have negatively affected the growth performance of African countries use the following arguments to support their position.

Africa is missing out on growth-inducing foreign investment

Foreign investors are believed to prefer to locate in economies with an abundant supply of scientists, engineers and highly skilled workforce. In other words, they prefer economies that are capable of absorbing and assimilating complex technologies. Since foreign direct investment (FDI) is strongly correlated with growth (Ramirez 2000; Chakrabarti 2001; Zhang 2001), it therefore implies that the surfeit of scientists and engineers in a country would spur growth through the attraction of larger flows of FDI. In his interviews with R&D managers of foreign corporations operating in China, Chen (2008: 628) notes that 'the primary motives underlying the establishment of advanced R&D centres in China concerned not the cost, but the availability of the required skilled labor'. Corroborating this point, the director of IBM China Research Labs pointed out that:

> the migration is not just about outsourcing for low labour rates. If it were just about low labour rates, we'd probably have R&D centres in places like Romania and the Philippines. China's advantage is not in low production costs. Production costs are even lower in India. China's advantage lies in the availability of the best talent.
>
> (Chen 2008: 628)

Because of their lack of technological capability, African countries attract FDI in low-end activities that do not generate substantial value added. FDI flows to Africa go mainly into low-end sectors such as tourism, agriculture, assembly-type manufacturing, mineral extraction, retail trade and banking (Onyeiwu and Shrestha 2004):

> The absolute number of skilled and educated workers in a developing country is one factor that *ceteris paribus* influences the amount of high-tech FDI a developing country can attract. One of the reasons Ireland was able to attract large inflows of high-tech FDI was the relatively large number of engineers and other highly trained people it could provide.
>
> (Paus 2005: 193)

Lack of technological capability weakens Africa's export performance

Growth in Africa has been constrained by weak export performance (UNCTAD 2008). Export performance, in turn, depends on technological capability and AC. Strong IC enables a country to produce high-tech or innovative products that can compete effectively on international markets. Technological capability also increases total-factor productivity, which subsequently enables a country to become cost-competitive abroad (Pack 1993). The experiences of the NICs of South East Asia have shown that export-led industrialization strategies are effective mechanisms for promoting economic growth (Krueger 1997). But an export-led industrialization strategy can only succeed with a strong AC and IC (Kim *et al.* 1987).

Low AC inhibits the growth of manufacturing value added

Economists who believe in the salience of AC and IC argue that the lack of technological capability and AC by African firms prevents them from generating significant levels of manufacturing value added, which has the effect of slowing down the economic growth of African countries. Lall *et al.* (1994) note that the failure of Ghanaian firms to develop skills, capabilities and technical support led to significant and costly deindustrialization in the country during the 1990s. Adei (1990) also found that the failure of the Bonsa Tyre Company in Ghana to enhance its efficiency and productivity was due to the firm's weak technological capability.

Strong AC promotes brain drain, investment in human capital and economic growth

Countries with strong AC (for instance, abundant scientists and engineers) usually experience brain drain, as their scientists and engineers seek better opportunities in other countries – particularly in Europe and North America. Easterly and Nyarko (2008) have shown that, rather than having a negative effect on growth, brain drain generates remittances to the country of origin of the migrant. The present value of these remittances, according to these authors' calculation, typically exceeds the cost of educating the migrant and thus leads to economic growth. Additionally, the prospect of earning a higher income abroad spurs private investment in human capital, thus enhancing AC and economic growth.

Historical evidence supports the salience of AC and IC

The history of growth suggests that technological change is a major determinant of growth. In his seminal article on the growth of the US economy, Solow (1956) showed that only about 12.5 per cent of the increase in labour productivity between 1909 and 1949 was due to an increase in capital intensity. The rest was attributable to 'technical change'. The experiences of the NICs have often been used to justify the salience of AC and IC in the growth process (Amsden 1989).

Arguments against the salience AC and IC

Those who subscribe to the notion that the lack of technological capability by African countries has not significantly affected the region's growth performance use the following evidence to make their case.

Oversupply of scientists and engineers in Africa

Some analysts believe that weak AC cannot be a constraint to Africa's economic growth, because there are too many unemployed scientists and engineers in African countries (Sender 1999). According to Amsden (1997), the abundant supply of scientific knowledge in developing countries has failed to generate demand necessary to employ it. According to these analysts, AC can be a constraint to growth only when there are shortages of scientists and engineers in a country. Such is not the case in contemporary Africa.

Innovation and technology diffuse easily across countries

A country need not develop indigenous technological capability, as long as it promotes openness of the economy. This argument is based on the fact that technology diffuses to open economies. By crafting effective technology transfer policies, a country can overcome its weak AC and IC. During the Meiji Restoration, Japan adopted FDI polices that allowed it to adapt foreign technologies to local conditions. Japan's rapid growth during the post-Second World War era is often attributed to its ability to acquire and effectively assimilate foreign technologies (Lawrence 1990).

Growth usually precedes AC and IC

There is a chicken-or-egg dilemma associated with the role of IC and AC in growth. Some have argued that growth has to occur first before a country can mobilize the resources needed to develop strong IC and AC. In the absence of growth, a country may need to borrow or seek foreign aid in order to invest in R&D or train scientists and engineers. Resort to borrowing increases a country's external indebtedness, with its negative impact on growth. Research has shown that aid dependency can stifle growth (Moyo and Ferguson 2009).

The arguments for and against the salience of IC and AC all have merit, but empirical analysis is needed to validate some of the contentions. In the next section, I use cross-country regressions to explore whether differences in AC and IC explain inter-country variations in Africa's growth performance.

Empirical analysis

Growth in Africa has not been uniform, both across countries and over time, with several African countries achieving negative growth rates in the 1990s, though countries such as Cape Verde, Equatorial Guinea and Eritrea achieved respectably high mean growth rates during this period (see Fosu 2009, his Table 1). There have been appreciable improvements in growth since the 1990s, however (ibid.). How might one explain the variation and the episodic nature of growth in Africa? Moss (2007) points out that answers to these questions are not only complex, but are sometimes inexplicable.[7] However, in the final analysis, what explains the longer-term growth among these countries, especially in the more recent period of growth resurgence?

A major goal of this section is to use cross-country regressions to investigate whether AC and IC explain the differences in the growth performance of African countries. To motivate the empirical analysis, I adopt the endogenous growth model proposed by Audretsch and Keilbach (2005). This model assumes that economic growth depends on four key variables: (i) investment in physical capital, (ii) the labour force, (iii) the volume of technological knowledge generated by the economy (represented by IC), and (iv) the rate by which that knowledge diffuses in the economy (represented by AC). The empirical challenge therefore becomes that of specifying growth equations that explicitly incorporate proxies for IC and AC, in addition to stylized variables that affect growth.

The following growth equation is used in this chapter to explore the salience of IC and AC for inter-country variation in the growth performance of Africa.

$$GRWT = \beta_0 + \beta_1 AC + \beta_2 IC + \beta_3 INV + \beta_4 POP + \beta_5 POLR + \beta_6 OPEN + \beta_7 GOV + \beta_8 AID$$

where: GRWT is mean rate of growth of GDP per capita; *AC* is absorptive capacity; *IC* is innovative capability; *INV* is investment in physical capital; *POP* is population growth; *POLR* is political risk; *OPEN* is openness of the economy; *GOV* is size of the government; and *AID* is foreign aid. The variables are measured as described in the following section.

Dependent variables

Given the boom-and-bust cycles that characterize growth in Africa, the dependent variable (GRWT) is the mean percentage rate of growth of (GDP) per capita for 31 SSA countries over the 2000–2008 period.

Explanatory variables

Absorptive capacity

Economic growth depends on a country's ability to absorb or assimilate new technologies (Audretsch and Keilbach 2005). AC is particularly crucial for African
countries, given their relatively weak capacity to innovate or introduce new technologies. The ideal measure of AC would be investment in R&D by African
countries (Cohen and Levinthal 1989). However, these data are not available for
most African countries. In this chapter, AC is proxied by the importation of
information and communication technology (ICT) goods as a percentage of total
imports. The use of this proxy is based on the assumption that countries with
strong AC tend to use ICT more extensively than countries with weak AC. Thus,
the higher the number of scientists, engineers and skilled workers in an economy,
the higher is its propensity to demand and import ICT goods. The coefficient of
AC is expected to be positive.

Innovative capability

The ability of a country to innovate and introduce new technologies (including
new products and services) to strengthen its competitiveness in foreign markets
is termed 'innovative capability' (IC). By boosting exports and foreign exchange
earnings, technological innovation promotes economic growth. In a study of
204 Korean firms, Young (1992) shows how 96 per cent of these firms succeeded
in upgrading their technologies and product quality, and subsequently gained
international competitiveness. South Korea has been able to sustain a respectable
growth rate mainly as a result of the technological capability of Korean firms (Pack
and Westphal 1986). IC is measured in this chapter by the total number of patents
granted each of the 31 countries in my sample during the period 2000–2008. The
coefficient of this variable is expected to be positive and significant.

Investment in physical capital

Investment in physical capital (INV) spurs growth not only by increasing labour
productivity, but also total-factor productivity. Physical capital can also influence
growth through its effects on trade (Baldwin and Seghezza 1996; Wacziarg and
Welch 2003). Studies on the growth performance of African countries often show
that low investment share of GDP is a major reason for the region's slow growth
(Levine and Renelt 1992). Investment in physical capital is proxied in this chapter
by the mean annual percentage growth of gross fixed capital formation during the
period 2000–2008. The coefficient of this variable is expected to be positive.

Population growth

It is widely believed in the development literature that Africa's high fertility rates
may be slowing down the region's growth (Moss 2007). With stagnant or declining

output, high fertility rates have the effect of reducing output per head. It may also lead to deficit spending, as the government tries to provide social services needed to support the high dependency ratio that comes with high fertility rates. Population is measured by the annual rate of growth of the population of the sample countries. The coefficient of population growth (POP) is expected to be negative.

Political risk

Studies have established a link between political risks (*POLR*), FDI and economic growth. Democratic and politically stable economies attract more FDI than despotic and unstable countries (Schneider and Frey 1985). Since FDI and growth tend to be positively related, greater political stability should then result in faster economic growth. Democratic regimes are also more likely to respect civil liberties, the rule of law and property rights – features that are more conducive to growth and investment. Ngowi (2001) argues that many developing countries have attracted little FDI and hence have achieved slow growth rates, because they are regarded as 'high risk and are characterized by a lack of political and institutional stability and predictability'. Fosu (2011) finds that the impact of political and civil rights on growth is rather complicated; it is U-shaped, though a linear specification of it still results in a significantly positive coefficient. I measure political risk by Freedom House's Index of Political Right. For each of the 31 countries in my sample, I calculated the mean of the index for 2000–2001. Because the index measures political rights on a scale of 1–7 (with 1 representing the highest levels and 7 the lowest), *POLR* is expected to be negatively correlated with economic growth.

Openness of the economy

Studies have shown that open economies attract more FDI and therefore grow faster, than closed economies (Morisset 2000; Chakrabarti 2001; Kandiero and Chitiga 2006). After controlling for endogeneity and country-fixed effects, Hoeffler (2002) found that openness (*OPEN*) is positively correlated with growth in Africa. Removal of capital controls and restrictive trade policies spur local firms to eliminate X-inefficiency and move closer to the international productivity frontier. I measure openness using trade as a percentage of GDP. I expect the coefficient of this variable to be positive.

Size of the government

The size of the government (*GOV*) can affect growth in Africa. As Moss (2007: 94) observes: 'by the early 1980s, it was believed that the cumulative effect of state intervention and unnecessary regulation was a major cause of African economic malaise'. Big government results in rent-seeking activities that crowd out productive investment (Ndulu and O'Connell 1999). They are also a breeding ground for corruption, cronyism and bureaucratic red tape. Conversely, smaller governments tend to reduce budget deficits, lower interest rates and hence boost private investment. The size of the government is measured by mean general government final consumption expenditure as a percentage of GDP, and its coefficient is expected to be negative.

Aid

There is controversy about the role of foreign aid in Africa's economic growth. Moyo and Ferguson (2009) argue that aid is detrimental to growth in Africa. They propose the immediate discontinuance of aid as a precondition for economic growth in the region. In contrast, Jeffrey Sachs (quoted in Munk 2013: 31) argues that aid flow to Africa since independence has been too meagre to make a significant difference to the region.[8] He therefore suggests the scaling-up of foreign aid so as to make a big push for growth in Africa. In this paper, aid is measured as a percentage of gross national income (GNI). Its coefficient is expected to be indeterminate a priori.

Data sources

With the exception of patents and political rights, data for the dependent and explanatory variables were collected from the World Development Indicators (WDI) database. The data were computed as means over the 2000–2008 period for each of the 31 sample SSA countries.[9] Data on patents and political rights were collected from the databases of the US Patent Office and the Heritage Foundation, respectively. The descriptive statistics for the dependent and explanatory variables are summarized in Table 3.5. As the table shows, the sample countries had a mean growth rate of about 1.7 per cent during the 2000–2008 period, with a

Table 3.5 Descriptive statistics

Variable	Observations	Mean	Std. Dev.	Minimum	Maximum
GRWT	31	1.66	2.43	−5.88	5.31
INV	31	8.60	9.25	−6.58	43.02
POP	31	2.21	0.83	0.08	3.78
GOV	31	15.20	7.26	6.39	45.35
OPEN	31	3.52	3.33	0.6	15.00
AID	31	9.85	8.06	0.34	31.45
POLR	31	4.80	1.57	1.00	7.00
AC	31	4.97	2.04	1.7	12.20
IC	31	38.54	198.41	0	1106

Source: Author's calculations.

Notes: GRWT, mean rate of growth of gross domestic product per capita; INV, investment in physical capital; POP, population growth; GOV, size of the government; OPEN, openness of the economy; AID, foreign aid; POLR, political risk; AC, absorptive capacity; IC, innovative capability.

maximum of 5.3 per cent, a minimum of –5.9 per cent and a standard deviation of 2.5 per cent.

Results and discussion

The OLS cross-country regression results are summarized in Table 3.6. Before discussing the results, it is important to acknowledge the fact that there may be econometric problems associated with small sample, cross-sectional OLS regressions. One such problem is heteroscedasticity, which might make estimates of the standard errors of the coefficients biased and thus render the test of significance relatively unreliable. Thus, the regression results presented below should be interpreted cautiously; however, the estimated coefficients should not be affected.The results suggest that AC, GOV and political rights are significant. Specifically, a 1 per cent increase in government consumption as a percentage of GDP reduces the growth rate by about 0.12 per cent. By the same token, a 1 per cent increase in the AC of an African country raises the growth rate by about 0.62 per cent. Conversely, a one-point increase in a country's index of political rights (or a deterioration in political rights ranking) reduces growth by about 0.57 per cent, though this effect is relatively weak at the 10 per cent level of significance. Surprisingly, there is no support for the notion that ICs, physical capital, population growth, openness of the economy or foreign aid explain inter-country variations in the growth performance of African countries.[10] The finding of a positive but insignificant coefficient of INV is consistent with that of Devarajan et al. (2003), who argue that 'low investment is not the constraint on African development'.

The empirical results suggest that growth in Africa is not simply a question of accumulating physical capital or promoting macroeconomic stability. While good policy is a *sine qua non* for growth (Collier and Gunning 1999; Fosu 2009),

Table 3.6 Results of cross-country OLS regression tests

Explanatory variables	Coefficient	Standard error	t	P> [t]
INV	0.015	0.054	0.29	0.772
POP	0.584	0.658	0.89	0.384
GOV	–0.125**	0.055	–2.27	0.034
OPEN	0.201	0.147	1.37	0.185
AID	0.012	0.065	0.19	0.852
POLR	–0.503*	0.283	–1.77	0.090
AC	0.646***	0.249	2.59	0.017
IC	–0.002	0.002	–0.98	0.338
CONS	0.607	2.065	0.29	0.771

Source: Author's calculations.

***Significant at the 1% level, **5% level and *10% level.

Notes: Dependent variable: mean growth of GDP per capita (2000–2008). Number of observations = 31; R^2 = 0.52; Adj R^2 = 0.35; $F(8, 22)$ = 2.99; Prob > F = 0.019; root mean square E = 1.97.

sustainable growth in Africa also requires the strengthening of the AC of African countries. In other words, growth can be accelerated if African firms succeed in developing the capacity to use technologies developed elsewhere. This result supports the view that investment in skills and knowledge is critical for growth in Africa (Schultz 1999). It also suggests that African governments should implement measures that would reduce brain drain. Currently, the brain drain from Africa is occurring at unprecedented high levels. About 13 per cent of skilled Africans reside outside the region, one of the highest levels of brain drain in the world (Easterly and Nyarko 2008).

The insignificance of foreign aid for growth in SSA is consistent with the reservations expressed by scholars about the effectiveness of aid in Africa. While some analysts argue that Africa needs to focus more on how to use aid more efficiently,[11] others contend that aid is completely inimical to African development (Moyo and Ferguson, 2009). The experiences of East Asia and Latin America suggest that the focus should not be on aid *per se*, but rather on private capital and investment.[12] Growth driven by private capital is often more sustainable and employment-generating than that driven by foreign aid. It is no secret that foreign aid in Africa usually ends up in the hands of bureaucrats and politicians who invest aid money in unproductive projects, if invested at all! President Paul Kagame of Rwanda could not have said it better when he asserted that 'aid has not delivered sustainable development. It is clear that trade and investment bring greater opportunity for wealth creation. We want investment that offers skills and jobs, encourages entrepreneurship, and provides the opportunity to improve millions of lives' (Kagame 2009).

Conclusions and policy implications

An important conclusion from this chapter is that AC matters for economic growth in Africa. Furthermore, the ability to innovate appears to be less important for growth in Africa than the ability to assimilate and effectively use new technologies.

In addition to addressing the stylized constraints to Africa's economic growth, policy makers and development practitioners should, therefore, take seriously the need to strengthen the AC of African countries.[13] The growth-enhancing attributes of technology are not necessarily manifested in the ability of African firms to produce innovative and patentable products. They are manifested in the ability of African firms to use technological knowledge to increase their total factor productivity, as well as to move faster along their learning curves. Rather than lead to major innovative breakthroughs, a stronger AC enables African firms to undertake incremental technical change that enhances their competitiveness in global markets.

Notes

1 Cohen and Levinthal (1990: 128) define AC as the 'ability of a firm to recognize the value of new, external information (or knowledge), assimilate it, and apply it to commercial ends'.

2 For instance, Collier and Gunning (1999: 7) did not mention technological factors in their list of the various factors that limit growth in Africa.
3 The literature on NIS is dominated by economists who use an interdisciplinary approach to study the impact of S&T policy on growth, income distribution, industrial development and international competitiveness.
4 Data on S&T indicators were obtained from the database of the United Nations Educational and Cultural Organization (UNESCO) at www.unesco.org.
5 See the UNESCO database on S&T indicators at www.unesco.org.
6 Based on patent data available at the US Patent Office, about 95 per cent of SSA countries received less than ten patents each during the past 30 years.
7 However, some observers attribute the dismal growth in the 1990s and early 1990s to 'policy syndromes' (Fosu 2009) and improvements during the 2000–2008 period to economic reform, good governance and a vibrant global economy that fuelled demand for Africa's exports (ibid.). This period also witnessed a big surge in the flow of FDI worldwide, including Africa.
8 In its 2005 summit in Gleneagles, Scotland, the G8 leaders pledged to double aid to Africa from US$25 billion to US$50 billion per annum by the year 2010.
9 Other countries were excluded from the sample because of the lack of data on some variables.
10 In their recent book, Moyo and Ferguson (2009) argue that aid is inimical to the growth and development of African countries.
11 See Jeffrey Sachs, 'Moyo's Confused Aid to Africa', *Huffington Post*, 27 May 2009.
12 These analysts also argue that if aid is to be sought it should be focused on project-level aid rather than arm's-length cash transfers, most of which end up in unproductive ventures.
13 It would be recalled from the empirical section that the coefficient on patents is not significant. This can be interpreted as implying that the ability to produce innovative products is not as important for growth as the ability to assimilate and use new knowledge and technologies developed elsewhere.

References

Adei, S. (1990). 'Technological Capacity and Aborted Industrialization in Ghana: The Case of Bonsa Tyre Company'. *World Development*, 18(11): 1501–11.
Amsden, A. (1989). *Asia's Next Giant: South Korea and Late Industrialization*. New York: Oxford University Press.
Amsden, A. (1997). 'Bringing Production Back in Understanding Government's Economic Role in Late Industrialisation'. *World Development*, 4(4): 469–80.
Audretsch, D.B. and M. Keilbach (2005). 'The Knowledge Spillover Theory of Entrepreneurship and Economic Growth'. Unpublished Manuscript. Jena: Max Planck Institute of Economics.
Baldwin, R. and E. Seghezza (1996). 'Testing for Trade-Induced Investment-Led Growth'. National Bureau of Economic Research Working Paper 5416. Cambridge, MA: NBER.
Chakrabarti, A. (2001). 'The Determinants of Foreign Direct Investment: Sensitivity Analyses of Cross-Country Regressions'. *Kyklos*, 54: 89–114.
Chen, Y.-C. (2008). 'Why Do Multinational Corporations Locate Their Advanced R&D Centres in Beijing?'. *Journal of Development Studies*, 44(5): 622–44.
Cohen W.M. and D.A. Levinthal (1989). 'Innovation and Learning: The Two Faces of R&D'. *The Economic Journal*, 99: 569–96.
Cohen W.M. and D.A. Levinthal (1990). 'Absorptive Capacity: A New Perspective on Learning and Innovation'. *Administrative Science Quarterly*, 35: 128–52.

Collier, P. and J. Gunning (1999). 'Why Has Africa Grown Slowly?'. *The Journal of Economic Perspectives*, 13(3): 3–22.

Devarajan, S., W. Easterly and H. Pack (2003). 'Low Investment Is Not the Constraint on African Development'. *Economic Development and Cultural Change*, 51(3): 547–71.

Easterly, W. and Y. Nyarko (2008). 'Is the Brain Drain Good for Africa?'. Global Working Papers 18. Washington, DC: Brookings Institution.

Fosu, A.K. (2009). 'Understanding the African Growth Record: The Importance of Policy Syndromes and Governance'. Discussion Paper 2009/02. Helsinki: UNU-WIDER.

Fosu, A.K. (2011). "Democracy and Growth in Africa: Evidence on the Impact of Political and Civil Rights," *The Empirical Economics Letters*, 10(1): 19–25.

Hoeffler, A. (2002). 'Openness, Investment and Growth'. *Journal of African Economies*, 10(4): 470–97.

Kagame, P. (2009). 'Why Africa Welcomes the Chinese'. *Guardian*, 2 November 2009, p. 31. Available at: http://www.theguardian.com/commentisfree/2009/nov/02/aid-trade-rwanda-china-west (accessed: 3 November 2009).

Kandiero, T. and M. Chitiga (2006). 'Trade Openness and Foreign Direct Investment in Africa'. *SAJEMS*, 9(3): 355–70.

Kim, L., J. Lee and J. Lee (1987). 'Korea's Entry into the Computer Industry and Its Acquisition of Technological Capability'. *Technovation*, 6: 5–16.

Krueger, A.O. (1997). 'Trade Policy and Economic Development: How We Learn'. *American Economic Review*, 87(1): 1–15.

Lall, S., G.B. Navaretti, S. Teitel and G. Wignaraja (1994). *Technology and Enterprise Development: Ghana under Structural Adjustment*. London: Macmillan.

Lawrence, R. (1990). 'Innovation and Trade: Meeting the Foreign Challenge'. In H.J. Aaron, J.E. Chubb, E.A. Hanushek, L.J. Korb, R.Z. Lawrence, T.E. Mann *et al.* (eds), *Setting National Priorities: Policy for the Nineties*. Washington, DC: Brookings Institution, pp. 145–84.

Levine, R. and D. Renelt (1992). 'A Sensitivity Analysis of Cross-Country Growth Regressions'. *American Economic Review*, 82(4): 942–63.

Moore, F.T. (1983). *Technological Change and Industrial Development*. Staff Working Paper 613. Washington, DC: World Bank.

Morisset, P. (2000). 'Foreign Direct Investment to Africa: Policies also Matter'. *Transnational Corporation*, 9: 107–25.

Moss, T.J. (2007). *African Development*. Boulder, CO: Lynne Rienner.

Moyo, D. and N. Ferguson (2009). *Dead Aid: Why Aid is Not Working and How There is a Better Way for Africa*. New York: Farrar, Straus, and Giroux.

Munk, N. (2013). *The Idealist – Jeffrey Sachs and the Quest to End Extreme Poverty*. New York: Doubleday.

Ndulu, B. and S. O'Connell (1999). 'Governance and Growth in Sub-Saharan Africa'. *The Journal of Economic Perspectives*, 13(3): 41–66.

Ngowi, H.P. (2001). 'Can Africa Increase its Global Share of Foreign Direct Investment (FDI)?'. *West African Review*, 2: 1–22.

Onyeiwu, S. and H. Shrestha (2004). 'Determinants of Foreign Direct Investment in Africa'. *Journal of Developing Societies*, 20(2): 89–106.

Oshikoya, T. (1992). 'Interest Rate Liberalization, Savings, Investment and Growth: The Case of Kenya'. *Savings and Development*, 16(3): 305–20.

Pack, H. (1993). 'Productivity and Industrial Development in Sub-Saharan Africa'. *World Development*, 21(1): 1–6.

Pack, H. and L.E. Westphal (1986). 'Industrial Strategy and Technology Change: Theory Versus Reality'. *Journal of Development Economics*, 22(1): 87–128.

Paus, E. (2005). *Foreign Investment, Development, and Globalization*. New York: Palgrave Macmillan.

Ramirez, M.D. (2000). 'Foreign Direct Investment in Mexico: A Co-integration Analysis'. *The Journal of Development Studies*, 37: 138–62.

Romer, P.M. (1986). 'Increasing Returns and Long-run Growth'. *Journal of Political Economy*, 94(5): 1002–37.

Sachs, J. (2009). 'Moyo's Confused Aid to Africa'. *Huffington Post*, 27 May. Available at: http://www.huffingtonpost.com/jeffrey-sachs/moyos-confused-attack-on_b_208222.html (accessed: 25 May 2011).

Sachs, J. and M. Warner (1999). 'Sources of Slow Growth in African Economies'. *Journal of African Economies*, 16: 335–76.

Scherer, F.M. (1984). *Innovation and Growth*. Cambridge, MA: MIT.

Schneider, F. and B.F. Frey (1985). 'Economic and Political Determinants of Foreign Direct Investment'. *World Development*, 13: 161–75.

Schultz, P.T. (1999). 'Health and Schooling Investments in Africa'. *The Journal of Economic Perspectives*, 13(3): 67–88.

Sender, J. (1999). 'Economic Performance Limitations of the Current Consensus'. *The Journal of Economic Perspectives*, 13(3): 89–114.

Solow, R. (1956). 'A Contribution to the Theory of Economic Growth'. *Quarterly Journal of Economics*, 70: 65–94.

UNCTAD (2008). *Economic Development in Africa*. New York: United Nations.

UNESCO Institute of Statistics (2001). *The State of Science and Technology in the World*, Paris: UNESCO.

Wacziarg, R. and K. Welch (2003). 'Trade Liberalization and Growth: New Evidence'. National Bureau of Economic Research Working Paper 10152. Cambridge, MA: NBER.

Young, S.-G. (1992). 'Import Liberalization and Industrial Adjustment'. In V. Corbo and S. M. Suh (eds), *Structural Adjustment in a Newly Industrialized Country*. Baltimore: The Johns Hopkins University Press, pp. 171–203.

Zhang, K.H. (2001). 'Does Foreign Direct Investment Promote Economic Growth? Evidence from East Asia and Latin America'. *Contemporary Economic Policy*, 19: 175–85.

4 Exchange-rate regimes and trade

Is Africa different?

*Mahvash Saeed Qureshi and
Charalambos G. Tsangarides*

Introduction[1]

The choice of exchange-rate regime and its macroeconomic implications – a well-debated subject since the collapse of the Bretton Woods system in the early 1970s – gained renewed interest with a series of financial crises in the late 1990s. The exchange-rate regimes adopted by the hardest hit countries were widely believed to have played a role in triggering the crisis, which led to a greater scrutiny of exchange-rate policy choices and their impact on the macroeconomy by both researchers and policy makers.

Most of the ensuing research focused on the influence of exchange-rate regimes on economic growth, inflation and macroeconomic stability. A notable exception to this is the seminal work of Rose (2000), which investigates the effect of currency unions on trade and finds that two countries having a common currency tend to trade about three times as much as they would otherwise. Frankel and Rose (2002) further show that the growth-enhancing benefits of currency unions (CUs) occur through increased trade only, and not through other channels (such as reduced inflation).

These findings have generated immense interest and controversy, and numerous studies have followed which, in general, find a smaller magnitude of the effect of CUs on trade than estimated by Rose (2000). More recently, Adam and Cobham (2007), Klein and Shambaugh (2006), and Qureshi and Tsangarides (2010) go beyond CUs and investigate the impact of other possible exchange-rate regimes on bilateral trade using the gravity model framework. They find that exchange-rate regimes with lower uncertainty and transaction costs, namely, CUs and pegs, are significantly more pro-trade than flexible exchange-rate regimes.

In this chapter, we revisit the link between exchange-rate regimes and trade in the context of Africa, where several monetary integration initiatives are under consideration. A key goal of the proposed African monetary unions is to boost international trade, but their feasibility has been questioned repeatedly on the basis of Mundell's (1961) optimum currency areas theory.[2] Indeed, while sharing a common currency may promote trade, it may also entail higher economic and institutional costs before and after the CU formation. Further, as is evident from the recent global financial crisis, not abiding with the institutional requisites could have destabilizing effects in the face of shocks not only for the country in question, but for the entire CU.

Our analysis therefore examines whether a suitable alternative exchange-rate arrangement exists for Africa – one that promotes trade through lower transaction costs, exchange-rate volatility and uncertainty, but retains some flexibility and places fewer demands for policy coordination – than CUs. Specifically, we empirically investigated the viability of *conventional pegs* as a possible choice for Africa to enhance bilateral trade and benchmark the trade-generating effects of both CUs and pegs for the region against the world. To this end, we constructed measures of CUs and pegs, using a novel dataset of the International Monetary Fund's (IMF) de jure and de facto exchange-rate-regime classifications for a sample of 159 countries from 1972 to 2006, to account for possible discrepancies between the officially announced and practically followed regimes, and their potentially different macroeconomic implications.[3]

Our empirical assessment also addresses some potential econometric concerns highlighted in earlier studies, particularly those pertaining to the treatment of omitted variables in bilateral trade models, and puts forward quantitative estimates obtained through a range of estimation methods, including controlling for country pair-fixed effects and the Hausman–Taylor (HT) approach, which permits the estimation of time-invariant variables.

Our findings could be summarized as follows: first, fixed exchange-rate regimes in the form of CUs and pegs increase trade for Africa relative to more flexible exchange-rate arrangements, and this effect is almost twice as large as for an average country in the world sample; second, the effect of CUs and pegs is above and beyond that of exchange-rate volatility indicating that other factors associated with more stable exchange-rate regimes such as lower transactions costs also play a significant role in promoting trade. Third, the effect of conventional pegs for the region appears to be at least as large as that of CUs, suggesting that conventional pegs could present a viable alternative to the region to promote trade without opting for more rigid exchange-rate arrangements in the form of CUs. Finally, we also find some evidence of an indirect effect of pegging with an anchor currency – typically realized through the stabilization of exchange rate against other currencies pegged to the same anchor – pointing to both direct and indirect bilateral trade gains achieved from pegging for Africa. These results are robust to a variety of specifications, estimation methods and variable definitions.

The following section provides a brief background to the study. The next sections outline the empirical methodology and data used in the chapter, present the estimation results and discuss the sensitivity analysis. The final section concludes.

Background

The literature on the impact of exchange-rate regimes on economic performance and crisis vulnerability burgeoned after the Asian financial crisis in the late 1990s. The existing studies, however, do not provide a consensus view on the subject, with results sometimes varying according to the classification of exchange-rate arrangements, the cross-country and time dimensions of the sample, model specification and estimation methodology. Ghosh *et al.* (1997), for example, find no systematic differences in output growth across regimes, but their results show that pegged regimes are associated with higher investment, lower productivity growth, lower inflation and higher volatility of growth and employment. Ghosh *et al.* (2003) find that pegs and intermediate regimes improve growth and inflation performance compared to floats, but pegged regimes also increase output volatility.

By contrast, Reinhart and Rogoff (2004) show that exchange-rate arrangements may be quite important for growth, trade and inflation. Levy-Yeyati and Sturzenegger (2003) note that hard pegs (such as currency boards) and those lasting 5 years or more are associated with lower inflation and slower growth in developing economies, but have no effect whatsoever in industrialized economies.[4] They also show that countries with short pegs underperform floats, since they grow slower without any gains in terms of inflation. Husain *et al.* (2005) argue that the economic implications of different exchange-rate regimes depend on the level of economic and institutional development. Their results indicate that greater exchange-rate flexibility improves economic growth in advanced economies, has no effect on growth and inflation in emerging economies, but lowers growth and increases inflation in developing economies.

In terms of crisis propensity, several studies document that less flexible exchange-rate regimes are significantly more likely to experience a banking or currency crisis than floats (Bubula and Ötker-Robe 2003; Ghosh *et al.* 2003, 2010; Angkinand and Willett 2011). Analysing the experience of emerging market economies before, during and after the global financial crisis, Ghosh *et al.* (2014) find that macroeconomic and financial vulnerabilities (such as real exchange-rate overvaluation, external imbalances, domestic credit booms, excessive foreign borrowing and greater domestic foreign currency lending) are significantly greater under less flexible exchange-rate regimes – including hard pegs (such as currency unions, currency boards and dollarized economies) – as compared to floats. Interestingly, they find that hard pegs are not especially susceptible to banking or currency crises, but are significantly more prone to growth collapses, while soft pegs (such as conventional single currency or basket pegs, bands and crawling arrangements) are the most susceptible to crises.

In the context of trade performance, an extensive body of literature in the late 1970s, through the 1980s, examines the effect of exchange-rate volatility on trade and finds mixed results (Hooper and Kohlhagen 1978; Cushman 1983; Kenen and Rodrik 1986; Thursby and Thursby 1987). Studies in the following decade, for example, Frankel (1997) and Frankel and Wei (1993), are more consistent in their findings and report negative, though small effects of exchange-rate volatility on trade. In his seminal work, Rose (2000) examines the issue from a different perspective and uses a gravity model of bilateral trade flows to investigate the impact of CUs on trade. He finds an economically large and statistically significant effect: two countries sharing a currency tend to trade about three times as much as they would otherwise. Rose and van Wincoop (2001), Frankel and Rose (2002), and Glick and Rose (2002) confirm this result and show that it is robust to various specifications and estimation techniques. Other studies have, however, challenged the size of the effect reported by Rose (2000) on methodological grounds, but generally agree with the existence of a common currency effect on trade.[5]

Some recent studies go beyond CUs and investigate the impact of other possible exchange-rate regimes on bilateral trade using the gravity model framework. For instance, Klein and Shambaugh (2006) use the de facto exchange-rate-regime classification developed by Shambaugh (2004) for the period 1973–1999 to estimate the impact of CUs and pegged exchange-rate arrangements on bilateral trade flows. They report statistically significant gains from CUs and direct pegs, but not a strong impact of indirect pegs on trade. Consistent with earlier studies, they also report a negative albeit small and diminishing effect of exchange-rate volatility on trade. Using Reinhart and Rogoff's (2004) de facto exchange-rate-regime classification, Adam and Cobham (2007) construct 27 different bilateral exchange-rate arrangements for countries during the period 1948 to 1998 and show that regimes with lower exchange-rate uncertainty and transactions costs are significantly more pro-trade than floating regimes.

For Africa, Masson and Pattillo (2004) examine the impact of CUs on trade and find that they promote intra-regional trade substantially. Tsangarides *et al.* (2009) support these findings and show that CU membership benefits Africa at least as much as it benefits the rest of the world. In addition, they find evidence that CUs are associated with trade creation and increased price co-movements among member countries, and that the duration of CU membership matters for trade: longer duration brings about greater benefits, but with some diminishing returns.

Methodology

To investigate the effect of CUs and pegged exchange-rate regimes on trade, we follow the existing literature and employ the gravity model of trade. The gravity model represents trade between two economies as a function of their respective economic masses and trading costs (commonly proxied by the distance between them). The basic model has been extended in recent years to incorporate a variety of other factors that may affect trading costs, for example, trade agreements, common language, historical ties, common border, geographical location and so forth. To the extent that exchange-rate policy influences currency conversion costs, exchange-rate volatility as well as inflation expectations, trading costs would also depend on the exchange-rate regime in place such that more stable exchange-rate regimes are expected to reduce these costs and affect bilateral trade.

We thus augment the conventional gravity model with measures of fixed exchange-rate regimes, specifically, CUs and pegs and estimate the benchmark specification of the following form:

$$\log(X_{ijt}) = \beta_0 + \sum_{k=1}^{N} \beta_k Z_{ijt} + \gamma CU_{ijt} + \delta DirPeg_{ijt} + \lambda_t + v_{ij} + u_{ijt} \qquad (4.1)$$

where X_{ijt} denotes real bilateral trade between countries i and j in year t; CU is a binary variable that is unity if i and j share a currency (and zero otherwise); *DirPeg* is also a binary variable that is unity if i's exchange rate is pegged to j, or vice versa (but i and j are not members of the same CU; and zero otherwise); and Z is a vector comprising traditional time-variant and -invariant determinants of trade between countries. The time-variant variables include the (log of) product of real gross domestic product (GDP) of the trading partners, the (log of) product of their real GDP per capita and a binary variable equal to one if the two countries share a free trade agreement (and zero otherwise). The time invariant variables include the (log of) bilateral distance, the (log of) product of geographical areas of the country pair, binary variables for the existence of common historical, geographical, and linguistic ties and the number of landlocked and island countries in the pair.[6]

In addition, Equation 4.1 includes country pair-specific effects (v_{ij}) – discussed in detail below – to account for any pro-trade omitted variables that are correlated with the explanatory variables, year-specific effects λ_t to control for any common shocks across countries over time and a random error term ($u_{ij} \sim N(0, \sigma)$).

Recognizing that both *CU*s and *DirPeg* may improve trade through channels other than reduced exchange-rate volatility (such as lower transaction costs), we also include a measure of real exchange-rate volatility *Vol* in Equation 4.1 to empirically determine the significance of the other channels. Further, while the variable *DirPeg* indicates the peg of a country's currency to a reference/anchor currency, this peg may lead to the stabilization of exchange rates vis-à-vis several other countries simultaneously, thereby generating other (indirect) peg relationships. Thus, for example, if two countries (B and C) are pegged to the same anchor currency (A), their currencies would also be stable relative to each other. Similarly, if another country, D, is pegged to B, then D would also have an exchange-rate link with countries A and C and so forth. To take into account such indirect peg relationships generated by a direct peg, we create another binary variable, $IndPeg_{ij}$ (which takes the value of 1 if i is indirectly related to j through its peg with an anchor currency; zero otherwise) and extend Equation 4.1 as follows:[7]

$$\log(X_{ijt}) = \beta_0 + \sum_{k=1}^{N} \beta_k Z_{ijt} + \gamma CU_{ijt} + \delta DirPeg_{ijt}$$
$$+ \varepsilon IndPeg_{ijt} + \varsigma Vol_{ijt} + \lambda_t + v_{ij} + u_{ijt} \qquad (4.2)$$

where, following Ghosh *et al.* (2003), *Vol* is defined over a specific horizon n and is constructed in two steps. First, for each month in a given year, we take the absolute value of the percentage change in the bilateral real exchange-rate R over the previous n months. Next, the mean of the absolute values over n months is taken to obtain a measure corresponding to that particular year, given by:

$$Vol_t = \sum_{p=1}^{n} \frac{\left|R_{t+p-1} - R_{n+p-1}\right|}{n} \quad (4.3)$$

where n represents two horizons – 12 and 36 months – to represent short- and long-run volatility, respectively.

The anchor currencies that we consider for the construction of both *DirPeg* and *IndPeg* variables include 12 globally, as well as regionally important currencies (Australian dollar, Belgian franc, Deutsche mark, French franc, Indian rupee, New Zealand dollar, Portuguese escudo, pound sterling, Russian rouble, Singapore dollar, Spanish peseta and South African rand). We focus on strict exchange-rate anchors, whereby countries serving as anchors of monetary policy or multiple anchors (basket pegs) are not included.

Further, since the depth or level of the indirect peg relation between a trading pair may imply a different impact on trade, we use two alternative coding schemes for indirect pegs. In the first scheme, we include the shortest indirect linkage where a dyad pegged to the same anchor currency is considered as having an indirect peg. In the second scheme, we also include longer indirect linkages, such as those between two countries that are pegged to different anchor currencies, but their anchor currencies are pegged to the same anchor country.[8] Overall, the four exchange-rat-regime categories considered in our estimation – CUs, direct pegs, indirect pegs and non-pegs – are mutually exclusive such that at a point in time, each country pair is coded as one of the three (with non-pegs considered as the reference category in the estimations).

Estimation issues

Estimation of the gravity model raises several methodological issues that have been discussed extensively in the literature, but foremost of which is the potential endogeneity of regressors, essentially arising from their correlation with the error term. There are two possible sources of this correlation: omitted variables and reverse causality.

The pooled ordinary least squares (OLS) approach essentially assumes that there is no unobserved individual heterogeneity across countries. However, if such heterogeneity exists and is correlated with bilateral trade as well as the regressors included in the gravity model, then the OLS estimator will be biased and inconsistent. Research following Rose (2000) attempts to control for this bias by introducing country-specific effects (CFE) in the gravity model – both for cross-sectional and panel estimations – but Glick and Rose (2002) argue that including CFE may not fully resolve the omitted variables problem. This is because the unobserved variables could be correlated with the bilateral characteristics of the dyads (such as the propensity to opt for a particular exchange-rate regime), as well as the trade between them. They therefore propose adding country pair-specific effects (CPFE) to the gravity equation, thereby controlling for any strong unobserved bilateral determinants of trade.

Estimating the gravity model with the CPFE, however, does not provide coefficient estimates for the time invariant variables. An alternative – which addresses concerns related to omitted variables and the estimation of time invariant (or with little variation) regressors – is the Hausman–Taylor (HT) (Hausman and Taylor 1981) estimation technique. The HT estimator – based on the instrumental variable approach – yields consistent and efficient estimates in the presence of correlation between some explanatory variables and the error term and is considered to outperform the OLS, random and fixed effects methods when applied to gravity models (see Egger and Pfaffermayr 2003; Serlenga and Shin 2007).[9]

The second potential source of endogeneity in Equation 4.1 stems from the dependence of exchange-rate regime itself on trade links between countries. While this source of endogeneity may be an important issue in cross-sectional studies, an advantage of using the panel specification is that it could be addressed through the inclusion of dyad-specific effects. Taking into account the dyadic-fixed effects captures the impact of all time invariant factors that are specific to the trading partners, but are likely to affect their trade as well as the exchange-rate arrangement between them. This makes the assumption of exogenous exchange-rate regime – that is, countries do not base their exchange-rate policy choices in response to random shocks to trade – much more plausible.[10] Nevertheless, to address any concerns that the exchange-rate regime responds to changes in trade due to time-varying bilateral effects not controlled for in the regression, we also estimate Equation 4.2 using the system generalized method of moments (GMM) estimator in the sensitivity analysis.

Data

An important issue in the empirical study of exchange-rate regimes is that of regime classification. Early literature used the de jure classification – the regime officially declared by the central bank and published in the IMF's *Annual Report on Exchange Arrangements and Exchange Restrictions (AREAER)*. However, since pervasive differences were highlighted between the officially announced and actually followed (or de facto) regimes, the use of the former in empirical analysis has been significantly reduced. Thereafter, de facto classifications that seek to categorize regimes based on movements in the exchange rate and/or international reserves have been developed – the best known of which include the IMF's de facto classification published since 1999; Ghosh *et al.* (2003), Levy-Yeyati and Sturzenegger (2003), Reinhart and Rogoff (2004), and Shambaugh (2004).

In our empirical analysis, we employ the IMF's de facto classification scheme – extended backwards for the period 1972–1999 by Bubula and Ötker-Robe (2003) and Anderson (2008) – which offers two notable advantages. First, it is the only available de facto classification which combines available information on a central bank's policy framework with the actual exchange-rate and foreign-reserves movements to form a judgement about the exchange-rate regime in place. In this respect, it is the only de facto classification that takes into account *central-bank* behaviour in addition to *exchange-rate* behaviour, where the necessary information is compiled from primary and secondary sources. Second, the available cross-country and time coverage for IMF's de facto classification is similar to that of the de jure classification, which ensures that any differences in results between the two are not driven by variation in country coverage or time period.[11]

A quick look at the IMF's de jure and de facto exchange-rate regime classification for the world and Africa samples reveals two interesting features (Figure 4.1). First, for both samples, the share of fixed exchange-rate regime in the de facto

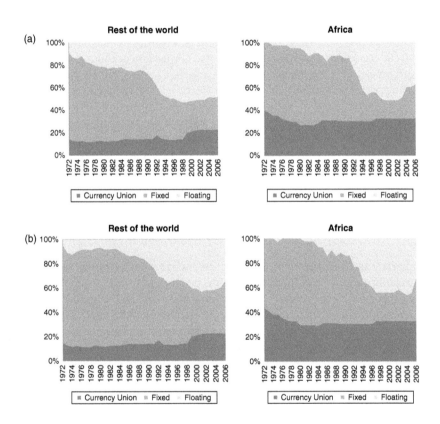

Figure 4.1 a, b Distribution of exchange rate regimes in Africa and the rest of the world, 1972–2006 (% of total observations): (a) IMF *de jure* classification; (b) IMF *de facto* classification

Source: Authors' estimates based on Anderson (2008).

Notes: Fixed exchange rate regimes include both conventional pegs as well as intermediate pegs (such as pegs within bands and crawling pegs).

Table 4.1 Distribution of regimes in the world and Africa sample (1972–2006)

Total	World	Africa	Currency unions	World	Africa
Observations	177,270	71,463	Observations	2,121	1,460
No. of country pairs	10,894	4,811	No. of country pairs	178	90
Percentage of world trade	100	4.30			
Direct pegs (de jure)			Direct pegs (de facto)		
Observations	1,192	490	Observations	1,625	539
No. of country pairs	124	36	No. of country pairs	143	40
Indirect pegs (de jure)			Indirect pegs (de facto)		
Observations	8,092	1,211	Observations	16,705	2,461
No. of country pairs	1,786	402	No. of country pairs	2,622	620

Source: Authors' calculations.

classification is consistently higher than in the de jure classification, supporting the 'hidden pegs' hypothesis of Levy-Yeyati and Sturzenegger (2003). Consequently, the share of de facto floating regimes is lower than the de jure floats throughout, as suggested by Calvo and Reinhart's (2002) 'fear of floating' hypothesis. Second, the share of fixed exchange-rate regime in both samples appears to have declined during the 1990s, but risen again in recent years. Specifically, about 60 per cent of the countries in Africa had a fixed exchange-rate regime (CU or peg) in place in 2006, which represents an increase of about 10 per cent from the previous decade.

Combining the regime classification for individual countries with the information on anchor currencies obtained from Anderson (2008), we construct bilateral binary variables for CUs, direct pegs and indirect pegs. Together with annual bilateral trade data obtained from the IMF's *Direction of Trade Statistics*, we obtain a rich and comprehensive bilateral dataset covering 159 countries from 1972 to 2006, yielding 10,894 country pairs and 177,270 observations – about 40 per cent of which belong to the Africa region.[12]

Table 4.1 presents the distribution of CUs, direct pegs and indirect pegs in the dyadic dataset used for estimation purposes. In the full sample, the number of observations coded as de facto pegs is higher than de jure pegs. Since one direct peg can generate several indirect pegs, we have 8,092 and 16,705 indirect pegs based on the de jure and de facto classifications, respectively. About 40 per cent of observations coded as direct pegs have at least one trading partner in the African region, while approximately 70 per cent of observations coded as sharing a common currency belong to Africa.

Empirical results

For comparative purposes, we estimate Equations 4.1 and 4.2 with the pooled OLS, CPFE and HT estimators, using both the de jure and de facto classifications.[13] To take into account probable correlation in the error term, we cluster the standard errors at the country-pair level in all estimations.

Table 4.2 Benchmark specification results for *de jure* classification (1972–2006)

Sample	World			Africa		
Estimation	OLS	CPFE	HT[a]	OLS	CPFE	HT[a]
CU	0.603*** (0.17)	0.298*** (0.08)	0.307*** (0.08)	1.191*** (0.21)	0.626* (0.32)	0.713*** (0.26)
Direct peg	0.398*** (0.11)	0.312*** (0.11)	0.309*** (0.11)	0.520*** (0.18)	0.860*** (0.33)	0.842*** (0.32)
Log (GDP)	1.126*** (0.01)	1.093*** (0.07)	1.210*** (0.05)	1.275*** (0.02)	1.548*** (0.15)	1.668*** (0.09)
Log (GDP per capita)	0.017 (0.01)	0.182** (0.07)	0.117* (0.06)	-0.070*** (0.02)	-0.510*** (0.15)	-0.584*** (0.11)
FTA	1.282*** (0.11)	0.241*** (0.05)	0.259*** (0.05)	1.706*** (0.16)	0.004 (0.13)	0.003 (0.13)
Current colony	-0.102 (0.58)	-0.365 (0.70)	-0.365 (0.70)	-2.878*** (1.06)	-2.643*** (1.02)	-2.668*** (1.02)
Log (distance)	-1.219*** (0.02)		-2.047*** (0.24)	-1.173*** (0.05)		-2.381*** (0.15)
Common language	0.494*** (0.05)		0.532*** (0.06)	0.423*** (0.07)		0.526*** (0.09)
Common border	0.625*** (0.14)		-0.486 (0.50)	1.141*** (0.22)		0.160 (0.35)
Landlocked	-0.305*** (0.03)		-0.153* (0.06)	-0.405*** (0.05)		-0.338*** (0.06)
Island	0.123*** (0.04)		0.476*** (0.09)	-0.291*** (0.07)		0.446*** (0.10)
Log (area)	-0.080*** (0.01)		-0.026 (0.04)	-0.209*** (0.01)		-0.378*** (0.05)
Common colony	0.756*** (0.08)		1.048*** (0.12)	0.629*** (0.10)		0.407*** (0.13)
Ever colony	1.221*** (0.14)		1.041*** (0.172)	1.637*** (0.21)		1.244*** (0.29)
Common country	1.603*** (0.57)		2.078*** (0.721)			
Observations	177,270	177,270	177,270	71,463	71,463	71,463
Number of dyads	10,894	10,894	10,894		4,811	4,811
R² (overall)	0.72	0.61		0.59	0.43	
Hausman test (*p*-value)[b]			1.00			1.00

Source: Authors' calculations.

***1 per cent, **5 per cent and *10 per cent significance levels.

a Variables instrumented: currency union (CU), direct peg, Log (GDP), Log (GDP per capita), Log (distance), FTA (Free Trade Agreement).

b Hausman test applied to the difference between the CPFE and HT estimators.

Notes: Dependent variable is log (real bilateral trade); time effects and constant included in all specifications; robust clustered (by dyad) standard errors in parentheses. CPFE, country pair-specific effects; HT, Hausman–Taylor estimation.

Table 4.3 Benchmark specification results for *de facto* classification (1972–2006)

Sample	World			Africa		
Estimation	OLS	CPFE	HT[a]	OLS	CPFE	HT[a]
CU	0.603*** (0.17)	0.302*** (0.08)	0.311*** (0.08)	1.191*** (0.21)	0.626* (0.32)	0.714*** (0.26)
Direct peg	0.389*** (0.10)	0.339*** (0.10)	0.336*** (0.10)	0.470*** (0.16)	0.791*** (0.27)	0.778*** (0.26)
Log (GDP)	1.126*** (0.01)	1.092*** (0.07)	1.209*** (0.05)	1.275*** (0.02)	1.549*** (0.15)	1.669*** (0.09)
Log (GDP per capita)	0.017 (0.01)	0.183** (0.07)	0.117* (0.06)	-0.069*** (0.02)	-0.511*** (0.15)	-0.584*** (0.11)
FTA	1.282*** (0.11)	0.242*** (0.05)	0.261*** (0.05)	1.705*** (0.16)	0.004 (0.13)	0.003 (0.13)
Current colony	-0.101 (0.58)	-0.364 (0.70)	-0.363 (0.70)	-2.893*** (1.06)	-2.644*** (1.02)	-2.669*** (1.02)
Log (distance)	-1.219*** (0.02)		-2.047*** (0.24)	-1.173*** (0.05)		-2.381*** (0.15)
Common language	0.494*** (0.05)		0.531*** (0.06)	0.423*** (0.07)		0.525*** (0.09)
Common border	0.621*** (0.14)		-0.488 (0.50)	1.141*** (0.22)		0.160 (0.35)
Landlocked	-0.306*** (0.03)		-0.153** (0.06)	-0.405*** (0.05)		-0.338*** (0.06)
Island	0.122*** (0.04)		0.475*** (0.09)	-0.291*** (0.07)		0.446*** (0.10)
Log (area)	-0.080*** (0.01)		-0.026 (0.04)	-0.209*** (0.01)		-0.378*** (0.05)
Common colony	0.755*** (0.08)		1.048*** (0.12)	0.629*** (0.10)		0.407*** (0.13)
Ever colony	1.221*** (0.14)		1.037*** (0.17)	1.654*** (0.20)		1.263*** (0.28)
Common country	1.601*** (0.57)		2.080*** (0.72)			
Observations	177,270	177,270	177,270	71,463	71,463	71,463
Number of dyads		10,894	10,894		4,811	4,811
R^2 (overall) Hausman–test	0.72	0.61		0.59	0.43	
(*p*–value)[b]			1.00			1.00

Source: Authors' calculations.

Notes: see Table 4.2.

The estimation results for the benchmark specification with both de jure and de facto classifications are presented in Tables 4.2 and 4.3, respectively. In both cases, for the OLS estimation, when only time effects are included along with the other gravity variables, CUs and direct pegs have a significantly positive effect on bilateral trade, with the effect of CUs being considerably larger than direct pegs in both samples. The signs and magnitude of the estimated coefficients of the traditional gravity variables are plausible and in line with earlier studies, and a majority of these variables are statistically significant at the 1 per cent level.

Controlling for the dyad-specific effects as in CPFE, we observe that the estimated trade-generating effects of CUs and direct pegs fall substantially for the world sample, but remain statistically significant. For Africa, the CU effect drops but that of direct pegs increases – interestingly, the direct effect of conventional pegs is almost 1.5 times larger than the CU effect. Nevertheless, using the CPFE approach, we lose the cross-sectional information of the data, and all time-invariant variables drop from the estimation. To take into account the cross-sectional dimension while allowing for the correlation of some regressors with the individual effects, we estimate Equation 4.1 with the HT approach. The Hausman-test results (as reported in the last row of Tables 4.2 and 4.3) suggest that the difference between the CPFE and HT estimators is not significant enough to reject the appropriateness of the HT estimator, which is thus our preferred estimator here.

The estimated trade-generating effect of CUs and direct pegs based on the HT method is quite similar to that obtained from the CPFE approach. We interpret the estimated coefficients to indicate that the membership of a CU, on average, increases bilateral trade for an average country in the world sample by about 35 per cent. This result is in line with the estimates of recent studies, which report a smaller effect than Rose (2000). Both de jure and de facto direct pegs have a significantly positive effect on bilateral trade, with the size of the estimated effect for the world sample (35–37 per cent) being close to that of CUs.

The HT estimation results for the de jure and de facto classifications for the Africa sample are broadly similar and indicate that the trade-generating effects of fixed exchange rates are on average more than double for Africa than for the world. Further, the effect of direct pegs appears to be at least as large as CUs for Africa. Thus, for example, CUs increase trade by almost 100 per cent between African trading partners, while direct pegs increase trade by about 130 per cent between an average country in Africa and its anchor country.

Next, we estimate the extended specification including measures of exchange-rate volatility and indirect pegs. The results reported in Tables 4.4 and 4.5 indicate that the estimated impact of long-run exchange-rate volatility is significantly negative for both samples, but the impact is larger for Africa as compared to an average country in the world sample. Notably, the estimated positive impacts of both CUs and direct pegs remain statistically significant despite controlling for exchange-rate volatility, supporting the findings of earlier studies and indicating

Table 4.4 Extended specification results for *de jure* classification (1972–2006)

Variables	World				Africa			
	CPFE	HT	CPFE	HTᵃ	CPFE	HT	CPFE	HTᵃ
CU	0.358***	0.369***	0.316***	0.332***	0.614*	0.678***	0.623*	0.694***
	(0.08)	(0.08)	(0.08)	(0.08)	(0.32)	(0.26)	(0.32)	(0.26)
Direct peg	0.316***	0.312***	0.306***	0.303***	0.876***	0.853***	0.883***	0.861***
	(0.11)	(0.11)	(0.11)	(0.11)	(0.33)	(0.32)	(0.33)	(0.32)
Volatilityᵇ	−0.253***	−0.246***	−0.254***	−0.245***	−0.344***	−0.333***	−0.344***	−0.334***
	(0.03)	(0.03)	(0.03)	(0.03)	(0.05)	(0.05)	(0.05)	(0.05)
Indirect peg			−0.152***	−0.149***			0.175*	0.189**
			(0.04)	(0.04)			(0.09)	(0.09)
Log (GDP)	1.061***	1.191***	1.039***	1.193***	1.470***	1.638***	1.486***	1.647***
	(0.07)	(0.05)	(0.07)	(0.05)	(0.15)	(0.08)	(0.15)	(0.08)
Log (GDP per capita)	0.193***	0.119*	0.214***	0.127**	−0.463***	−0.570***	−0.476***	−0.578***
	(0.07)	(0.06)	(0.07)	(0.06)	(0.15)	(0.11)	(0.15)	(0.109)
FTA	0.234***	0.254***	0.248***	0.268***	0.020	0.014	0.019	0.016
	(0.05)	(0.05)	(0.05)	(0.05)	(0.13)	(0.13)	(0.133)	(0.13)
Current colony	−0.371	−0.371	−0.376	−0.383	−2.640**	−2.676**	−2.631**	−2.664**
	(0.70)	(0.70)	(0.70)	(0.70)	(1.05)	(1.04)	(1.05)	(1.04)
Log (distance)		−2.133***		−1.809***		−2.370***		−2.355***
		(0.24)		(0.13)		(0.15)		(0.15)
Common language		0.519***		0.549***		0.531***		0.528***
		(0.06)		(0.05)		(0.09)		(0.09)
Common border		−0.660		−0.015		0.144		0.170
		(0.50)		(0.305)		(0.35)		(0.35)
Landlocked		−0.181***		−0.155***		−0.356***		−0.355***
		(0.06)		(0.05)		(0.06)		(0.06)

(Continued)

Table 4.4 (Continued)

Variables	World				Africa			
	CPFE	HT	CPFE	HTª	CPFE	HT	CPFE	HTª
Island		0.496***		0.374***		0.431***		0.431***
		(0.09)		(0.07)		(0.10)		(0.10)
Log (area)		-0.013		-0.028		-0.360***		-0.365***
		(0.04)		(0.03)		(0.05)		(0.05)
Common colony		0.994***		1.076***		0.394***		0.395***
		(0.12)		(0.10)		(0.13)		(0.13)
Ever colony		1.080***		1.070***		1.300***		1.298***
		(0.17)		(0.17)		(0.28)		(0.28)
Common country		2.142***		2.007***				
		(0.72)		(0.72)				
Observations	177,270	177,270	177,270	177,270	71,463	71,463	71,463	71,463
Number of dyads	10,894	10,894	10,894	10,894	4,811	4,811	4,811	4,811
R^2– (overall)	0.61	0.46	0.61	0.78	0.43		0.43	
Hausman–test (p–value)ᶜ		0.46		0.78		1.00		1.00

Source: Authors' calculations.

a Variables instrumented: CU, Direct peg, Log (GDP), Log (GDP per capita), Log (distance), FTA.

b Volatility refers to long-run volatility computed over 36-month horizon.

c Hausman-test applied to the difference between the FE and HT estimators.

Notes: see Table 4.2.

Table 4.5 Extended specification results for *de facto* classification (1972–2006)

Variables	World				Africa			
	CPFE	HT	CPFE	HT^a	CPFE	HT	CPFE	HT^a
CU	0.363***	0.373***	0.291***	0.306***	0.614*	0.678***	0.617*	0.673***
	(0.08)	(0.08)	(0.08)	(0.08)	(0.32)	(0.26)	(0.32)	(0.26)
Direct peg	0.344***	0.341***	0.329***	0.327***	0.809***	0.793***	0.811***	0.795***
	(0.10)	(0.10)	(0.10)	(0.10)	(0.27)	(0.26)	(0.27)	(0.26)
Volatility^b	−0.254***	−0.246***	−0.249***	−0.240***	−0.344***	−0.333***	−0.346***	−0.335***
	(0.03)	(0.03)	(0.03)	(0.03)	(0.05)	(0.05)	(0.05)	(0.05)
Indirect peg			−0.228***	−0.228***			0.046	0.046
			(0.03)	(0.03)			(0.07)	(0.07)
Log (GDP)	1.060***	1.190***	1.027***	1.175***	1.471***	1.639***	1.477***	1.637***
	(0.07)	(0.05)	(0.07)	(0.05)	(0.15)	(0.08)	(0.15)	(0.08)
Log (GDP per capita)	0.194***	0.120*	0.228***	0.146**	−0.464***	−0.570***	−0.469***	−0.566***
	(0.07)	(0.06)	(0.07)	(0.06)	(0.15)	(0.11)	(0.15)	(0.11)
FTA	0.236***	0.255***	0.262***	0.283***	0.020	0.014	0.020	0.013
	(0.05)	(0.05)	(0.05)	(0.05)	(0.13)	(0.13)	(0.13)	(0.13)
Current colony	−0.369	−0.369	−0.382	−0.387	−2.642**	−2.677***	−2.639**	−2.672**
	(0.70)	(0.70)	(0.70)	(0.70)	(1.05)	(1.04)	(1.05)	(1.04)
Log (distance)		−2.133***		−1.884***		−2.371***		−2.389***
		(0.24)		(0.17)		(0.15)		(0.15)
Common language		0.518***		0.543***		0.530***		0.529***
		(0.06)		(0.05)		(0.09)		(0.09)
Common border		−0.663		−0.157		0.144		0.113
		(0.50)		(0.37)		(0.35)		(0.35)
Landlocked		−0.181***		−0.172***		−0.356***		−0.353***
		(0.06)		(0.06)		(0.06)		(0.06)

(Continued)

Table 4.5 (Continued)

Variables	World				Africa			
	CPFE	HT	CPFE	HT^a	CPFE	HT	CPFE	HT^a
Island		0.495***		0.388***		0.432***		0.435***
		(0.09)		(0.07)		(0.10)		(0.10)
Log (area)		-0.013		-0.0151		-0.360***		-0.359***
		(0.04)		(0.03)		(0.05)		(0.05)
Common colony		0.995***		1.062***		0.395***		0.396***
		(0.12)		(0.11)		(0.126)		(0.13)
Ever colony		1.076***		1.062***		1.318***		1.312***
		(0.17)		(0.17)		(0.275)		(0.28)
Common country		2.144***		2.043***				
		(0.72)		(0.72)				
Observations	177,270	177,270	17,7270	17,7270	71,463	71,463	71,463	
Number of dyads	10,894	10,894	10,894	10,894	4,811	4,811	4,811	4,811
R^2 (overall)	0.61		0.61	0.62		0.43		
Hausman−test (p−value)^c							1.00	

Source: Authors' calculations.

a Variables instrumented: CU, Direct peg, Log (GDP), Log (GDP per capita), Log (distance), FTA.

b Volatility refers to long-run volatility computed over 36-month horizon.

c Hausman-test applied to the difference between the FE and HT estimators.

Notes: see Table 4.2.

Table 4.6 Sensitivity analysis for Africa sample (1972–2006)

De jure classification

	Short–run volatility[a]	Indirect peg[b]	Quadratic income[c]	Quadratic volatility[d]	Vol2[e]	SGMM[f]	Shambaugh[g]
CU	0.678*** (0.27)	0.652** (0.26)	0.429* (0.24)	0.629** (0.26)	0.703** (0.26)	0.580*** (0.20)	
Direct peg	0.839*** (0.30)	0.862*** (0.32)	0.939*** (0.33)	0.857*** (0.32)	0.859*** (0.32)	0.980*** (0.29)	
Indirect peg	0.184** (0.09)	0.122** (0.05)	0.191** (0.09)	0.186** (0.09)	0.189** (0.09)	0.191 (1.45)	
Volatility[a]	−0.238*** (0.04)	−0.338*** (0.05)	−0.335*** (0.05)	−0.835*** (0.13)	−0.183*** (0.03)	−0.011 (0.16)	
De facto classification							
CU	0.659*** (0.20)	0.647** (0.26)	0.417* (0.24)	0.611** (0.26)	0.680*** (0.26)	0.768*** (0.30)	0.572** (0.257)
Direct peg	0.774*** (0.14)	0.785*** (0.26)	0.869*** (0.27)	0.804*** (0.27)	0.791*** (0.26)	0.823*** (0.18)	0.409*** (0.110)
Indirect peg	0.033 (0.04)	−0.082* (0.05)	0.060 (0.07)	0.048 (0.07)	0.041 (0.07)	0.126 (0.41)	−0.093* (0.06)
Volatility[a]	−0.237*** (0.03)	−0.328*** (0.05)	−0.337*** (0.05)	−0.838*** (0.13)	−0.183*** (0.03)	−0.042 (0.05)	−0.333*** (0.05)
Observations	71,318	71,463	71,463	71,463	71,463	64,114	71,463
Number of pairs	4,811	4,811	4,811	4,811	4,811	4,406	4,811

Source: Authors' calculations.

Notes: Results obtained from HT estimator; Robust clustered (by dyad) standard errors in parentheses; time effects and other control variables included in all specifications.
***, ** and * indicate significance at the 1, 5 and 10 per cent levels, respectively.
a Short–run volatility over the 12–month horizon.
b Deeper indirect peg links (relation 2,3,4 and 5) as in Figure 4A.1.
c Includes quadratic terms for log real GDP and real GDP per capita.
d Includes quadratic term for exchange rate volatility.
e Vol2 is defined as the standard deviation of the first difference of (logs of) the real exchange rate.
f System–GMM dynamic panel estimation.
g Using Shambaugh's (2004) de facto exchange rate regime classification.

that more stable exchange-rate regimes promote trade through channels in addition to reduced exchange-rate volatility.

The impact of indirect pegs appears to be strongly negative for the world sample. This result, somewhat surprisingly, is similar to that obtained by Klein and Shambaugh (2006) and Qureshi and Tsangarides (2010). The latter, however, observe that the negative effect stems from the indirect pegs generated through the US dollar, which largely comprise non-industrialized dyads that are geographically located far apart (for example, those between trading partners in East Asia and Latin America). This is in contrast to the indirect pegs generated through, for example, the Deutsche mark and the French franc that are mostly between trading partners in Europe and Africa, with comparatively smaller distances. Geographical location could play an important role in determining the effect of indirect pegs, as the benefits associated with greater exchange-rate stability vis-à-vis the partner countries may diminish if other trading costs, such as transportation and information, increase.[14]

This explanation appears plausible in our case, since we observe the effect of indirect pegs – largely generated through the French franc – to be positive for Africa. This is true for both the de jure and de facto classification, though the effect is statistically significant for the former classification only.

Sensitivity analysis

The results presented in Tables 4.2 to 4.5 verify the robustness of our estimates to various estimation methods (OLS, CPFE and HT). However, several other concerns pertaining to model specification, methodology, variable definitions and sample coverage raised in earlier literature may be relevant to our analysis. In what follows, we attempt to address these concerns through a range of sensitivity checks, and we report the results in Table 4.6.

Alternate variable definitions

The results reported in Table 4.6 (column 1) show that using the measure of short-run exchange-rate volatility (defined over a one-year period) instead of long-run volatility in Equation 4.1 does not alter the results in a significant manner. The estimated coefficients of both CUs and direct pegs for the Africa sample retain statistical significance, but the estimated coefficient of short-run exchange-rate volatility is somewhat smaller than long-run volatility, indicating that exchange-rate volatility over a long horizon is more damaging for trade activity.

Table 4.6 (column 2) presents the results of the extended specification with an alternate definition of exchange-rate volatility (the standard deviation of the first difference of (logs of) the real exchange rate) and given by:

$$Vol2_t = SD[r_{t+p-1} - r_{t+p-2}],$$ (4.4)

where r is the natural log of bilateral real exchange rate between countries i and j, and the first difference is computed over 1 month (with end-of-month data), while the standard deviation is calculated over 36 months to measure long-run volatility. The results show that using *Vol2* does not affect the estimated coefficients of CUs and pegs in a significant manner, and the effect of exchange-rate volatility also remains significantly negative.

Reassuringly, the results are also robust to an alternative measure for indirect pegs, which includes more distant relationships created through pegging with an anchor currency (specifically, relations 3, 4 and 5 in Figure 4A.1). Table 4.6 (column 3) shows that the positive effect of indirect pegs for Africa holds though the magnitude of the estimated coefficient of indirect pegs becomes smaller indicating, as expected, lower benefits from more distant indirect links created through pegging.

Alternate model specification

To address concerns related to the non-linear relationship between trade and output, and exchange-rate volatility, we modify our extended specification and include quadratic terms for (log) real GDP and GDP per capita, as well as for exchange-rate volatility. The results reported in columns 4 and 5 of Table 4.6 show that this has no effect whatsoever on the estimation results for *CUs*, *DirPeg* and *IndPeg* for both de jure and de facto classifications. (The estimated coefficient for the quadratic term of exchange-rate volatility is, however, significantly positive – not reported here – indicating that the negative effect of exchange-rate volatility on bilateral trade diminishes gradually as volatility increases.)

Simultaneity concerns

Next, we address any simultaneity concerns using the system GMM estimator – proposed by Blundell and Bond (1998) – which transforms the model by taking first differences to eliminate the fixed effects and supplements it with the levels equation (using lagged levels as instruments for the differenced equation and lagged differences as instruments for the levels equation). The results, presented in Table 4.6 (column 6), show that the strong positive impact of fixed exchange-rate arrangements on bilateral trade is robust to GMM estimation and the dynamic panel specification of the model. For both the de jure and de facto classifications, the coefficients for CU and direct pegs are significantly positive. However, the estimated coefficient for exchange-rate volatility, though negative, becomes statistically insignificant.

Alternate exchange-rate regime classification

Taken together, the estimates reported in Tables 4.2 to 4.6 suggest that CUs in Africa increase bilateral trade in the range of about 50–115 per cent, while (de jure and de facto) direct pegs promote trade by about 115–55 per cent. These estimates are, however, based on the IMF exchange-rate-regime classification and may be sensitive to other available exchange-rate-regime classifications. To test the robustness of our results to the regime classification, we use the de facto classification developed by Shambaugh (2004). Specifically, Shambaugh (2004) considers a country to have a pegged regime in place, if in a given calendar year, that country's monthly official bilateral exchange rate remains within a 2 per cent band of a 'base' currency (and a non-peg otherwise). Hence, in contrast to the IMF's de facto classification, Shambaugh (2004) categorizes the regime solely based on the actual behaviour of the exchange rate.[15]

The results obtained from this alternate classification for the Africa sample are presented in the last column of Table 4.6. The estimated coefficients for the CU and direct peg dummy variables are significantly positive, but the effect of indirect pegs in this case is weakly negative. Although the magnitude of the estimated coefficient for the direct peg variable appears smaller, we are unable to reject the hypothesis of the equality of both coefficients through an F-test, which supports the result obtained earlier that the effect of direct pegs, is at least as large as CUs for Africa. Further, the results for the world sample obtained using Shambaugh's classification (not reported here) are very similar to those reported in Table 4.5 – in particular, the effect of fixed exchange-rate regimes on bilateral trade appears to be larger for Africa than for the world sample.[16]

Conclusion

This chapter empirically examines the effect of monetary unions vis-à-vis conventional peg regimes on Africa's bilateral trade using both de jure and de facto classifications from 1972 to 2006. Our analysis, based on an augmented version of the gravity model, shows that currency unions and direct pegs have a strong trade-generating effect on Africa, which is almost twice as large as for an average country in the world sample. The effect stems through reduced exchange-rate volatility as well as through other possible channels (such as lower transaction costs). We find that the trade-generating effect of direct pegs for the region is at least as large as that of CUs and also find some evidence of beneficial indirect gains achieved through pegging as well.

From a policy perspective, the positive and relatively large effect of direct pegs for Africa's trade may have important implications for the ongoing debates on regional currency union formation, a subject that is at the forefront of economic policy agendas across Africa. Viewed in the context of the policy option to choose hard or soft pegs, countries aspiring to expand cross-border trade activity through more stable exchange-rate regimes, while retaining some flexibility, could consider pegs as a viable alternative to complete (and rigid) monetary integration. Notwithstanding the trade benefits of fixed exchange-rate regimes, countries need to carefully weigh the pros and cons of fixed exchange-rate regimes and the available policy options in the face of possible real shocks, before opting for any form of fixed exchange-rate arrangement.

Appendix 4A: Data Description

Table 4A.1 Variable description and data sources

Variable	Description	Source
Dependent variable		
lrtrade$_{ijt}$	Log of the mean value of real bilateral trade between i and j at time t	IMF's *Direction of Trade (DoT)*: Average of exports from a to b, and b to a; and import into a from b, and to b from a. Deflated by US CPI for urban consumers
Explanatory variables		
CU$_{ijt}$	Binary variable which is unity if i and j share currency at time t	Anderson (2008)
Direct peg (de jure)$_{ijt}$	Binary variable which is unity if i and j are pegged to each other at time t	Anderson (2008)
Direct peg (de facto)$_{ijt}$	Binary variable which is unity if i and j are pegged to each other at time t	Anderson (2008)
Volatility	Exchange rate volatility	Based on exchange-rate data obtained from the Information Notice System
Lrgdp$_{ijt}$	Log of the product of real GDP of i and j at time t	World Bank's *World Development Indicators (WDI)*
Lrgdp$_{ijt}$	Log of the product of real GDP per capita of i and j at time t	*WDI*
Ldist$_{ij}$	Log of the distance between i and j	CEPII (www.cepii.fr/anglaisgraph/bdd/distances.htm)
Ldist_cap$_{ij}$	Log of the distance between capital cities of i and j	CEPII (www.cepii.fr/anglaisgraph/bdd/distances.htm)
Ldist_wces$_{ij}$	Log of population weighted distance between the largest cities of i and j	CEP I(www.cepii.fr/anglaisgraph/bdd/distances.htm)
Lang$_{ij}$	Binary variable which is unity if i and j have a common language	Tsangarides et al. (2009)
Comborder$_{ij}$	Binary variable which is unity if i and j share a land border	Tsangarides et al. (2009)
Landl	Number of landlocked countries in the country-pair (0, 1, or 2)	Tsangarides et al. (2009)
Island	Number of island nations in the country-pair (0, 1, or 2)	Tsangarides et al. (2009)
Larea$_{ij}$	Log of product of land area of i and j	Tsangarides et al. (2009)

(Continued)

Table 4A.1 (Continued)

Variable	Description	Source
Comcol$_{ij}$	Binary variable which is unity if i and j were colonies after 1945 with the same colonizer	Tsangarides et al. (2009)
Curcol$_{ij}$	Binary variable which is unity if i and j are colonies at time t	Tsangarides et al. (2009)
Evercol$_{ij}$	Binary variable which is unity if i colonized j or vice versa	Tsangarides et al. (2009)
Comcty$_{ij}$	Binary variable which is unity if i and j remained part of the same nation during the sample	Tsangarides et al. (2009)
Fta$_{ij}$	Binary variable which is unity if i and j belong to the same regional trade agreement	WTO (http://rtais.wto.org/UI/ PublicMaintainRTAHome.aspx)

Source: Authors' compilation.

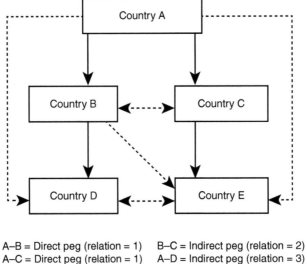

A–B = Direct peg (relation = 1) B–C = Indirect peg (relation = 2)
A–C = Direct peg (relation = 1) A–D = Indirect peg (relation = 3)
B–D = Direct peg (relation = 1) A–E = Indirect peg (relation = 3)
C–E = Direct peg (relation = 1) B–E = Indirect peg (relation = 4)
C–D = Indirect peg (relation = 4)
D–E = Indirect peg (relation = 5)

Figure 4A.1 Direct- and indirect-peg relations across countries

Source: Qureshi and Tsangarides (2010).

Notes

1 We thank Atish Ghosh, Badi Baltagi, Michael Bleaney, Augustin Fosu, colleagues at the International Monetary Fund, and participants at the CSAE 2009 (Oxford University) and NEUDC 2009 (Tufts University) conferences for helpful comments and suggestions. Special thanks to Harald Anderson for generously making his data on exchange-rate regime classification available to us. The views expressed in this chapter are those of the authors and do not necessarily represent those of the IMF or IMF policy. All errors are the authors' responsibility.

2 The regional integration initiatives in Africa include the creation of the Economic Community of West African States, for which a second monetary area – the West African Monetary Zone – comprising non-member countries of the existing West African Economic Monetary Union is envisaged by 2015. Members of the East African Community also aim to create a currency union by 2015, and an extension of the southern Common Monetary Area, which links Lesotho, South Africa and Swaziland to other states in the region, is also a possibility in the long run. See Bénassy-Quéré and Coupet (2005), Debrun *et al.* (2005), and Tsangarides and Qureshi (2008) for a discussion on the feasibility of the proposed monetary unions.

3 While the de facto exchange-rate regime affects actual trading costs, the de jure exchange-rate regime may also have an effect on trade flows by influencing market expectations about risk and inflation.

4 Levy-Yeyati and Sturzenegger (2003) argue that in the presence of short-run price rigidities, exchange-rate flexibility facilitates resource allocation in the face of real shocks, thereby improving growth prospects. Broda (2001) and Edwards and Levy-Yeyati (2005) support this finding and respectively show that the inability of rigid regimes to absorb shocks results in more volatile output paths and lower growth.

5 See Nitsch (2002), Tenreyro (2001) and Tsangarides *et al.* (2009).

6 See Table 4A.1 for a detailed description of the variables and data sources.

7 The definition of indirect pegs used here is similar to that in Klein and Shambaugh (2006) and Qureshi and Tsangarides (2010); see Figure 4A.1.

8 Specifically, the first definition of indirect peg includes relation 2 between pairs in Figure 4A.1. The second definition includes indirect relations 2, 3, 4 and 5. The results for the second definition are presented in the sensitivity analysis.

9 The HT approach instruments the endogenous time-varying variables with the deviation from their means, and the endogenous time-invariant variables with the deviation of the exogenous time-varying variables from their means. The set of endogenous variables could be determined by a Hausman-test, which is based on the comparison of the HT estimator with the within (fixed effects) estimator (Baltagi 2001).

10 In the context of CUs in Africa, the assumption of exogeneity is even more plausible considering that the decision to form CUs has been driven largely by political considerations (Masson and Pattillo 2004).

11 The de jure classification, formally available until 1998, has been updated to 2007 by Anderson (2008). For a detailed comparison of IMF's de facto classification with other popular classifications, see Ghosh *et al.* (2010).

12 The full sample covers all countries for which the required data are available, while the Africa sample comprises those observations where at least one trading partner is in Africa.

13 We also estimate the benchmark specification (1) with the random effects model. The Hausman-test – based on the differences between the fixed and random effects models – however, fails to confirm the hypothesis that the explanatory variables are uncorrelated with the unobserved omitted variables.

14 Qureshi and Tsangarides (2010) examine if the effect of indirect pegs is conditional on distance by including an interaction term of indirect pegs and bilateral distance, and find support for the conjecture that geographical distance dampens the effect of exchange-rate stability created through indirect peg relationships.

15 Considerable differences appear to lie in the coding of direct (and consequently indirect) pegs between the IMF's de facto and Shambaugh's classifications, with the latter in general generating more peg relationships. In the dyadic sample, for example, there is agreement on only 36 per cent of the observations for direct pegs.
16 In addition to the reported robustness tests, we also use alternate samples, which exclude oil exporters and small states (with populations less than one million), and employ other estimation methods to take into account zero trade observations between countries (such as the Tobit method). The results for these exercises are not reported here for brevity, but remain very similar to those reported in Tables 4.2 and 4.3.

References

Adam, C. and D. Cobham (2007). 'Exchange Rate Regimes and Trade'. *The Manchester School*, 75: 44–63.

Anderson, H. (2008). 'Exchange Policies before Widespread Floating (1945–89)'. Unpublished manuscript. Washington, DC: International Monetary Fund.

Angkinand, A. and T. Willett (2011). 'Exchange Rate Regimes and Banking Crises: The Channels of Influence Investigated'. *International Journal of Finance and Economics*, 16: 256–74.

Baltagi, B. (2001). *Econometric Analysis of Panel Data*, 2nd edition. Bognor Regis: Wiley.

Bénassy-Quéré, A. and M. Coupet (2005). 'On the Adequacy of Monetary Arrangements in Sub-Saharan Africa'. *World Economy*, 28: 349–73.

Blundell, R.W. and S.R. Bond (1998). 'Initial Conditions and Moment Restrictions in Dynamic Panel Data Models'. *Journal of Econometrics*, 87: 115–43.

Broda, C. (2001). 'Coping with Terms of Trade Shocks: Pegs versus Floats'. *American Economic Review*, 91(2): 376–80.

Bubula, A. and I. Ötker-Robe (2003). 'Are Pegged and Intermediate Regimes More Crisis Prone?'. Working Paper 03/223. Washington, DC: International Monetary Fund.

Calvo, G. and C.M. Reinhart (2002). 'Fear of Floating'. *Quarterly Journal of Economics*, 107: 379–408.

Cushman, D.O. (1983). 'The Effects of Real Exchange Rate Risk on International Trade'. *Journal of International Economics*, 15: 45–63.

Debrun, X., P. Masson and C. Pattillo (2005). 'Monetary Union in West Africa: Who Might Gain, Who Might Lose, and Why?'. *Canadian Journal of Economics*, 38: 454–81.

Edwards, S. and E. Levy-Yeyati (2005). 'Flexible Exchange Rates as Shock Absorbers'. *European Economic Review*, 49(8): 2079–105.

Egger, P. and M. Pfaffermayr (2003). 'The Proper Panel Econometric Specification for the Gravity Equation: A Three-Way Model with Bilateral Interaction Effects'. *Empirical Economics*, 28(3): 571–80.

Frankel, J. (1997). *Regional Trading Blocs in the World Economic System*. Washington, DC: Institute for International Economics.

Frankel, J.A. and S.J. Wei (1993). 'Trade Blocks and Currency Blocks'. National Bureau of Economic Research Working Paper 4345. Cambridge, MA: NBER.

Frankel, J.A. and A.K. Rose (2002). 'An Estimate of the Effect of Common Currencies on Trade and Income'. *Quarterly Journal of Economics*, 117: 437–66.

Ghosh, A., A. Gulde, J. Ostry and H. Wolf (1997). 'Does the Nominal Exchange Rate Regime Matter?' National Bureau of Economic Research Working Paper 5874. Cambridge, MA: NBER.

Ghosh, A., A. Gulde and H. Wolf (2003). *Exchange Rate Regime: Choices and Consequences*. Cambridge, MA: MIT Press.

Ghosh, A., J. Ostry and C. Tsangarides (2010). 'Exchange Rate Regime and the Stability of the International Monetary System.' Occasional Paper No. 270. Washington, DC: International Monetary Fund.

Ghosh, A., J. Ostry and M.S. Qureshi (2014). 'Exchange Rate Management and Crisis Susceptibility: A Reassessment.' Working Paper No. 14/11. Washington, DC: International Monetary Fund.

Glick, R. and A. Rose (2002). 'Does a Currency Union Affect Trade? The Time-series Evidence'. *European Economic Review*, 46: 1125–51.

Hausman, J. and W.E. Taylor (1981). 'Panel Data and Unobservable Individual Effects'. *Econometrica*, 49(6): 1377–98.

Hooper, P. and S.W. Kohlhagen (1978). 'The Effect of Exchange Rate Uncertainty on the Prices and Volume of International Trade'. *Journal of International Economics*, 8: 483–511.

Husain, A., A. Mody and K. Rogoff (2005). 'Exchange Rate Regime Durability and Performance in Developing versus Advanced Economies'. *Journal of Monetary Economics*, 52: 35–64.

Kenen, P. and D. Rodrik (1986). 'Measuring and Analyzing the Effects of Short-term Volatility in Real Exchange Rates'. *Review of Economics and Statistics*, 68: 311–15.

Klein, M. and J. Shambaugh (2006). 'Fixed Exchange Rates and Trade'. *Journal of International Economics*, 70: 359–83.

Levy-Yeyati, E. and F. Sturzenegger (2003). 'To Float or to Fix: Evidence on the Impact of Exchange Rate Regimes on Growth'. *American Economic Review*, 93(4): 1173–93.

Masson, P. and C. Pattillo (2004). *The Monetary Geography of Africa*. Washington, DC: Brookings Institution.

Mundell, R.A. (1961). 'A Theory of Optimum Currency Areas'. *American Economic Review*, 53: 657–64.

Nitsch, V. (2002). 'Honey, I Shrunk the Currency Union Effect on Trade'. *The World Economy*, 25(4): 457–74.

Qureshi, M.S. and C. Tsangarides (2010). 'The Empirics of Exchange Rate Regimes and Trade: Words vs. Deeds'. Working Paper 10/48. Washington, DC: International Monetary Fund.

Reinhart, C. and K. Rogoff (2004). 'A Modern History of Exchange Rate Regimes: A Reinterpretation'. *Quarterly Journal of Economics*, 119(1): 1–48.

Rose, A.K. (2000). 'One Money One Market: Estimating the Effect of Common Currencies on Trade'. *Economic Policy*, 15: 7–46.

Rose, A.K. and E. van Wincoop (2001). 'National Money as a Barrier to International Trade: The Real Case for Currency Union'. *American Economic Review*, 91(2): 386–90.

Serlenga, L. and Y. Shin (2007). 'Gravity Models of Intra-EU Trade: Application of the CCEP-HT Estimation in Heterogeneous Panels with Unobserved Common Time-Specific Factors'. *Journal of Applied Econometrics*, 22: 361–81.

Shambaugh, J. (2004). 'The Effects of Fixed Exchange Rates on Monetary Policy'. *Quarterly Journal of Economics*, 119(1): 301–52.

Tenreyro, S. (2001). 'On the Causes and Consequences of Currency Unions'. Unpublished manuscript. Cambridge, MA: Harvard University.

Thursby, M.C. and J.G. Thursby (1987). 'Bilateral Trade Flows, the Linder Hypothesis, and Exchange Risk'. *Review of Economics and Statistics*, 69: 488–95.

Tsangarides, C. and M.S. Qureshi (2008). 'Monetary Union Membership in West Africa: A Cluster Analysis'. *World Development*, 36: 1261–79.

Tsangarides, C., P. Ewenczyk, M. Hulej and M.S. Qureshi (2009). 'Are Africa's Currency Unions Good for Trade?' *IMF Staff Papers*, 56: 876–918.

5 Interrelationships between health, environmental quality and economic activity

What consequences for economic convergence?

Alassane Drabo

Introduction

Environmental protection is an important issue that is gradually becoming more present in development strategies. It occupies a significant place in the economic policy of many countries and constitutes a major concern for the international community. This concern, expressed at international level, is illustrated at many international meetings and conferences: two Nobel Peace prizes were awarded to personalities who raised public awareness on environmental issues – Wangari Maathai in 2004 and Al Gore in 2007 – and it is one of the eight Millennium Development Goals (MDGs) adopted by the United Nations (UN) in 2000. In fact, 192 UN member states undertook in 2000 to integrate the principles of sustainable development into country policies and programmes, reverse loss of environmental resources, reduce biodiversity loss and halve, by 2015, the proportion of people without sustainable access to safe drinking water and basic sanitation (United Nations 2013). This great interest is explained by the fact that the environment is intimately connected to a viable ecosystem as explained by the UN Secretary General in the UN Environmental Programme 2007 Annual Report: 'it keeps the climate stable, clothes our backs, provides the medicines we need, and protects us from radiation from space'(UNEP 2007: 3).

Although environmental protection is nowadays an important emerging concept, the search for large and sustainable pro-poor economic growth remains a necessity and a priority for all economies. The simultaneous pursuit of these two objectives, which is the wish of all countries, gives rise to at least one question: what is the relationship between economic activity and environmental degradation? During the early decades, many studies tried to give theoretical and empirical responses to this question and the most popular remains the environmental Kuznets curve hypothesis (EKC). The EKC (Grossman and Krueger 1995; Torras and Boyce 1998) describes the relationship between declining environmental quality and income as an inverted-U; that is, in the course of economic growth and development, environmental quality initially worsens, but ultimately improves with improvements in income levels.

The relationship between income and environmental quality should not be limited to the EKC; the environmental degradation in turn can have significant effects on economic activity (Bovenberg and Smulders 1995, 1996; Bruvoll *et al.*

1999). These effects impact growth through many channels, among which is health status. Health occupies a dominating role in the economic policy of many developing countries. This importance is illustrated through its weight among the MDGs. Some studies estimate the cost of pollution and argue that morbidity and mortality should be considered (Scapecchi 2008).

The aim of this chapter is to assess the relationship between health, the environment and economic activity, and the consequences of this relationship on economic convergence. In fact, given the EKC hypothesis, in the early stages of economic development, the gain from income growth could be cancelled or mitigated by environmental degradation through a population's health (and other channels) and create a vicious circle in economic activity unlike in developed countries. This in turn could slow down economic convergence.

Very few studies have shown interest, in a simultaneous way, in these three elements – health, the environment and economic activity – in spite of the importance demonstrated by the international community. Most studies on this relationship, nevertheless, focus on the EKC hypothesis. Moreover, to the best of my knowledge, this is the first study investigating the association between economic convergence and environmental degradation.

The current chapter shows that there is a feedback relationship between economic activity and environmental quality, on the one hand, and between health and economic activity on the other hand. Health status remains an important channel through which environmental degradation affects economic growth, even if it is not the only factor. Environmental degradation affects negatively economic activity and reduces the ability of poor countries to economically catch up with their developed counterparts.

The rest of this chapter is organized in five sections. First there is a review of the literature on the relationship between economic activity, health and the environment. Following this is a section devoted to empirical design – we investigate the association between environmental indicators and economic convergence, before examining the relationship between health, environmental degradation and economic growth. The penultimate section presents the results and the final section, the conclusion.

Literature review

In this section, we review the literature on the link between economic outcomes and environmental quality. Then, we explain how pollution affects population health. Finally, we examine the association between health and economic performance.

Economic growth and environment

Growth and economic convergence

Economic convergence – a concept introduced in the economic literature by Solow (1956) – has been tested many times. It was generalized by Barro and

Sala-i-Martin (1992), Mankiw *et al.* (1992), and Levine and Renelt (1992) through the conditional convergence notion. Conditional convergence implies that countries would reach their respective steady states. Hence, in looking for convergence in a cross-country study, it is necessary to control for the differences in steady states of different countries. The choice of control variables is very important because the statistical significant level as well as the coefficient amplitude of the variable of interest is sensitive in this choice (Levine and Renelt 1992). In 1992, Mankiw *et al.* provided an analysis of economic convergence by adding human capital, represented by education level, to the Solow (1956) model and showed that their results fit better to the predictions of the Solow model. Knowles and Owen (1995) complemented this work by adding health as a second human capital.

All these improvements are important, but not important enough. They fail to take into account the role that omitted variables could play, in particular environmental quality. This omission has aroused a renewed interest in recent years in the light of the natural resources curse and EKC hypotheses.

Consideration of the environmental aspect

The existence of an intrinsic relation between economic activity and environmental quality remains evident. At the theoretical level, several authors tried to give an explanation on the way environmental degradation could impact economic activity (Bovenberg and Smulders 1995, 1996; Hofkes 1996; Resosudarmo and Thorbecke 1996; Bruvoll *et al.* 1999; Geldrop and Withagen 2000). These studies can be divided into four major categories following Panayotou (2000). Optimal growth models, as the first category, build on a Ramsey (1928) model and extensions by Koopmans (1963) and Cass (1965) (Keeler *et al.* 1971; Mäler 1974; Gruver 1976; Brock 1977; Becker 1982; Tahvonen and Kuuluvainen 1993; Selden and Song 1995; Stokey 1998). These are dynamic optimization models, in which the utility-maximization problem of the consumer with an infinite time horizon is solved using the techniques of optimal control theory. Some of these models considered the effects of pollution on the growth path (Keeler *et al.* 1971; Gruver 1976; Van der Ploeg and Withagen 1991), whereas others focused on natural resources depletion (Dasgupta and Heal 1974; Solow 1974). In general, models of pollution and optimal growth suggest that some abatement or curtailment of growth will be optimal.

The second category not only considers pollution as an argument of the production and utility functions, but also includes environment itself as a factor of production (Chichilinsky 1994; Lopez 1994; Geldrop and Withagen 2000). This measure of environmental quality can be conceptualized as a stock that is damaged by production or pollution. The presence of environmental stock in the production function means that optimal pollution taxes or regulations that do not account for environmental quality are not sufficient to achieve the optimal level of environmental quality in the steady state.

The third group is constituted by endogenous growth models that relax the neoclassical specification of the production function assumed in the optimal growth models (Gradus and Smulders 1993; Ligthart and Van der Ploeg 1994; Bovenberg and Smulders 1995, 1996; Hofkes 1996; Stokey 1998). Based on Romer (1986, 1990), these models are characterized by constant or increasing returns to scale to some factors, or a class of factors, because private returns on investment may differ from social returns on investment, often because of externality effects. This category consists of extending this new growth theory to include environment or pollution as a factor of production and environmental quality as an argument of the utility function. Bovenberg and Smulders (1995, 1996) modify the Romer (1986) model to include environment as a factor of production. Gradus and Smulders (1993), Ligthart and Van der Ploeg (1994), and Stockey (1998) extend the simple 'AK' used by Barro by including environment, while Victor *et al.* (1993) apply Romer (1990) to include environmental quality. In general, optimal pollution control requires a lower level of growth than would be achieved in the absence of pollution.

Finally, there are other models that connect environmental degradation and economic growth. This category includes the overlapping generation model based on Diamond (1965), as well as John and Pecchenino (1994). We also have a two-country general equilibrium model of growth and environment in the presence of trade (Copeland and Taylor 1994). These models reinforce the results of the optimal growth models that incorporate environmental quality.

At the empirical level, some economists have tried to assess this impact of the environmental degradation on the economic activity. Bruvoll *et al.* (1999) estimated the cost of environmental constraints – called environmental drag – to the Norwegian economy through a dynamic resource environment applied model. Their simulation indicates that the environmental drag reduces the annual economic growth rate by about 0.1 of a percentage point and annual growth in wealth, including environmental wealth, is reduced by 0.23 of a percentage point until 2030. Resosudarmo and Thorbecke (1996) show, through the social environmental accounting matrix, that the improvement of environmental quality reduces health problems and therefore stimulates economic growth.

The best way to understand how environmental degradation can affect economic growth is to explain the channels through which this occurs. In the economic literature we can find implicitly or explicitly some of these channels. Most of the channels found in the literature are labour supply and labour productivity.[1] Air pollution by carbon dioxide (CO_2), sulphur dioxide (SO_2), nitrogen oxides (NO_x), carbon monoxide (CO), traffic noise and so on affect health and leave people unable to work over short or long periods and reduce the productivity of those who work.

The other channels have not been broadly developed in the literature. Among them, we have the deterioration of physical capital (Bovenberg and Smulders 1996; Bruvoll *et al.* 1999). In fact, some pollutants such as SO_2 induce corrosion on capital equipment and increase road depreciation and thus depreciation of public capital. This increases the burden on public expenditure and eventually crowds out private activity (Bruvoll *et al.* 1999). Another channel is welfare degradation. People receive utility from environmental services like recreational values. Some pollutants, such as SO_2 and NO_x, contribute to acidification of lakes and forests and others such as CO and particulate matter (PM_{10}), provoke health-related suffering. This can discourage foreign direct investment and skilled labour. Finally, environmental quality improvement affects saving behaviour and therefore investment (Ricci 2007).

The EKC hypothesis

It is now clear that environmental quality affects economic performance. Economic activity in turn deteriorates environmental quality, and this occurs in almost all the economic sectors (Shafik 1994; Repetto and Baliga 1996; Yadav 1997; Hettige *et al.* 1998; Mansour 2004). This effect of economic activity on environmental quality is complex and depends on such factors as preferences, production technology and the economic structure which are intrinsically linked to the development level. The pollution level depends on the gross domestic product (GDP) composition, which itself is linked to the development level (EKC hypothesis).

During earlier decades, several studies investigated theoretical and empirical effects of economic development on pollution, with the most popular hypothesis being the EKC (Grossman and Krueger 1995; Torras and Boyce 1998). This hypothesis describes the relationship between declining environmental quality and income as an inverted-U, that is, in the course of economic growth and development, environmental quality initially worsens, but ultimately improves with improvements in income levels.

The first explanation for the EKC relationship is that the environment can be thought of as a luxury good. In the early stages of economic development a country would be unwilling to exchange consumption for investment in environmental regulation, hence environmental quality declines. When the country reaches a threshold level of income, its citizens start to demand improvements in environmental quality. Another explanation of the EKC hypothesis is that countries pass through technological life cycles, as they move from highly polluting technology (agriculture-based economies) to less polluting technology (service-based systems). In addition to these macroeconomic explanations, the EKC hypothesis is supported by microeconomic foundations (Andreoni and Levinson 1998).

Health and environment

A healthy labour force is essential for the development of an economy and requires a healthy environment (clean air, water, recreation and wilderness). As argued by Pearce and Warford (1993), the immediate and most important consequences of environmental degradation are damage to human health through different forms of diseases. For example, air pollution may increase the mortality rate (Woodruff *et al.* 1997; Gangadharan and Valenzuela 2001; Chay and Greenstone 2003; Aunan and Pan 2004; Jerrett *et al.* 2005). Jerrett *et al.* (2005) investigated whether chronic exposure to particulate air pollution is significantly associated with mortality when the effects of other social, demographic and lifestyle confounders are taken into account. They found substantively large and statistically significant health effects for women and men. Other studies have also uncovered links between pollution and particular illnesses, such as cardio-respiratory diseases (Burnett and Krewski 1994; Aunan and Pan 2004; Jerrett *et al.* 2005), asthma (Nauenberg and Basu 1999) and congenital anomalies (Rankin *et al.* 2009).

Health and economic development

The association between income and population health has been largely studied in the economic literature for many decades. Several channels through which health affects the level of output in a country have been identified. The first is that healthier people are more productive and available as labour. Indeed, they can work harder and longer, and think more clearly. Health may also improve economic outcome through its effect on education. Improvements in health raise the motivation to attend high-level schooling, since the returns to investment in schooling are valuable over a longer working life. Healthier students also have higher school attendance and higher cognitive functioning, and thus receive a better education for a given level of schooling. Furthermore, lower mortality rates and higher life expectancy encourage saving for retirement, thus raising the levels of investment and capital per worker.

Certain scholars assess empirically how health indicators may influence economic returns in a specific region using individual or household data, while others measure the same effect at a more aggregated level, between countries or regions. All these studies could be divided according to the health indicators considered. Indeed, a number of studies utilized health inputs (Weil 2007), whereas others used health outcomes themselves. Health inputs, according to Weil (2007), are the physical factors that influence an individual's health and comprise nutrition variables, exposure to pathogens and the availability of medical care. Health outcomes are characteristics that describe the health status of an individual or a given population. These include health indicators broadly considered such as life expectancy, mortality indicators, the ability to work hard, cognitive functioning, as well as specific illness prevalence such as malaria, AIDS/HIV, guinea worm and so on.

Using indicators that represent all causes of health outcomes, researchers generally conclude that population health remains an important predictor of economic outcomes (Cuddington and Hancock 1994; Barro 1996; Bloom and Malaney 1998; Bloom *et al.* 2000; Arora 2001; Bloom *et al.* 2005; Acemoglu and Johnson 2007, 2009; Bloom *et al.* 2009). Acemoglu and Johnson (2007) provide, however, another point of view and present opposing results, indicating that increases in life expectancy have no significant effect on economic output per capita. Even though Bloom *et al.* (2009) disagree with their results through a comment, they maintained their position in their 2009 paper.

The second branch of the literature assessed the importance of health in economic development by looking at health inputs rather than health outcomes.

These studies found a positive association between health variables and income, with richer countries using more health inputs than poorer countries. Some of these studies focused on malnutrition and economic productivity. They generally established that calorie intake and anthropometric indicators are positively correlated with economic output (Alderman and Behrman 2006).

There is therefore a link between environmental quality, population health and economic performance. This chapter discusses the consequences of this interrelationship on economic convergence. In fact, this interrelationship provokes different consequences depending on the development level if the EKC hypothesis is verified. In countries below the EKC income threshold, all attempts to boost economic growth (without abatement) will result in greater environmental degradation. And this will burden economic growth through health and other channels, creating a vicious circle. However, when countries above the EKC income threshold try to boost their economic growth, their environmental quality will be improved and therefore they will be in a virtuous circle. That will penalize poor countries by slowing down the speed of convergence if they do not take care of environmental concerns.

Empirical analysis

Estimation methodology

This section is devoted to the econometric specifications. The analysis is subdivided into four main steps. First, the effect of environmental quality on economic outcomes is assessed through the introduction of pollution indicators in an augmented neoclassical growth model. Then, we evaluate how these variables affect the ability of poor countries to catch up with rich ones by adding to the previous model the interaction term between initial GDP per capita and environmental variable. The third model investigates the role played by health in the impact of environmental variables on economic outcomes. Finally, we develop an explanation to this effect of pollution on convergence by estimating simultaneously a growth equation, a health equation and an environmental equation, and highlight the interrelationships between these three variables.

Economic growth and environment

Based on the neoclassical augmented growth model, the effect of environment on economic growth could be specified as follows:

$$gdpc_{it} = \alpha_1 gdpc_{it-1} + \alpha_2 envir_{it} + \alpha_k X'_{kit} + v_{it} \tag{5.1}$$

where $gdpc_{it}$ and $envir_{it}$ represent, respectively, the logarithmic form of GDP per capita and the environmental quality of country i in period t. X is the matrix of the control variables introduced which have been used frequently in the empirical literature.[2] v_{it} is the error term. The coefficient of the economic catch-up variable α_1 is expected to be between 0.0 and 1.0 $(0 < \alpha_1 < 1)$ in order to confirm economic convergence. We expect α_2 to be less than 0 $(\alpha_2 < 0)$ when environment quality is measured by pollution indicators.

This econometric model could be estimated using panel data with ordinary least squares. But the application of this estimator to our model suffers from three problems. First, it does not take into account country-specific and time-invariant heterogeneity. When we take advantage of the panel structure of the data, and when country-fixed effects are controlled for, the following model is estimated:

$$gdpc_{it} = \alpha_1 gdpc_{it-1} + \alpha_2 envir_{it} + \alpha_k X'_{kit} + \mu_i + K_t + v_{it} \tag{5.2}$$

The country- and time-fixed effects are represented respectively by μ_i and K_t.

Even though country-fixed effects limit the bias induced by time-invariant unobservable variables, the second drawback comes from the endogeneity of the environmental variable. This problem arises for two main reasons. There is probably a reverse causality in the relationship between environment and economic outcomes. In fact, according to the EKC hypothesis, the development level of a country has significant effects on its level of pollution (Grossman and Krueger 1995). The environmental indicator could also be a proxy for certain variables that have significant effects on economic growth, such as the technology use and the structure of the economy. The instrumental variable method's two-state least squares (2SLS) estimator seems appropriate. This estimator applied to our model raises the third problem because of its dynamic characteristic. Indeed it leads to a biased estimation of α_1, since $gdpc_{it-1}$ and v_{it} are probably correlated. The generalized method of moments (GMM) applied for dynamic panel data is suitable to estimate consistently the parameter α_1 and also the coefficients of predetermined and endogenous variables. We use the system–GMM estimator, which combines equations in levels and equations in differences and then exploits additional moment conditions (Blundell and Bond 1998). Predetermined and endogenous variables are instrumented by both their lagged values in levels and lagged values in differences.[3] Two specification tests check the validity of the instruments: the first is the standard Sargan-Hansen test of overidentifying restrictions; the second examines the hypothesis that there is no second-order serial correlation in the first difference residuals.

Economic convergence and environment

To assess the impact of environmental quality on economic convergence, we introduce the interaction term between lag GDP per capita and environment as an additional variable into the previous model:

$$gdpc_{it} = \alpha_1 gdpc_{it-1} + \alpha_2 envir_{it} + \alpha_3 (gdpc_{it-1})$$
$$* (envir_{it}) + \alpha_k X'_{kit} + \mu_i + K_t + v_{it} \tag{5.3}$$

In this model the catch-up coefficient is:

$$\frac{\partial(gdpc_t)}{\partial(gdpc_{t-1})} = \alpha_1' + \alpha_3 * envir$$

and this is a function of environmental quality. α_1' is expected to be $0 < \alpha_1' < 1$, $\alpha_2 < 0$ and $\alpha_3 > 0$. This model is also estimated with the GMM.

Explanation through the role of health variable

These models allowed us to assess the impact of environmental degradation on economic growth and economic convergence when health status is among the control variables. However, this remains insufficient, because it does not take into account the interrelation between health, environment and economic growth. Moreover, it does not permit us to assess the impact of environmental degradation which affects growth through health. To assess this, we add to previous equations two others: an equation of health and one of environment.

Through these additional equations, we estimate the impact of income and environmental degradation on health. Generally, it is assumed that health outcomes of a population improve when the economy grows and these improvements are made easier by the rise in the general standard of living (access to educational opportunities and health services). Health depends also on the quality of the physical environment such as the amount of air pollution and the quality of drinking water. At the same time, the quality of a country's physical environment is a result of certain growth factors in the economy (intensive use of land, forest, air and water pollution). We follow Gangadharan and Valenzuela (2001) by expressing health as a function of income, physical environmental quality and other control variables:

$$h_{it} = f(gdpc_{it}, envir_{it}(gdpc_{it}, Z_{it}), w_{it}) \tag{5.4}$$

where h is a health indicator, z the non-economic variables that determine environmental quality and w the non-economic variables that determine health status (provision and access to health services, number of physicians, immunization rate, education). The above health equation can be written as:

$$h_{it} = \beta_0 + \beta_1 gdpc_{it} + \beta_2 envir_{it} + \beta_3 w_{it} + \rho_{it} \tag{5.5}$$

Here our purpose is to highlight the relation between economic development and environmental quality. Economic growth is generally made at the cost of a deterioration of the quality of the natural environment. Several studies have assessed empirically and theoretically the effect of economic development on environmental quality (Grossman and Krueger 1995; Andreoni and Levinson 1998; Torras and Boyce 1998). Generally, they found that income is linked to environmental quality through an inverted-U relationship. In our model environmental quality is explained by income and social variables:

$$envir_{it} = c + \gamma_1 gdpc_{it} + \gamma_1 gdpc^2_{it} + \gamma_3 z_{it} + n_{it} \tag{5.6}$$

where z is the non-economic (social) variables that could affect environmental quality such as population density. These two equations are estimated simultaneously with 2SLS.

Interrelationships between income, health and environment

To verify the robustness of our results, we also estimate using three-stage least squares (3SLS), involving Equations 5.2, 5.5 and 5.6. This method further takes into account the interrelationships between gdpc, h and envir. In fact, in our system the variable for economic activity is both used as a dependent and explanatory variable, and similarly for health and environmental quality. This simultaneity bias can be corrected by use of the 2SLS or the 3SLS.

Variables and data

This study is based on panel data of 117 developed and developing countries for which data are available from 1971 to 2000, subdivided into 5-year periods.[4] The economic outcome is measured by GDP per capita based on purchasing power parity (PPP) in constant 2005 international dollars. This indicator is taken from the World Development Indicators of the World Bank (2008). Environmental quality is represented by three indicators, carbon dioxide emission in metric tons per capita (CO_2) and sulphur dioxide emission milligrams per GDP (SO_2) for air pollution and biological oxygen demand in milligrams per worker (BOD) for water pollution. BOD is a measure of the oxygen used by micro-organisms to decompose waste. Micro-organisms such as bacteria are responsible for decomposing organic waste. When organic matter such as dead plants, leaves, grass clippings, manure, sewage, or even food waste is present in a water supply, the bacteria will begin the process of breaking down this waste. If there is a large quantity of organic waste in the water supply, there will also be a lot of bacteria working to decompose this waste. In this case, the demand for oxygen will be high (due to all the bacteria) so the BOD level will be high (CIESE).[5] The BOD and CO_2 data are also taken from World Bank (2008), while SO_2 emission is from the dataset compiled by David Stern[6] in 2006. As health indicator, we use the logistic form of infant mortality rate. In fact the infant mortality indicator is limited asymptotically, and an increase in this indicator does not represent the same performance when its initial level is weak or high; the best functional form to examine is that where the variable is expressed as a logit (Grigoriou 2005):

$$\log it(IMR) = \log\left(\frac{IMR}{1-IMR}\right)$$

We also use as control variables the gross fixed capital formation as percentage of GDP, annual population growth rate, economic openness (ratio of the sum of import and export to GDP), household final consumption per capita, financial development (money and quasi money as a ratio of GDP), inflation rate, immunization rate against DPT, the number of physicians per 1,000 inhabitants and female fertility rate, all taken from a World Bank database (2008). Income inequality is measured by the Gini coefficient taken from the database created by Galbraith and Kum (2005) and known as the University of Texas inequality project database. Our institution's quality indicator is from polity IV and the variable we use is polity2. Finally, the variable of education quality is from Barro and Lee (2000). The definitions and sources of these variables, as well as the list of countries sampled, are presented in Appendix 5A.

Econometric results

We begin by discussing the results from the estimation of the growth model, then we carry out the results of the simultaneous estimation of the health and environmental equations. Finally, we present the results obtained with the simultaneous estimation of the three equations.

Economic growth and environment

The results obtained from the estimation of Equation 5.2 are presented in the first three columns of Table 5.1. The dependent variable is GDP per capita and our variable of interest is environmental quality, measured by three different indicators (SO_2 per GDP, CO_2 per capita and BOD per worker). This equation is estimated with the two-step system–GMM estimator, and environmental variables are taken as endogenous and then instrumented by at least their second-order lags.[7]

These results suggest that environmental degradations have a negative and statistically significant effect on economic growth whatever the environmental indicator considered. Infant mortality rate also has a negative and significant effect on economic growth. Another interesting result is the coefficient of the catch-up variable. Indeed, the coefficient of lagged GDP per capita is around 0.91; this corresponds to a rate of convergence of about 2 per cent per year.[8] That means each year poor countries reduce their gap to their steady state by 2 per cent. This convergence rate is close to that found in the literature. All other relevant variables of control present expected signs and are statistically significant at the 10 per cent level, except the education and inflation variables, whose coefficients display unexpected or unstable signs.

Economic convergence and environmental quality

As previously argued, environmental quality may reduce the ability of poor countries to catch up with developed ones economically. To assess empirically whether pollution affects the speed of convergence, we estimate Equation 5.3 with the two-step system–GMM estimator and environmental variables and the interaction

Table 5.1 Two-step system–generalized method of moments results of the economic convergence effect of environmental variables

Variables	Dependent variables: GDP per capita PPP in constant value 2005					
	SO_2 per GDP (1)	CO_2 per capita (2)	BOD per worker (3)	SO_2 per GDP (4)	CO_2 per capita (5)	BOD per worker (6)
Log initial GDP per capita	0.913*** (14.73)	0.917*** (8.73)	0.907*** (42.12)	0.903*** (13.40)	0.936*** (5.19)	0.675*** (6.74)
(Environment) × (initial GDP)	-0.622** (2.00)	-0.007* (1.93)		2.313** (2.36)	0.013*** (2.98)	0.910** (2.40)
Environmental variables			-0.666* (1.66)	-16.547** (2.36)	-0.128*** (2.94)	-7.692** (2.42)
Population growth	-0.000 (0.06)	0.003 (0.53)	-0.008 (0.99)	0.001 (0.33)	-0.002 (0.26)	0.006 (0.53)
Log schooling	0.013* (1.94)	0.005 (0.45)	0.011 (1.16)	0.005 (0.75)	0.002 (0.19)	0.014 (1.07)
Log investment	-0.015 (0.44)	0.091*** (3.68)	0.051 (1.64)	0.090*** (3.26)	0.134*** (3.36)	0.064* (1.85)
Logit health	-0.048*** (4.03)	-0.044*** (4.15)	-0.028* (1.77)	-0.040*** (3.26)	-0.035*** (2.66)	-0.080*** (2.63)
Openness	0.056** (2.32)	0.018 (0.75)	0.037 (1.53)	0.023 (1.46)	0.018 (0.72)	-0.036 (0.95)
Log consumption	0.049 (0.88)	0.050 (0.59)	0.043** (2.36)	0.041 (0.76)	0.018 (0.13)	0.078 (1.15)
Financial development	-94.851 (1.25)	-66.054 (1.41)	-132.090*** (2.95)	-83.703 (1.19)	-102.375 (1.60)	151.914 (1.37)
Polity2	0.001 (1.31)	0.002** (2.21)	0.002** (1.98)	0.003*** (2.76)	0.002** (2.17)	0.002* (1.72)
Inflation	0.005* (1.72)	-0.003*** (5.44)	-0.003*** (5.91)	-0.002*** (5.18)	-0.003*** (3.70)	-0.002*** (2.60)
Constant	0.228 (1.31)	-0.066 (0.30)	0.357 (1.93)	0.106 (0.69)	-0.067 (0.17)	1.732*** (2.85)
Observations	235	239	203	235	239	203
Countries	68	69	63	68	69	63
AR1	0.019	0.009	0.014	0.004	0.010	0.010
AR2	0.127	0.094	0.117	0.128	0.115	0.151
Hansen p-value	0.388	0.156	0.259	0.389	0.285	0.139
Number of instruments	26	17	15	17	17	19

Source: Author's calculation.

Notes: Robust t-statistics in parentheses. Standard errors are corrected by the Windmeijer (2005) method designed for finite sample bias in a two-step system–GMM estimator. * $p < 0.10$, ** $p < 0.05$, *** $p < 0.01$.
AR1, AR2, Arellano–Bond test for autocorrelation of order 1 and 2, respectively, in differenced residuals, BOD, biological oxygen demand; GDP, gross domestic product; PPP, purchasing power parity.

term are taken as endogenous and then instrumented by at least their second-order lags. The results obtained are summarized in the last three columns (4, 5 and 6) of Table 5.1. The coefficients of our variables of interest have the correct signs and are statistically significant. Indeed, the lag of GDP per capita and its interaction term with environmental indicators have positive coefficients, while pollution variables have negative coefficients. This means that the speed of convergence of an economy depends on its pollution level. More precisely, a high level of environmental degradation increases the marginal effect of lag GDP per capita on its current level and therefore reduces the speed of convergence. Environmental quality

Table 5.2 Two-step system–GMM results of the economic convergence effect of environmental variables without education

Variables	Dependent variables: GDP per capita PPP in constant value 2005		
	SO_2 per GDP (1)	CO_2 per capita (2)	BOD per worker (3)
Log Initial GDP per capita	0.891***	0.870***	0.797***
	(10.59)	(5.83)	(12.29)
(Environment) × (initial GDP)	1.520*	0.010*	0.690*
	(1.66)	(1.94)	(1.94)
Environmental variables	−11.060*	−0.105*	−5.832*
	(1.69)	(1.94)	(1.96)
Population growth	−0.000	−0.003	−0.001
	(0.07)	(0.38)	(0.11)
Log investment	0.068**	0.124***	0.056*
	(2.28)	(2.81)	(1.92)
Logit health	−0.031***	−0.014	−0.050**
	(2.71)	(0.84)	(2.47)
Openness	0.031	0.067*	−0.013
	(1.27)	(1.79)	(0.40)
Log consumption	0.055	0.078	0.015
	(0.78)	(0.67)	(0.54)
Financial development	−45.268	−131.795*	103.831
	(0.76)	(1.72)	(1.10)
Polity2	0.002**	0.002	0.002*
	(1.99)	(1.63)	(1.74)
Inflation	−0.003***	−0.002***	−0.003***
	(5.88)	(3.73)	(7.03)
Constant	0.214	0.131	1.315**
	(1.19)	(0.35)	(2.18)
Observations	287	292	233
Countries	84	86	73
AR1	0.006	0.017	0.003
AR2	0.129	0.150	0.106
Hansen p-value	0.191	0.210	0.545
Number of instruments	13	18	14

Source: Author's calculation.

Note: Robust t-statistics in parentheses. Standard errors are corrected by the Windmeijer (2005) method designed for finite sample bias in a two-step system–GMM estimator. * $p < 0.10$, ** $p < 0.05$, *** $p < 0.01$.

can be viewed as an obstacle for developing countries by reducing their ability to get closer to developed countries economically, given the EKC hypothesis.

Regarding the control variables, only investment, health, institutional quality and inflation rate appear statistically significant. In fact, investment and institutional quality increase economic growth, while high mortality and inflation rates reduce it.

The scarcity of education data for many countries reduces the number of countries in our sample. To deal with this potential degrees-of-freedom problem, we conduct the estimation without the education variable. The results are presented in Table 5.2. The sample size increases from 68 countries to 86 and the results remain unchanged.

Role of health outcomes

To take the interrelationships between health, environment and economic growth into account, and to assess the impact of environmental degradation which affects growth through health, we estimate simultaneously a health and an environment equation with 2SLS estimator. We perform the Hausman specification test (Hausman 1978) to make our choice between the random and fixed effects models. When the p-value of this test is superior to 10 per cent, the random effects model estimator is better; this is the case of the specification with SO_2 and BOD. Otherwise, we choose the fixed effect estimator. The results obtained through 2SLS are summarized in Table 5.3.

Columns 1 and 2 of Table 5.3 present the results when SO_2 per GDP is used as the environmental indicator. These results show that lagged income per capita, immunization rate, urbanization and number of physicians are factors that contribute to improve health status. However, environmental degradation worsens it. The negative coefficient of environmental variable confirms our theoretical argument, namely health is an important channel through which health affects economic growth. The result of the first-step regression (environmental quality equation in column 2) indicates that the coefficient of lagged income per capita is positive and significant at 1 per cent, showing that economic activity deteriorates environmental quality. But the negative and significant coefficient of lagged income square indicates that the negative effect of GDP on environmental quality is conditioned to an income threshold above which the effect becomes positive and income improves environmental quality confirming the EKC hypothesis. The four last columns of this table present the results when carbon dioxide per GDP (columns 3 and 4) and the biological oxygen demand (columns 5 and 6) are used as environmental variables. All the environmental variables have the correct sign, and the EKC hypothesis is verified in each case.

The 2SLS estimations of these two equations allow us to draw some conclusions: there is an inverse causality between economic activity and environmental degradation, and health status is an important channel through which environmental degradation affects economic growth even if it is not alone. The effect of economic activity on environmental quality is dependent on the income level. Countries whose income levels are below the EKC income threshold will be caught in a poverty trap due to environmental degradation. However, those with income levels

Table 5.3 2SLS estimation of the health effect of environmental degradation and environmental Kuznets-curve hypothesis

Variables	Random effects		Fixed effects		Random effects	
	Inf. mort. rate (1)	SO_2 per GDP (2)	Inf. mort. rate (3)	CO_2 per capita (4)	Inf. mort. rate (5)	BOD per worker (6)
Immunization	-0.837***	0.0013	-0.670***	0.090	-1.000***	0.011
	(4.22)	(0.45)	(3.82)	(0.06)	(3.39)	(0.57)
Physician	-0.539***	0.002***	-0.570***	2.265***	-0.052	0.0036
	(6.67)	(2.59)	(7.02)	(3.77)	(0.76)	(0.77)
Urban population	-1.135*	0.008	-1.372**	5.296	0.173	-0.039
	(1.70)	(0.90)	(2.06)	(0.89)	(0.44)	(-1.49)
Log fertility rate	-0.282	0.009***	0.152	-1.072	0.312	0.0371***
	(1.16)	(3.88)	(1.05)	(-0.70)	(1.51)	(3.41)
Log GDP per capita lag	-0.124	0.0414***	-0.221	26.05***	-0.445***	0.111***
	(0.82)	(2.78)	(1.57)	(2.75)	(5.33)	(2.65)
Environment	52.782**		0.055**		11.746***	
	(2.53)		(2.17)		(3.38)	
Log GDP per capita square lag		-0.0026***		-1.583***		-0.0063**
		(-3.08)		(-2.99)		(-2.55)
Income inequality		-0.0005		-0.111***		0.0013***
		(-0.79)		(-2.83)		(3.05)
Constant	-0.607	-0.1703**	-0.101	-100.2**	-1.701**	-0.369**
	(0.53)	(-2.55)	(0.08)	(-2.32)	(1.98)	(-2.10)
Observations	253	253	259	259	257	257
Countries	113	113	117	117	117	117
Hausman test (*p*-value)	0.99		0.00		0.29	

Source: Author's calculation.

Note: Robust *t*-statistics in parentheses. * $p < 0.10$, ** $p < 0.05$, *** $p < 0.01$.
2SLS, two-state least squares; Inf. mort., infant mortality.

Table 5.4 3SLS estimation of the interrelationships between health, environment, and economic activity

Variables	3SLS estimation of the relationships between health, environment, and economic activity								
	GDP per capita (1)	Inf. mort. rate (2)	SO₂ per GDP (3)	GDP per capita (4)	Inf. mort. rate (5)	CO₂ per capita (6)	GDP per capita (7)	Inf. mort. rate (8)	BOD per worker (9)
Pop. growth	-0.00696			0.00187			-0.00570		
	(-1.197)			(0.408)			(-1.008)		
Initial GDP	0.920***			0.979***			0.905***		
	(54.32)			(29.17)			(67.29)		
Schooling	0.0245***			0.0244***			0.0244**		
	(2.900)			(3.214)			(2.545)		
Investment	0.0884***			0.113***			0.0454**		
	(5.016)			(4.898)			(2.007)		
Inf. mort.	-0.0910***			-0.154***			-0.0897***		
	(-4.594)			(-7.337)			(-3.033)		
Log cons.	-0.00927			-0.00996			0.0269*		
	(-0.393)			(-0.593)			(1.869)		
Financial dev.	-129.5			-17.75			-28.18		
	(-1.473)			(-0.473)			(-0.584)		
Polity2	0.00119			0.000830			0.00203***		
	(1.322)			(1.143)			(2.826)		
Inflation	-0.000972			-0.00229			-0.00214		
	(-0.630)			(-1.418)			(-1.383)		
Immunization		-0.850***			-0.331***			-0.493***	
		(-5.272)			(-2.729)			(-3.417)	
Physician		-0.0789*			-0.0596			-0.136***	
		(-1.951)			(-1.577)			(-3.014)	

(Continued)

Table 5.4 (Continued)

Variables	3SLS estimation of the relationships between health, environment, and economic activity								
	GDP per capita (1)	Inf. mort. rate (2)	SO_2 per GDP (3)	GDP per capita (4)	Inf. mort. rate (5)	CO_2 per capita (6)	GDP per capita (7)	Inf. mort. rate (8)	BOD per worker (9)
Fertility rate		0.645*** (6.697)			0.925*** (8.245)			0.602*** (5.263)	
Environment	-0.0692*** (-3.180)	0.465*** (6.216)		-0.0550** (-2.568)	0.458*** (5.114)		-0.0992 (-1.281)	0.845*** (3.298)	
Log GDP per capita		-0.197*** (-3.520)	4.045*** (5.464)		-0.948*** (-9.285)	4.455*** (7.825)		-0.359*** (-7.731)	0.308 (1.615)
Log GDP per square capita			-0.268*** (-6.089)			-0.185*** (-5.588)			-0.0213* (-1.875)
Inequality			-0.00165 (-0.169)			-0.005 (0.60)			0.0125*** (4.511)
Constant	-0.252** (-2.518)	0.887* (1.755)	-20.36*** (-6.573)	-0.615** (-2.291)	3.655*** (4.684)	-23.34*** (-9.858)	-0.0273 (-0.353)	0.832 (1.371)	-3.202*** (-4.087)
Observations	179	179	179	216	216	216	180	180	180
R^2	0.993	0.724	0.197	0.994	0.798	0.817	0.997	0.840	0.262

Source: Author's calculation.

Note: Robust t-statistics in parentheses. * $p < 0.10$, ** $p < 0.05$, *** $p < 0.01$. All the independent variables are in natural logarithmic form, except health variable, population growth, polity2 and inflation rate.
3SLS, three-stage least squares.

above this threshold will be in a virtuous circle due to the improvement of environmental quality. This result suggests that the ability of poor countries to catch up with rich ones would be reduced. Any ambitious economic policy must take into account environmental concerns in order to avoid potential perverse effects.

Interrelationships between income, health and environment

In order to confirm the results already analysed, we estimate simultaneously all the three equations (growth, health and environment equations) with the 3SLS estimator.[9] The results are presented in Table 5.4.

These results are similar to those reported previously in Tables 5.1 to 5.3. The first three columns present the results when SO$_2$ per GDP is used as an environmental indicator. This environmental indicator affects negatively and significantly economic activity as presented in column 1 and degrades health status (column 2). And the EKC hypothesis is confirmed in column 3.

The six other columns of this table present the results when carbon dioxide per GDP (columns 4, 5 and 6) and the biological oxygen demand (columns 7, 8 and 9) are used as environmental variables. All the environmental variables have the correct sign and the EKC hypothesis is verified in each case.

Conclusion

The main goal of this chapter is the analysis of the interrelationships between health, income and environmental quality, and the consequences on the economic convergence process. We introduce an environmental variable in a growth model in order to observe its effect on economic growth. Our results show that environmental degradation negatively affects economic activity and reduces the ability of poor countries to reach developed ones economically. This reinforces our theoretical argument according to which environmental quality improvement plays a considerable role in the economic convergence process. Two-step GMM and least square estimations of health and environment equations allow us to confirm the inverse causality between environmental quality and economic growth and between economic growth and health. Health status remains an important channel through which environmental degradation affects economic growth even if it is not alone. Poor countries which have chosen rapid economic growth at the price of environmental quality will penalize themselves and have little chance to reach their goal. Such a policy can reduce growth through health and other related channels.

Poor countries cannot postpone attending to environmental concerns in the hope that the environment will improve with increased incomes and avoid poverty traps due to environmental degradation. Policy makers in these countries should, on the contrary, take into account environmental concerns as promoted by the international community through the MDGs.

This chapter can also be placed into the debate about development aid effectiveness. In fact, development assistance based on less polluting production technology will help poor countries to avoid the vicious circles shown in this chapter.

Appendix 5A

Table 5A.1 Descriptive statistics

Variable	Obs.	Mean	Std. dev.	Min.	Max.
GDP per capita	259	11212.43	10918.89	355.8692	55491.52
Inf. mort. rate	259	36.90442	33.55625	3.48	138.656
SO$_2$ per GDP	253	0.0069203	0.017175	0.0000922	0.1760821
CO$_2$ per capita	259	5.060414	5.543132	0.0319344	35.87007
BOD per worker	256	0.1950967	0.0519381	0.0694487	0.4478187
Pop. growth	259	1.337404	3.075527	−44.40836	5.603235
School	211	23.11564	22.01362	0	84.1
Investment	258	20.90701	5.34708	9.488747	40.29905
Openness	256	68.85741	39.29941	2.003065	238.6728
Consumption	219	4469.355	5270.451	87.23995	22281.84
Financial dev.	221	44.7538	32.07666	9.198633	227.4642
Polity2	226	3.879646	6.691901	−10	10
Inflation rate	254	38.59134	190.1751	−1.659683	2342.221
Immunization	259	81.51004	16.49692	24	99
Physician	259	1.445306	1.155825	.0198895	4.173381
Fertility rate	259	3.132003	1.578447	1.152	7.845
Inequality	259	42.36337	6.444149	26.135	64.2473

Source: Author's compilation.

Table 5A.2 Definitions of variables and their sources

Variables	Characteristics	Sources
GDP per capita	Gross domestic product per capita	World Bank (2008)
Inf. mort. rate	Infant mortality rate	UNICEF
SO$_2$ per GDP	Sulphur dioxide emission per GDP	Stern (2006)
CO$_2$ per capita	Carbon dioxide emission per capita	World Bank (2008)
BOD per worker	Biological Oxygen Demand per worker	World Bank (2008)
Pop. growth	Population growth rate	World Bank (2008)
School	Percentage of 'no schooling' in the total population	Barro and Lee (2000)
Investment	Gross fixed capital formation	World Bank (2008)
Openness	Ratio of the sum of export and import to	World Bank (2008)
Consumption	Household final consumption rate per capita	World Bank (2008)
Financial dev.	Money and quasi money as a ratio of GDP	World Bank (2008)
Polity2	Institution quality	Polity IV
Inflation rate	Consumption index price	World Bank (2008)
Immunization	Immunization rate against DPT	World Bank (2008)
Physician	Number of physicians per 1,000 inhabitants	World Bank (2008)
Fertility rate	Women's fertility rate	World Bank (2008)
Inequality	Gini coefficient of income	University of Texas

Source: Author's illustration.

List of countries in the sample

Albania	Greece	New Zealand
Algeria	Guatemala	Oman
Argentina	Honduras	Pakistan
Armenia	Haiti	Panama
Australia	Hungary	Peru
Austria	Indonesia	Philippines
Azerbaijan	India	Papua New Guinea
Belgium	Ireland	Poland
Bangladesh	Islamic Republic of Iran	Portugal
Bulgaria	Iceland	Paraguay
Bahrain	Israel	Romania
Belize	Italy	Russian Federation
Bolivia	Jamaica	Rwanda
Brazil	Jordan	Saudi Arabia
Bhutan	Japan	Senegal
Botswana	Kenya	Singapore
Central African	Kyrgyz Republic	El Salvador
Republic	Korea Republic	Spain
Canada	Kuwait	Suriname
Chile	Sri Lanka	Slovak Republic
China	Lithuania	Slovenia
Côte d'Ivoire	Luxembourg	Sweden
Cameroon	Latvia	Swaziland
Democratic Republic of	Morocco	Syrian Arab Republic
the Congo	Moldova	Thailand
Colombia	Madagascar	Tonga
Cape Verde	Mexico	Trinidad and Tobago
Costa Rica	FYR Macedonia	Tunisia
Croatia	Malta	Turkey
Cyprus	Myanmar	United Kingdom
Denmark	Mongolia	Uganda
Ecuador	Mozambique	Ukraine
Arab Republic of Egypt	Mauritius	Uruguay
Ethiopia	Malawi	United States of America
Finland	Malaysia	St. Vincent and the
Fiji	Namibia	Grenadines
France	Nigeria	Venezuela
Gabon	Netherlands	South Africa
Germany	Norway	Zambia.
Ghana	Nepal	

Notes

1 This channel will be the object of particular attention in this chapter.
2 These variables are listed in the next subsection, Economic convergence and environment.

3 The paper uses the two-step system–GMM estimator with the Windmeijer (2005) correction for finite sample bias.
4 The time periods are 1971–1975, 1976–1980, 1981–1985, 1986–1990, 1991–1995, 1996–2000.
5 According to the Center for Improved Engineering and Science Education (CIESE): http://ciese.org/curriculum/waterproj/bod/ (accessed: 19 November 2014).
6 We thank David Stern for the provision of data.
7 To prevent the problem of the proliferation of instruments commonly faced in this methodology, we restrict the maximum number of lags at 5, which leads us to a maximum number of instruments equal to 26.
8 The theoretical coefficient of the lagged GDP per capita is $\exp(-\lambda t)$, where *exp* is the exponential function, λ is the speed of convergence and t is the time. Given that we are using 5-year periods in the study, the speed of convergence is 1.88%.
9 Here the environmental indicators are expressed in natural logarithmic form to be interpreted as elasticity.

References

Acemoglu, D. and J. Johnson (2007). 'Disease and Development: The Effect of Life Expectancy on Economic Growth'. *Journal of Political Economy*, 115(6): 925–85.
Acemoglu, D. and J. Johnson (2009). 'Disease and Development: The Effect of Life Expectancy on Economic Growth'. In M. Spence and M. Lewis (eds), *Health and Growth*. Washington, DC: World Bank, Commission on Growth and Development, pp. 77–129.
Alderman, H. and J.R. Behrman (2006). 'Reducing the Incidence of Low Birth Weight in Low-Income Countries Has Substantial Economic Benefits'. *World Bank Research Observer*, 21(1): 25–48.
Andreoni, J. and A. Levinson (1998). 'The Simple Analytics of the Environmental Kuznets Curve'. *Journal of Public Economics*, 80(2): 269–86.
Arora, S. (2001). 'Health, Human Productivity, and Long-Term Economic Growth'. *The Journal of Economic History*, 61: 699–749.
Aunan, K. and X.C. Pan (2004). 'Exposure-Response Functions for Health Effects of Ambient Air Pollution Applicable for China – A Meta-Analysis'. *Science of the Total Environment*, 329: 3–16.
Barro, R. (1996). *Health and Economic Growth*. Cambridge, MA: Harvard University.
Barro, J.R. and X. Sala-i-Martin (1992). 'Convergence'. *Journal of Political Economy'*, C: 223–51.
Barro, R.J. and J.-W. Lee (2000). 'International Data on Educational Attainment: Updates and Implications'. Working Paper 42. Cambridge, MA: Harvard University, CID.
Becker, R.A. (1982). 'Intergenerational Equity: The Capital-Environment Trade-Off'. *Journal of Environmental Economics and Management*, 9: 165–85.
Bloom, D. and P.N. Malaney (1998). 'Macroeconomic Consequences of the Russian Mortality Crisis'. *World Development*, 26: 2073–85.
Bloom, D.E., D. Canning and G. Fink (2009). 'Disease and Development Revisited'. Working Paper 15137. Cambridge, MA: Harvard School of Public Health.
Bloom, D.E., D. Canning and P.N. Malaney (2000). 'Demographic Change and Economic Growth in Asia'. *Population and Development Review*, 26 (supp.): 257–90.
Bloom, D.E., D. Canning and J. Sevilla (2005). 'The Effect of Health on Economic Growth: A Production Function Approach'. *World Development*, 32(1): 1–13.
Blundell R. and S. Bond (1998). 'Initial Conditions and Moment Restrictions in Dynamic Panel Data Models'. *Journal of Econometrics*, 87: 115–43.

Bovenberg, A.L. and S. Smulders (1995). 'Environmental Quality Pollution-Augmenting Technological Change in a Two Sector Endogenous Growth Model'. *Journal of Public Economics*, 1: 369–91.

Bovenberg, A.L. and S. Smulders (1996). 'Transitional Impacts of Environmental Policy in an Endogenous Growth Model'. *International Economic Review*, 37: 861–93.

Brock, W.A. (1977). 'A Polluted Golden Age'. In V. Smith (ed.), *Economics of Natural Environmental Resources*. New York: Gordon and Breach, pp. 441–62.

Bruvoll, A., S. Glomsrod and H. Vennemo (1999). 'Environmental Drag: Evidence from Norway'. *Ecological Economics*, 30: 235–49.

Burnett, R. and D. Krewski (1994). 'Air Pollution Effects on Hospital Admission Rates: A Random Effects Modeling Approach', *The Canadian Journal of Statistics*, 22(4): 441–58.

Cass, D. (1965) 'Optimal Growth in an Aggregate Model of Capital Accumulation'. *Review of Economic Studies*, 32: 233–40.

Chay, K.Y. and M. Greenstone (2003). 'The Impact of Air Pollution on Infant Mortality: Evidence from Geographic Variation in Pollution Shocks Induced by a Recession'. *The Quarterly Journal of Economics*, 118(3): 1121–67.

Chichilnisky, G. (1994). 'North-South Trade and the Global Environment'. *The American Economic Review*, 84(4): 851–74.

Copeland, B.R. and M.S. Taylor (1994). 'North-South Trade and the Environment'. *Quarterly Journal of Economics*, 109(3): 755–85.

Cuddington, J.T and J.D. Hancock (1994). 'Assessing the Impact of AIDS on the Growth of the Malawian Economy'. *Journal of Development Economics*, 43: 363–68.

Dasgupta, P. and G. Heal (1974). 'The Optimal Depletion of Exhaustible Resources'. *Review of Economic Studies*, 3–28.

Diamond, P. (1965). 'National Debt in a Neoclassical Growth Model'. *American Economic Review*, 55: 1126–50.

Galbraith, J.K. and H. Kum (2005). 'Estimating the Inequality of Household Incomes: A Statistical Approach to the Creation of a Dense and Consistent Global Data Set'. *Review of Income and Wealth*, 51(1): 115–43.

Gangadharan, L. and M.R. Valenzuela (2001). 'Interrelationships between Income, Health and the Environment: Extending the Environmental Kuznets Curve Hypothesis'. *Ecological Economics*, 36: 513–31.

Geldrop, V. and C. Withagen (2000). 'Natural Capital and Sustainability'. *Ecological Economics*, 32(3): 445–55.

Gradus, R. and S. Smulders (1993). 'The Trade off between Environment Care and Long-Term Growth – Pollution in the Three Prototype Growth Models'. *Journal of Economics*, 58(1): 25–51.

Grigoriou, C. (2005). 'Essais sur la Vulnérabilité des Enfants dans les Pays en Développement: L'Impact de la Politique Économique'. PhD Thesis. Auvergne: Université d'Auvergne, Centre d'Etudes and de Recherches sur le Développement International.

Grossman, G. and A.B. Krueger (1995). 'Pollution Growth and the Environment'. *Quarterly Journal of Economics*, 110: 353–77.

Gruver, J.W. (1976). 'Optimal Investment in Pollution Control Capital in a Neoclassical Context'. *Journal of Environmental Economics and Management*, 3: 165–77.

Hausman, J. (1978). 'Specification Test in Econometrics'. *Econometrica*, 46: 1251–71.

Hettige, H., M. Mani and D. Wheeler (1998). 'Industrial Pollution and Economic Development', Policy Research Working Paper 1876. Washington, DC: World Bank.

Hofkes, M.W. (1996). 'Modelling Sustainable Development: An Economy-Ecology Integrated Model'. *Economic Modelling*, 13: 333–53.

Jerrett, M., M. Buzzelli, R.T. Burnett and P.F. DeLuca (2005). 'Particulate Air Pollution, Social Confounders and Mortality in Small Areas of an Industrial City'. *Social Science & Medicine*, 60: 2845–63.

John, A. and R. Pecchenino (1994). 'An Overlapping Generation Model of Growth and the Environment'. *The Economic Journal*, 104: 1393–1410.

Keeler, E., M. Spence and D. Garnham (1971). 'The Optimal Control of Pollution'. *Journal of Economic Theory*, 4: 19–34.

Knowles, S. and P.D. Owen (1995). 'Health Capital and Cross-Country Variation in Income Per Capita in the Mankiw-Romer-Weil Model'. *Economics Letters*, 48(1): 99–106.

Koopmans, T.C. (1963). 'On the Concept of Optimal Economic Growth'. In *The Econometric Approach to Development Planning*. North-Holland and Rand McNally, pp. 226–87. A reissue of *Pontificiae Academiae Scientiarum Scripta Varia*, 28 (1963): 225–300.

Levine R. and D. Renelt (1992). 'A Sensitivity Analysis of Cross Country Growth Regressions'. *American Economic Review*, 82: 942–63.

Ligthart, J.E. and F. Van Der Ploeg (1994). 'Pollution, the Cost of Public Funds and Endogenous Growth'. *Economics Letters*, 46(4): 339–49.

Lopez, R. (1994). 'The Environment as a Factor of Production: the Effect of Economic Growth and Trade Liberalization'. *Journal of Environmental Economics and Management*, 27: 163–84.

Mäler, K.G. (1974). *Environmental Economics: A Theoretical Inquiry*. Baltimore, MA: The Johns Hopkins University Press.

Mankiw, N., G. Romer and D.N. Weil (1992). 'A Contribution to the Empirics of Economic Growth'. *The Quarterly Journal of Economics*, 107: 407–37.

Mansour S.A. (2004). 'Pesticide Exposure – Egyptian Scene'. *Toxicology*, 198: 91–115.

Nauenberg, E. and K. Basu (1999). 'Effect of Insurance Coverage on the Relationship between Asthma Hospitalizations and Exposure to Air Pollution'. *Public Health Reports*, 114(2): 135–48.

Panayotou, T. (2000). 'Economic Growth and the Environment'. Working Paper 56. Cambridge, MA: Harvard University, CID.

Pearce, D.W. and J.J. Warford (1993). *World without End: Economics, Environment and Sustainable Development*. Oxford: Oxford University Press.

Ramsey, F.P. (1928). 'A Mathematical Theory of Saving'. *Economic Journal*, 38: 543–59.

Rankin, J., T. Chadwick, M. Natarajan, D. Howel, P. Pearce, and T. Pless-Mulloli (2009). 'Maternal Exposure to Ambient Air Pollutants and Risk of Congenital Anomalies'. *Environmental Research*, 109: 181–87.

Repetto, R. and S.S. Baliga (1996). *Pesticide and Immune System: The Public Health Risk*. Washington, DC: World Resources Institute.

Resosudarmo, B.P. and E. Thorbecke (1996). 'The Impact of Environment Policies on Household Income for Different Socio-Economic Classes: The Case of Air Pollutants in Indonesia'. *Ecological Economics*, 17(2): 83–94.

Ricci, F. (2007). 'Channels of Transmission of Environmental Policy to Economic Growth: A Survey of the Theory'. *Ecological Economics*, 60(4): 688–99.

Romer, P.M. (1986). 'Increasing Returns and Long Run Growth'. *Journal of Political Economy*, 94: 1002–37.

Romer, P.M. (1990). 'Endogenous Technological Change'. *Journal of Political Economy* 71–101.

Scapecchi, P. (2008). 'The Health Costs of Inaction with Respect to Air Pollution'. Environment Working Papers 2. Paris: OECD.

Selden, T.M. and D. Song (1995). 'Neoclassical Growth, the J Curve for Abatement, and the Inverted U Curve for Pollution'. *Journal of Environmental Economics and Management*, 29: 162–8.

Shafik, N. (1994). 'Economic Development and Environment Quality: An Econometric Analysis'. *Oxford Economic Paper*, 46: 757–73.

Solow, R.M. (1956). 'A Contribution to the Theory of Economic Growth'. *Quarterly Journal of Economics*, LXX: 65–94.

Solow, R.M. (1974). 'Intergenerational Equity and Exhaustible Resources'. *The Review of Economic Studies* (Symposium Issue): 29–46.

Stern, D. (2006). 'Reversal in the Trend of Global Anthrogenic Sulfur Emissions'. *Global Environmental Change*, 16(2): 207–20.

Stokey, N.L. (1998). 'Are There Limits to Growth?'. *International Economic Review*, 39: 1–31.

Tahvonen, O. and J. Kuuluvainen (1993). 'Economic Growth, Pollution and Renewable Resources'. *Journal of Environmental Economics and Management*, 24: 101–18.

Torras, M. and J. K. Boyce (1998). 'Income, Inequality and Pollution: A Reassessment of the Environment Kuznets Curve'. *Ecological Economics*, 25: 147–60.

United Nations (2013). The Millennium Development Goals Report 2013. United Nations, New York.

United Nations Environment Programme (UNEP) (2007). 'Annual Report'. Nairobi: UNEP.

Van der Ploeg, F. and C. Withagen (1991). 'Pollution Control and the Ramsey Problem'. *Environmental and Resource Economics*, 1: 215–36.

Victor, T.Y.H., P. Chang and K. Blackburn (1993). 'Endogenous Growth, Environment and R&D'. Nota di Lavoro 23.93. Milan: Fondazione ENI Enrico Mattei.

Weil, D. (2007). 'Accounting for the Effect of Health on Economic Growth'. *The Quarterly Journal of Economics*, 122(3): 1265–306.

Windmeijer, F. (2005). 'A Finite Sample Correction for the Variance of Linear Efficient Two-Step GMM Estimators'. *Journal of Econometrics* 126: 25–51.

Woodruff, T.J., J. Grillo and K.C. Schoendorf (1997). 'The Relationship between Selected Causes of Postneonatal Infant Mortality and Particulate Air Pollution in the United States'. *Environmental Health Perspectives*, 105(6): 608–12.

World Bank (2008). *World Development Indicators Online*. Washington, DC: World Bank.

Yadav, S.N. (1997). 'Dynamic Optimization of Nitrogen Use when Groundwater Contamination is Interlised at the Standard in the Long Run', *American Journal of Agricultural Economics*, 79(1997): 931–45.

6 Emerging evidence on the relative importance of sectoral sources of growth in Sub-Saharan Africa

Eric Kehinde Ogunleye

Introduction

Sub-Saharan Africa (SSA) is one of the most widely investigated regions of the world with respect to determinants and constraints of economic growth and development. These interests are sparked by the fact that, despite different policy prescriptions and implementation, sustained economic growth and development remains slow in the region, falling almost consistently behind other developing regions until recently. This plethora of studies sometimes yields varied, diverse and inconsistent results. While some believe that Africa's colonial history is responsible for its slow growth, others heap the blame on physical geography and climate. Yet others conclude that tribal divisions, poor quality of governance and institutions, and conflicts resulting from resource abundance are the important factors. Thus, these findings yield several policy prescriptions that are as diverse, contradictory and inconsistent as the findings. Implementing them has led to mixed results, generating several myths and realities on economic growth and development in the region.

Within the diverse theoretical and empirical literature on economic growth and development in SSA, there are also diverse views on the relative importance of sectoral drivers of growth. While some believe that agriculture is the most important driver, others advocate industrialization, especially manufacturing, with the emerging view giving prominence to the role of services. The Industrial Revolution that laid the foundation for sustainable economic growth and development in Europe naturally induced the policy thinking that industrialization was the most important driver of growth. Thus, beginning from the 1950s, SSA countries were encouraged to pursue industrialization, originally aimed at satisfying the markets of the advanced economies. Most of these countries vigorously pursued the import substitution industrialization (ISI) strategy and later the Export Promotion strategy. Inappropriate policies and economic realities in SSA countries vis-à-vis the industrialized countries being copied, led to structural economic problems that resulted in stagnation and even retrogression. Adjustment was imperative and came at the heels of the Bretton Woods institutions that recommended agriculture as the important driver of growth. Again, appropriate, effective and successful policies aimed at improving productivity in this sector remain the daunting challenge. Discussions on the role of services as a potential driver of growth are relatively new. However, the new, robust and consistent reality emanating from our findings reveals that this sector was the most important driver of growth in SSA between 1980 and 2007.

Understanding the relative importance of sectoral drivers of growth in SSA countries has serious policy implications. Without this understanding, policies will be misdirected. The goal of this study is to determine the relative importance of agriculture, manufacturing and services as drivers of economic growth in selected SSA countries. This study contributes to the growth literature in SSA by providing a deeper understanding of the relative importance of sectoral drivers of growth in the region. Attempts are also made to identify the channels through which these effects occur for services, the most important sectoral driver of growth identified in this study. In order of importance, services, agriculture and manufacturing are the sources of growth in SSA countries, while openness and the labour force are the greatest constraints on services in influencing economic growth. Anecdotal evidence suggests that employment is the possible channel through which services impact on growth.

The chapter is organized as follows. The next section on myths and realities on economic growth in Africa emphasizes the determinants of growth and the shifting focus on sectoral drivers of growth. The nature and structure of economic growth in SSA countries is the focus in the following section. The next section discusses theoretical and empirical methodology and data issues and is followed by a presentation and discussion of the empirical findings. The penultimate section presents a set of policy issues and recommendations, then the final section is the conclusion.

Myths and realities on economic growth in Africa

Several myths exist about economic growth in SSA countries. Some of these myths originate from mere hearsay; others are based on personal beliefs, opinions and convictions. While these myths exist, the realities of economic growth in Africa also exist. The aim of this section is to provide realities confirming or debunking some of the myths about economic growth in SSA countries, with focus on the determinants of economic growth and illusions about the sectoral drivers of growth.

Determinants of economic growth

Initial conditions

Initial conditions in African countries are believed to play an important role in explaining the region's economic performance. For instance, the colonial legacy and ethnic divisions of African countries are assumed to influence growth through poor choices of economic policy (Sachs and Warner 1997). Long years of colonialism created the conditions that induced the slow growth still being experienced by some African countries today despite the recent growth success in several countries. The nature of colonial rule and the policies they adopted created artificial and polarized countries, forcing together people that are culturally, socially, and ideally different and divided. A classic example is Nigeria. In fact, an opposition leader in the 1970s and 1980s once referred to the country as a mere geographic expression. The inherited initial conditions continue to haunt the country to the present day as demonstrated by the incessant ethnic and religious clashes. Colonial policies also created a dichotomous society based on a sentimental construct of ethnicity that engendered the spirit of superiority of one ethnic group over the other. To cite such an example, the concept of Hutus and Tutsis rhetoric in Rwanda was invented by the colonial leaders. This concept created a porous and volatile society resulting from deep-seated animosity between the groups with a penchant for power and dominance. The genocides were manifestation of this. SSA countries also inherited a dependent economy structured to satisfy the market needs of the industrialized countries, especially raw materials. Thus, infrastructure development, education and human resource development were structured to achieve this aim.

The realities, some of which are already mentioned above, demonstrate the truthfulness that initial conditions are an important factor of economic growth and development in SSA countries. This is an important factor in explaining the rapid progress made by Botswana and economic stagnation in countries such as Nigeria until recently. Botswana was never polarized nor did the country lose its traditional ways of doing things. These remain the basis for institutional, economic, social and political decision-making. However, where doubts about the importance of initial conditions are admissible is when we look at a country such as Ethiopia that was never colonized. Despite this status, economic performance in this country is not significantly different from other SSA countries with the initial conditions constraint. Somalia is a similar example of a country that was never formally colonized. In contrast, there are countries that were enmeshed in this initial condition constraint but have succeeded in overcoming this obstacle to growth. Examples of these countries include Rwanda and Mauritius, and to some extent Ghana. Mauritius, for instance, despite its initial conditions, has grown from a poor, agriculture-based economy to a diversified, middle-income economy, with rapidly growing industrial, financial and tourist sectors.

Governance and institutions

There is empirical evidence establishing that poor governance, weak institutions and poor policies explain a large part of the slow growth in SSA countries, with the strong belief that better policies would contribute to stronger economic performance (Sachs and Warner 1997). These variables exert both a direct and an indirect influence on economic performance. Indirectly, they spur growth through increasing domestic and foreign investment, improving the performance of public and private institutions and increasing the size and efficiency of the domestic economic base. Demonstrating the importance of institutions in growth studies, Levine and Renelt (1992) noted that a set of these policy variables are rarely jointly insignificant in a growth regression. The current debate on the role of governance, leadership and institutions on economic performance now tilts heavily towards quality, where capability, commitment and credibility are the main issues.

To a large extent, the failure of SSA countries to attain sustainable high economic growth and development is almost synonymous with the failure of governance. Barro and Lee (1993) argued that there exists a feedback relationship between economic stability and political stability. Using Ghana as a case study, Aryeetey and Tarp (2000) demonstrated that political instability contributes significantly to macroeconomic instability. Several issues are identifiable here. First is the legitimacy of governance. For a long time, governance in most SSA countries has been through coups, counter-coups and military 'revolutions', sometimes bringing to power leaders with less governance experience. Thus, the process that generated these leaders was not representative and as such illegitimate. Second is the objective functions of political leaders which are often at variance with those they represent. While the objective function of the people is social welfare maximization and optimal allocation of public goods, the leaders have a diametrically different objective, namely, enriching and amassing wealth for themselves through illegal means. Third, given the first two issues raised above, political leaders in SSA countries were often corrupt, lacked political will, dedication and the capability for effective governance. Thus, they lacked the required thought processes and strategies for economic growth and transformation.

In addition to governance, quality of institutions is also often used in explaining economic growth in SSA countries. North (1981: 201–2) defines institutions as 'a set of rules, compliance procedures, and moral and ethical behavioural norms designed to *constrain* the behaviour of individuals in the interests of maximizing the wealth or utility of principals'.

This definition provides a clearer picture of the concept of institutions. Institutions in SSA countries, both private and public, are evidently and generally weak. This notion can be traced to Lewis (1955) where problems of economic growth and its proximate causes were explored. These proximate causes of economic growth were linked to several issues including social, institutional, historical, psychological and biological issues. The realities show that countries with stronger and less distorted social, political and economic institutions tend to perform better than those whose institutions are weak and disturbed through external interventions. For instance, the strong institutions in Botswana which are enshrined in its traditional, pre-colonial period are believed to be a major factor behind the country's high economic performance. The Tswana tribes, for example, have strong traditional institutions that allowed for implicit bargain between their leaders and the people. There were established forums for consultation between the chief and his people through a public forum known as the *kgotla* (Du Toit 1995: 21), where all affairs of interest to all parties were openly discussed. This has provided the basis for the transparent, accountable and responsive governance practised in this country, with its very positive effects on economic performance. Other SSA countries had similar institutional arrangements. However, external interventions through colonialism destroyed these institutions and bequeathed these countries a foreign, strange and incomprehensible system which they find difficult to understand.

Geography

Two geographical factors that are often cited as the sources of slow growth in SSA countries are the landlocked and tropical climatic natures of most of these countries. This is based on the fact that about one-third of all SSA countries are landlocked, while almost all of them are tropical. The landlocked nature of SSA countries is believed to be even more important given that none of the fast growing Asian economies possess this feature. The channel through which land-lockedness influences growth is the constraints it imposes on openness to trade due to the higher costs and inconvenience of international activities, especially shipping and transport logistics. The tropical climatic nature of SSA countries is associated with higher prevalence of diseases that affect both humans and crops. This suggests that workers will fall sick more often, thus significantly reducing their real and potential productivity. Similarly, agricultural crops in this region are prone to attacks from tropical pests and insects which could drastically reduce output. Tropical countries are also characterized by low soil quality and less reliable rain. It is worth mentioning that it was Lewis (1955, 1977) who first used the terms 'tropical economies', 'countries of temperate settlement', 'the wet tropics' and 'the dry tropics' as variables in explaining economic growth.

The reality, however, is that Africa is not different because of its geography: landlockedness is not peculiar to the region. To begin with, only 15 of the 53 countries in Africa[1] are landlocked, representing less than 30 per cent. Although this is the highest in any continent, the fact remains that other continents of the world also have some landlocked countries, and this has not resulted in stagnation of the continent. In Europe, Austria, Luxembourg and Switzerland are landlocked countries. Yet, they are not in any way falling behind other non-landlocked countries in terms of growth and general economic performance. In fact, Luxembourg has been consistently ranked number one economy in the world on the basis of per capita income. While the small size of the economy and low population could be advantageous, the consistency suggests that the landlocked nature of the country is not a constraint to economic performance and should not be to SSA countries.

To further counter the argument of the role of geographic factor in economic performance, there are no less than four landlocked African countries that are serving as role models of economic performance, suggesting that landlockedness is not a constraint to growth as purported. These countries are Botswana, Ethiopia, Rwanda and Uganda. From 1993 to 2007, these four countries recorded gross domestic product (GDP) growth that is consistently above 5 per cent, with the exception of 2003 for Rwanda and a few years for Ethiopia. On the other hand, several coastal countries are reporting consistently poor economic performance compared with the landlocked countries. For instance, despite its long coastal line, Nigeria's real per capita income has been hovering in the neighbourhood of US$300–US$400 annually between 1960 and 2007, with the highest peak of US$472 in 2007. The picture is even gloomier when we consider the Democratic Republic of Congo (DRC). The picture is not any better in Cote d'Ivoire. With a peak of over US$1,100 real GDP in 1978, the figure has witnessed a systematic decline by more than half to reach an all-time low of less than US$550 in 2007. This demonstrates that the notion of landlockedness as a cause of slow growth needs to be re-examined.

External factors

External factors that have been advanced as impinging on economic growth in SSA countries are the international commodity market and the international financial system. International commodity market conditions influence growth negatively through openness of SSA economies. The extent of negative impact is demonstrated by Fosu (1998: 31), who wrote:

> the 'contagion' effect can be substantial and the 'speculative attacks' may lead to overshooting of the long-run equilibrium exchange rates. Such short-run equilibria can be destabilizing and highly deleterious to both economic and political institutions. It is thus conceivable that these 'short-run' disturbances would have medium or even long-term adverse impacts on affected economies.

However, the empirical evidence on the effect of export instability originating from fluctuations in foreign demands or in world prices in SSA is inconclusive. While Gyimah-Brempong (1991) found a statistically significant negative impact during 1960–1986, Fosu (1992) established a statistically insignificant negative impact for 1970–1986, with earlier studies establishing similar results and a concluding argument that the effects of exports instability on growth is substantial only when it is transmitted into capital (investment) instability (Fosu 1991). On the other hand, there appears to be an unambiguous negative effect of import instability on growth (see Helleiner 1986; Fosu 2001). Nor are prices of exports the source of the poor economic growth in Africa (Fosu 1991, 1992, 1997). My position here on the reality about the negative effect of export instability on growth in SSA countries is that it is self-induced through concentration in primary commodities that are subject to the vagaries of international market prices. With the exception of very few, most SSA countries are engaged in production and exports of the same kind of commodities. Diversification is the key to breaking out of this constraint. However, apart from a few SSA countries such as Mauritius, not many African countries have made a conscious effort to pull themselves out of this quagmire.

Another external factor is external aid dependency and debt. While some authors have claimed that aid has a harmful effect on growth (Griffin and Enos

1970; Mosley *et al.* 1987; Krueger *et al.* 1989), others have established a positive effect (Grinols and Bhagwati 1976; Levy 1987; Pack and Pack 1990). These opposing submissions have been harmonized by Burnside and Dollar (1997) who argued that the effectiveness of aid on growth works through the policy environment with the finding that aid is effective in a good policy environment. On a general note, negative effect of external debt on economic growth has been established (see Ojo and Oshikoya 1995; Elbadawi *et al.* 1996: 49–76; Fosu 1996, 1999; Iyoha 1999). Again, the reality is that the external debt burden was self-inflicted. It is a price to pay for the poor economic policy management and choices that characterized most of these economies in the 1960s and 1970s. These wrong economic policy choices resulted in structural imbalances that necessitated the adjustment which ultimately resulted in large external debt accumulation. This growth constraint would have been avoided by most of these countries if they had carefully considered the long-term impact of their policy choices.

Policies

Blame for the poor sustained economic growth of SSA countries has also been heaped on the direct policy interventions of the Bretton Woods institutions and the donor countries through the structural adjustment program (SAP) designed to help countries to overcome their structural economic crises and imbalance of the 1970s and 1980s. It is imperative to point out at this juncture the complicity of African leaders and elites in the bad shape that the African economies found themselves during this period which necessitated this foreign intervention. The import substitution industrialization (ISI) policy adopted in the 1960s and 1970s was questionable. The ISI was a development paradigm developed originally for the Latin American and Caribbean countries. This policy was adopted by SSA countries without questioning its veracity and appropriateness to the social, economic, cultural and political realities in the continent. Moreover, systematic application of this policy to African countries was missing. For ISI to succeed and generate the intended impact, several multilevel policies, coordination, targets and human capital are required. However, all of these were ignored. This is not surprising given that adoption of this policy seemed to have been motivated by an anti-colonial and socialist struggle and a strong desire to quickly overcome the colonial inheritance and legacies as demonstrated in the case of Ghana in the Seven-Year Development Plan (1957–1966). There was thus no objectivity in assessing the realities of the economies before adopting the policy. Granted, the concept of ISI was not bad in itself but fault lay with the nature of its implementation in SSA countries which favoured massive state support, exchange controls, overvalued exchange rate, quotas, state subsidies and highly penalized exports. Corruption, tribalism and nepotism on the part of elites who were saddled with the responsibility of running the state-owned enterprises led to complete run down of these institutions.

Shifting focus on sectoral driver of growth and development in Africa

In the 1950s, when most African countries were colonies of Great Britain, Arthur Lewis's two-sector growth model designed for British colonies was the economic development paradigm that informed policies. The policy was developed originally for Latin American and Caribbean countries, and later for African countries and was based on the belief that developing countries should naturally follow the path taken by the industrialized economies at the end of the Second World War. More importantly, these colonies were believed to have very small domestic markets, insufficient capital and a shortage of skilled human capital. Therefore, it was thought that the best model of development was the infusion of physical capital, human capital and technology from the capital-rich industrialized countries into African countries for the purpose of producing exports to satisfy the demand in the industrialized countries. Based on this understanding, the logic was simple: industrialization was the driver of economic growth and development in SSA. The view was that African countries faced daunting challenges to industrialization, resulting from the shortage or absence of physical and human capital, entrepreneurial skills and technological know-how, and that these challenges were to be surmounted through foreign outsourcing, from industrialized countries; SSA would then experience growth and development.

As African countries began emerging from colonial rule, they guided themselves with the thinking that industrialization was the key to economic development. This explains why Ghana, under Dr. Kwame Nkrumah, recruited Arthur Lewis to fashion an industrial policy for the country at independence. Lewis's (1955) solution was simple: structurally transform the subsistence-based agricultural economy into a modern industrial economy. This development paradigm was given an impetus by Prebisch (1950) and Singer (1950). Thus, several African countries vigorously pursued an import substitution industrialization (ISI) policy as a means to attain economic growth. This policy option made sense in that it was irrational to import, at very high costs, manufactured goods that were produced with primary products that had been originally exported from these countries at very low prices.

A discernible weakness inherent in this policy was the incorrect assumption that economies of SSA countries were similar to those of the industrialized countries and should therefore follow their growth path. Second, the model favoured foreign capital and foreign investors, thus inducing over-reliance on foreign capital and capital flight. Finally, this development thinking did not take cognizance of the natural resource endowments and comparative advantage of SSA countries.

The outcomes of the implementation of the ISI confirmed the veracity of our position above. The emphasis on industrialization led to a major neglect of agriculture and food production. Food imports rose and so too did the bills. The industries created were over-protected through unrealistic exchange rates and trade policies and through substantial subsidies granted by the government as incentives to produce. Domestic innovation and invention were absent, implying a high cost of imported machinery. All these factors reinforced themselves to make these firms highly uncompetitive. It is worth stressing at this juncture that the ISI policy was not bad in itself but rather the fault lay with the mode of its implementation.

Beginning in the mid-1970s, most economies of SSA countries began to manifest structural problems emanating from both internal and external sources. Some of these structural problems include: a low economic and export base; excessive focus on the industrial sector to the neglect of agriculture and services; a declining balance of payments, stemming from a consistent fall in the prices of agriculture and raw material exports relative to the rising prices of imported manufactured goods; existence of over-intrusive, bloated, inefficient and corrupt state-owned enterprises that enjoyed state protection as large monopolies and oligopolies; and a serious drain on fiscal revenues through large state subsidies, foreign credits and a reduced drive for tax collection.

The World Bank/IMF intervened in helping African countries solve the perceived structural rigidities in their economies through the adoption of the SAP. One of the pillars of this policy prescription was that African countries should focus on agriculture as the driver of growth and development. One important factor behind the belief that agriculture was or could be the sectoral driver of economic growth in SSA is the fact that apart from Southern Africa, approximately over 60 per cent of the economically active population in the continent was engaged in agriculture with an even higher percentage of the population living in rural areas. There were two possible channels through which agriculture could drive growth in SSA. Employing the analysis of Arthur Lewis, modernizing agriculture would provide a means of employing less of this army of unemployed and underemployed workforce engaged in the sector, while releasing the majority of the workforce for more productive use in non-agricultural sectors such as industry. For earlier views on the role of agriculture in economic growth, see Rosenstein-Rodan (1943), Lewis (1955), Rostow (1960), Fei and Ranis (1964), and Harris and Todaro (1970).

Another factor behind the thinking that agriculture holds the key to economic growth in SSA is its role as a productive sector and its high contribution to economic activity, measured in terms of GDP. On average, between 15 and 20 per cent of GDP was derived from agriculture. This has remained so since these countries attained political independence, demonstrating little structural transformation of the economy. This naturally led to the worrying fact that the sector contributes more to employment than it does to output, implying that productivity per worker is very low relative to other sectors. In fact Gollin (2009) finds a striking difference in output and income per worker between agriculture and non-agriculture activities. Specifically, 13 countries have *mean* agricultural output per worker that is less than US$1 per day and 17 countries recorded US$2 per day. Removing perceived obstacles to productivity and modernizing the sector, therefore, holds the key to improving productivity in the sector for improved contribution to economic growth.

Agriculture is also thought to be of high importance to economic growth in SSA given its potential for feeding the teeming population in the region. Schultz (1953) argued that many poor countries, most of which are found in Africa are in a situation of high food drain, that is, 'a level of income so low that a critically large proportion of the income is required for food'. For instance, undernourishment and complete lack of food is closely linked to the poverty and underdevelopment that was prevalent in Africa. And this can become a vicious cycle where undernourishment and malnutrition leads to low cognitive functioning, poor education and physical stamina. This implies subsequent low supply of labour and poor quality of the labour supplied. This, in turn, leads to poor productivity, poverty and economic growth. Low productivity in agriculture induces higher prices of food and other basic needs and increases food imports bills that ultimately hinder economic growth.

Another important argument that is pertinent to economic growth in Africa is whether agricultural productivity improvements precede economic growth or are preceded by it. Industrial revolution is often cited as an instance in establishing the nature of causation between agricultural productivity improvements and economic growth. This remains inconclusive (see Kuznets 1966; Chenery and Syrquin 1975; Syrquin 1988).

Thoughts about services as a possible driver of growth in African countries are informed by the increasing role of services in the global economy and the fact that economies dominated by high service industries typically tend to be knowledge intensive. Tomlinson and Ndhlovu (2003) demonstrated that there has been a steady rise in the share of service sector in GDP in all regions, developed and developing. Financial services, trading and recently tourism are the major activities in this sector. An important factor that has given impetus to the emergence of this sector as a possible growth-inducing activity in Africa is the recent reforms especially in the financial sector. Pioneering work on the possible contribution of financial services to economic growth was carried out by Gurley and Shaw (1967), McKinnon (1973) and Shaw (1973). These studies emphasized financial intermediation, monetization and capital formation as the important channels through which financial services could impact on growth. The thinking here is that as economy develops, demand for financial services both in terms of quantity and quality increases. This sends signals to players in the sector to be innovative in their efforts to develop better financial products. It was also conceived that a developing financial sector could help induce higher economic growth by providing financial services for more productive and higher economic activities, suggesting a possible feedback relationship between financial services development and economic growth.

Another factor that has led to the emergence of the service sector as a possible sectoral driver of growth is the technological and communication revolution that began in the 1980s. This has led to significant productivity of labour engaged in the sector. In countries such as Singapore, services based on improved technology have gained so much prominence that they contributed up to US$27.5 billion to the economy in 2000. Thus, in 2002 the country's Economic Review Committee recommended a focus on developing this sector, especially finance, logistics and tourism, with the projection that these activities would add 0.4 per cent to the country's annual GDP growth and create an additional 200,000 jobs by 2012.[2]

Several studies have confirmed the long-term positive effects of tourism services on economic growth (see Tosun 1999; Balaguer and Cantavella-Jordá 2002; Dritsakis 2004; Gunduz and Hatemi 2005; Oh 2005; Proenca and Soukiazis 2005). A study has established that countries with tourism services grow faster than Organisation for Economic Co-operation and Development (OECD), oil-exporting and least developed countries (LDC) (Brau *et al.* 2003). It is important to point out that most of these studies are based on the experiences of countries outside the SSA. There remains a dearth of studies examining this relationship for SSA countries.

Nature and structure of economic growth in SSA

Economic growth across African countries has been relatively strong in recent times (see Table 6.1). GDP in SSA averaged about 5 per cent between 2000 and 2007, with a peak of more than 6 per cent in 2007. Similarly, per capita GDP averaged less than 3 per cent, with a peak of about 4 per cent during the same period. Overall, most countries recorded positive GDP growth rates as opposed to the pervasive negative growth rates in previous decades. We can classify economic performance of SSA countries during this period as strong performers[3] (those with 5 per cent mean and above), good performers[4] (those with growth rate between 3 per cent and 4.99 per cent), low performers[5] (those with growth between 1 per cent and 2.99 per cent) and poor performers[6] (less than 1 per cent and negative growth). From this simple exercise, it is possible to identify countries that are driving growth in Africa. Prominent among these are Angola, Equatorial Guinea, Ethiopia, Mozambique, Sierra Leone and Sudan, all of which recorded an average of over 7 per cent growth rates during this period. This heart-warming development about strong economic performance in SSA countries has been attributed to several factors. These include a benign external economic environment, favourable and rising global market prices of resources, favourable policies, stronger institutions, improved governance, and reduced civil and armed conflicts. Going forward, further improvement in these policy variables and exogenous factors are expected to help consolidate the gains made so far.

However, the downside to the sustainability of this brilliant performance is the sluggish recovery from the financial crisis that rocked the global economy

Table 6.1 Economic growth in sub-Saharan Africa, 1961–2012

	1961–69	*1970–79*	*1980–89*	*1990–99*	*2000–09*	*2010*	*2011*	*2012*
GDP growth (annual)	4.57	4.17	1.74	1.98	5.14	5.02	4.07	4.29
GDP per capita growth	2.04	1.40	−1.10	−0.74	2.41	2.25	1.33	1.54

Source: Based on World Development Indicators Database.

in 2008–2009. The channels through which the crisis negatively impacted on the sources of economic growth in SSA countries were trade, falling commodity prices, FDI inflows, aid inflows and remittances (IMF 2009). But for the quick interventions by African countries and multilateral institutions such as the African Development Bank, this could have eroded all the gains made over the last few years and return SSA countries to another decade of slump economic performance as economic growth.

In recent years there has been a mild shift in the structure and composition of GDP in most African countries, from agriculture towards services in most countries and towards industry in the case of a few countries, notably Mauritius. In 2007, for instance, services (44.3 per cent) accounted for the largest share of GDP, followed by industry (41.7 per cent) and agriculture (14 per cent). Compared with 2000, the relative shares of agriculture, manufacturing and services declined in 2007. This shortfall was compensated for by increasing mineral and oil outputs in the resource-endowed countries. In terms of growth performance, all sectors showed improved growth over time (see Table 6.2). While agriculture recorded the highest mean annual growth in the 1990s, the structure has since changed in favour of services with this sector now leading, followed by manufacturing and agriculture. The sectoral performance has also witnessed relatively impressive growth as all sectors recorded improved performance over time. Again, the strongest performance was recorded in services followed by industry, particularly mining, which includes petroleum.

The overall picture of economic growth in SSA countries reveals a volatile and unsustainable growth pattern. In many countries, strong growth in a year is usually followed by very poor growth performance the following year and negative growth in many cases. For most of the countries, it is very difficult to understand and identify a pattern for economic performance and growth. This is a cause for worry. It implies that policies aimed at influencing performance of economic growth are still not having the desired result. It also suggests that SSA countries are still unable to mitigate and leverage the negative effects of exogenous shocks on their economies.

Juxtaposing economic growth in SSA with those of other developing regions of the world, it is evident that performance in SSA has not been consistently behind other developing regions as is generally believed. Per capita GDP growth was relatively good compared with other developing regions from 1960 until about 1974 (see Figure 6.1). The growth pattern was also relatively stable compared

Table 6.2 Sectoral growth rates in Africa, 1990–2007

Sector	1990–99	2000–05	2006	2007
Agriculture	2.9	3.7	4.9	4.5
Manufacturing	1.6	3.4	4.6	4.9
Services	2.5	5.1	6.6	5.6

Source: Based on African Development Bank 2008.

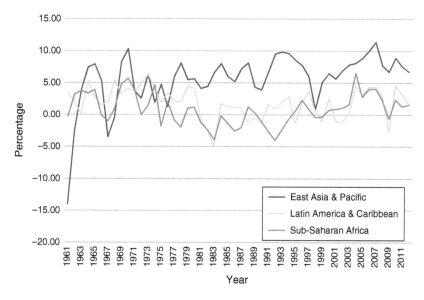

Figure 6.1 Per capita GDP growth pattern in sub-Saharan Africa and other developing
regions, 1961–2012 (%)

Source: Based on World Bank's World Development Indicators database (accessed 2 June 2014).

with other developing regions. Beginning in 1975, a steady downward pattern is
discernible which became worse in the early 1980s, with growth rates staying
almost permanently negative throughout. A rebound set in from 1999 with a slow
but steady rise. Though the global economic meltdown presented a major risk to
the sustainability of growth, the pragmatic action taken globally, especially by
African countries, helped mitigate the risk, thus relaunching the economies on
the path of sustainable growth.

Several issues emerge from this brief exposé on growth and economic performance of African countries. One, while poor economic performance of African
countries has been long recognized, these countries are yet to fully comprehend
both the nature of factors constraining economic growth in their economies and
the appropriate policy prescriptions to tackle them. Two, economic growth in
SSA countries is characterized by high volatility and has been greatly unsustainable. This is partly due to policy inconsistencies, policy reversals and exogenous
shocks emanating from international politics and commodity prices.

Theoretical and empirical methodology and data issues

The theoretical basis for this analysis is the conventional neoclassical growth model
with the traditional determinants of economic growth, but modified to accommo-
date per capita productivity growth in agriculture, manufacturing and services.

Following the standard Solow growth model (Solow 1956) of the Cobb-Douglas form, we have:

$$Y(t) = K(t)^{\alpha}\{A(t)L(t)^{1-\alpha} \tag{6.1}$$

where Y is output, K is physical capital stock, A is knowledge that enhances productivity and L represents the number of workers. Time affects output only through K, L and A, while AL is effective labour. In this study, A represents productivity in the respective sectors and is the channel through which the relative effects and importance of productivity in the agriculture, manufacturing and service sectors on economic growth in SSA countries is being investigated.

We follow the empirical methodology often used in the growth literature, though rarely used for studies based on SSA countries. This model specification will be extended to account for interaction terms between agriculture, manufacturing and services growth and the level of income of SSA countries to allow the growth effect of productivity in these activities to vary with the income level. The standard growth regression usually estimated in the growth literature which we estimate for the selected SSA countries is as follows:

$$\ln Y_{i,t} = a_0 + \partial \ln Y_{i,t-1} + \beta' X_{i,t} + \lambda_i + \lambda_t + \varepsilon_{i,t} \tag{6.2}$$

The dependent variable (Y_{it}) is per capita real GDP of SSA country i at time t. The explanatory variables are the initial per capita GDP (Y_{it-1}) and a set of other explanatory variables (X_{it}) that vary across both countries and time. The term λ_i represents the unobserved country-specific effects such as policies and institutions that may be important determinants of growth. On the other hand, λ_t is an unobserved time-specific effect, while ε_{it} is the time-varying regression residual. The subscripts i and t denote SSA country and time period respectively, while ln symbolizes logarithm.

The presence of the lagged dependent variable (Y_{it-1}) combined with that of the fixed effects (λ_i) renders the OLS estimator inconsistent, given that λ_i is by construction correlated with the error term (ε_{it}). There is also the high likelihood that other explanatory variables might be correlated with the fixed effects. Thus, every coefficient has the potential of being biased. The challenge, therefore, is to estimate a consistent and unbiased dynamic growth model for the selected countries. The first step to achieve this is to eliminate the fixed effects. But then, the within-OLS estimator which could do this is no better a technique since the equation is in differenced form, implying that the new error term ($\varepsilon_{it}-\varepsilon_{it-1}$) is by construction correlated with the lagged dependent variable $Y_{it-1}-Y_{it-2}$ (see Equation 6.2). Thus, neither the OLS estimator nor the within-OLS estimator is appropriate for estimating dynamic growth equations.

Another problem we have to grapple with is omitted variables, which could be variant or invariant. The inclusion of the fixed effects λ_i allows us to control for invariant omitted variables. There is also the probability of endogeneity of some of the explanatory variables. For instance, faster-growing SSA countries might adopt technologies and innovations that would induce increased productivity growth in agriculture, manufacturing and services.

Many studies in the empirical growth literature address all these issues by relying on the Arellano–Bond Generalized Method of Moments (GMM) estimator proposed by Arellano and Bond (1991). This estimator technique controls for omitted invariant variables and corrects for the potential endogeneity of some explanatory variables by using internal instruments. In addition, the procedure controls and eliminates the unobserved individual-specific effects λ_i by first-differencing the growth equation. Despite these weaknesses in the use of OLS to estimate this type of model and the strength of the GMM methodology to correct for these weaknesses, very few studies employ this latter technique of analysis in estimating growth equations in Africa, prominent among which are Hoeffler (1999) and O'Connell and Ndulu (2000).

The estimated growth equation is of this form:

$$\ln y_{i,t} - \ln y_{i,t-1} = a_0 + \alpha(\ln y_{i,t-1} - \ln y_{i,t-2}) + \beta'(X_{i,t} - X_{i,t-1})$$
$$+ (\lambda_i - \lambda_i) + (\lambda_t - \lambda_{t-1}) + (\varepsilon_{i,t} - \varepsilon_{i,t-1}) \qquad (6.3)$$

In this framework, the explanatory variables assumed to be endogenous or predetermined can be instrumented and the validity of such instruments can be tested. To correct for the endogeneity problem, the Arellano–Bond GMM procedure employs lagged values of the corresponding endogenous variables as internal instruments. More specifically, endogenous variables are instrumented by lags from at least two periods and deeper and a predetermined variable is instrumented by lags from at least one period and deeper. This demands some assumptions on the endogeneity or exogeneity of the explanatory variables included in the growth model. The explanatory variables can be strictly exogenous to growth or predetermined or endogenous.

For the purpose of this study, the following differenced GMM model is specified for estimation:

$$\ln \Delta Y_{i,t} = a_0 + \partial \ln \Delta Y_{i,t-1} + \beta' \Delta X_{i,t} + \Delta \lambda_i + \Delta \lambda_t + \Delta \varepsilon_{i,t} \qquad (6.4)$$

It is pertinent at this juncture to elucidate on the explanatory variables (X). These are: agriculture, manufacturing and services productivity growth; labour measured as the economically active population; capital measured as the gross fixed capital formation; institution; governance; infrastructure, measured as the number of both telephone lines and mobile telephone subscribers per 100 persons; human capital denoted by the secondary school enrolment rate; urbanization; and trade openness. The model is estimated with the robust option to correct for heteroscedasticity.

The consistency of GMM estimation holds only if lagged values of explanatory variables are valid instruments. To ascertain this, two post-estimation diagnostic tests are provided. The Sargan test for the overall validity of the instruments is reported to determine whether lagged and first-differenced values of endogenous or predetermined explanatory variables are valid instruments. Another specification test examines whether the residual of the regression in differences is second-order serially correlated. While first-order serial correlation is expected, second-order serial correlation must be rejected to confirm the correctness of our model specification.

For the empirical purpose of this study, 38 SSA countries[7] were chosen, based on data availability. All data are annual across the selected countries, spanning 1980–2007. Growth is the central focus of this study and is measured as annual per capita GDP growth in percentages. Agriculture, manufacturing and services are measured as the growth in the value added of each of these variables expressed in percentages. These variables are expected to exert positive influences on per capita GDP growth.

There is no final judgement on the best measure of infrastructure in growth and development studies in SSA. However, we are constrained by data availability to use the number of telephone lines available, measured as both landlines and mobile telephone subscribers per 100 persons. A positive sign is anticipated. In our measure of human capital, we use education attainment, measured as the gross total secondary school enrolment ratio expressed in percentages. A positive relationship is expected between human capital and economic growth.

To capture issues of governance and institutions, we employ the Polity IV Project Database. The Revised Combined Polity Score, otherwise known as Polity 2, is used as a measure of governance. This score is computed by subtracting the institutionalized autocracy indicator from the institutionalized democracy value indicator. The score ranges from –10 to 10, where higher score implies better governance. A positive sign indicates that governance makes a positive contribution to economic growth. To capture the effects of institutions, we follow Tabellini (2005) in using constraints on the Executive, as defined in the Polity IV Database. According to this criterion, better political institutions means that the holder of executive powers is accountable to bodies of political representatives, and government authority is constrained by checks and balances and by the rule of law. The value varies from 1 (= unlimited authority) to 7 (= accountable executives constrained by checks and balances). Higher values thus correspond to better institutions. For details on the governance and institution data, its components and computations, see Marshall and Jaggers (2009).

Empirical results and discussions

We begin the discussions of our empirical findings by first examining the basic statistical characteristics of the model (see Table 6.3). Given the period (1980–2007) and country (38) of coverage of the study and frequency of the data (annual), there are 1,064 observations. The mean per capita GDP growth in the selected countries over the period was about 0.5 per cent. This demonstrates the poor economic growth in SSA during the period under review. Given a standard deviation of more than 5, growth in these countries can be said to be volatile over the entire period. Rwanda recorded both the lowest and highest per capita GDP

Table 6.3 Summary of descriptive statistics of the variables

Variable	Variable description and sources	Mean	Standard deviation	Minimum	Maximum
GDP growth per capita	This is based on 2005 US dollars. It is the sum of gross value added by all resident producers in the economy plus any product taxes and minus any subsidies not included in the value of the products. Sourced from World Bank's World Development Indicators (WDI).	0.49	5.44	−47.00	38
Agriculture value added growth	This refers to annual percentage growth in agriculture value added at 2005 constant US dollars. It is the net output of agriculture after adding up all outputs and subtracting intermediate inputs and determined by the International Standard Industrial Classification (ISIC), revision 3 and corresponds to divisions 1–5 and includes forestry, hunting and fishing, as well as cultivation of crops and livestock production. Sourced from WDI.	2.73	9.12	−37.00	68.00
Manufacturing value added growth	Manufacturing productivity refers to annual percentage growth in manufacturing value added at 2005 constant US dollars. It is the net output of manufacturing industrial activities after adding up all outputs and subtracting intermediate inputs and determined by the International Standard Industrial Classification (ISIC), revision 3 and corresponds to divisions 15–37. Sourced from WDI.	3.76	10.03	−54.00	66.00
Services value added growth	This refers to annual percentage growth in services value added at 2005 constant US dollars. It is the net output of manufacturing industrial activities after adding up all outputs and subtracting intermediate inputs and determined by the International Standard Industrial Classification (ISIC), revision 3 and corresponds to divisions 50–99. The activities include: wholesale and retail trade (including hotels and restaurants); transport; government; financial, professional and personal services such as education, health care and real estate services. It also includes imputed bank service charges, import duties and other statistical discrepancies noted by national compilers, as well as discrepancies arising from rescaling. Sourced from WDI.	3.48	7.78	−57.00	48.00

(Continued)

Table 6.3 (Continued)

Variable	Variable description and sources	Mean	Standard deviation	Minimum	Maximum
Telephone lines	Telephone lines are fixed telephone and mobile lines connecting a subscriber's terminal equipment to the public switched telephone network and that have a port on a telephone exchange. This variable is measured as number of lines per 100 people and includes integrated services digital network channels and fixed wireless subscribers. Sourced from WDI.	4.29	11.11	0	99
Secondary school enrolment	This is a proxy for human capita and is measured in percentage. It is total enrolment for both sexes. Data are sourced from African Development Bank's 2008 Selected Statistics on African Countries.	26.51	18.81	2.7	95.4
Governance	The Revised Combined Polity Score, otherwise known as Polity 2, is used as a measure of governance. This score is computed by subtracting the institutionalized autocracy indicator from the institutionalized democracy value indicator. The score ranges from −10 to 10, where higher score implies better governance. A positive sign indicates that governance makes a positive contribution to economic growth. Data are extracted from the Polity IV Project Database.	−1.49	6.01	−10.00	10.00
Institution	This is measured as the constraints on the Executive extracted from the Polity IV Database. The variable posts that better political institutions means that the holder of executive powers is accountable to bodies of political representatives, and government authority is constrained by checks and balances and by the rule of law. The value varies from 1 (unlimited authority) to 7 (accountable executives constrained by checks and balances). Higher values thus correspond to better institutions.	−2.31	21.22	−88.00	7.00
Physical capital	This is the annual percentage growth of capital formation based on 2005 constant US dollars. It consists of outlays on additions to the fixed assets of the economy plus net changes in the level of inventories. Fixed assets include: land improvements; plant, machinery and equipment purchases; and the construction of roads, railways and the like, including schools, offices, hospitals, private residential dwellings, and commercial and industrial buildings. On the other hand, inventories are stocks of goods held by firms to meet temporary or unexpected fluctuations in production or sales, and 'work in progress.' Extracted from WDI.	6.25	23.92	−22.10	64.64

(Continued)

Table 6.3 (Continued)

Variable	Variable description and sources	Mean	Standard deviation	Minimum	Maximum
Labour force	This is the total labour force participation rate as a percentage of total population aged 15–64 that are economically active. It includes all people who supply labour for the production of goods and services during the year. Data on this variable are sourced from WDI.	71.83	10.86	48.4	91.5
Openness	Openness is trade openness measured as the sum of exports and imports of goods and services in percentage of GDP Data are extracted from WDI.	73.35	52.33	6.32	531.74
Urbanization	This is the annual percentage growth of urban population. Urban population refers to people living in urban areas as defined by national statistical offices of each country. It is calculated using World Bank population estimates and urban ratios from the United Nations World Urbanization Prospects. Data are sourced from WDI.	4.52	1.93	0.57	9.47

Source: Author's calculations.

Note: The sample covers 1980–2007 for 38 SSA countries.

growth of –47 per cent in 1994 at the height of the genocide and 38 per cent in 1995 as the economy experienced a rebound at the end of the genocide.

Agriculture, manufacturing and services productivity growth recorded a respective mean of 2.73 per cent, 3.76 per cent and 3.48 per cent over the entire sample period in the selected countries. This suggests that manufacturing recorded the highest mean growth, while agriculture had the least average growth. Again, this brings into the limelight the low productivity rate that characterizes the agriculture sector across SSA countries. Agricultural production in SSA countries is dominated by small subsistent, often fragmented farms, on which the peasant farmholders' mode of production is usually crude and output is usually for consumption.

Most African countries recorded a near-zero number of fixed telephone lines and mobile telephone subscriptions per 100 persons in the 1980s and 1990s. The big relief came in the early 2000s with the infusion of the Global System for Mobile communications (GSM). This has substantially increased the number of mobile telephone lines, although some of these countries recorded a decrease in telephone landline subscriptions. This development explains the mean subscription rate that stood at 11 per 100 persons during the period of study. South Africa, Gabon, Mauritius and Botswana are the trailblazers with over 80 subscribers per 100 persons in 2007. South Africa stood tallest with 99 subscriptions per 100 persons in the same year. School enrolment averaged 26.5 per cent over the entire period across the selected countries, revealing low enrolment rates. South Africa recorded the highest enrolment rate of over 95 per cent in 1995, while Burundi has the lowest rate of 2.7 per cent in 1980. African countries are characterized by poor governance and institutions, explaining the low scores in these variables over the entire period. However, African countries are beginning to witness the emergence of good governance and efficient institutions in recent times.

The results of the estimated growth models based on annual growth rates in agriculture, manufacturing and services productivity for the 38 selected SSA countries based on the Arellano–Bond first differenced GMM estimates of Equation 3 are reported in Table 6.4.[8] Sargan tests are conducted and the results are reported with a view to assessing the validity of the overidentifying restrictions. The results reveal a failure to reject the null hypothesis that the overidentifying restrictions are valid in all cases. We also take cognizance of the fact that the validity of the GMM estimation is based on the condition that there is no second-order correlation, even though first-order autocorrelation is expected. The results confirm the absence of second-order autocorrelation. Consequently, the estimated coefficients reflect the true (efficient and unbiased) relationship between growth in agriculture, manufacturing and services productivity (our variables of interest) and the traditional predetermined and endogenous determinants of growth, on the one hand, and per capita GDP growth, on the other. To establish the relative importance of productivity in the sectors as drivers of growth in SSA, we standardize all the regressors so that they have mean zero (0) and standard deviation one (1).

Columns 1–3 in Table 6.4 report the individual impact of agriculture, manufacturing and services productivity on economic growth in the 38 selected SSA

Table 6.4 Panel data estimation of the sources of growth in 38 selected SSA countries for 1980–2007 using the Arellano–Bond GMM estimator

Explanatory variables	Models: Dependent variable is Y_{it} per capita GDP growth						
	(1) GMM	(2) GMM	(3) GMM	(4) GMM	(5) GMM	(6) GMM	(7) GMM
Y_{it-1}	-0.00.0133	-0.1217***	-0.0501	-0.0338	-0.0030	-0.0835***	-0.0179
	(0.00.0355)	(0.0328)	(0.0498)	(0.0282)	(0.0268)	(0.0276)	(0.0239)
AgriProd	0.3591***			0.3589***	0.3167***		0.3213***
	(0.0321)			(0.0257)	(0.0241)		(0.0213)
ManuProd		0.0415***		0.3939***		0.2935***	0.2997***
		(0.0032)		(0.0262)		(0.0288)	(0.0244)
ServProd			0.1540***		0.5431***	0.4853***	0.4414***
			(0.0538)		(0.02901)	(0.0323)	(0.0279)
Physical Capital	0.1376***	0.1654***	0.1598***	0.1450***	0.1025***	0.0869***	0.0952***
	(0.0371)	(0.0348)	(0.0479)	(0.0286)	(0.0289)	(0.0305)	(0.0258)
Human Capital	0.0514	-0.0109	-0.0928	0.0138	-0.0395	-0.0492	-0.0552
	(0.1579)	(0.1407)	(0.1375)	(0.1240)	(0.1144)	(0.1200)	(0.0994)
Labour Force	-0.4390***	-0.5244***	-0.3484***	-0.3812***	-0.3195***	-0.3852***	-0.2651***
	(0.0610)	(0.0573)	(0.0798)	(0.0473)	(0.0457)	(0.0492)	(0.0431)
Governance	-0.0517	-0.0302	0.0708	-0.0389	-0.0694	-0.0615	-0.0396
	(0.0745)	(0.0683)	(0.1326)	(0.0557)	(0.0551)	(0.0584)	(0.0486)
Institution	0.0550	0729**	-0.0403	0.0572*	0.0028	0.0192	0.0043
	(0.0364)	(0.0337)	(0.0482)	(0.0301)	(0.0268)	(0.0293)	(0.0245)
Infrastructure	-0.0616	0.0684	0.1447	0.0305	0.0219	0.0624	0.0375
	(0.1255)	(0.1089)	(0.0919)	(0.0955)	(0.0879)	(0.0924)	(0.0777)

(Continued)

Table 6.4 (Continued)

Explanatory variables	Models: Dependent variable is Y_{it} per capita GDP growth						
	(1) GMM	*(2) GMM*	*(3) GMM*	*(4) GMM*	*(5) GMM*	*(6) GMM*	*(7) GMM*
Openness	−0.1578	−0.3674***	0.0545	−0.2637***	−0.0499	−0.1719*	−0.0265
	(0.1098)	(0.1031)	(0.1128)	(0.0926)	(0.0878)	(0.0913)	(0.0752)
Urbanization	0.3517***	0.4002***	0.1962*	0.2270***	0.1547***	0.2135***	0.0888*
	(0808)	(0.0715)	(0.1201)	(0.0617)	(0.0589)	(0.0618)	(0.0539)
Number of obs.	626	593	243	655	594	588	577
Sargan test, *p*-level	00.2594	00.2412	00.1237	00.3194	00.2435	00.1429	00.2542
AR(1) test, *p*-level	00.0000	00.0000	00.0000	00.0000	00.0000	00.0000	00.0000
AR(2) test, *p*-level	00.6805	00.9899	00.2347	00.5883	00.2812	00.1662	00.7470

Source: Author's calculations.

Note: Standard errors in parentheses; ***, **, * respectively represents statistical significance at 1 per cent, 5 per cent and 10 per cent.

countries. Each of these variables has a positive and statistically significant effect on growth. The estimated coefficients are, respectively, 0.36, 0.04 and 0.15. This tends to suggest that when the sectors are entered separately in the regression, agriculture has the highest effect, followed by services and then manufacturing. It seems, however, that the reason for this outcome is that longer lags were used as instruments in the services model to correct for autocorrelation. In other models where service appears with either agriculture or manufacturing, or with both of them, it consistently records the highest coefficient. Columns 4–6 combine two of these variables of interest in each of the models. Services consistently recorded the highest coefficient in all the models where it appeared. In column 4, where only agriculture and manufacturing are featured, manufacturing is observed to have outperformed agriculture.

Our most preferred model is column 7, where all the three sector variables of interest appear together. Agriculture, manufacturing and services all have the expected positive sign with statistically significant estimated coefficients of 0.32, 0.30 and 0.44, respectively. It is obvious that the estimate effect of services is considerably higher than those of the other sectors. This result then suggests that the service sector has been the leading driver of growth in SSA countries, at least over the sample period considered here.[9]

There are five possible factors that may have led to the emergence of services as the leading sectoral driver of growth in SSA: a reduction in conflict and insecurity, which has improved tourism; increased trade in services; growth in urbanization, which induces higher labour participation in service-related sectors; large capital and aid inflows that have led to a rise in prices of non-tradables; emergence of middle-class Africans with a voracious demand for diverse goods and services; and recent increased Chinese activities in the services sector. In recent times, especially beginning with the previous decade, there has been a drastic reduction in civil, ethnic and political conflict in most SSA countries. Military despotism has significantly been contained, giving way to liberal democracy with its associated dividend of freedom. Such positive developments have led to increased interest in tourism in these countries. Tourism has been an increased source of income for countries such as Botswana, Mauritius, Ghana, Kenya, Namibia, South Africa and Tanzania. And, there are prospects for further development. The World Tourism Organization has indicated that SSA countries have largely untapped potential for seaside, environmental, cultural, sports and discovery tourisms, and ecotourism.

Increased trade in services is another possible factor behind the importance of services as the leading driver of growth. For instance, between 2000 and 2005, trade in services as a percentage of GDP recorded an annual mean growth of over 13 per cent for SSA countries and over 11 per cent between 1977 and 2005. The World Trade Organization (WTO) has acknowledged that trade in services is the largest and most dynamic component of the economies of both developed and developing countries. This high importance explains the inclusion of trade in services as a subject of multilateral trade negotiations by the WTO since 2000. To demonstrate the high importance of services to African economies, in 2007 the region recorded 22 per cent growth in exports of commercial services and 31 per cent in transport services.

Furthermore, growth in urbanization which has induced huge rural–urban migration has resulted in people engaging more in services than in agriculture, for instance. Most people, especially youths, who move to urban areas usually find it difficult to obtain formal employment. In most cases they end up in services-related activities such as trading, hair-cutting, driving, hair-dressing, sewing and so on. In addition, the mass movement to the cities leads to a high demand for housing. This has created a new and rapidly moving estate development and real-estate sector services, with a booming construction sector in most cities in SSA countries.

More importantly, SSA countries have witnessed increased activities in high-end services such as information and communication technology (ICT) services. While these activities accounted for negligible percentage of GDP and were, indeed, non-existent for some countries up to the 1990s, they have witnessed an upsurge in the 2000s. For example, telephone lines increased from about 2.4 million to over 12 million between 1980 and 2007. Similarly, Internet users per 100 persons increased from 0.07 in 1996 to 3.8 at the end of 2007. The rise in these upper-end services in economic activities has induced flow of labour to the sector in addition to the attendant increased productivity in other sectors resulting from these engagements.

Beginning in the 1980s, SSA countries have witnessed unprecedented capital inflows in the form of aid and private capital. Most of these were in the form of humanitarian aid to the countries in conflict and those implementing structural adjustment. Others received large foreign exchange from natural resource booms, notably oil and minerals. These factors reinforced themselves to induce a rise in the real foreign exchange rate of these countries. This phenomenon, christened Dutch disease, increased prices of domestic tradables relative to their foreign substitutes, while driving up the price of non-tradables. With this, labour, human, and factors of production moved from production of tradables to the non-tradable sectors dominated by services. This structural shift towards non-tradable services would lend a prominent role to services in economic activities.

The highly voracious African middle-class is emerging in almost all countries, estimated to reach 40 million by 2030. These households have a penchant for consumption in almost all goods and services, ranging from basic necessities such as food and clothing to exotic wines and luxurious cars, homes and holidays. In a bid to serve this rising market, several retail service-oriented activities have emerged. These include diverse retail outlets, supermarkets and restaurants that include global brands. Also, individual Africans are complementing these highbrow retailers with increased retail trading activities, engaging in frequent travel to traditional markets of developed countries and recently emerging countries to buy the goods in demand with a view to selling them in the local market. All of these have significantly increased the relative importance of trading services as a driver of growth in SSA.

Finally, the recently intensified activities of China in Africa, which are heavily concentrated in mining and services, have added impetus to the role of services in economic activities in SSA countries. China's engagements in the service sector are mostly in wholesale/retail trading and financial services. In fact, the highest single investment in Africa from China to date is the Industrial and Commercial Bank of China's US$5 billion purchase of a 20 per cent stake in South Africa's Standard Bank. In addition, China had initiated several other similar, though of less magnitude, engagements in Nigeria and Kenya. Chinese service-related activities are also found in trading, providing an avenue for the sale of products made in China. In several African countries, these traders own and operate small, medium and large businesses engaged in almost all trading activities from the most sophisticated electrical, electronic, computer and auto-mobile equipment to very simple products such as hurricane lanterns, canned juice and household utensils. The proliferation of Chinese trading activities and the cheap prices of the wide range of products they provide have fuelled trading, with a possible positive impact on economic growth.

The finding that services are the leading driver of growth in SSA could be a consequence of the period of analysis. Beginning from the 1980s, African countries have been engaging in heightened activities in the services sector, given the limited success of earlier industrial-led and agriculture-led growth policies of ISI and SAP, respectively. Relative diversification away from these activities into services since then may be a possible factor here. Another plausible explanation is that this finding could be an indication of a gradual maturity of African economies, given the theoretical proposition that as economies mature, services become more prominent and important economic activities.

Channels of impact

Having established that the service sector is the most important driver of growth in SSA countries, we pursue the analysis further by seeking to establish the channels through which this occurs. To achieve this objective, services variable is interacted with selected variables. Five interaction variables are created and the results are reported in Table 6.5. In columns 1–5, the impact of each interacted variable is examined in turn, while, in column 6, the combined effects of all the variables are simultaneously examined.

In columns 1–5, all the estimated interacted variables are negative except for governance. Of these, all of them are statistically significant except governance and institutions. In column 6, all the interacted variables maintained their previous signs except infrastructure, which turned out with a positive sign. However, only openness and labour force have statistically significant coefficients. This result demonstrates that openness, institutions and labour force constrain the impact of services on economic growth in SSA countries.

Openness and labour force appear to be the most important constraints given their consistent negative sign and high statistically significant estimated coefficients. This result implies that trade openness could be detrimental to growth in SSA countries when services are an important component of trade. This makes sense given the state of development of African economies where most of the trade in services involves imports with little or nothing to export. This finding supports some of the arguments made by Rodríguez and Rodrik (2001) and

Table 6.5 Panel data estimation of the sources of growth in SSA countries for 1980–2007 using the Arellano–Bond GMM estimator and including interaction variables

Explanatory variables	Models					
	(1) GMM	(2) GMM	(3) GMM	(4) GMM	(5) GMM	(6) GMM
Y_{it-1}	0.0016	-0.0115	-0.0119	0.0104	-0.0043	0.0217
	(0.0203)	(0.0209)	(0.0209)	(0.0200)	(0.0208)	(0.0196)
Agrivad	0.3364***	0.3358***	0.3352***	0.3268***	0.3358***	0.3279***
	(0.0186)	(0.0192)	(0.0192)	(0.0183)	(0.0190)	(0.0177)
Manuvad	0.2702***	0.2747***	0.2758***	0.2616***	0.2711***	0.2552***
	(0.0193)	(0.0199)	(0.0203)	(0.0189)	(0.0197)	(0.0188)
Servad	0.4482***	0.4414***	0.4407***	0.4084***	0.4126***	0.4228***
	(0.0231)	(0.0247)	(0.0239)	(0.0229)	(0.0246)	(0.0241)
Physical capital	0.0462**	0.0499**	0.0496**	0.0415**	0.0417**	0.0394**
	(0.0198)	(0.0205)	(0.0205)	(0.0194)	(0.0204)	(0.0190)
Human capital	-0.0150	-0.0279	-0.0291	-0.0220	-0.0095	-0.0013
	(0.0923)	(0.0956)	(0.0953)	(0.0904)	(0.0945)	(0.0880)
Labour force	-0.3110***	-0.3288***	-0.3347***	-0.3461***	-0.3262***	-0.3236***
	(0.0328)	(0.0359)	(0.0338)	(0.0321)	(0.0335)	(0.0313)
Governance	-0.0280	-0.0436	-0.0454	-0.0580	-0.0462	-0.0386
	(0.0392)	(0.0406)	(0.0407)	(0.0384)	(0.0400)	(0.0376)
Institutions	0.0068	0.0059	0.0092	0.0170	0.0067	0.0114
	(0.0226)	(0.0234)	(0.0257)	(0.0222)	(0.0231)	(0.0237)
Infrastructure	0.0261	0.0095	0.0095	0.0112	0.0647	0.0214
	(0.0731)	(0.0756)	(0.0754)	(0.0715)	(0.0762)	(0.0709)
Openness	-0.1406***	-0.0212	-0.0209	0.0675	-0.0696	-0.0158
	(0.0197)	(0.0682)	(0.0698)	(0.0668)	(0.0701)	(0.0662)

(Continued)

Table 6.5 (Continued)

Explanatory variables	Models					
	(1) GMM	(2) GMM	(3) GMM	(4) GMM	(5) GMM	(6) GMM
Urbanization	0.1367***	0.1658***	0.1649***	0.1928***	0.1466***	0.1665***
	(0.0427)	(0.0439)	(0.0439)	(0.0418)	(0.0438)	(0.0409)
Interaction variables						
Openness* services	−0.1405***					−0.1341***
	(.0197)					(0.0208)
Governance* services		0.0029				0.0264
		(0.0273)				(0.0261)
Institutions* Services			−0.0033			−0.0008
			(0.0164)			(0.0159)
Labour force* services				−0.0734***		−0.0745***
				(0.0091)		(0.0093)
Infrastructure* services					−0.1815***	0.1341***
					(0.0477)	(0.0208)
Sargan test, p-level	0.2442	0.2195	0.2318	0.1645	0.2750	0.2247
AR(1) test, p-level	0.0000	0.0000	0.0000	0.0000	0.0000	0.0000
AR(2) test, p-level	0.4556	0.7616	0.7490	0.7660	0.6584	0.7948

Source: Author's calculations.

Note: Standard errors are in parentheses. ***, ** and * represent respectively statistical significance at the 1 per cent, 5 per cent and 10 per cent levels.

Chang *et al.* (2005) that certain forms of trade could be detrimental to economic growth. It also tends to corroborate the traditional assertion that for trade to be beneficial, trading partners should specialize in activities in which a country has comparative advantage. Presently SSA countries do not have comparative advantage in services vis-à-vis their trading partners. Competence in specific services activities needs to be further developed in order to increase comparative and competitive advantages in this sector. Moreover, SSA countries do not have a sufficiently well trained and specialized labour force in services as a result of the non-traditional nature of the sector in these economies. Increasing the amount of specialized training in specific service activities within the labour force is imperative for relaxing this constraint. Infrastructure development also promises high impact on growth through increased services productivity. This demonstrates the positive effect improved infrastructure would have on growth.

The role of the financial service sector is likely to be paramount through increased employment in the observed prominence of services for growth. In recent times, the financial services sector has witnessed a rapid increase in most African countries, especially in Nigeria and South Africa with strong penetration into other countries. This development has seen the emergence of large and various money and financial market institutions and activities. Given the underdeveloped nature of this sector where technology is highly deficient, engagements are highly labour-intensive. In Nigeria, for instance, this sector has been the major employer of graduates in the past ten years as employment in other sectors is generally low. In addition, staff compensation in this sector is higher than the average obtainable in other sectors of the economy apart from oil and gas, thus its further attraction to graduates from all disciplines. Moreover, the recent developments in telecommunication, especially the GSM, have further served as a high employment avenue for Africans. Firms operating in this sector pay very competitive salaries that are in the same range with the banking sector. They also provide employment for many graduates from all disciplines. These are people that would have otherwise been unemployed. They have also provided millions of jobs for the recharge cards vendors and roadside GSM call operators and others engaged in the telecom value chain. Their activities have sparked other peripheral businesses such as mobile phone sale and repairs and servicing companies producing recharge cards. Given the communal nature of African societies, the millions of jobs thus created are highly welfare-improving and have a poverty-reducing effect, not only on the employee, but also on their several dependants, who are sponsored in schools or who are assisted to establish businesses, and through 'domestic remittances'.

Policy issues and recommendations

Financial services

Given the importance of the service sector, especially the financial services, as a driver of growth in SSA, there is a need for fundamental reform of this sector to further position it for better performance. The financial sector in SSA countries has traditionally been weak and among one of the least developed. It is heartening that several SSA countries have commenced the process of reforms and restructuring in this sector. However, money and capital market institutions remain weak with a low range of financial products and small asset base. A large proportion of the people, especially those in rural areas are either under-banked or non-banked. Access to credit remains a big challenge not just for individuals but also for most small and medium enterprises. Financial depth remains shallow and inefficient, further constraining the monetary policy-making process and rendering it very costly. Overall, this reduces welfare and further increases poverty among Africans. Conscious policy efforts must be targeted at strengthening the financial systems to generate and ensure domestic savings are channelled to productive uses. Specifically reforms should focus on: reducing or eliminating distortions arising from interest rate controls, controlled lending and supervisory forbearance; improving efficiency of supervision, as demonstrated in the recent experience in Nigeria, in order to prevent actions that could lead to systemic failure; promoting, improving and supporting activities of microfinance enterprises; and undertaking legal reforms that would facilitate access to credit through the use of alternative instruments to overcome the bottlenecks of collateral.

More specifically, information asymmetries, imperfect enforcement mechanisms, low savings and inefficient markets characterized by poor business practices and high risks, associated with financial transactions, remain the major challenges in the financial sector of most SSA countries. Necessary reforms aimed at mitigating these downsides are imperative. Another very important policy issue is the development and integration of the informal financial sector. SSA countries have a plethora of varying purpose-oriented, informal financial institutions designed to satisfy the demands of distinct clientele. Systematic efforts are required to harmonize the activities of these institutions and integrate them with the formal financial sector.

The recent global financial crisis offers additional reason for conscious efforts in strengthening the governance, management and oversight of players in the sector. Frequent and routine stress-test assessments of all financial institutions in each country should be conducted with a view to avoiding sudden collapse that could have a contagious effect on the entire industry. The banks should also be required to be more transparent in reporting their transactions and disclosing sources of risks in their engagements. This will help in identifying possible sources of crisis and fixing them before they get out of hand.

Telecommunication

The role of the telecommunication services subsector and its role in socio-economic development in Africa especially in recent times, cannot be overemphasized. To further improve the performance of this subsector and strengthen its impact on economic growth there is a need for specific policies targeted at: regulating the activities of operators in the sector, further improvements in infrastructure development to relax the cost of operations, sector reforms to create competition and efficiency in services, the removal of market entry barriers through liberalization, and incentives to encourage innovation and punish sluggish and exploitative service providers.

Tourism

To better position tourism as a major driver of economic growth in SSA, sound policies and practices are required at all levels and in all sectors. Lack of human capital specific to the tourism sector could be a barrier to the rapid development of this sector. Improvement in skills peculiar to tourism might be lacking, given the fact that tourism is not a traditional sector in SSA countries but is a relatively new sector compared with economies of Europe, North America, Middle East and Asia. Specific technical and administrative skills in the tourism sector should be developed to create a pool of high-, medium- and low-level skills in this sector. In this respect, each country should conduct a needs-based assessment of the available human resources in the sector. More training institutions for human capital development in tourism and hospitality industries should be encouraged. Such initiatives could be implemented at subregional levels given the fact that investment may not be feasible at the national levels.

So far, only Southern Africa as a subregion has made substantial efforts towards a regional policy on sustainable tourism. These include the South African Development Company (SADC) Protocol on Tourism, the Regional Tourism Organisation of Southern Africa (RETOSA) and the New Partnership for Africa's Development (NEPAD) Tourism Action Plan. All these initiatives are helping in consolidating collaboration and maximizing the positive effects of these efforts in the subregion. For instance, the SADC Protocol provides a regional consensus on several tourism-facilitating issues, including the need to make entry and travel within countries in the region as smooth as possible for visitors. Similarly, RETOSA is mandated to promote the combined tourism interests of all member states. It is interesting to note that RETOSA is promoting three innovative tourism-enhancing initiatives, namely, community-based tourism, trans-frontier conservation areas tourism and the introduction of a single visa for tourists in all SADC members. These are laudable efforts and examples of best practice that should be emulated in Central, Eastern and Western Africa.

Promotion of global awareness of the tourism potentials of SSA countries is imperative and so is infrastructure development to support this emerging sector. The need for tourism-promoting infrastructure is underscored below given the importance of infrastructure, not only to the tourism subsector, but also to other services within the wider sector. On tourism promotion, SSA countries need to do more both individually and collectively in creating awareness on the tourism potentials and must see destinations on the continent. For instance, how many people in the world know that Ghana has the biggest man-made lake in the world? This is just one of the many must-see tourist destinations in Africa. The years 2009 and 2010 presented a very unique opportunity for African countries to create this awareness with the continent hosting three major World Cup events, namely, the under-17, under-20 and the senior World Cup finals. The nature of football and the enthusiasm it elicits from people around the world provide an excellent avenue for this promotion. It is interesting to note that some Southern African countries made good use of the opportunity to showcase to the world their tourism potentials. It is recommended that SSA countries organize an annual tourism fair with hosting rotation among the countries. This will help exhibit the tourism potential in the countries, promote regional tourism infra-structure development and integrate the region with the world tourism market and value chain. There is also a need for active participation in the World Trade Tourism Fairs.

Infrastructure

Infrastructure deficiency is a major risk to the services sector's continued contri-bution to sustainable economic growth in SSA. In Nigeria, for instance, and pre-sumably in several other SSA countries, several artisans and skilled providers of services such as electronics repairers, barbers, cobblers, welders, tailors and so on have resorted to commercial motorcycling because of incessant power failures and an unpredictable power supply. Even in sensitive locations such as industrial and university areas, stable power supply is not guaranteed. There is no doubt that there are several communities in SSA countries where they do not have access to power supply for more than 15 minutes in a whole week! Conscious effort has to be made towards developing strategies for a comprehensive overhaul of regional and continental infrastructure in SSA countries. Also, the incorrect notion that the private sector will promote infrastructure investment that will transform the sector must be reconsidered. The region must articulate a compre-hensive infrastructure development policy and strategy that will link the whole continent, or at least the Western, Central, Eastern and Southern regions. It is interesting to note that China has emerged as an important source of infrastruc-ture gap-filling development finance partner in SSA. For instance, Foster *et al.* (2009) showed that total Chinese finance commitments in African infrastructure averaged approximately US$0.5 billion for 2001–2003; these reached an annual mean of US$1.5 billion in 2004 and 2005, peaking at US$7 billion in 2006, before plummeting to US$4.5 billion the following year. These infrastructure development efforts are concentrated on power, the sector with the highest financing needs; transportation – railways and roads; and ICT. Bilateral and multilateral synergies and private–public infrastructure development initiatives are critical to successful comprehensive infrastructural development in SSA countries.

In addition to using the Chinese engagements as a lever to further infra-structure development, there is a need for national and regional initiatives to advance infrastructure development. For instance, given its oil wealth, Nigeria can afford to, and therefore should, assume the role of developing an infrastruc-ture development master plan for West Africa similar to its National Integrated

Infrastructure Master Plan (NIIMP). The several million metric tons of gas being flared should be effectively utilized to generate electricity across the subregion, thus reducing the incessant power outages that could be a great disincentive to the development of tourism and telecommunication activities. Moreover, the country should help midwife the development of a ring-railway connecting all the major cities and tourist areas in the West African subregion. This would further integrate the region in trading services and promote subregional tourism.

I am not by this suggesting the replacement of agriculture with services. Agriculture remains the SSA countries' area of comparative advantage given the arable land endowment, the congenial weather conditions and biophysical environment and its mass of strong and hard-working people. However, the full potential of this sector is yet to be unleashed due to a lack of proper reform and modernization of activities within the sector. Production in this sector continues to be dominated by fragmented, subsistent, small landholding farmers with a heavy reliance on crude equipment. Agricultural activities are also viewed as development activity rather than business. Specific policy and institutional reforms targeted directly at the agricultural sector will help lessen and possibly remove these obstacles. These could be in the form of property rights definition with respect to landholding through a Land Use Act, the development of indigenous knowledge systems in the practice of agriculture, and mechanization through public, private and foreign investments. All agriculture reform and modernization efforts must, however, take cognizance of the peculiar biophysical, historical, social, economic, political and institutional complexities of SSA countries. Policies from other countries, developed or developing, should not be superimposed on SSA countries. Rather, thoughtful and critical reflection and adaptation to suit the social, economic and environmental demands and needs of the countries are encouraged.

Conclusion

Sound understanding of the sources and drivers of growth is critical for policy in any economy. The fractured and unsustainable growth experience of most SSA countries over the years rests partly on misunderstandings about the relative importance of sectoral drivers of growth. This study investigated and tested the general belief that agriculture is the leading sectoral driver of growth in SSA given its dominance in most SSA countries. Employing the Arellano–Bond dynamic GMM panel technique, we found that, contrary to this belief, it is rather the services sector that is the leading driver of growth in the region, followed by agriculture and manufacturing. Important service activities behind this observed phenomenon include tourism, financial services, construction, telecommunication services and trading. To further position this sector for an improved and sustainable performance, particular attention and emphasis should be paid to the specific policies required to help improve the performance of this sector.

Notes

1 These countries are Botswana, Burkina Faso, Burundi, Central African Republic, Chad, Ethiopia, Lesotho, Malawi, Mali, Niger, Rwanda, Swaziland, Uganda, Zambia and Zimbabwe.
2 http://findarticles.com/p/articles/mi_hb4692/is_200210/ai_n17601912/ (accessed:)
3 Angola, Botswana, Burkina Faso, Cape Verde, Chad, Equatorial Guinea, Ethiopia, Ghana, Mali, Mozambique, Nigeria, Rwanda, Sierra Leone, Sudan, Tanzania and Uganda.
4 Benin, Cameroon, Democratic Republic of Congo, Republic of Congo, Djibouti, The Gambia, Kenya, Lesotho, Liberia, Madagascar, Mauritania, Mauritius, Namibia, Niger, Senegal, South Africa and Zambia.
5 Burundi, Comoros, Gabon, Guinea, Guinea-Bissau, Malawi, Swaziland and Togo.
6 Central African Republic, Cote d'Ivoire, Eritrea, Seychelles and Zimbabwe.
7 Angola, Benin, Botswana, Burkina Faso, Burundi, Cameroon, Central African Republic, Chad, Comoros, Democratic Republic of Congo, Republic of Congo, Cote d'Ivoire, Ethiopia, Gabon, The Gambia, Ghana, Guinea, Guinea-Bissau, Kenya, Lesotho, Madagascar, Malawi, Mali, Mauritania, Mauritius, Mozambique, Namibia, Niger, Nigeria, Rwanda, Senegal, South Africa, Sudan, Swaziland, Togo, Uganda, Zambia and Zimbabwe.
8 Estimations of the Arellano-Bond dynamic GMM models are based on the Xtabond command provided in STATA software.
9 The results also show diverse result in other estimated coefficients. Physical capital has the right sign and exerts significant effects on growth. Institution, infrastructure, openness and urbanization have the right signs but the coefficients are not statistically significant. Human capital, labour force and governance do not have the expected coefficients.

References

African Development Bank (2008). *Selected Statistics on African Countries 2008*, Volume XXVII. Tunis: AfDB.
Arellano, M. and S. Bond (1991). 'Some Tests of Specification for Panel Data: Monte Carlo Evidence and an Application to Employment Equations'. *Review of Economic Studies*, 58(2): 277–97.
Aryeetey, E and F. Tarp (2000). 'Structural Adjustment and After: Which Way Forward?'. In E. Aryeetey, J. Harrigan and M. Nisanke (eds), *Economic Reforms in Ghana: The Miracle and the Mirage*. Oxford: James Currey and Woeli Publishers, pp. 344–365.
Balaguer, J. and M. Cantavella-Jordá (2002). 'Tourism as a Long-run Growth Factor: The Spanish Case'. *Applied Economics*, 34(7): 877–84.
Barro, R. and J.-W. Lee (1993). 'International Comparisons of Educational Attainment'. *Journal of Monetary Economics*, 32(3): 363–94.
Brau, R., A. Lanza and F. Pigliaru (2003). 'How Fast are the Tourism Countries Growing? The Cross-Country Evidence'. CRENoS Centro Ricerche Economiche Nord Sud, Working Paper, NO03-09. Cagliari, Italy: CRENoS.
Burnside, C. and D. Dollar (1997). 'Aid, Policies, and Growth'. World Bank Policy Research Working Paper No. 569252. Washington DC: World Bank.
Chenery, H.B. and M. Syrquin (1975). *Patterns of Development, 1950–1970*. Oxford: Oxford University Press.
Dritsakis, N. (2004). 'Tourism as a Long-run Economic Growth Factor: An Empirical Investigation for Greece'. *Tourism Economics*, 10(3): 305–16.
Du Toit, P. (1995). 'State Building and Democracy in Southern Africa: Botswana, Zimbabwe and South Africa'. Washington, DC: United States Institute of Peace.

Elbadawi, I.A., B.J. Ndulu and N. Ndung'u (1996). 'Debt Overhang and Economic Growth in Sub-Saharan Africa'. In Z. Iqbal and R. Kanbur (eds), *External Finance for Low Income Countries*. Washington DC: IMF, pp. 49–76.

Fei, J.C.H. and G. Ranis (1964). 'Development of the Labour Surplus Economy: Theory and Policy'. Economic Growth Center, Yale University. Homewood, IL: Richard D. Irwin.

Foster, V., W. Butterfield, C. Chen and N. Pushak (2009). *Building Bridges: China's Role as Infrastructure Financier for Sub-Saharan Africa*. Washington DC: World Bank.

Fosu, A.K. (1991). 'Capital Instability and Economic Growth in Sub-Saharan Africa'. *Journal of Development Studies*, 28(1): 74–85.

Fosu, A.K. (1992). 'Effect of Export Instability on Economic Growth in Africa'. *Journal of Developing Areas*, 26(3): 323–32.

Fosu, A.K. (1996). 'The Impact of External Debt on Economic Growth in Sub-Saharan Africa'. *Journal of Economic Development*, 21(1): 93–118.

Fosu, A.K. (1997). 'Instabilities and Economic Growth in Contemporary Africa: The Role of Export Price Instability'. In T.D. Boston (ed.) *A Different Vision: Race and Public Policy*. London and New York: Routledge, pp. 401–409.

Fosu, A.K. (1998). 'Joys and Sorrows of Openness: A Review Essay – Comment'. Paper presented at the Seminar on Economic Growth and its Determinants, Ministry for Development Co-operation, The Hague, organized by the Netherlands Economic Institute.

Fosu, A.K. (1999). 'The External Debt Burden and Economic Growth in the 1980s: Evidence from Sub-Saharan Africa'. *Canadian Journal of Development Studies*, 20(2): 307–18.

Fosu, A.K. (2001). 'Economic Fluctuations and Growth in Sub-Saharan Africa: Importance of Import Instability'. *Journal of Development Studies*, 37(3): 71–84.

Gollin, D. (2009). 'Agriculture as an Engine of Growth and Poverty Reduction: What We Know and What We Need to Know'. A Framework Paper for the African Economic Research Consortium Project on 'Understanding Links between Growth and Poverty Reduction in Africa'. Nairobi, Kenya: African Economic Research Consortium.

Griffin, K. and J. Enos (1970). 'Foreign Assistance: Objectives and Consequences'. *Economic Development and Cultural Change*, 18: 313–27.

Grinols, E. and J. Bhagwati (1976). 'Foreign Capital, Savings and Dependence'. *Review of Economics and Statistics*, 58: 416–24.

Gunduz, L. and A. Hatemi (2005). 'Is the Tourism-led Growth Hypothesis Valid for Turkey?'. *Applied Economics*, 12: 499–504.

Gurley, J. and E. Shaw (1967). 'Financial Structure and Economic Development'. *Economic Development and Cultural Change*, 15: 257–68.

Gyimah-Brempong, K. (1991). 'Export Instability and Economic Growth in Sub-Saharan Africa'. *Economic Development and Cultural Change*, 39(4): 815–28.

Harris J. and M. Todaro (1970). 'Migration, Unemployment & Development: A Two-Sector Analysis'. *American Economic Review*, 60(1): 126–42.

Helleiner, G. K (1986). 'Outward Orientation, Import Instability and African Economic Growth: An Empirical Investigation'. In S. Lall and F. Stewart (eds), *Theory and Reality in Development*. London: Macmillan, pp. 139–159.

Hoeffler, A. (1999). 'The Augmented Solow Model and the African Growth Debate'. Background paper, Centre for the Study of African Economies, University of Oxford.

IMF (2009). 'Impact of the Global Financial Crisis on Sub-Saharan Africa'. International Monetary Fund, Africa Department.

Iyoha, M.A. (1999). 'External debt and economic growth in sub-Saharan African countries: An econometric study'. AERC Research Paper No. 90. Nairobi: African Economic Research Consortium.

Krueger, A.O., C. Michalopoulos and V. Ruttan (1989). *Aid and Development*. Baltimore, MD: Johns Hopkins University Press.

Kuznets, S. (1966). *Modern Economic Growth*. New Haven: Yale University Press.

Levine, R. and D. Renelt (1992). 'A Sensitivity Analysis of Cross-Country Growth Regressions'. *American Economic Review*, 82(4): 942–63.

Levy, V. (1987). 'Does Concessionary Aid Lead to Higher Investment Rates in Low Income Countries?'. *Review of Economics and Statistics*, 69: 152–56.

Lewis, W.A. (1955). *The Theory of Economic Growth*. London: Allen and Unwin.

Lewis, W.A. (1977). *The Evolution of the International Economic Order*. Princeton: Princeton University Press.

Marshall, M.G. and K. Jaggers (2009). *Polity IV Project: Dataset Users' Manual*. Center for Global Policy, School of Public Policy, George Mason University and Center for Systemic Peace.

McKinnon, R.I. (1973). *Money and Capital in Economic Development*. Washington, DC: Brookings Institution.

Mosley, P., J. Hudson and S. Horrel (1987). 'Aid, the Public and the Market in Less Developed Countries'. *Economic Journal*, 97: 616–41.

North, D.C. (1981). *Structure and Change in Economic History*. New York: Norton.

O'Connell, S. and B.J. Ndulu (2000). '*Africa's Growth Experience: A Focus on Sources of Growth*'. AERC, Nairobi: Mimeo.

Oh, C. (2005). 'The Contribution of Tourism Development to Economic Growth in the Korean Economy'. *Tourism Management*, 26(1): 39–44.

Ojo, O. and T. Oshikoya (1995). 'Determinants of Long-Term Growth: Some African Results'. *Journal of African Economies*, 4(2): 163–91.

Pack, H. and J.R. Pack (1990). 'Is Foreign Aid Fungible? The Case of Indonesia'. *Economic Journal*, 82: 188–94.

Prebisch, R. (1950). *The Economic Development of Latin America and Its Principal Problems*. New York: United Nations.

Proenca, S. and E. Soukiazis (2005). 'Tourism as an Alternative Source of Regional Growth in Portugal'. Centro de Estudos da Uniao Europeia Faculdade de Economia da Unversidade de Coimbra, Discussion paper No. 34.

Rodríguez, F. and D. Rodrik (2001). 'Trade Policy and Economic Growth: A Sceptic's Guide to the Cross-national Evidence'. In B.S. Bernanke and K. Rogoff (eds), *NBER Macroeconomics Annual 2000*. Cambridge, MA: National Bureau of Economic Research.

Rosenstein-Rodan, P.N. (1943). 'Problems of Industrialization of Eastern and South-Eastern Europe'. *Economic Journal* (Juneto September): 204–7. Reprinted in G.M. Meier, *Leading Issues in Economic Development Sixth Edition*, Oxford University Press (1995).

Rostow, W.W. (1960). *The Stages of Economic Growth*. Cambridge: Cambridge University Press.

Sachs, J.D. and A.M. Warner (1997). 'Sources of Slow Growth in African Economies'. *Journal of African Economies*, 6(3): 335–76.

Schultz, T.W. (1953). *The Economic Organization of Agriculture*. New York: McGraw-Hill.

Shaw, E. (1973). *Financial Deepening in Economic Development*. Oxford: Oxford University Press.

Singer, H.W. (1950). 'U.S. Foreign Investment in Underdeveloped Areas: The Distribution of Gains between Investing and Borrowing Countries'. *American Economic Review*, Papers and Proceedings, 40: 473–85.

Solow, R. (1956). 'A Contribution to the Theory of Economic Growth'. *Quarterly Journal of Economics*, 70: 65–94.

Syrquin, M. (1988). 'Patterns of Structural Change'. Chapter 7. In H. Chenery and T.N. Srinivasan *Handbook of Development Economics*. Vol. I. Amsterdam: Elsevier Science, pp. 203–273.

Tabellini, G. (2005). 'The Role of the State in Economic Development'. *KYKLOS*, 58(2): 283–303.

Tomlinson, M. and T. Ndhlovu (2003). 'Do Services Matter for African Economic Development'. In M. Muchie, P. Gammeltoft and B.A. Lundvall (eds), *Putting Africa First: The Making of African Innovation Systems*. Aalborg: Aalborg University Press, pp. 305–320.

Tosun, C. (1999). 'An Analysis of Contributions of International Inbound Tourism to the Turkish Economy'. *Tourism Economics*, 5: 217–50.

7 Tourism and economic growth

African evidence from panel vector autoregressive framework

Boopen Seetanah, Kesseven Padachi and Sawkut Rojid

Introduction

Worldwide tourism grew phenomenally from 25 million arrivals in 1950 to more than one billion in 2013, with a mean annual growth rate of 6.5 per cent (UNWTO 2013). The contribution of travel and tourism to gross domestic product (GDP) is expected to rise from 9.5 per cent to 10.5 per cent by 2018,[1] and the contribution of the travel and tourism economy to total employment is expected to rise from 8.4 per cent to 9.2 per cent, or to 1 in every 10.8 jobs, by 2018.

Pioneering studies from Lea (1988) and Sinclair (1998) have highlighted the potential of the tourism sector in promoting growth, creating jobs and generating revenue for the government. In fact the tourism-led growth hypothesis postulates that international tourism is considered as a potential strategic factor for economic growth.[2] Tourist spending, as an alternative form of exports, is believed to contribute to the balance of payments through foreign exchange earnings and proceeds generated from tourism expansion and can represent a significant income source for a national economy (Balaguer and Cantavella-Jordá 2002). Foreign exchange earnings from tourism can subsequently also be used to import capital goods to produce goods and services, which in turn lead to economic growth (McKinnon 1964). Other economic benefits derived from tourism activity include tax revenues, employment (it tends to be labour-intensive) and additional sources of income (Khan *et al.* 1990; Uysal and Gitelson 1994; Archer 1995; Durbarry 2002). Theoretical analysis tends to posit that tourism expansion should make a positive contribution to economic growth (Balaguer and Cantavella-Jordá 2002; Dritsakis 2004).

This issue has attracted great interest only recently, and there are a number of empirical papers confirming the tourism industry's contribution to a country's economic growth (see Balaguer and Cantavella-Jordá 2002; Dritsakis 2004; Gunduz and Hatemi-J 2005; Kim *et al.* 2006; Noriko and Mototsugu 2007). Similarly, Soukiazis and Proença (2005) examined the impact of tourism at the regional level, and Shan and Wilson (2001) study the causality between tourism and trade. However, it should also be pointed out that few authors could not establish any positive link between tourism and economic growth (see Chen and Devereux 1999; Oh 2005; Lee and Chang 2008).

Despite the belief in tourism-led economic development, relatively speaking, few studies have rigorously investigated a causal relationship between tourism and economic growth.[3] Moreover, most studies have indeed been dealing with samples of developed countries and despite the increasing importance of tourism for African economies, few, if any, studies[4] have been found to rigorously assess the relationship. We have not come across any research analysing the role of tourism on economic performance that focuses exclusively on rigorous cross-sectional and panel data analysis for developing country cases, particularly for the case of Africa. Furthermore, most of the related studies have failed to take into account the endogeneity issues and indirect benefits from tourism. Mauritius' success story is also attributed in part to the booming tourism sector, and the country thus represents an interesting candidate to investigate, more so given its small-island developing-state nature, with all its associated specificities and vulnerabilities.

The aim of this chapter is to supplement the literature, by establishing the empirical link of the extent to which the tourism industry can spur economic growth while accounting for the conventional sources of economic growth using standard theory for a sample of African economies. In an attempt to attain this objective, our study makes use of data from 40 economies[5] over a period of 17 years (1990–2006). The basis for the selection of the sample is purely based on existence and availability of comparable data. Another research contribution of this study lies in the fact that so far we have not come across any research which has adequately dealt with the issues of dynamics, causality and endogeneity in the tourism development and economic growth link. The study thus innovatively adopts a panel vector autoregression (VAR) framework to account for the above, largely ignored issues, while at the same time allowing for country-specific unobserved heterogeneity in the levels of the variables. Empirical studies of this nature certainly add to the growing body of literature on the debate of tourism development and growth, and as such also bring new evidence from the sample of African economies.

The rest of the chapter is organized as follows: a review of selected literature, followed by an overview of tourism in Africa, then in the next section we specify an augmented Solow growth model which incorporates tourism as one of the sources of growth. It also presents the results from the panel VAR which reflects both the dynamic nature of the data and endogeneity of some of the conventional growth sources. The last section summarizes the results and draws conclusions.

Related literature

Research analysing the relationship between tourism activity and economic growth has been flourishing recently. For instance, using Spanish data from 1975 to 1997, Balaguer and Cantavella-Jordá (2002) discovered a stable long-run relationship between tourism and economic growth. Dritsakis (2004) examined the impact of tourism on the long-run economic growth of Greece, using Granger causality tests based on error correction models, and also found a strong causal relationship between international tourism earnings and economic growth, as well as a causal relationship between economic growth and international tourism earnings, thus supporting both tourism-led economic development and economic-driven tourism growth.

Tosun (1999) and Gunduz and Hatemi (2005) confirmed empirical support for the tourism-led growth hypothesis for Turkey. Using a cointegration, Kim *et al.* (2006) reported similar results for Taiwan and further found a bidirectional causality between growth and tourism. Brida *et al.* (2008) also confirmed the tourism-led growth hypothesis through cointegration and causality testing for the case of Mexico. Durbarry (2004) is among the very few who focused on the case study of an African state, namely Mauritius. Using cointegration and causality tests, Durbarry's results lend support to the contention that tourism has promoted growth and development.

At the regional level, employing the convergence approach based on an analysis by Barro and Sala-i-Martin (1992), Soukiazis and Proença (2005) drew the conclusion that tourism can be considered as an alternative solution for enhancing regional growth in Portugal. Cortes-Jimenez (2006) found that both domestic and international tourism have a significant and positive role in regional economic growth for the Spanish and Italian regions. Other studies, using various samples of countries, also reported a positive contribution of tourism to growth. For instance, Cunado and Perez de Garcia (2006) found some evidence of conditional convergence towards the African regional average and the US average for some countries in their African sample. Brau *et al.* (2003) compared the relative growth performance of 14 'tourism countries' within a sample of 143 countries and documented that tourism countries grow faster than all the subgroups. Eugenio-Martin *et al.* (2004) also analysed the relationship for the case of Latin America for the period 1985 to 1998. The author showed that the tourism sector is adequate for the economic growth of medium- or low-income countries, though not necessarily for developed countries. More recent studies can be traced back from Seetanah (2011), who confirmed the positive impact of tourism on growth for the case of island economies.

A few studies could not establish the viable contribution of tourism to economic growth. Lee (2008), for instance, using the bounds test developed by Pesaran *et al.* (2001), is among those who could not find a cointegrating relationship between tourism and economic growth, but rather found support for the growth-led tourism hypothesis. Oh (2005) also disagreed with the tourism-led growth theory and, using South Korean data in a cointegration analysis, the author rejected any long-run link between tourism receipts and economic growth over the period from 1975 to 2001. Chen and Devereux (1999) yet argued that tourism may reduce welfare for trade regimes dominated by export taxes or import subsidies. Using a theoretical framework, they demonstrated that foreign direct investment (FDI) in the form of tourism is, for the most part, beneficial while tourist immiserization is still possible in sub-Saharan Africa (SSA). Based on panel data analysis, Sequeira and Campos (2005) also accounted for the endogeneity problem and concluded that tourism, on its own, cannot explain the higher growth rates of the sample of countries.

Tourism in Africa

While tourist arrivals worldwide reached more than the 1 billion mark in 2012, with a mean annual growth rate of 6.5 per cent (WTO 2012), tourist arrivals in Africa for the same period registered only around 52 million, representing around 5 per cent of world share. This compares with around 50 per cent of arrivals in Europe, 20 per cent in Asia/Pacific, 15 per cent in the Americas and around 5 per cent in the Middle East. Table 7.1 provides a summary of tourist arrivals by region for the period 1995–2012. Meanwhile, in 2012, tourism spending in Africa reached US$70 billion, representing around a 3 per cent world share, compared with more than 50 per cent for Europe, 20 per cent for Asia/Pacific and 3.5 per cent for the Middle East (UNWTO 2013).

In terms of contribution to GDP, travel and tourism direct-GDP contribution in Africa reached US$75 billion in 2013, greater than the combined GDP contribution of Africa's banking, communications, chemicals manufacturing and auto-manufacturing sectors. Including its indirect and induced impacts, travel and tourism generated US$179 billion in GDP, or 8.9% of Africa's GDP, in 2013.

African travel and tourism GDP contribution has registered a steady increase over the years, with a mean increase of over 50 per cent since 2005 (although to a lesser extent for the case of direct industry GDP contribution). This compares with a mean increase of around 25 per cent for the world in real terms. The continent's 10-year annualized growth of this sector averaged around 5 per cent (more or less comparable with other parts of the world). Table 7.2 shows the contribution of travel and tourism in GDP in billions of US dollars since the year 1990.

Tourism has also been an important job provider for the continent. With 8 million direct employees in Africa, travel and tourism is one of the leading employers in the region, surpassing the direct job creation of most African industries. Including its indirect and induced impacts, travel and tourism in Africa sustained 20 million jobs in 2013. Table 7.3 shows that jobs in this sector have increased from 10 million to 32 million over the period 2000–13, with an annualized mean growth of around 2 per cent (WTTC 2013).

Table 7.1 International tourist arrivals (millions) by region

	1995	2000	2005	2010	2011	2012
World	563	678	805	956	996	1035
Africa	19	26	35	50	49	52
Europe	307	389	447	488	517	535
Asia/Pacific	82	110	154	205	216	233
Americas	109	128	137	150	156	162
Middle East	14	24	36	59	55	53

Source: Based on UNWTO (2013).

Table 7.2 Travel and tourism (T & T) contribution to gross domestic product (GDP), Africa

Year		1990	1995	2000	2005	2010	2011	2012	2013
T&T direct contribution to GDP									
SSA	US$ bn	5.548	8.954	9.406	21.151	31.088	33.869	36.413	36.63
North Africa	US$ bn	7.452	8.004	13.671	22.619	36.902	34.906	37.639	34.951
Total		13	16.958	23.077	43.77	67.99	68.775	74.052	71.581
T&T total contribution to GDP									
SSA	US$ bn	13.537	22.153	23.376	54.009	82.711	89.33	95.625	95.733
North Africa	US$ bn	13.917	16.443	27.652	46.201	77.94	74.855	79.829	74.998
Total		27.454	38.596	51.028	100.21	160.651	164.185	175.454	170.731
Visitor exports									
SSA	US$ bn	4.279	7.499	8.266	17.952	25.129	27.988	30.214	29.391
North Africa	US$ bn	4.951	6.32	9.165	15.99	25.435	21.083	22.419	18.742
Total		9.23	13.819	17.431	33.942	50.564	49.071	52.633	48.133
Domestic T&T spending									
SSA	US$ bn	7.224	10.92	10.053	21.999	33.523	35.862	38.272	39.147
North Africa	US$ bn	5.972	5.525	9.981	15.603	26.345	28.034	30.822	30.938
Total		13.196	16.445	20.034	37.602	59.868	63.896	69.094	70.085

Source: Based on UNWTO (2013).

Table 7.3 Travel and tourism employment, Africa

	2000	2005	2010	2011
SSA	6,506,000	14,963,000	20,813,000	23,183,000
North Africa	3,822,000	7,037,000	9,661,000	9,521,000
Total	10,328,000	22,000,000	30,475,000	32,705,000

Source: Based on UNWTO (2013).

Notes: SSA, sub-Saharan Africa.

Econometric framework and data sources

Economic model

Based on the principles of some earlier growth studies (see Barro and Lee 1994; Temple 1999; Levine *et al.* 2000; Wachtel 2001; Eugenio-Martin *et al.* 2004; Durbarry 2004; Seetanah 2008), we adopt an augmented Solow growth model in this study. We thus include the conventional sources of economic growth, namely investment in physical capital (*IVTGDP*), human capital (*EDU*) and a measure of the openness of the economy (*OPEN*). The economic model is further augmented to include a measure for economic freedom (*EF*) and tourism development (*TOUR*). The dependent variable Y is a measure of the country national income, proxied by the GDP in real terms.

The model takes the following form:[6]

$$Y = f(IVTGDP, OPEN, EDU, EF, TOUR) \tag{7.1}$$

There exists in the growth literature a near-unanimous consensus (see Reinhart 1989; De Long and Summers 1990, 1994; and more recently Arin 2004) of the role of private investment (*IVTGDP*) in promoting economic performance. The gross fixed capital formation as a percentage of real GDP is used to measure investment in physical capital. Also included in the model is *OPEN*, defined as the ratio of the sum of exports and imports to GDP, proxies for the level of openness of the country. According to Dollar (1992), Sachs and Warner (1995) and Edwards (1998), for instance, increased trade openness raised economic growth through a country's access to: the advances of technological knowledge of its trade partners; bigger markets; and vital investment and intermediate goods.

We added a measure of education (*EDU*) to account for the quality of labour. This follows the arguments and empirical evidence of Mankiw *et al.* (1992), Barro (1998) and more recently Temple (2001). Workers with higher levels of education or skills should, *ceteris paribus*, be more productive, inventive and innovative. *EDU* is measured by secondary school enrolment.

Owen (1987) and Sen (1999) argued that freedom – political, economic, social, transparency and security – is a necessary condition for economic growth. This concept is captured by including in the model the economic freedom index, *EF*, obtained from Holmes *et al.* (2008).[7] We expect the effect of *EF* to be positive.

The main variable of interest to the present study is *TOUR*, which is a measure of tourism development. The total tourist arrivals are utilized as a proxy for tourism expansion, consistent with previous studies (Wang and Godbey 1994; Kim *et al.* 2006). As a robustness test we also employed another commonly used tourism proxy, namely, tourism receipts per capita. All data were obtained from the World Bank Development Indicators (WDI 2007) CDROM, except for *EF* (which is taken from the Heritage Foundation) and for tourism (available from the World Tourism Organization).

The econometric specification can be written as:

$$y_{it} = \beta_0 + \beta_1 ivtgdp_{it} + \beta_2 open_{it} + \beta_3 edu_{it} + \beta_4 ef_{it} + \beta_5 tour_{it} + \varepsilon_{it}$$

where *i* denotes the different countries in the sample and *t* denotes the time dimension. The small letters denote the natural logarithm of the variables implying a double log-linear specification for ease of interpretation (that is in percentage terms). The sample comprises 40 African economies for the period 1990–2006.

To ensure stationarity of the variables, we applied the Im *et al.* (1995) panel unit root tests to our panel data. This test, also confirmed by the Fisher–ADF and Fisher–PP panel unit root tests, rejected at the 5 per cent significance level for each variable the null hypothesis that the time series in levels had a unit root. Thus each of the variables was considered stationary, and it was therefore judged safe to continue with the panel-data estimation.

Endogeneity issues and the panel vector autoregressive model

To account for possible interrelationships among variables, including endogeneity and causality, we apply VAR to the panel data.[8] Panel data VAR combines the traditional VAR approach, which treats all the variables in the system as endogenous, with the panel data approach, which allows for unobserved individual heterogeneity. We specify a first-order VAR model as follows

$$Z_{it} = \Gamma_0 + \Gamma_1 Z_{it-1} + \mu_i + \varepsilon_t \tag{7.2}$$

where z_t is a six-variable vector *(y, ivtgdp, open, edu, ef, tour)* and the variables are as defined previously.

In applying the VAR procedure to panel data, we need to impose the restriction that the underlying structure is the same for each cross-sectional unit. This constraint is likely to be violated in practice, however. One way to overcome the restriction on parameters is to allow for 'individual heterogeneity' in the levels of the variables by introducing fixed effects, denoted by μ_i in the model (Love and Zicchino 2006). Since the fixed effects are correlated with the regressors due to lags of the dependent variables, the mean differencing procedure commonly used to eliminate fixed effects would create biased coefficients. To avoid this problem we use forward mean differencing, also referred to as the 'Helmert procedure' (see Arellano and Bover 1995). This procedure removes only the forward mean, that is, the mean of all the future observations available for each country year. The transformation preserves the orthogonality between trans-formed variables and lagged regressors, so we can use lagged regressors as instruments and estimate the coefficients by the system of generalized method of moments (GMM).[9]

Estimation and analysis

We estimated the coefficients of the system given in Equation 7.2 after the fixed effects had been removed, and Table 7.4 reports the results of the model.

Analysis

Referring to the output equation, tourism, as proxied by the number of tourist arrivals, has made a positive contribution to economic growth of African coun-tries. The coefficient of 0.15, a measure of output elasticity, denotes that a 1 per cent increase in tourist arrivals contributed directly to, on average, a 0.15 per cent increase in the GDP of African economies. This result is consistent with those of

Table 7.4 Results from the panel vector autoregression (VAR) model (1990–2006)

Response to [→]

Response of [↓]	*Constant*	y_{t-1}	$ivtgdp_{t-1}$	$open_{t-1}$	edu_{t-1}	ef_{t-1}	$tour_{t-1}$
y	−0.53	0.33	0.46	0.27	0.19	0.14	0.15
	(1.53)	(2.23)**	(2.11)**	(2.31)***	(1.98)*	(1.86)*	(1.98)*
ivtgdp	0.43	0.23	0.58	0.09	0.12	0.11	0.30
	(1.86)*	(2.15)**	(2.21)**	(1.01)	(1.71)*	(1.89)*	(1.82)*
open	0.54	0.11	0.07	0.66	0.04	0.11	0.05
	(1.91)*	(2.18)**	(1.13)	(1.99)*	(1.78)*	(1.21)	(0.65)
edu	1.12	0.14	0.09	0.04	0.56	0.03	0.04
	(1.87)*	(2.33)**	(1.23)	(0.55)	(1.98)*	(0.32)	(1.02)
ef	−0.34	0.09	0.03	0.10	0.15	0.51	0.06
	(1.23)	(1.78)*	(1.12)	(1.54)	(2.15)**	(1.99)*	(1.01)
tour	0.61	0.12	0.11	0.06	0.15	0.13	0.45
	(1.69)*	(2.25)**	(1.94)*	(1.24)	(1.99)*	(2.02)*	(2.45)***

Source: Authors' calculation.

Notes: Number of observations, 680; number of countries, 40.
The VAR model is estimated by GMM and fixed effects are removed prior to estimation. Reported numbers show the coefficients of regressing the row variables on lags of the column variables. Heteroscedasticity-adjusted *t*-statistics are in parentheses. *** significant at the 1% level, ** at 5%, and *** at 10%, respectively. The small letters denote variables in natural logarithmic terms and *t*-values (absolute) are in parentheses.
IVTGDP is a measure of physical capital, EDU is a measure of human capital, OPEN proxies the openness of the economy, EF measures economic freedom and TOUR is our variable of concern, which measures tourism development. The dependent variable *Y* measures the output level of the economy. The small letters denotes that the variables have been transformed in logarithmic terms.

Dritsakis (2004), Eugenio-Martin *et al.* (2004) and Kim *et al.* (2006), for Greece, Latin America and Taiwan, respectively. The remaining explanatory variables also display the expected signs and are significant. It should be noted, however, that the magnitude of the tourism coefficient remains relatively small, as compared with, for instance, those of private investment and openness, which remain the major growth drivers.

The VAR framework enables us to gauge additional insights, including those on endogeneity and indirect effects. While it has been shown here that tourism influences growth (tourism-led growth), a reverse causation also exists (see 'tour' equation), with output in turn serving as a determinant of tourism. The output level, which proxies for economic well-being and the level of development, may thus play an important role in attracting tourists. These bicausal results are consistent with those obtained by Dritsakis (2004), Oh (2005), Kim *et al.* (2006) and Lee (2008) for Greece, Korea, Taiwan and Singapore, respectively. The 'tour' equation can also be viewed as a tourist-demand equation with income, education attainment, economic freedom and the investment level being other determinants. Thus, increasing the levels of these determinants could also enhance tourism, with further positive implications for growth.

For example, the 'investment equation' reports positive indirect effects of tourism on private investment. This finding supports the view that tourism encourages private investment, presumably in the tourism sector, and hence additional growth. An estimated 'tour' coefficient of 0.3 in the investment equation denotes that a percentage increase in tourism could lead to a 0.3 per cent increase in private investment. Given that the direct effect is a 0.43 per cent increase in GDP growth for a 1 per cent increase in private investment, there should be a 0.3 × 0.43 or 0.13 per cent increase in output growth. This is an estimate of the additional indirect effect of tourism on output via the private capital channel.

Summary and policy implications

Using a panel VAR model to take account of indirect effects, causality and endogeneity issues, this chapter investigated whether tourism, as measured by the number of tourist arrivals, has contributed to the national income of a sample of 40 African countries over the period 1990–2006.

Results from the study suggest that tourism is an important determinant of African development, although private investment, openness and human capital remain the main drivers. While the tourism-led growth hypothesis is supported, a reverse causation exists, as output level is seen to be also a determinant of tourism, thus supporting a bicausal and reinforcing relationship. Moreover, in addition to income, enhancing education attainment, economic freedom and investment could also raise the level of tourism which may in turn increase growth. A broad policy implication of this study is that African economies can improve their economic growth performance, not only by investing in the traditional sources of growth such as investment in physical and human capital, and trade, but also by strategically enhancing the tourism industry.

Appendix 7A

List of sub-Saharan African countries:

Algeria	Mauritius
Angola	Mozambique
Benin	Malawi
Botswana	Mali
Burundi	Morocco
Cameroon	Namibia
Congo	Niger
Central Africa	Nigeria
Côte D'Ivoire	Rwanda
Gabon	Senegal
Gambia	Seychelles
Ghana	South Africa
Guinea-Bissau	Sudan
Egypt	Swaziland
Ethiopia	Tanzania
Kenya	Togo
Lesotho	Tunisia
Libya	Uganda
Madagascar	Zambia, and
Mauritania	Zimbabwe.

Notes

1 Real GDP growth for the travel and tourism economy was expected to be 3.0 per cent in 2008, down from 4.1 per cent in 2007, but to average 4.0 per cent per annum over the coming 10 years.
2 Refer to Sinclair and Stabler (2002) for a good theoretical treatment.
3 Oh (2005) argued that it is necessary to investigate the hypothesis in numerous destination countries for the purpose of generalization.
4 Studies on developing countries and Africa have mostly focused on the examination of the tourism sector by estimating and forecasting tourism demand and income generation via the multiplier process (Sinclair 1998; Bezmen 2006).
5 The list of selected countries is given in Appendix 7A.
6 In a separate specification, not reported here, we also estimate the Arellano–Bond dynamic panel data model by including year dummies to capture the effect of time trend. The results do not differ appreciably from the present ones. Moreover, we also included FDI in an alternative specification and again the results were similar.
7 The economic freedom index is calculated as the weighted average of 10 categories related to business, trade, fiscal government size, monetary, investment, financial, property rights, corruption and labour freedoms. It is measured on a scale of 0–10, with a larger value representing a higher level of freedom.
8 Powell et al. (2002) and Love and Zicchino (2006) used a similar approach in their respective studies. The former studied the interrelationships between inflows and outflows of capital and other macro variables and the latter, that of financial development and dynamic investment behaviour.

9 In our case the model is 'just identified'; that is, the number of regressors equals the number of instruments, therefore system GMM is numerically equivalent to equation-by-equation 2SLS.

References

Archer, B. (1995). 'Importance of Tourism for the Economy of Bermuda'. *Annals of Tourism Research*, 22(4): 918–30.

Arin, K.P. (2004). 'Fiscal Policy, Private Investment and Economic Growth: Evidence from G-7 Countries'. Available at SSRN: http://ssrn.com/abstract=438785 (accessed: 6 May 2013).

Arellano, M. and O. Bover (1995). 'Another Look at the Instrumental Variable Estimation of Error-Components Models'. *Journal of Econometrics*, 68: 29–51.

Balaguer, J. and M. Cantavella-Jordá (2002). 'Tourism as a Long-run Economic Growth Factor: The Spanish Case'. *Applied Economics*, 34: 877–84.

Barro, R. and J.W. Lee (1994). 'Data Set for a Panel of 138 Countries'. Mimeo. Boston, MA: Harvard University.

Barro, R. and X. Sala-i-Martin (1992). 'Public Finance in Models of Economic Growth'. *Review of Economic Studies*, 59: 645–62.

Barro, R.J. (1998). 'Notes on Growth Accounting'. Working Paper 6654. Cambridge, MA: NBER.

Bezmen, T. (2006). 'Estimating the Impact of Tourism on Economic Development in Latin America'. Paper presented at the Academy of Economics and Finance, Houston, TX, February 2006.

Brau, R., A. Lanza, and F. Pigliaru (2003). 'How Fast are the Tourism Countries Growing? The Cross-Country Evidence'. Working Paper [AQ]NO03-09. Cagliari: Centro Ricerche Economiche Nord Sud.

Brida, J.G., E.S. Carrera, and W.A. Risso (2008). 'Tourism's Impact on Long-run Mexican Economic Growth'. *Economics Bulletin*, 3(21): 1–8.

Chen, L.L. and J. Devereux (1999). 'Tourism and Welfare in Sub-Saharan Africa: A Theoretical Analysis'. *Journal of African Economies*, 8: 209–27.

Cortes-Jimenez, I. (2006). 'Tourism and Economic Growth at Regional Level: The Cases of Spain and Italy'. ERSA Conference Paper ersa06p61. Vienna: European Regional Science Association.

Cunado, J. and F. Perez de Garcia (2006). 'Real Convergence in Africa in the Second-Half of the 20th Century'. *Journal of Economics and Business*, 58: 153–67.

Dollar, D. (1992). 'Outward-Oriented Developing Economies Really Do Grow More Rapidly: Evidence from 95 LDCs, 1976–1985'. *Economic Development and Cultural Change*, 40(3): 523–44.

De Long, J. and L. Summers (1990). 'Equipment Investment and Economic Growth'. Working Paper 3515. Cambridge MA: NBER.

De Long, J. and L. Summers (1994). 'Equipment Investment and Economic Growth: Reply'. *Quarterly Journal of Economics*, 109(3): 803–7.

Dritsakis, N. (2004). 'Tourism as a Long-run Economic Growth Factor: An Empirical Investigation for Greece Using Causality Analysis'. *Tourism Economics*, 10(3): 305–16.

Durbarry, R. (2002). 'The Economic Contribution of Tourism in Mauritius'. *Annals of Tourism Research*, 29(3): 862–65.

Durbarry, R. (2004). 'Tourism and Economic Growth: The Case of Mauritius'. *Tourism Economics*, 10(3): 389–401.

Edwards, S. (1998). 'Openness, Productivity and Growth: What Do We Really Know?'. *Economic Journal*, 108: 383–98.

Eugenio-Martin, J.L., N.M. Morales and R. Scarpa (2004). 'Tourism and Economic Growth in Latin American Countries: A Panel Data Approach'. Working Paper 26. Milano: FEEM.

Gunduz, L. and A. Hatemi-J (2005). 'Is the Tourism-Led Growth Hypothesis Valid for Turkey?'. *Applied Economics Letters*, 12: 499–504.

Holmes, K.R., E.J. Feulner and M.A. O'Grady (2008). *Index of Economic Freedom*. Heritage Foundation and the Wall Street Journal.

Im, K., H. Pesaran and Y. Shin (1995). 'Testing for Unit Roots in Heterogeneous Panels'. Working Papers Amalgamated Series 9526. Cambridge: University of Cambridge, DAE.

Khan H., C.F. Seng and W.K. Cheong (1990). 'The Social Impact of Tourism on Singapore'. *Service Industries Journal*, 10(3): 541–48.

Kim, H.J., M. Chen and S. Jan (2006). 'Tourism Expansion and Economic Development: The Case of Taiwan'. *Tourism Management*, 27: 925–33.

Lea, J. (1988). *Tourism and Development in the Third World*. New York: Routledge.

Lee, C.-C. and C.-P. Chang (2008). 'Tourism Development and Economic Growth: A Closer Look at Panels'. *Tourism Management*, 29(1): 180–92.

Lee, C.G. (2008). 'Tourism and Economic Growth: The Case of Singapore, Regional and Sectoral Economic Studies'. *Euro-American Association of Economic Development*, 8(1): 89–98.

Levine R., N. Loayza and T. Beck (2000). 'Financial Intermediation and Growth: Causality and Causes'. *Journal of Monetary Economics*, 46: 31–77.

Love, I. and L. Zicchino (2006). 'Financial Development and Dynamic Investment Behavior: Evidence from Panel VAR'. *The Quarterly Review of Economics and Finance*, 46: 190–210.

Mankiw, N.G., D. Romer and D.N. Weil (1992). 'A Contribution to the Empirics of Economic Growth'. *The Quarterly Journal of Economics*, CVI(2): 407–37.

McKinnon, R. (1964). 'Foreign Exchange Constraints in Economic Development and Efficient Aid Allocation'. *Economic Journal*, 74: 388–409.

Noriko, I. and F. Mototsugu (2007). 'Impacts of Tourism and Fiscal Expenditure to Remote Islands: The Case of the Amami Islands in Japan'. *Applied Economics Letter*, 14: 661–66.

Oh, C. (2005). 'The Contribution of Tourism Development to Economic Growth in the Korean Economy'. *Tourism Management*, 26(1): 39–44.

Owen, E. (1987). *The Future of Freedom in the Developing World*. Oxford: Pergamon Press.

Pesaran, M.H., Y. Shin and R.J. Smith (2001). 'Bounds Testing Approaches to the Analysis of Level Relationships'. *Journal of Applied Econometrics*, 16: 289–326.

Powell, J., P. Selman and A. Wragg (2002). 'Protected Areas: Reinforcing the Virtuous Circle'. *Planning Practice and Research*, 17(3): 279–25.

Reinhart, C.M. (1989). 'Private Investment and Economic Growth in Developing Countries'. Working Paper 89/60. Washington, DC: IMF.

Sachs, G. and T. Warner (1995). 'Natural Resource Abundance and Economic Growth'. Working Paper 5398. Cambridge, MA: NBER.

Seetanah B. (2008). 'Financial Development and Economic Growth: An ARDL Approach for the Case of the Small Island State of Mauritius'. *Applied Economics*, 15(10): 809–19.

Seetanah B. (2011). 'Assessing the Dynamic Economic Impact of Tourism for Island Economies'. *Annals of Tourism Research*, 38(1): 291–308.

Sen, A.N. (1999). *Development as Freedom*. New York: Alfred A. Knopf.

Sequeira, T.N. and C. Campos (2005). 'International Tourism and Economic Growth: A Panel Data Approach'. Working Paper 141. Milano: FEEM.

Shan, J. and K. Wilson (2001). 'Causality Between Trade and Tourism: Empirical Evidence from China'. *Applied Economics Letters*, 8: 279–83.

Sinclair, M.T. (1998). 'Tourism and Economic Development: A Survey'. *Journal of Development Studies*, 34(5): 1–51.

Sinclair, M.T. and M. Stabler (2002). *The Economics of Tourism*. London: Routledge.

Soukiazis, E. and S. Proença (2005). 'Tourism as an Alternative Source of Regional Growth in Portugal: A Panel Data Analysis at Nuts II and III Levels'. *Portuguese Economic Journal*, 6(2): 43–61.

Temple, J.R.W. (1999). 'The New Growth Evidence'. *Journal of Economic Literature*, 37(1): 112–56.

Temple, J.R.W. (2001). 'Generalizations that Aren't? Evidence on Education and Growth'. *European Economic Review*, 45(4–6): 905–18.

Tosun, C. (1999). 'An Analysis of Contributions of International Inbound Tourism to the Turkish Economy'. *Tourism Economics*, 5: 217–50.

Uysal, M. and R. Gitelson (1994). 'Assessment of Economic Impacts: Festivals and Special Events'. 2(1): 3–10.

Wachtel, P. (2001). 'Growth and Finance: What Do We Know and How Do We Know It?'. *International Finance*, 4(Winter): 335–62.

Wang P. and G. Godbey (1994). 'A Normative Approach to Tourism Growth to the Year 2000'. *Journal of Travel Research*, 33: 32–7.

World Development Indicators (WDI) (2007). New York and Geneva: World Bank.

WTO (2012). WTO Annual Report 2012. Geneva: World Tourism Organisation. http://www2.unwto.org/publication/unwto-annual-report-2012 (accessed: 4 April 2014).

World Tourism Organization (UNWTO) (2013). 'Yearbook of Tourism Statistics'. Madrid: UNWTO.

WTTC (2013). WTTC Travel and Tourism Economic Impact 2013. Available at: www.wttc.org (accessed: 4 April 2014).

8 Hunting for leopards

Long-run country income dynamics in Africa

Jorge Arbache and John Page

Introduction

After stagnating for much of its post-colonial history, economic performance in sub-Saharan Africa (SSA) has markedly improved. Since 1995, mean economic growth has been close to 5 per cent per year. Countries with at least 4 per cent gross domestic product (GDP) growth now constitute about 70 per cent of the region's total population and 80 per cent of its GDP. Per capita income grew by 1.6 per cent a year in the late 1990s and by 2–3 per cent in each year since 2000.

Recent popular and academic writing has suggested that Africa may be at a turning point in its long economic decline (see Commission for Africa 2005; Ndulu *et al.* 2007). But predictions of Africa's imminent economic recovery or demise have proved wrong on numerous occasions in the past 40 years. Growth in Africa since 1975 has been lower and more volatile than in any other region of the world – developed or developing (Table 8.1). And, unlike East and (more recently) South Asia, it has had few regional 'champions' to serve as models of successful, rapidly growing economies.[1]

Using the most recent purchasing power parity (PPP) data for 44 SSA countries, this chapter examines country-level dynamics of long-run growth in Africa between 1975 and 2005. The next section describes our data and the characteristics of Africa's long-run growth. Here we confirm previous findings that the major characteristics of growth in Africa are its low long-run trend and its extreme volatility at the country level. We find no persuasive evidence of growth persistence within countries and only weak evidence of persistence at the regional level since 1990.

'Rich country, poor country' examines how growth recovery has affected the distribution of income among countries in the region. We describe the country-level distribution of income in Africa and test for convergence in per capita income levels between richer and poorer countries. We find no evidence that poorer countries in Africa are converging to the income levels of their richer neighbours. We find persuasive evidence of inertia in per capita incomes for economies in Africa. Where countries began in terms of relative income in 1975 is an excellent predictor of where they ended up in 2005. Because the rich economies are growing faster than their poorer neighbours, we also find that inter-country distribution of income has become less equal over time.

Table 8.1 Gross domestic product (GDP) per capita and growth by region (weighted data)

Region	1975–80	1981–85	1986–90	1991–95	1996–2000	2001–05
GDP per capita						
Sub-Saharan Africa	1,928	1,844	1,782	1,648	1,668	1,768
East Asia & Pacific	905	1,227	1,686	2,407	3,399	4,595
Latin America & Caribbean	6,020	6,295	6,315	6,450	6,978	7,205
Middle East & North Africa	4,179	4,180	4,055	4,326	4,651	5,197
South Asia	1,132	1,268	1,505	1,745	2,110	2,530
Low & middle income	2,278	2,560	2,881	3,045	3,513	4,219
Growth						
Sub-Saharan Africa	−0.06	−1.60	−0.21	−1.64	0.79	1.79
East Asia & Pacific	5.26	6.12	5.76	9.10	5.63	7.06
Latin America & Caribbean	3.31	−0.95	−0.43	1.61	1.53	1.21
Middle East & North Africa	−0.20	2.41	−1.20	1.18	1.91	2.78
South Asia	1.03	3.14	3.89	3.01	3.59	4.65
Low & middle income	2.79	1.99	1.93	1.56	3.23	4.58

Source: Authors' computations.

Note: All sub-Saharan African countries are included in calculations.

In the section entitled Hunting for leopards, we discuss how one indication that Africa has indeed reached a turning point, would be evidence that a group of African economies with high and accelerating long-run growth – 'leopards', the regional equivalent of Asia's 'tigers' – is beginning to emerge. We first identify four groups of countries according to their income levels and growth experiences, and we look for some common characteristics that are associated with these groups. Two distinct and stable income groups or 'clubs', rich and poor, are identifiable in the data. Our most striking finding is that transitions from low-income to higher-income levels have been rare in the last 30 years. Only two countries, both oil exporters, made the transition.

We then use the approach to growth accelerations and decelerations developed by Arbache and Page (2007), to see if a subset of countries with a high frequency of rapid growth accelerations emerges during 1995–2005. Based on our results for income transitions, growth thresholds and growth accelerations, we identify six economies that show the potential to be Africa's growth leaders. The final section is the conclusion.

Chaos without change: Africa's long-run growth, 1975–2005

This section examines long-run trends in per capita income growth for 44 African economies. Data on GDP per capita at 2000 international PPP prices are taken from the *World Development Indicators* and span the years 1975 to 2005.[2] Our sample contains all SSA countries for which PPP GDP data exist. There are no GDP per capita PPP data for Liberia, San Tomé and Principe and Somalia, therefore they are excluded from the analysis.[3] The unweighted mean GDP per capita between 1975 and 2005 for the 44 countries in our sample was US$2,306. Mean GDP per capita using GDP-weighted data was US$1,702.[4] Table 8A.1 presents descriptive statistics for income and growth at the country level.

Figure 8.1 presents the timepaths of unweighted and GDP-weighted per capita income growth rates.[5] Although the trajectories of the unweighted and weighted series appear similar, their means and variances are significantly different. The region's unweighted mean growth rate was 0.71 per cent and its standard deviation (SD) was 6.32 per cent. The mean and SD of the weighted data are −0.17 per cent and 1.7 per cent, respectively, reflecting the fact that Africa's bigger economies grew more slowly than its smaller ones. Between 1975 and 2005, South Africa, which represents, on average, 42 per cent of the region's GDP, grew in per capita terms by an mean of only 0.12 per cent a year; and Nigeria, the region's second-largest economy, (13.50 per cent of GDP) grew by 0.28 per cent.

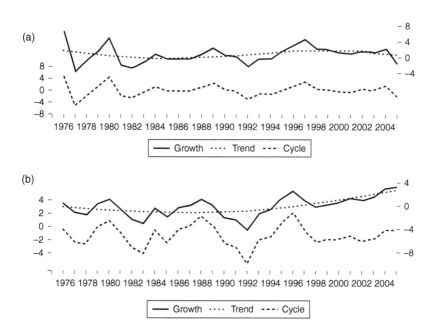

Figure 8.1 Gross domestic product per capita growth, 1975–2005: (a) unweighted data; (b) weighted data

Source: Authors' computations.

Both the unweighted and weighted series show a positive trend beginning in the mid-1990s. In the period 1995–2005, unweighted mean GDP growth per capita was 1.81 per cent, more than twice the long-run mean. In order to test for statistically meaningful breaks in the mid-1990s, we ran recursive residual estimations and other stability tests. Figure 8.2 shows the recursive estimation for the growth series. There is statistical evidence that growth accelerated around 1995. Both the Chow breakpoint and forecast tests support the conclusion that a structural break in the income growth series occurred in the mid-1990s.[6]

Growth rates for individual countries were low and the coefficient of variation was high, indicating that growth was highly erratic (Table 8A.1). Figure 8.3 shows that African economies have by far the least predictable growth globally,

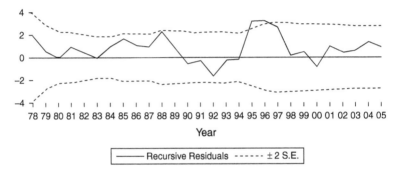

Figure 8.2 Stability test: recursive residual estimation of growth rates

Source: Authors' computations.

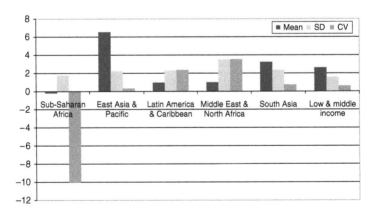

Figure 8.3 Gross domestic product per capita growth: means, standard deviation (SD) and coefficient of variation (CV) by region (weighted data), 1975–2005

Source: Authors' computations.

Table 8.2 Decomposition of standard deviation of GDP per capita and growth
        1975–2005

Variable	Mean	Standard deviation		
		Overall	Between countries	Within countries
GDP per capita	2,306	2,633	2,490	809
GDP per capita growth	0.71	6.32	2.26	5.95

Source: Authors' computations.

Notes: Statistics calculated from panel data.

as measured by the coefficient of variation (CV). Countries with different levels of income (such as South Africa and Malawi), geographical locations (such as Mali and Senegal), resource endowments (such as Nigeria and Ethiopia) and long-run GDP per capita growth patterns (like Gabon, Niger, Madagascar and Swaziland) share a common characteristic, high growth volatility.

Table 8.2 decomposes the standard deviation of GDP per capita and its growth into within- and between-country components. Growth is highly unstable in individual countries; the ratio of the within-country SD to the total SD of growth rates is 94 per cent. The Comoros (–22.6), Ethiopia (18.4), Guinea-Bissau (–11.9), Malawi (24.6), Mauritania (34.6), Namibia (19.8), Nigeria (18.7) and South Africa (20.6) are notable for their extremely high volatility, even by regional standards.

Only three economies – Botswana (0.5), Cape Verde (0.8) and Mauritius (0.4) – have coefficients of variation of less than 1.0. These three economies are also notable for their high long-run growth rates, ranking second to fourth out of the sample in terms of their overall rate of per capita income growth, 1975–2005.[7]

Kernel densities of the distribution of per capita GDP growth rates at 10-year intervals are shown in Figure 8.4a–d. The growth acceleration of 1995–2005 is clearly visible in the rightward shift of the distribution.

The most striking change in the distribution over time, however, is the extent to which growth rates have converged (Figure 8.4a). The 1976 distribution is remarkably flat. Since then, there have been increasingly more acute peaks around the mean (Figure 8.4b–d).

The SD of growth rates dropped from 8.2 per cent in 1976 to 3.6 per cent in 2005. Two sets of outliers – high performers and economies in decline – also appear to be emerging in the 1995 and 2005 distributions (Figure 8.4c and d).

An important question with respect to long-run growth is whether it has been persistent. Figure 8.5 shows the results of regressing mean GDP per capita growth on growth in the first year of our series, 1975–1976:

$$\Delta \overline{Y}_i = \alpha + \beta (\Delta Y_i^{76}) + \varepsilon \tag{8.1}$$

where $\Delta \overline{Y}_i$ is the mean growth of country i and ΔY_i^{76} is the growth rate of country i in 1976, the first year in our series. Not surprisingly, given the extreme variability

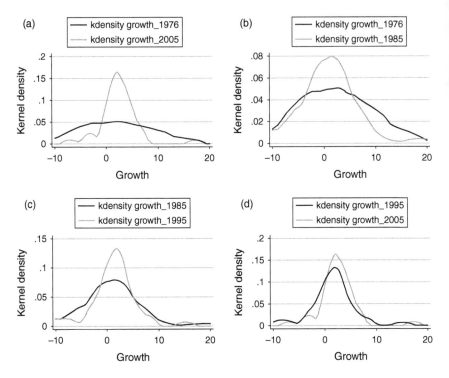

Figure 8.4 Density of gross domestic product per capita growth across countries: (a) 1976 compared with 2005; (b) 1976 compared with 1985; (c) 1985 compared with 1995; (d) 1995 compared with 2005

Source: Author's computations.

of growth rates, there is no evidence of growth persistence. The coefficient of β is close to zero and insignificant ($\beta = 0.061$, $t = 1.65$).[8] Growth in 1976 for the representative African country fails to predict mean growth in the subsequent 30 years.

We also stratify the data before and after 1995 to assess whether there was evidence of persistence during either of the two subperiods:

$$\Delta \bar{Y}_i^{76-94} = \alpha + \beta (\Delta Y_i^{76}) + \varepsilon \tag{8.2}$$

$$\Delta \bar{Y}_i^{95-05} = \alpha + \beta (\Delta Y_i^{95}) + \varepsilon \tag{8.3}$$

where $\Delta \bar{Y}_i^{76-94}$ is mean GDP per capita growth between 1976 and 1994, $\Delta \bar{Y}_i^{95-05}$ is mean GDP per capita growth between 1995 and 2005, and ΔY_i^{76} and ΔY_i^{95} are the growth rate of country i in 1976 and 1991.

The results are shown in Figure 8.6a and b. The coefficients of β are 0.06 (1.38) and 0.21 (3.06), respectively, for the first and second periods, suggesting that

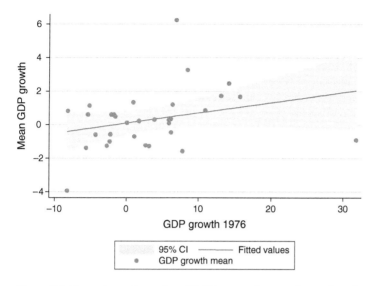

Figure 8.5 Gross domestic product (GDP) per capita growth as a function of initial conditions

Source: Authors' computations.

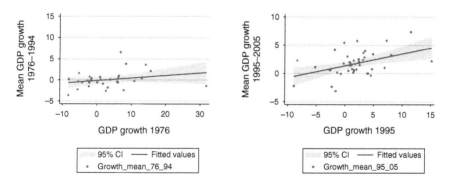

Figure 8.6 Mean growth as a function of initial conditions by time period

Source: Author's computations.

growth became more predictable from the mid-1990s on, a result that is in line with the kernel density exercises.[9]

As an additional check for persistence at the individual country level, we calculate the correlation coefficients of growth over time for individual countries. Statistically significant coefficients indicate that country growth rates follow predictable patterns. The very large majority of correlation coefficients before 1995 are not statistically significant, but about a third of the coefficients of 1995–2005 are significant (Arbache and Page 2008). This suggests that at the individual country level, growth was generally erratic, although there was increased persistence between 1995 and 2005.[10]

In sum for the region as a whole, and for the vast majority of African economies, growth from 1975 to 2005 has been both disappointing and volatile. Growth on average has accelerated and has shown a weak tendency to become more persistent over time, but for the individual African country, past growth helps very little to predict future growth.

Rich country, poor country

Africa's mean GDP per capita had a slowly rising long-run trend, consisting of about 20 years of virtual stagnation with an inflexion point upward in the mid-1990s (Figure 8.7).[11] Income per person in the average African economy declined towards the middle of the 1990s and then recovered. Weighting by GDP (Figure 8.7b) gives a U-shaped pattern of GDP per capita, reaching a minimum in the mid-1990s.

Africa's largest economies, measured in terms of GDP, experienced some of its greatest income declines between 1975 and 1994. By 2005, income weighted GDP per capita had not yet recovered to the levels observed in the mid-1970s.

For most individual African economies, GDP per capita registered only modest increases between 1975 and 2005, and many countries – such as the Democratic Republic of Congo, Côte d'Ivoire and Zimbabwe – had declining per capita incomes

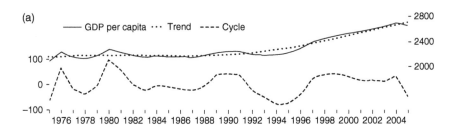

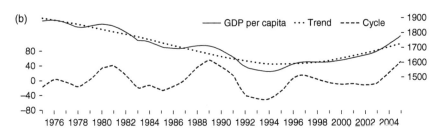

Figure 8.7 Gross domestic product per capita, 1975–2005: (a) unweighted data; (b) weighted data

Source: Authors' computations.

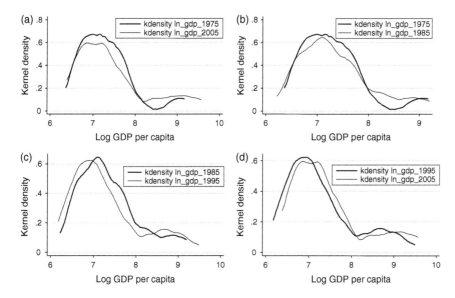

Figure 8.8 Density of gross domestic product per capita across countries: (a) 1975 compared with 2005; (b) 1975 compared with 1985; (c) 1985 compared with 1995; (d) 1995 compared with 2005

Source: Authors' computations.

over the period. The SD of income per capita was generally low, and the CV of many countries is close to zero. Most of the variation (69 per cent) in Africa's average income per person occurs between countries (Table 8.2) rather than within them.

Figure 8.8 shows comparative kernel density plots of GDP per capita for at 10-year intervals between 1975 and 2005. The kernel plot is helpful in identifying shifting patterns in the distribution of country-level incomes per capita, such as the formation of identifiable groups or 'clubs' (Quah 1993a, 1993b). The slight movement towards the right of the GDP per capita plot of 2005 compared with that of 1975 (Figure 8.8a) reflects the region's slow economic growth. Most of that movement took place between 1995 and 2005, when we observe a noticeable slide to the right, reflecting increasing incomes throughout Africa (Figure 8.8d). Since the mid-1990s, the variance of income per capita also appears to have declined.

Since 1975 there has been a pronounced bimodality in the distribution of income among countries in Africa. The twin peaks observed in each of the panels of Figure 8.8 define two groups of countries, rich and poor, which are relatively stable over the 30-year period. The most significant shift towards polarization of the country-level distribution occurred between 1985 and 1995 (Figure 8.8c), a period when many countries were devastated by conflicts. Polarization was reduced somewhat between 1995 and 2005.

The second peak virtually disappears in each 10-year period when we remove Botswana, Cape Verde, Gabon, Mauritius, Namibia, the Seychelles and South

Africa from the data. Thus these seven countries form a stable, rich country club.[12] With the exception of South Africa, the members of the club are small economies, and they have relatively little in common with one another. Botswana, Cape Verde and Mauritius had high growth – even by global standards – and low-growth volatility. The Seychelles had more moderate growth with high volatility. Namibia and South Africa barely grew but were highly erratic growers, and Gabon declined with high volatility. Cape Verde, Mauritius and the Seychelles are islands; Botswana is landlocked and resource rich.

Table 8.3 shows, for 43 countries, the ratio of their GDP per capita to that of South Africa, the richest African economy in 1975.

These data show little upward income mobility among African countries. Despite South Africa's long period of slow growth, only nine countries – Botswana, Cape Verde, Equatorial Guinea, Lesotho, Mauritius, the Seychelles, Sudan, Swaziland and Uganda – had an increase in their GDP per capita of at least 5 percentage points relative to South Africa. Of these, only Sudan and Uganda are not members of the rich country club identified above. Botswana, Mauritius and the Seychelles

Table 8.3 GDP per capita relative to South Africa

Country	1975 (or earliest year)	2005 (or most recent year)	Country	1975 (or earliest year)	2005 (or most recent year)
Angola	0.19	0.21	Lesotho	0.12	0.30
Benin	0.09	0.10	Madagascar	0.13	0.08
Botswana	0.19	1.12	Malawi	0.06	0.06
Burkina Faso	0.08	0.11	Mali	0.08	0.09
Burundi	0.08	0.06	Mauritania	0.20	0.20
Cameroon	0.18	0.21	Mauritius	0.40	1.14
Cape Verde	0.23	0.52	Mozambique	0.07	0.11
Central African Republic	0.17	0.11	Namibia	0.65	0.68
Chad	0.10	0.13	Niger	0.10	0.07
Comoros	0.19	0.18	Nigeria	0.10	0.10
Congo, Dem. Rep.	0.23	0.06	Rwanda	0.09	0.11
Congo, Rep.	0.10	0.11	Senegal	0.15	0.16
Côte d'Ivoire	0.25	0.15	Seychelles	0.76	1.45
Equatorial Guinea	0.13	0.73	Sierra Leone	0.10	0.07
Eritrea	0.09	0.10	Sudan	0.12	0.19
Ethiopia	0.09	0.09	Swaziland	0.32	0.43
Gabon	0.97	0.63	Tanzania	0.05	0.07
Gambia, The	0.16	0.17	Togo	0.18	0.14
Ghana	0.20	0.22	Uganda	0.08	0.13
Guinea	0.19	0.21	Zambia	0.14	0.09
Guinea-Bissau	0.11	0.07	Zimbabwe	0.29	0.18
Kenya	0.10	0.11			

Source: Authors' computations.

Note: The ratio is the fraction of GDP per capita to South Africa's.

were the only economies to overtake South Africa in terms of per capita income. An important 'neighbourhood effect' is apparent in the data: Botswana, Lesotho and Swaziland, all to a large degree integrated into the South African economy, are among the faster converging economies.

Twenty-three countries experienced little or no change in their income levels relative to South Africa, and 11 – including Côte d'Ivoire, Gabon, Madagascar and Zimbabwe – had sharp deteriorations. The increase in income divergence was particularly sharp in Côte d'Ivoire, the Democratic Republic of Congo and Gabon. A majority of resource-rich countries (including oil exporters) did not improve their relative positions (Angola, Chad, Democratic Republic of the Congo, Nigeria and Zambia), providing support to the arguments of Collier (2007) and others that the 'natural resource curse' is particularly relevant in Africa.

A more formal test of whether the income per capita of poorer African countries is converging towards the region's richer ones can be conducted using the following unconditional convergence model:

$$\Delta \overline{Y}_i = \alpha + \beta Y_i^{75} + \varepsilon, \tag{8.4}$$

where $\Delta \overline{Y}_i$ is the mean growth rate of country i, and Y_i^{75} is the GDP per capita of country i in 1975. For convergence to occur, poor countries have to grow faster (Barro 1991; Barro and Sala-i-Martin 1991), making the predicted sign of β in Equation 8.4 negative.

The regression, shown in Figure 8.9, offers no evidence of unconditional convergence. The estimated coefficient is not significantly different from zero ($\beta = -0.122$, $t = -0.29$), indicating that in Africa the initial level of income alone has no effect on the growth rate.[13]

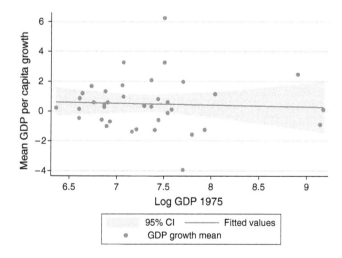

Figure 8.9 Mean growth as a function of initial conditions

Source: Author's computations.

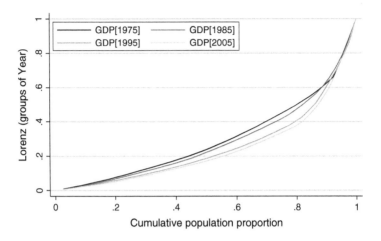

Figure 8.10 Lorenz curves: GDP per capita

Source: Author's computations.

These results confirm our heuristic evidence of substantial inertia in the income distribution and are consistent with other research. For example, McCoskey (2002) finds no evidence of unconditional convergence in Africa using long-run panel data. We also test for convergence in the period 1995–2005 – due to the structural break that took place in the growth series at about that point – by regressing mean growth during 1995–2005 on income in 1995. The results (β = 0.43, t = 0.19) are essentially the same as those reported for Equation 8.4.[14] Africa's poorer economies were not converging towards the income levels of their richer neighbours, even after the growth acceleration.

The lack of income convergence over the past 30 years has led to an increase in inequality of per capita incomes among countries across Africa. Lorenz curves of the GDP per capita at 10-year intervals from 1975 to 2005 are presented in Figure 8.10. These show increasing income inequality in each 10-year period. The sharpest rise in inter-country inequality took place between 1985 and 1995. This is consistent with the growing polarization of income and the emergence of the rich country club shown in the kernel densities.

The ratio of income of the richest 10 per cent of countries to the poorest 10 per cent of countries rose from 10.5 in 1975 to 18.5 in 2005. In 1975–2000 South Africa's GDP per capita (then the highest in the region) was 17 times higher than that of Malawi. In 2000–2005, the gap between the highest GDP per capita country, the Seychelles, and Malawi had grown to 24 times.

Where you start is where you end up

The previous sections identified some stylized facts about long-run GDP per capita growth and the distribution of income at the country level in Africa. These stylized facts – low and volatile growth, the formation of clubs, lack of convergence in income levels and rising inter-country income inequality – point towards little dynamism in income growth. In this section, we examine the income dynamics of countries in greater detail.

We begin by asking the question: How stable is the per capita income of a typical country in Africa? To test for income stability we ran the following regression:

$$\bar{Y_i} = \alpha + \beta Y_i^{75} + \varepsilon \qquad (8.5)$$

where $\bar{Y_i}$ is the mean GDP per capita of country i and Y_i^{75} is the GDP per capita of country i in 1975. Given our prior evidence of little income dynamism, we expect that average income in a typical African economy will be close to its initial income in 1975.[15] If so, the coefficient estimate of β should be close to 1. A region with a large number of dynamic economies would have an estimated coefficient of significantly more than 1, indicating that initial income under-predicts average income.

The result, presented in Figure 8.11, shows a line near 45 degrees ($\beta = 0.901$, $t = 7.41$). Apart from a few cases, the mean GDP per capita 1975–2005 closely mirrors that of 1975, reflecting a high degree of inertia.[16] There are some positive outliers, such as Botswana, Cape Verde, Lesotho, Mauritius and Namibia, whose mean GDP per capita is well above their 1975 levels. Negative outliers such as the Côte d'Ivoire, Democratic Republic of the Congo, Eritrea, Gabon,

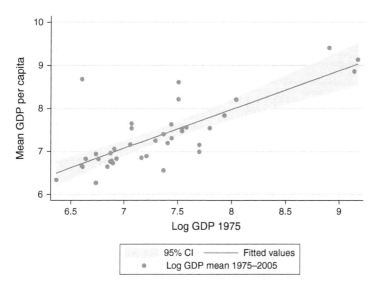

Figure 8.11 Mean gross domestic product (GDP) per capita as a function of GDP per capita in 1975

Source: Authors' computations.

Madagascar and Zambia, had mean GDP per capita well below their initial levels of income.[17]

To check whether there was a change in income stability accompanying the growth acceleration after 1995, we ran the same stability tests for mean GDP per capita for the subperiods 1975–1994 and 1995–2005, by regressing average income in those periods on the initial level of income in 1975. The results are highly significant and close to 1 (estimated coefficients of 0.891 and 0.909, respectively). These are virtually identical to the results of Equation 8.5, implying that the income structure remained highly stable, even after the break in the income and growth series in around 1995.

Hunting for leopards

Our results up to this point are somewhat discouraging from the perspective of identifying a major turn-around in Africa's economic fortunes. We find no evidence of income convergence and very little evidence of significant income mobility across countries in the region. Low and volatile growth in Africa has been associated with a remarkably stable structure of incomes. For the most part, initial income in 1975 equals average income for the entire period 1975–2005 and average income during 1995–2005.

It is possible, however, that within this stable overall structure, individual countries stand out by exhibiting more dynamic behaviour. These 'leopards' – Africa's equivalent of Asia's tigers – might be expected to have made the transition from low-income to higher-income status, common to China, Korea, Malaysia and other newly industrializing Asian economies. Korea, for example, began its rapid growth period at levels of income well below that of the average Asian economy (and equal to that of Ghana) and finished at levels well above.

In an attempt to identify dynamic economies, we constructed a typology based on income levels. We split the time series into two subperiods, 1975–1994 and 1995–2005. For each year, we calculate SSA's median GDP per capita and then check whether each country's GDP per capita was above or below the median. A country whose GDP per capita remained above the median for the majority of years in 1975–1994 is assigned to category 'A', meaning that its GDP per capita was generally 'above' the benchmark. A country whose GDP per capita remained below the median for most years is assigned category 'B', meaning 'below'.[18] The same exercise is carried out for 1995–2005. Because it is possible for a country to switch categories, we have four possible combinations:[19]

AA – Countries with GDP per capita above Africa's median GDP per capita for most years of the first and second periods;

BB – Countries with GDP per capita below Africa's median GDP per capita for most years of the first and second periods;

BA – Countries with GDP per capita that switches from below to above Africa's median GDP per capita from the first to the second period;

AB – Countries with GDP per capita that switches from above to below Africa's median GDP per capita from the first to the second period.

The results of this classification exercise are presented in Table 8.4. Figure 8.12 shows the GDP per capita by country group over time. Basic statistics on the country groups are presented in Table 8A.4.

Again, we find evidence of two clubs – rich nations and poor nations – with little mobility between them.[20] GDP per capita is four times higher in AA countries than in BB countries, and *t*-statistics reject the equality of means of GDP per capita between the two groups. There was also increasing divergence in income levels between the two groups over time (Figure 8.12). Income per capita on average remained largely stagnant for AA countries between 1975 and 1995, but it increased substantially thereafter. The average per capita income of the BB countries declined until around 1995, after which there was a slight recovery, but the average real income of the BB group was the same in 2005 as in 1975. The CV of GDP per capita of AA countries increased from 0.77 in 1975–1994 to 0.87 in 1995–2005. The CV of the BB group increased from 0.26 to 0.30. Thus, part of the increasing income inequality identified above, in Rich country, poor country, is driven by the large and rising income dispersion among countries in the richer group.

The AA group had higher mean growth over the whole period 1975–2005 (0.85 per cent) than BB (0.39 per cent). Growth was more erratic in the poorer countries. The coefficient of variation of growth is 4.67 for the BB category and 1.37 for the AA group. Given the high variance of growth rates, we cannot reject the hypothesis of equal mean growth rates in AA and BB countries between 1975 and 2005. Between 1995 and 2005 the two groups had virtually identical growth rates of about 1.60 per cent per year. Within each group there is a wide diversity of growth performance. Growth rates in the AA group, for example, range from 6.24 per cent for Botswana to –1.26 per cent for Zimbabwe. The range of growth outcomes is somewhat more compact for the BB group, varying between 2.07 per cent for Mozambique and –1.38 per cent for Madagascar. All five of the region's fastest growing economies for the period 1975–2005 are in the AA group.

One striking, and disappointing, feature from the point of view of hunting for leopards is the small number of transitional cases (BA or AB). BA countries comprise only Equatorial Guinea and Sudan, both oil exporters. These economies grew on average by 4.4 per cent a year over the entire period, but their expansion was driven by very rapid growth in 1995–2005, when annual growth was 8.3 per cent (from 1.8 per cent in the first period). That boom enabled their GDP per capita to increase by 60 per cent between 1975 and 2005. The AB economies – the Central African Republic and the Democratic Republic of the Congo – collapsed, mainly as a result of conflicts, leading mean GDP per capita to shrink by more than half.

Given the diversity of growth experiences within our stable lower- and higher-income groups, it is possible our leopards are emerging within groups rather than between the groups. To continue our search for growth leaders, we use a variation of the methodology developed by Hausmann *et al.* (2005) to identify growth

Table 8.4 Countries by country groups, growth and other characteristics

Country group	Shrinking economies (mean growth below 0)		Stagnant economies (mean growth between 0 & 0.71%)		Growing economies (mean growth above 0.71%)	
AA	Comoros[c]	(−0.14)	Angola[a]	(0.70)	Botswana[b]	(6.24)
	Côte d'Ivoire[a]	(−1.57)	Gambia[c]	(0.29)	Cape Verde[c]	(3.26)
	Gabon[a]	(−0.91)	Ghana[c]	(0.60)	Cameroon[a]	(0.81)
	Togo[c]	(−0.60)	Guinea[b]	(0.62)	Lesotho[d]	(3.27)
	Zimbabwe[d]	(−1.26)	Mauritania[c]	(0.10)	Mauritius[c]	(4.22)
			Senegal[c]	(0.36)	Namibia[b]	(1.15)
			South Africa[c]	(0.12)	Seychelles[c]	(2.47)
					Swaziland[d]	(1.15)
BB	Burundi[d]	(−1.26)	Benin[c]	(0.60)	Burkina Faso[d]	(1.21)
	Guinea-Bissau[c]	(−0.70)	Congo[a]	(0.61)	Chad[a]	(1.34)
	Madagascar[c]	(−1.38)	Ethiopia[d]	(0.42)	Eritrea[c]	(1.96)
	Niger[d]	(−1.00)	Kenya[c]	(0.48)	Mali[d]	(0.86)
	Sierra Leone[b]	(−0.57)	Malawi[d]	(0.22)	Mozambique[c]	(2.07)
	Zambia[b]	(−1.16)	Nigeria[a]	(0.29)	Rwanda[d]	(1.68)
					Tanzania[c]	(1.69)
					Uganda[d]	(1.92)
BA					Equatorial Guinea[a]	(10.55)
					Sudan[a]	(1.72)
AB	Central African Rep.[d]	(−1.27)				
	DRC[d]	(−3.95)				

Source: Authors' computations.

Notes: 0.71% is the mean growth rate in 1975–2005; Mean growth rate in parentheses;
a Oil exporter.
b Non-oil resource intensive.
c Non-resource intensive, coastal country.
d Non-resource intensive, landlocked country.

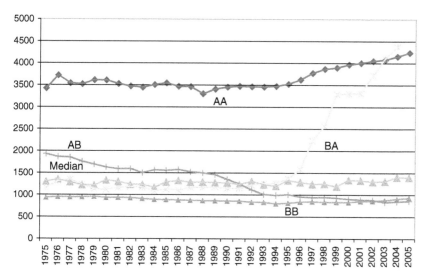

Figure 8.12 GDP per capita by country group

Source: Authors' computations.

accelerations (good times) and decelerations (bad times). Our approach (Arbache and Page 2007) differs from theirs and that of researchers applying their method to Africa (IMF 2007) in two important respects. First, it identifies both growth accelerations *and* decelerations in a cross-section of countries. Second, it does not use a common threshold growth rate to identify growth accelerations. Instead, it defines good and bad times relative to each country's long-run economic performance. This seems appropriate in Africa's volatile, low-growth environment.

Four conditions define good times for a given country:

– First, the 4-year forward-moving average of GDP per capita growth minus the four-year backward-moving average is greater than zero for a given year;
– Second, the 4-year forward-moving average of growth is above the country's long-run trend;
– Third, the 4-year forward-moving average of GDP per capita exceeds the 4-year backward-moving average; and
– Fourth, the first three conditions are satisfied for at least 3 years in a row, followed by the 3 subsequent years after the last year that satisfies the first three conditions.

Growth decelerations – bad times – are defined by the opposites of the first three conditions for good times and the presence of the fourth.

Table 8.5 shows the relative frequency of accelerations and decelerations, and their respective growth rates, for different periods. Between 1975 and 2005, there

Table 8.5 Likelihood and growth rates of economic acceleration and deceleration in Africa, 1975–2005

Period	All country–years in the period		Country–years with acceleration		Country–years with deceleration		Country–years with trend growth	
	Observations (country–yrs)	Growth rate	Frequency (of country–yrs)	Growth rate	Frequency (of country–yrs)	Growth rate	Frequency (of country–yrs)	
1995–2005 (after trend break)	494	1.88	0.42	3.76	0.12	−1.29	0.46	
1975–94 (before trend break)	749	−0.07	0.14	3.39	0.29	−3.14	0.57	
1985–94	433	−0.23	0.21	3.21	0.36	−3.18	0.43	
1975–84	316	0.13	0.04	4.61	0.18	−3.06	0.78	
1975–2005 (all years)	1,243	0.7	0.25	3.64	0.22	−2.74	0.53	

Source: Authors' computations.

was a slightly higher probability that the representative African economy was in a growth acceleration than a deceleration: 25 per cent of the 1,243 total observations per country per year identify growth accelerations, while 22 per cent identify growth decelerations.[21] The remaining country-year observations reflect normal economic times with countries growing at about their trend growth rate. Countries that experienced growth accelerations managed to grow on average by 3.6 per cent per year during those episodes, compared with the region-wide mean of 0.7 per cent. During decelerations, countries contracted on average by –2.7 per cent. Consistent with the region's long-run growth trend, the period 1995–2005 saw a substantial increase in the frequency of growth accelerations and a corresponding reduction in growth declines compared with the previous 20 years.

Table 8.6 shows the frequency of growth accelerations by country for the three periods of our analysis. Most countries experienced a higher frequency of growth accelerations after 1995 compared with 1975–1994. Burkina Faso and Ghana were in a growth acceleration during the entire period 1995–2005, and Mali, Namibia, Nigeria, Sao Tome and Principe, Sudan and Tanzania accelerated at a frequency above 70 per cent. Burundi, Congo, Guinea-Bissau, Kenya, Lesotho, Mauritius and Swaziland in contrast had a reduction in the frequency of growth accelerations relative to earlier periods.

Table 8.7 presents information on growth rates by country on average and during acceleration episodes for the relevant time periods. The last two columns show the deviation of the growth rate during accelerations from trend (1975–2005).[22]

We could attempt to use the increase in the relative frequency of growth accelerations as a criterion for identifying potential leopards. Using that criterion alone would lead us towards picking such dramatically improved performers as Burkina Faso, Ghana, Mali, Sudan and Tanzania, for example. It would, however, also lead us to exclude such historically strong economies as Botswana, Lesotho and Mauritius. This is partly an artefact of our method of identifying growth accelerations. Because we define an acceleration (or deceleration) relative to an economy's own long-run trend growth rate, a sustained small improvement from a low long-run trend, while clearly beneficial, would not qualify for leopard status.

Rather, we identify potential leopards as those countries that had both sustained long-run growth and a high frequency of growth accelerations using the following four criteria:

- The mean growth for the economy equals or exceeds mean per capita growth for the entire period 1975–2005 (0.71 per cent).
- The mean growth rate for the economy in the period 1995–2005 equals or exceeds mean per capita growth for 1979–2005 (1.88 per cent).
- The frequency of growth accelerations for the economy during 1995–2005 equals or exceeds the mean frequency for 1995–2005 (0.42).
- The growth rate of the economy during growth accelerations in 1995–2005 equals or exceeds the mean for all growth accelerations 1975–2005 (3.64 per cent).

Table 8.6 Likelihood of growth acceleration by country

Country	1975–2005	1975–1994	1995–2005	Frequency of growth acceleration (1995–2005) above the region's average of 0.42?
Angola	0.48	0.43	0.55	Yes
Benin	0.27	0.11	0.55	Yes
Botswana	0.43	0.37	0.55	Yes
Burkina Faso	0.43	0.11	1.00	Yes
Burundi	0.20	0.32	0.00	No
Cameroon	0.23	0.00	0.64	Yes
Cape Verde	0.42	0.23	0.64	Yes
Central African	0.23	0.00	0.64	Yes
Chad	0.20	0.00	0.55	Yes
Comoros	0.24	0.00	0.55	Yes
Congo, Dem. Rep.	0.00	0.00	0.00	No
Congo, Rep.	0.20	0.32	0.00	No
Côte d'Ivoire	0.20	0.05	0.45	Yes
Equatorial Guinea	0.42	0.22	0.60	Yes
Eritrea	0.00	0.00	0.00	No
Ethiopia	0.25	0.15	0.36	No
Gabon	0.00	0.00	0.00	No
Gambia, The	0.00	0.00	0.00	No
Ghana	0.43	0.11	1.00	Yes
Guinea	0.37	0.25	0.45	Yes
Guinea-Bissau	0.23	0.37	0.00	No
Kenya	0.20	0.32	0.00	No
Lesotho	0.23	0.37	0.00	No
Madagascar	0.00	0.00	0.00	No
Malawi	0.23	0.16	0.36	No
Mali	0.33	0.05	0.82	Yes
Mauritania	0.00	0.00	0.00	No
Mauritius	0.28	0.50	0.00	No
Mozambique	0.32	0.07	0.64	Yes
Namibia	0.32	0.00	0.73	Yes
Niger	0.00	0.00	0.00	No
Nigeria	0.53	0.37	0.82	Yes
Rwanda	0.20	0.00	0.55	Yes
Senegal	0.27	0.05	0.64	Yes
Seychelles	0.53	0.53	0.55	Yes
Sierra Leone	0.20	0.00	0.55	Yes
South Africa	0.23	0.00	0.64	Yes
Sudan	0.30	0.00	0.82	Yes
Swaziland	0.27	0.42	0.00	No
Tanzania	0.47	0.00	0.73	Yes
Togo	0.20	0.05	0.45	Yes
Uganda	0.30	0.25	0.36	No
Zambia	0.23	0.00	0.64	Yes
Zimbabwe	0.20	0.11	0.36	No
Total	0.25	0.14	0.42	

Source: Authors' computations.

Table 8.7 Growth rate during acceleration, by country

Country	Growth rate (%)			Growth rate during acceleration (%)			Deviation from growth acceleration trend (%)	
	Average	1975–1994	1995–2005	1975–2005	1975–1994	1995–2005	1975–1994	1995–2005
Angola	0.70	-3.34	5.84	3.93	1.55	6.30	-60.49	60.49
Benin	0.60	0.07	1.50	1.60	0.22	2.07	-86.43	28.81
Botswana	6.24	6.50	5.78	6.87	7.41	6.24	7.85	-9.16
Burkina Faso	1.21	0.96	1.66	1.39	-0.06	1.66	-104.39	18.98
Burundi	-0.46	0.58	-2.26	1.48	1.48	NA	NA	NA
Cameroon	0.81	0.14	1.97	2.21	NA	2.21	NA	0.00
Cape Verde	3.26	3.14	3.40	3.57	3.19	3.73	-10.52	4.51
Central African Republic	-1.27	-1.81	-0.34	0.89	NA	0.89	NA	0.00
Chad	1.34	-0.30	4.18	7.66	NA	7.66	NA	0.00
Comoros	-0.14	-0.36	0.13	0.11	NA	0.11	NA	0.00
Congo, Dem. Rep.	-3.95	-4.85	-2.38	NA	NA	NA	NA	NA
Congo, Rep.	0.61	0.75	0.37	10.05	10.05	NA	0.00	NA
Côte d'Ivoire	-1.57	-2.47	-0.02	1.82	-2.12	2.61	-216.47	43.29
Equatorial Guinea	10.55	0.66	19.45	20.88	3.09	26.81	-85.19	28.40
Eritrea	1.96	17.24	-0.82	NA	NA	NA	NA	NA
Ethiopia	0.42	-1.37	2.54	3.71	8.16	1.49	119.81	-59.90
Gabon	-0.91	-1.43	-0.01	NA	NA	NA	NA	NA
Gambia, The	0.29	0.04	0.73	NA	NA	NA	NA	NA
Ghana	0.60	-0.40	2.31	2.15	1.30	2.31	-39.67	7.21
Guinea	0.97	0.31	1.46	1.78	0.28	2.39	-84.30	33.72
Guinea-Bissau	-0.70	0.08	-2.05	0.76	0.76	NA	0.00	NA
Kenya	0.48	0.39	0.64	1.76	1.76	NA	0.00	NA
Lesotho	3.27	3.78	2.39	3.83	3.83	NA	0.00	NA
Madagascar	-1.38	-2.26	0.14	NA	NA	NA	NA	NA
Malawi	0.22	-0.89	2.15	1.68	-3.54	5.59	-310.57	232.93
Mali	0.86	-0.29	2.85	2.75	-1.75	3.25	-163.73	18.19

(Continued)

Table 8.7 (Continued)

Country	Growth rate (%)			Growth rate during acceleration (%)			Deviation from growth acceleration trend (%)	
	Average	1975–1994	1995–2005	1975–2005	1975–1994	1995–2005	1975–1994	1995–2005
Mauritania	0.10	−0.42	0.99	NA	NA	NA	NA	NA
Mauritius	4.22	4.67	3.65	5.65	5.65	NA	0.00	NA
Mozambique	2.07	−0.61	5.49	5.08	3.08	5.37	−39.32	5.62
Namibia	0.15	−1.12	1.75	2.14	NA	2.14	NA	0.00
Niger	−1.00	−1.55	−0.07	NA	NA	NA	NA	NA
Nigeria	0.28	−0.57	1.74	1.99	2.01	1.97	1.09	−0.85
Rwanda	1.68	−0.51	5.47	2.27	NA	2.27	NA	0.00
Senegal	0.36	−0.64	2.08	1.75	0.22	1.96	−87.61	12.52
Seychelles	2.47	3.58	0.54	4.01	4.27	3.58	6.43	−10.72
Sierra Leone	−0.57	−1.56	1.15	7.95	NA	7.95	NA	0.00
South Africa	0.12	−0.61	1.38	1.96	NA	1.96	NA	0.00
Sudan	1.72	0.39	4.02	3.90	NA	3.90	NA	0.00
Swaziland	1.15	1.56	0.45	4.63	4.63	NA	0.00	NA
Tanzania	1.69	−0.69	2.98	3.69	NA	3.69	NA	0.00
Togo	−0.60	−1.39	0.76	4.27	12.03	2.71	182.01	−36.40
Uganda	1.92	0.73	3.21	3.69	2.67	4.45	−27.66	20.74
Zambia	−1.23	−2.60	1.13	2.35	NA	2.35	NA	0.00
Zimbabwe	−1.26	−0.18	−3.14	2.61	2.95	2.45	12.89	−6.45

Source: Authors' computations.

We believe that these criteria reflect some of the most important characteristics of successful countries to emerge from our analysis of growth dynamics. A country meeting all four criteria would have grown faster than the regional average, both from 1975 to 2005, showing some growth persistence, and during 1995–2005, showing average growth above the rising trend. It would also have had a higher than average frequency of growth accelerations in 1995–2005 and would have grown during those accelerations at a rate that exceeded the overall regional average.

Eight countries – Angola, Botswana, Cape Verde, Chad, Mozambique, Equatorial Guinea, Sudan and Tanzania – (18.2 per cent of our sample) meet all four criteria.[23] This is a small enough set of countries, set sufficiently apart from their regional neighbours to provide a basis for identifying them as high performers.[24] The criteria are sufficiently restrictive that only an additional four countries in the sample – Cameroon, Mali, Rwanda and Uganda – meet three out of four. The remaining 32 countries (73 per cent of the sample) meet two or fewer criteria.

There are some surprises in the results, at least from the perspective of popular views on recent African growth. Burkina Faso, Ethiopia, Ghana, Rwanda, Senegal and Uganda, all praised in recent donor publications as good performers (see for example World Bank 2007), do not appear among our leopard candidates, although most meet at least two of the criteria and Rwanda and Uganda meet three. Mauritius and Lesotho, sustained growers for the past 30 years, fail to make the cut due to the absence of growth accelerations in 1995–2005.

In terms of our prior classification of countries by income groups, both transitional (BA) economies, Equatorial Guinea and Sudan, meet our four criteria. The remaining countries are drawn equally from the growing economies of both the AA and BB classifications (Table 8.4). Angola, Botswana and Cape Verde are growing AA economies; Chad, Mozambique and Tanzania are growing BB economies. Angola, Chad, Botswana, Equatorial Guinea and Sudan are resource rich. Cape Verde, Mozambique and Tanzania are more diversified, coastal economies. Botswana is the only landlocked country.

Have we found the leopards in these six economies? In light of the income dynamics described above, we should be cautious before declaring the hunt over. Perhaps the most worrying feature of our set of high performers is the presence of five resource-rich economies among the eight. One of these, Botswana, is a perennial growth leader, not just in Africa but globally. It certainly has much to offer to other resource-rich countries in Africa in terms of lessons of 30 years of experience in transforming natural resource wealth into economic growth. But, given the history of resource abundant economies in Africa – and the negative income dynamics we note for several mineral dependent economies – we are somewhat reluctant to identify the other resource-rich economies in the sample as long-run growth leaders. Elsewhere (Arbache and Page 2007) we have shown that conflicts are associated with a higher probability of growth declines. Angola, Chad and Sudan all have a recent history of conflicts, making the durability of their growth uncertain.

Of the diversified, coastal economies, Cape Verde has the longest history of economic success, but it is extremely small (although so too were Hong Kong and

Singapore at one time) and highly dependent on international migrant remittances for much of its income growth. Mozambique and Tanzania, both of which are diverse relatively large economies by African standards, may offer greater prospects of emerging as models for other coastal countries.

We may also have excluded some longer-term good performers such as Lesotho, Mauritius, Rwanda and Uganda unfairly, by placing substantial weight on the frequency and pace of recent growth accelerations. Because our definition of growth accelerations is relative to the long-run rate of growth of the economy, these long-run growers may be victims of their own success; by growing relatively fast achieving further accelerations is made that much more difficult. Alternatively, had we placed even greater weight on growth accelerations, we might have included Burkina Faso, Ghana, Mali, Namibia and Nigeria among the list of countries with increasing growth potential, given the high frequency with which they experienced accelerated growth in 1995–2005.

To sum up, we believe that our hunt for leopards has been a moderate success. Not surprisingly, many of Africa's potential growth leaders are rich in natural resources. For them – to the extent that oil and minerals prices remain high – the challenge will be less about maintaining growth than about using resource rents well. Botswana has shown that this is possible, but, given the history of natural resource revenue management in Africa, it may be the only true leopard to emerge from this group. We are somewhat more optimistic about the group of diversified economies. Cape Verde has a long track record of good and accelerating economic growth. Mozambique and Tanzania clearly have shown growth potential. If we add the 'near misses' – Lesotho, Mauritius, Rwanda and Uganda – to the list, we have a group of economies from which some leopards seem likely to emerge.

Conclusions

This chapter has examined some long-run features of the growth and distribution of GDP per capita among countries in sub-Saharan African. Our main goal was to identify the long-run patterns and regularities in income dynamics across countries and to search for leopards—economies that stood out with respect to the speed and persistence of their growth. Our main findings are as follows:

–   *Growth has been low and volatile.* African countries have erratic growth around a low mean. Growth is extremely volatile across Africa, and this phenomenon is not restricted to economies with any specific economic or geographic attributes.
–   *Growth has accelerated since the mid 1990s.* A structural break in both the per capita income and growth series for the region took place around 1995, when the growth rate accelerated significantly across the continent. More countries experienced more frequent growth accelerations relative to their long-run trend, and the distribution of growth rates began to converge.
–   *There is significant inertia in the distribution of income across countries.* Our econometric results indicate that there is no convergence of incomes taking place across Africa, and that at the individual country level there is a

high degree of inertia in average per capita incomes. Income in 1975 is a good predictor of average income for both the whole of 1975–2005 and for 1995–2005.

– *Africa's cross-country income distribution is becoming less equal.* Africa can be divided into rich and poor income clubs. Despite recent improvements in growth performance in poor countries, the richest countries have grown more in the long-run, and that has increased the income gap. As a consequence, the distribution of incomes among countries in Africa is becoming less equal.

– *Initial conditions matter a great deal for income distribution but not for growth.* Initial conditions, represented by the economy's 1975 level of income, seem to be the single most important factor explaining income levels. Whatever the mechanics behind this phenomenon, it exerts a strong and persistent influence on income determination and on the structure of income among countries. We do not find evidence that initial conditions are associated with long-run growth.

– *A small number of countries have emerged as possible 'leopards', but we remain uncertain as to the durability of their growth.* Using a combination of income transitions, growth thresholds and growth accelerations, we identify eight economies as Africa's potential growth leaders. Five of the eight, however, are resource-rich economies, which our analysis of growth dynamics suggests may underperform their potential. One of these, Botswana, is a long-time high performer. The four other resource-rich economies – Angola, Chad, Equatorial Guinea and Sudan – meet our criteria, but we are somewhat reluctant to identify them as leopards. Of the diversified coastal economies, Cape Verde has the longest history of economic success, but is highly dependent on international remittances for much of its income growth. Mozambique and Tanzania may offer prospects of emerging as models for other African economies.

We began this chapter by asking whether the growth turn-around in Africa marked a reversal of the nearly three-decade decline in Africa's economic fortunes. We found evidence of a statistically significant rise in growth and per capita incomes for the region, but we are left wondering whether the good times will last. While growth on average has accelerated and volatility has declined since 1995, we still find considerable inertia in Africa's income dynamics, even post-1995. The level where the typical country had started in 1975 pretty much determined where it ended up in terms of average income. The rich and poor country clubs were remarkably stable and there were very few transitional cases. The rich were getting a bit richer, but the poor were getting richer more slowly, which led to rising inequality in the country-level distribution of incomes. We identify a small number of high performing economies, but most of these were resource rich. And, while we find some potential leopards among the region's more diversified economies, Africa will need more growth leaders, drawn from a wider variety of geological and geographical circumstances, before we can confidently assert that it has turned the corner.

Appendix 8A

Table 8A.1 Descriptive statistics for the countries sampled, 1975–2005

Country	GDP per capita					GDP per capita growth				
	1975	2005	Mean annual	Standard deviation	Coefficient of variation	Mean annual	Standard deviation	Min	Max	Coefficient of variation
Angola	860	2,077	1,608	242.5	0.151	0.70	8.31	-27.13	17.21	11.92
Benin	–	1,015	914	56.3	0.062	0.60	2.96	-7.64	6.38	4.95
Botswana	1,820	11,021	5,474	2637.0	0.482	6.24	3.36	-0.58	16.07	0.54
Burkina Faso	763	1,079	918	81.5	0.089	1.21	3.30	-4.36	7.16	2.72
Burundi	738	622	785	104.1	0.133	-0.46	4.65	-8.92	9.18	-10.02
Cameroon	1,702	2,045	2,054	345.6	0.168	0.81	6.51	-10.51	18.42	8.00
Cape Verde	–	5,162	3,686	799.0	0.217	3.26	2.52	-1.56	8.51	0.77
CAR	1,646	1,089	1,330	201.6	0.152	-1.27	4.42	-10.70	6.47	-3.48
Chad	972	1,270	879	133.9	0.152	1.34	9.57	-23.04	25.23	7.13
Comoros	–	1,773	1,845	107.1	0.058	-0.14	3.23	-7.85	6.24	-22.65
Congo, Dem. Rep.	2,214	635	1,271	539.4	0.425	-3.95	5.07	-16.59	3.54	-1.28
Congo, Rep.	998	1,123	1,163	181.6	0.156	0.61	6.77	-11.77	19.76	11.14
Côte d'Ivoire	2,433	1,466	1,881	429.3	0.228	-1.57	4.51	-15.14	7.81	-2.87
Equatorial Guinea	–	–	2,859	2110.0	0.738	10.55	17.62	-6.16	67.09	1.67
Eritrea	–	986	1,078	134.5	0.125	1.96	9.11	-16.30	20.92	4.66
Ethiopia	–	938	817	76.7	0.094	0.42	7.78	-13.87	16.43	18.41
Gabon	9,323	6,187	7,041	1389.3	0.197	-0.91	9.60	-26.25	31.80	-10.60
Gambia, The	1,584	1,709	1,633	50.9	0.031	0.29	2.92	-6.09	7.24	9.90
Ghana	1,885	2,206	1,756	201.1	0.115	0.60	3.78	-10.08	6.70	6.33
Guinea	1,019	2,060	1,873	122.0	0.065	0.97	1.55	-2.64	3.41	1.59
Guinea-Bissau	–	736	921	104.3	0.113	-0.70	8.36	-29.98	14.81	-11.95
Kenya	963	1,103	1,051	39.7	0.038	0.48	2.29	-3.89	5.49	4.78
Lesotho	1,176	2,967	2,102	517.8	0.246	3.27	5.47	-5.77	19.04	1.67
Madagascar	1,290	821	947	154.6	0.163	-1.38	4.68	-15.19	6.92	-3.39

(Continued)

Table 8A.1 (Continued)

Country	GDP per capita					GDP per capita growth				
	1975	2005	Mean annual	Standard deviation	Coefficient of variation	Mean annual	Standard deviation	Min	Max	Coefficient of variation
Malawi	579	593	565	40.1	0.071	0.22	5.41	−11.03	15.13	24.57
Mali	742	919	764	80.0	0.105	0.86	5.49	−13.45	10.92	6.36
Mauritania	1,963	1,988	1,915	63.1	0.033	0.10	3.40	−6.62	6.96	34.58
Mauritius	–	11,312	7,318	2327.4	0.318	4.22	1.66	1.69	8.46	0.39
Mozambique	–	1,105	704	168.7	0.24	2.07	7.34	−17.45	14.75	3.54
Namibia	–	6,749	5,875	415.9	0.071	0.15	2.89	−5.11	5.03	19.82
Niger	985	695	829	150.5	0.181	−1.00	5.45	−19.42	10.04	−5.43
Nigeria	961	1,003	865	90.6	0.105	0.28	5.15	−15.54	8.20	18.67
Rwanda	840	1,073	1,031	123.9	0.12	1.68	12.25	−47.00	37.48	7.28
Senegal	1,468	1,594	1,408	80.3	0.057	0.36	4.12	−6.77	12.19	11.57
Seychelles	7,363	14,329	12,113	2954.6	0.244	2.47	6.91	−9.23	19.28	2.80
Sierra Leone	935	717	770	166.8	0.217	−0.57	7.97	−19.26	21.82	−14.04
South Africa	9,625	9,884	9,242	517.5	0.056	0.12	2.41	−4.33	4.17	20.64
Sudan	1,161	1,853	1,287	220.6	0.171	1.72	5.52	−8.80	13.09	3.21
Swaziland	3,103	4,292	3,664	578.0	0.158	1.15	3.64	−5.19	11.13	3.17
Tanzania	–	662	529	53.3	0.101	1.69	2.65	−2.73	5.06	1.57
Togo	1,708	1,340	1,490	182.5	0.123	−0.60	6.44	−17.14	12.05	−10.68
Uganda	–	1,293	976	181.3	0.186	1.92	3.15	−6.59	8.09	1.64
Zambia	1,351	910	981	182.3	0.186	−1.23	4.01	−10.92	4.31	−3.26
Zimbabwe	2,784	1,813	2,526	253.2	0.1	−1.26	5.71	−11.25	10.46	−4.53

Table 8A.2 GDP per capita and median by year

	Angola	Benin	Botswana	Burkina Faso	Burundi	Cameroon	Cape Verde	CAR	Chad	Comoros	Congo, Demi. Rep.
1975		860	1,820	763	738	1,702	–	1,646	972		2,214
1976		845	1,946	812	784	1,563	–	1,698	981	–	2,031
1977		863	2,107	798	856	1,726	–	1,722	983	–	1,982
1978		849	2,328	818	829	2,044	–	1,700	959	–	1,817
1979		878	2,523	831	820	2,105	–	1,616	738	–	1,768
1980	1,909	909	2,731	821	805	2,005	–	1,503	679	1,861	1,753
1981	1,728	967	2,880	838	875	2,282	2,409	1,439	672	1,883	1,742
1982	1,667	956	3,123	898	837	2,386	2,492	1,505	692	1,951	1,684
1983	1,677	883	3,419	881	839	2,481	2,704	1,344	782	1,993	1,660
1984	1,719	921	3,593	845	812	2,593	2,922	1,431	778	2,021	1,703
1985	1,725	958	3,730	894	877	2,724	3,086	1,449	923	2,014	1,662
1986	1,726	947	3,913	944	876	2,824	3,097	1,465	861	1,999	1,690
1987	1,817	903	4,250	905	894	2,683	3,112	1,362	816	1,979	1,685
1988	1,874	905	4,933	937	911	2,401	3,230	1,356	914	1,980	1,642
1989	1,836	850	5,423	918	898	2,290	3,341	1,353	930	1,867	1,571
1990	1,782	848	5,633	878	907	2,089	3,289	1,292	864	1,912	1,418
1991	1,709	856	5,894	927	931	1,954	3,257	1,253	910	1,762	1,253
1992	1,541	858	5,911	904	923	1,842	3,283	1,142	954	1,872	1,079
1993	1,123	856	5,877	919	851	1,737	3,429	1,115	780	1,888	900
1994	1,127	862	5,949	902	807	1,650	3,578	1,140	834	1,751	836
1995	1,209	872	6,074	918	735	1,663	3,754	1,192	819	1,776	817
1996	1,311	892	6,279	957	670	1,705	3,813	1,118	813	1,717	789
1997	1,382	919	6,784	980	655	1,751	3,927	1,152	833	1,749	729
1998	1,443	933	7,374	963	681	1,800	4,121	1,182	864	1,727	704
1999	1,455	949	7,795	1,000	666	1,839	4,373	1,202	832	1,740	660
2000	1,462	974	8,349	986	650	1,877	4,555	1,209	801	1,718	601
2001	1,469	991	8,724	1,013	648	1,923	4,618	1,208	855	1,739	574
2002	1,635	1,003	9,184	1,024	659	1,962	4,717	1,183	894	1,773	578
2003	1,641	1,009	9,761	1,056	630	2,003	4,893	1,079	991	1,779	594
2004	1,772	1,008	10,354	1,063	639	2,039	4,994	1,080	1,241	1,737	615
2005	2,077	1,015	11,021	1,079	622	2,045	5,162	1,089	1,270	1,773	635

(Continued)

Table 8A.2 (Continued)

Congo, Rep.	Côte d'Ivoire	Equatorial Guinea	Eritrea	Ethiopia	Gapon	Gambia, The	Ghana	Guinea	Guinea–Bissau	Kenya	Lesotho
998	2,433				9,323	1,584	1,885		1,019	963	1,176
977	2,623	–	–	–	12,288	1,646	1,783	–	1,030	948	1,276
862	2,687	–	–	–	10,435	1,648	1,792	–	916	1,000	1,519
889	2,842	–	–	–	7,696	1,697	1,912	–	993	1,030	1,755
947	2,775	–	–	–	7,506	1,622	1,827	–	973	1,068	1,761
1,079	2,355	–	–	–	7,469	1,668	1,790	–	790	1,086	1,669
1,230	2,324	–	–	909	7,614	1,668	1,676	–	907	1,084	1,637
1,473	2,220	–	–	891	7,155	1,602	1,507	–	923	1,059	1,633
1,510	2,036	–	–	935	7,326	1,718	1,387	–	873	1,033	1,539
1,564	1,894	–	–	886	7,632	1,719	1,454	–	933	1,012	1,657
1,497	1,896	1,266	–	764	7,220	1,644	1,478	–	950	1,018	1,701
1,350	1,880	1,188	–	807	6,934	1,648	1,507	1,717	921	1,051	1,677
1,310	1,802	1,209	–	897	5,561	1,625	1,534	1,728	924	1,075	1,708
1,290	1,756	1,219	–	868	6,073	1,633	1,575	1,787	942	1,102	1,859
1,282	1,745	1,185	–	827	6,380	1,664	1,610	1,802	973	1,115	1,982
1,254	1,667	1,201	–	814	6,496	1,659	1,618	1,818	1,002	1,124	2,080
1,244	1,614	1,161	–	721	6,674	1,650	1,656	1,770	1,022	1,104	2,134
1,236	1,560	1,255	804	621	6,254	1,646	1,673	1,748	1,000	1,061	2,205
1,185	1,510	1,301	913	723	6,205	1,638	1,706	1,744	988	1,033	2,255
1,085	1,478	1,334	1,104	722	6,225	1,585	1,716	1,758	988	1,030	2,305
1,102	1,538	1,487	1,126	739	6,465	1,545	1,742	1,803	1,000	1,046	2,377
1,112	1,612	1,875	1,210	806	6,606	1,526	1,779	1,834	1,085	1,062	2,581
1,069	1,658	3,133	1,277	815	6,796	1,547	1,811	1,880	1,124	1,041	2,756
1,073	1,693	3,729	1,263	761	6,758	1,549	1,854	1,929	787	1,050	2,597
1,007	1,679	5,149	1,221	791	6,188	1,595	1,893	1,978	826	1,050	2,577
1,055	1,582	5,103	1,022	814	6,175	1,631	1,920	1,974	863	1,033	2,592
1,061	1,553	5,058	1,071	859	6,208	1,674	1,954	2,009	840	1,049	2,662
1,077	1,505	5,813	1,031	841	6,100	1,572	1,997	2,048	757	1,032	2,750
1,053	1,459	6,516	1,046	798	6,159	1,634	2,056	2,028	739	1,041	2,834
1,059	1,462	7,005	1,021	879	6,149	1,671	2,126	2,037	732	1,067	2,927
1,123	1,466	–	986	938	6,187	1,709	2,206	2,060	736	1,103	2,967

(Continued)

Table 8A.2 (Continued)

	Madagascar	Malawi	Mali	Mauritania	Mauritius	Mozambique	Namibia	Niger	Nigeria	Rwanda
1975	1,290	579	742	1,963	–	–	–	985	961	840
1976	1,217	589	823	2,080	–	–	–	962	1,018	972
1977	1,213	597	855	1,991	–	–	–	1,006	1,047	959
1978	1,149	633	823	1,933	–	–	–	1,107	957	1,013
1979	1,228	640	889	1,977	–	–	–	1,150	992	1,096
1980	1,204	623	831	1,994	4,038	706	6,573	1,090	1,004	1,156
1981	1,057	574	775	2,013	4,170	724	6,502	1,064	848	1,183
1982	1,009	573	722	1,919	4,355	659	6,347	1,048	823	1,172
1983	989	578	738	1,944	4,438	544	6,094	968	759	1,208
1984	978	589	751	1,837	4,513	501	5,911	780	703	1,121
1985	961	589	650	1,849	4,744	501	5,743	815	751	1,128
1986	953	557	688	1,910	5,097	488	5,772	840	748	1,138
1987	937	532	668	1,904	5,528	560	5,707	815	722	1,082
1988	942	517	662	1,893	5,915	608	5,489	844	770	1,083
1989	953	497	722	1,939	6,200	645	5,338	826	802	1,058
1990	955	506	691	1,861	6,511	643	5,245	790	844	1,036
1991	869	537	685	1,850	6,825	658	5,462	785	859	1,048
1992	854	491	723	1,839	7,096	582	5,655	711	860	1,187
1993	847	535	689	1,900	7,406	599	5,366	699	855	1,183
1994	822	476	677	1,795	7,629	617	5,582	704	833	627
1995	811	548	700	1,920	7,872	616	5,635	699	831	862
1996	804	576	703	1,978	8,196	640	5,638	699	845	932
1997	809	583	730	1,847	8,568	692	5,702	694	846	974
1998	816	589	754	1,846	8,987	762	5,724	741	841	957
1999	829	589	782	1,914	9,391	801	5,767	712	830	940
2000	843	583	785	1,894	9,673	799	5,838	678	854	931
2001	869	541	854	1,891	10,100	885	5,868	701	860	951
2002	737	544	863	1,856	10,286	938	6,163	698	854	1,012
2003	788	564	900	1,901	10,504	992	6,295	711	924	1,005
2004	807	591	892	1,941	10,904	1,046	6,592	687	959	1,030
2005	821	593	919	1,988	11,312	1,105	6,749	695	1,003	1,073

(Continued)

Table 8A.2 (Continued)

Senegal	Seychelles	Sierra Leone	South Africa	Sudan	Swaziland	Tanzania	Togo	Uganda	Zambia	Zimbabwe	Median
1,468	7,363	935	9,625	1,161	3,103	–	1,708	–	1,351	2,784	1,290
1,559	8,406	914	9,631	1,313	2,942	–	1,634	–	1,387	2,708	1,313
1,480	7,753	898	9,422	1,352	2,879	–	1,708	–	1,282	2,445	1,480
1,388	9,248	902	9,503	1,233	2,825	–	1,850	–	1,248	2,306	1,388
1,449	10,560	925	9,649	1,134	2,822	–	1,708	–	1,172	2,305	1,449
1,365	9,984	951	10,051	1,115	3,075	–	1,897	–	1,170	2,546	1,586
1,313	9,062	961	10,335	1,159	2,994	_	1,772	–	1,201	2,759	1,538
1,473	8,872	989	10,041	1,187	2,917	–	1,646	844	1,130	2,723	1,505
1,463	8,643	950	9,606	1,173	2,888	–	1,498	865	1,071	2,658	1,463
1,364	8,961	968	9,837	1,080	2,976	–	1,521	834	1,033	2,505	1,454
1,374	9,884	894	9,469	985	2,994	–	1,547	779	1,015	2,577	1,464
1,394	9,797	880	9,231	1,013	3,260	–	1,516	754	990	2,533	1,465
1,406	10,158	915	9,193	1,132	3,623	–	1,471	755	983	2,470	1,406
1,433	10,629	826	9,353	1,106	3,746	501	1,516	787	1,012	2,564	1,395
1,372	11,727	811	9,365	1,180	3,962	503	1,529	807	971	2,611	1,363
1,385	12,438	824	9,147	1,092	4,169	520	1,481	829	938	2,710	1,339
1,341	12,645	836	8,869	1,147	4,146	513	1,432	846	912	2,783	1,253
1,334	13,379	675	8,501	1,194	4,066	499	1,342	846	872	2,470	1,236
1,270	14,003	685	8,426	1,219	4,080	488	1,112	887	907	2,442	1,183
1,273	13,663	672	8,514	1,202	4,087	480	1,246	915	808	2,614	1,140
1,304	13,302	616	8,592	1,244	4,111	482	1,305	989	766	2,572	1,209
1,337	13,753	642	8,765	1,286	4,139	491	1,374	1,047	799	2,793	1,286
1,347	15,218	524	8,793	1,336	4,160	496	1,517	1,068	806	2,827	1,336
1,372	16,177	511	8,633	1,389	4,162	503	1,429	1,087	774	2,872	1,372
1,420	16,160	459	8,626	1,445	4,185	509	1,414	1,140	774	2,738	1,414
1,427	16,790	463	8,764	1,506	4,167	524	1,358	1,167	785	2,498	1,358
1,458	16,404	527	8,841	1,567	4,150	546	1,315	1,185	808	2,411	1,315
1,440	16,121	642	9,064	1,636	4,191	573	1,332	1,219	820	2,289	1,332
1,498	15,270	670	9,229	1,695	4,224	602	1,332	1,234	848	2,039	1,332
1,553	14,815	691	9,533	1,750	4,258	631	1,337	1,257	879	1,950	1,337
1,594	14,329	717	9,884	1,853	4,292	662	1,340	1,293	910	1,813	1,317

Table 8A.3 Gross domestic product per capita and median by year: country-group assignment

	Period 1: 1975–1990																Period 2: 1991–2005															Code
	1975	1976	1977	1978	1979	1980	1981	1982	1983	1984	1985	1986	1987	1988	1989	1990	1991	1992	1993	1994	1995	1996	1997	1998	1999	2000	2001	2002	2003	2004	2005	
Angola	1	1	1	1	1	1	1	1	1	1	0	0	0	0	0	0	0	0	1	1	0	0	0	0	0	0	0	0	0	0	0	AA
Benin	0	0	0	1	0	0	0	0	0	0	1	1	1	1	1	1	1	1	1	1	1	1	1	1	1	1	1	1	1	1	1	BB
Botswana	1	1	1	0	0	1	0	0	0	0	0	0	0	0	0	0	0	0	0	0	0	0	0	0	0	0	0	0	0	0	0	AA
Burkina Faso	1	1	1	1	1	1	1	1	1	1	1	1	1	1	1	1	1	1	1	1	1	1	1	1	1	1	1	1	1	1	1	BB
Burundi	1	1	1	1	1	1	1	1	1	1	1	1	1	1	1	1	1	1	1	1	1	1	1	1	1	1	1	1	1	1	1	BB
Cameroon	0	0	0	0	0	0	0	0	0	0	0	0	0	0	0	0	0	0	0	0	0	0	0	0	0	0	0	0	0	0	0	AA
Cape Verde	0	0	0	0	0	0	0	0	0	0	0	0	0	0	0	0	0	0	0	0	0	0	0	0	0	0	0	0	0	0	0	AA
CAR	0	0	0	0	0	0	0	0	0	0	0	0	0	0	0	0	1	1	1	1	1	1	1	1	1	1	1	1	1	1	1	AB
Comoros	0	0	0	0	0	0	0	0	0	0	0	0	0	0	0	0	0	0	0	0	0	0	0	0	0	0	0	0	0	0	0	AA
Congo, D. R.	1	1	1	1	1	1	1	1	1	1	1	1	1	1	1	1	1	1	1	1	1	1	1	1	1	1	1	1	1	1	1	AB
Congo, Rep.	0	0	1	0	0	0	0	0	0	0	0	0	0	0	0	0	0	0	0	0	0	0	0	0	0	0	0	1	1	1	1	BB
Côte d'Ivoire	0	0	0	0	0	0	0	0	0	0	0	0	0	0	0	0	0	0	0	0	0	0	0	0	0	0	0	0	0	0	0	AA
Ethiopia	0	0	0	0	0	0	1	1	1	0	0	0	0	0	0	0	1	1	1	1	1	1	1	1	1	1	1	1	1	1	1	BB
Gabon	0	0	0	0	0	0	0	0	0	0	0	0	0	0	0	0	0	0	0	0	0	0	0	0	0	0	0	0	0	0	0	AA
Gambia, The	0	0	0	0	0	0	0	0	0	0	0	0	0	0	0	0	0	0	0	0	0	0	0	0	0	0	0	0	1	0	0	AA
Ghana	0	0	0	0	0	0	0	0	1	0	0	0	0	0	0	0	0	0	0	0	0	0	0	0	0	0	0	0	0	0	0	AA
Guinea	0	0	0	0	0	0	0	0	0	0	0	0	0	0	0	0	0	0	0	0	0	0	0	0	0	0	0	0	0	0	0	AA
Guinea-Bissau	1	1	1	1	1	1	1	1	1	1	1	1	1	1	1	1	1	1	1	1	1	1	1	1	1	1	1	1	1	1	1	BB
Kenya	1	1	1	1	1	1	1	1	1	1	1	1	1	1	1	1	1	1	1	1	1	1	1	1	1	1	1	1	1	1	1	BB
Lesotho	1	0	0	0	0	0	0	0	0	0	0	0	0	0	0	0	0	0	0	0	0	0	0	0	0	0	0	0	0	0	0	AA
Madagascar	1	1	1	1	1	1	1	1	1	1	1	1	1	1	1	1	1	1	1	1	1	1	1	1	1	1	1	1	1	1	1	BB
Malawi	1	1	1	1	1	1	1	1	1	1	1	1	1	1	1	1	1	1	1	1	1	1	1	1	1	1	1	1	1	1	1	BB
Mali	1	1	1	1	1	1	1	1	1	1	1	1	1	1	1	1	1	1	1	1	1	1	1	1	1	1	1	1	1	1	1	BB
Mauritania	0	0	0	0	0	0	0	0	0	0	0	0	0	0	0	0	0	0	0	0	0	0	0	0	0	0	0	0	0	0	0	AA

(Continued)

Table 8A.3 (Continued)

	Period 1: 1975–1990																Period 2: 1991–2005															Code
	1975	1976	1977	1978	1979	1980	1981	1982	1983	1984	1985	1986	1987	1988	1989	1990	1991	1992	1993	1994	1995	1996	1997	1998	1999	2000	2001	2002	2003	2004	2005	
Mauritius	1	1	1	1	1	0	0	0	0	0	0	0	0	0	0	0	0	0	0	0	0	0	0	0	0	0	0	0	0	0	0	AA
Niger	1	1	1	1	1	1	1	1	1	1	1	1	1	1	1	1	1	1	1	1	1	1	1	1	1	1	1	1	1	1	1	BB
Nigeria	1	1	1	1	1	1	1	1	1	1	1	1	1	1	1	1	1	1	1	1	1	1	1	1	1	1	1	1	1	1	1	BB
Rwanda	1	1	1	0	0	1	1	1	1	1	1	1	1	1	1	1	1	0	0	1	1	1	1	1	1	1	1	1	1	1	1	BB
Senegal	0	0	0	0	0	0	0	0	0	0	0	1	0	0	0	0	0	0	0	0	0	0	0	0	0	0	0	0	0	0	0	AA
Seychelles	0	0	0	0	0	0	0	0	0	0	0	0	0	0	0	0	0	1	0	0	0	0	0	0	0	0	0	0	0	0	0	AA
Sierra Leone	1	1	1	1	1	1	1	1	1	1	1	1	1	1	1	1	1	1	1	1	1	1	1	1	1	1	1	1	1	1	1	BB
South Africa	0	0	0	0	0	0	0	0	0	0	0	0	0	0	0	0	0	0	0	0	0	0	0	0	0	0	0	0	0	0	0	AA
Sudan	1	1	1	1	1	1	1	1	1	1	1	1	1	1	1	1	1	1	0	0	0	0	0	0	0	0	0	0	0	0	0	BA
Swaziland	0	0	0	0	0	0	0	0	0	0	0	0	0	0	0	0	0	0	0	0	0	0	0	0	0	0	1	0	0	0	0	AA
Tanzania	1	1	1	1	1	1	1	1	1	1	1	1	1	1	1	1	1	1	1	1	1	1	1	1	1	1	1	1	1	1	1	BB
Togo	0	0	0	0	0	0	0	0	0	0	0	0	0	1	1	1	1	1	1	1	1	1	0	1	0	0	0	0	0	0	0	AA
Uganda			0	1	1	1	1	1	1	1	1	1	1	1	1	1	1	1	1	0	0	0	0	0	0	1	1	1	1	1	0	BB
Zambia	0	0	1	1	1	1	1	1	1	1	1	1	1	1	1	1	1	1	1	0	0	1	1	1	0	1	1	1	1	1	1	BB
Zimbabwe	0	0	0	0	0	0	0	0	0	0	0	0	0	0	0	0	0	0	0	0	0	0	0	0	0	0	0	0	0	0	0	AA

Table 84.4 Country groups: basic statistics

	No. of countries	(countries)	Mean GDP per capita			Mean growth			SD of growth	CV of growth	Share of Africa's GDP (%)		Share of Africa's population (%)	
			1975	2005	1975–2005	1976–1994	1995–2005	1976–2005	1976–2005	1976–2005	1975–1980	2000–2005	1975	2005
AA	20	Angola, Botswana, Cameroon, Cape Verde, Comoros, Côte d'Ivoire, Gabon, Gambia, Ghana, Guinea, Lesotho, Mauritania, Mauritius. Namibia, Senegal, Seychelles, South Africa, Swaziland, Togo, and Zimbabwe	3,424	4,241	3,648	0.38	1.58	0.85	1.44	1.37	64.3	62.6	31.7	31.1
BB	20	Benin, Burkina Faso, Burundi, Chad, Congo, Eritrea, Ethiopia, Guinea-Bissau, Kenya, Madagascar, Malawi, Mali, Mozambique, Niger, Nigeria, Rwanda, Sierra Leone, Tanzania, Uganda, and Zambia.	931	933	880	–0.4	1.56	0.39	1.73	4.67	28.3	32.1	56.2	56.7
BA	2	Equatorial Guinea and Sudan	1,161	1,853	1,787	1.81	8.27	4.43	9.16	2.25	3.1	4	4.8	4.5
AB	2	Central African Republic and Democratic Republic of Congo	1,930	862	1,301	–3.33	–1.35	–2.6	3.46	–1.32	4.3	1.4	7.3	7.6

Source: Authors' computations.

The authors would like to thank the participants at the UNU-WIDER Development Conference on Southern Engines of Global Growth: China, India, Brazil and South Africa, held in Helsinki, Finland, 7–8 September 2008, for helpful comments and suggestions on an early version of this study.

Notes

1 Botswana and Mauritius are notable exceptions to this statement, a theme to which we shall return below.
2 1975 is the first year available for this indicator.
3 We thus have a panel of data with 44 countries and 31 time periods. Our sample accounts for 98.4 per cent of population and 99 per cent of regional GDP in 2005. Although Equatorial Guinea is in our sample, we removed the country from charts, econometrics and aggregate descriptive statistics, because its extremely high growth rates in recent years distort many of the results.
4 Although there are differences between GDP per capita at PPP and non-PPP, those differences are confined to levels and do not affect growth trajectories. PPP and non-PPP growth data share similar statistical properties. See Arbache and Page (2008) for a fuller discussion.
5 We employ the Hodrick–Prescott filter in Figure 8.1 to smooth the estimate of the long-run trend component of the GDP growth series.
6 We also find evidence of a structural break in the per capita income series at about the same time.
7 Equatorial Guinea, which ranks first, and Lesotho, which ranks fifth, have the same coefficient of variation of growth of about 1.7.
8 Gabon grew 31 per cent in 1976, biasing the results. Thus we removed it from the regression.
9 We have removed Rwanda from the regression and Figure 8.6b, because it grew by 37.5 per cent in 1995, distorting the results.
10 Easterly *et al.* (1993) find for a worldwide sample that correlation of growth across decades is also very low, averaging 0.3.
11 We employ the Hodrick-Prescott filter in Figure 8.7.
12 In 2005, those countries hosted about 8.5 per cent of the regional population, but produced 44 per cent of regional GDP.
13 The statistical and qualitative results remain the same when we remove outliers such as Botswana and the Democratic Republic of Congo from the regression.
14 We also split the sample into subperiods before 1990 and after 1990, and regress average growth in each period on the level of income in 1975. The estimated coefficients of both equations are not significant.
15 For countries for which GDP data were not available in 1975, we use the earliest available year.
16 We also calculate the year-to-year correlation coefficients of GDP per capita within countries over time. Most coefficients are large and significant, thus supporting the finding of significant inertia in income levels.
17 We also run the same model while controlling for growth SD, and the results are virtually the same.
18 Bosworth and Collins (2003) have a similar method for grouping countries. They group 84 countries from all regions as higher income and lower income, according to the per capita income above or below the median. However, they take the income per capita in 1960, their first year, as reference for grouping. Garner (2006) uses mean long-run growth rates to classify African countries. We also have tested other criteria for grouping countries, using means instead of medians, growth instead of GDP per capita level,

and clustering analysis, among others; but the present exercise provides the most robust results. We run the median exercise removing South Africa, but the classification of countries remains basically the same.

19 Tables 8A.2 and 8A.3 show the countries' GDP per capita and median by year and respective assignments to country groups.

20 To test the robustness of the country group classification we estimate pooled and fixed-effect regression models. Country group coefficients for income levels are statistically significant at the 5 per cent level; they are sizable and have the expected signs. These results suggest that the country group classifications are relevant and highly stable in predicting income levels (Arbache and Page 2008).

21 As a means of checking the robustness of the results, growth accelerations and decelerations are also identified by replacing 0 with +1 per cent and −1 per cent for acceleration and deceleration, respectively, in condition 1, but the results do not change substantially. Therefore, only the base-case results are reported, because they are less restrictive.

22 Burundi, Côte d'Ivoire, Malawi and Mali show negative mean growth rates during accelerations in 1975–1994. This is due to negative growth rates in the first year(s) of the acceleration episodes.

23 As Angola misses the first criterion by only 0.01, we decided to include it in the list.

24 These countries represented 16.5 per cent of the population and 15.6 per cent of regional GDP in 2005.

References

Arbache, J.S. and J. Page (2007). 'More Growth or Fewer Collapses? A New Look at Long Run Growth in Sub-Saharan Africa'. WB Policy Working Paper 4384. Washington, DC: World Bank.

Arbache, J.S. and J. Page (2008). 'Patterns of Long Term Growth in Sub-Saharan Africa'. In D. Go and J. Page (eds), *Africa at a Turning Point? Growth, Aid and External Shocks*. Washington, DC: World Bank.

Barro, R. (1991). 'Economic Growth in a Cross Section of Countries'. *Quarterly Journal of Economics*, 106(2): 407–43.

Barro, R.J. and X. Sala-i-Martin (1991). 'Convergence across States and Regions'. *Brooking Papers on Economic Activity*, 1: 107–82.

Bosworth, B.P. and S.M. Collins (2003). 'The Empirics of Growth: An Update'. *Brookings Papers on Economic Activity*, 2: 113–206.

Collier, P. (2007). *The Bottom Billion – Why the Poorest Countries are Failing and What Can Be Done about It*. New York: Oxford University Press.

Commission for Africa (2005). *Report of the Commission for Africa*.

Easterly, W., M. Kremer, L. Pritchett and L.H. Summers (1993). 'Good Policy or Good Luck? Country Growth Performance and Temporary Shocks'. *Journal of Monetary Economics*, 32(3): 459–83.

Garner, P. (2006). 'Economic Growth in Sub-Saharan Africa'. Rexburg, Idaho: Brigham Young University. Mimeo.

Hausmann, R., L. Pritchett and D. Rodrik (2005). 'Growth Accelerations'. *Journal of Economic Growth*, 10(4): 303–29.

IMF (International Monetary Fund) (2007). 'Sub-Saharan Africa Regional Economic Outlook: Fall 2007'. Document SM/07/319. Washington, DC: IMF.

McCoskey, S.K. (2002). 'Convergence in Sub-Saharan Africa: a Nonstationary Panel Data Approach'. *Applied Economics*, 34(7): 819–29.

Ndulu, B.J., L. Chakraborti, L. Lijane, V. Ramachandran and J. Wolgin (2007). *Challenges of African Growth – Opportunities, Constraints, and Strategic Directions*. Washington, DC: World Bank.

Quah, D. (1993a). 'Empirical Cross-Section Dynamics in Economic Growth'. *European Economic Review*, 37(2–3): 426–34.

Quah, D. (1993b). 'Galton's Fallacy and Tests of the Convergence Hypothesis'. *Scandinavian Journal of Economics*, 95(4): 427–43.

World Bank (2007). 'Accelerating Development Outcomes in Africa Progress and Change in the Africa Action Plan'. Development Committee Paper, Spring Meeting, 2007. Washington, DC: World Bank.

9 Growth and distributional aspects of poverty reduction in South Africa

Fiona Tregenna

Introduction

The South African government has targeted the halving of poverty by 2014. This study uses income and expenditure microdata to frame this goal in terms of specific measures of the poverty gap and poverty headcount ratio. This forms the basis for an analysis of under what growth and distributional scenarios the target could be achieved.

The disappointing record of income poverty reduction since democratization in South Africa highlights the challenge of significantly cutting poverty. Halving poverty by 2014 in South Africa, as per government's commitment in the Accelerated and Shared Growth Initiative – South Africa (AsgiSA) (Presidency of the Republic of South Africa 2006), would seem to require a serious shift in policy.

The actual policies that could be implemented to reduce poverty fall outside of the scope of this chapter. Rather, the focus is on what the commitment to halving poverty means in terms of growth and distribution, and under what growth–distributional scenarios these targets can be achieved.

I start by reviewing briefly the empirical literature on poverty trends in South Africa, and discussing the international literature on the relationships between poverty, growth and inequality. The next section analyses current poverty levels in South Africa, as a baseline for the discussion in the following section of the meaning of halving poverty. The section 'Growing out of poverty' assesses whether poverty can feasibly be halved through growth alone. With the answer in the negative, the section following that sets out a methodology for simulating pro-poor distributional changes. 'What combinations of growth and pro-poor distributional change could halve poverty?' discusses the effects on poverty of combining these distributional changes with various growth scenarios, before conclusions are presented.

Literature

The existing literature mostly points to an increase in poverty in South Africa in the late 1990s (see Leibbrandt et al. 2004; Meth and Dias 2004; Hoogeveen and Özler 2005; Ardington et al. 2005; Pauw and Mncube 2007). A study published by the South African government (Government of the Republic of South Africa 2008) claims decreases in the poverty gap and the poverty headcount ratio between 1995 and 2005, attributing these primarily to government's social welfare grants. Some studies, such as that of Van der Berg et al. (2005), point to a decline in poverty between 2000 and 2004.

There is international literature on each of the dimensions of the triangular relationship between growth, distribution/inequality, and poverty. In terms of the relationship between growth and poverty, Adams (2004) finds that economic growth reduces poverty in developing countries, but the rate of this reduction is highly sensitive to how growth is defined and measured. Fosu (2008) finds that greater income equality would positively affect the impact of growth on poverty reduction in African countries, with considerable heterogeneity among countries. Fanta and Upadhyay (2009) find that growth reduces poverty, with estimated elasticities between −0.5 and −1.1, in a sample of 16 African countries.

There is a corpus of literature on the effects of inequality on growth, and another concerning the effects of growth on inequality. The impact of growth on distribution is a priori indeterminate, and would be contingent on country-specific factors such as relative factor endowments and rewards (such as to capital and labour, and to various categories of labour). The effects of growth on inequality are also affected by the sectoral nature of growth, in terms of relative productivity in different sectors and the distributional characteristics of the sectors in which growth is highest. Broader political economic and institutional issues, such as the relative power of various groups, also affect the way in which growth affects distribution.

Empirically, according to Bourguignon (2004) there is too much country specificity in the impact of growth on inequality to allow for any generalization. Similarly, Ravallion (1995) finds that there are no systematic effects of growth on poverty.

The classical conception of the relationship between inequality and growth was expressed in Kuznets' (1955) inverted-U curve, according to which inequality initially rises with income per capita but falls at higher levels of income per capita. Especially in the earlier literature, this was interpreted as pointing to a trade-off between growth and equity, up to the turning point of the inverted-U. According to Bourguignon and Morrisson (1998), the inverted-U hypothesis was borne out empirically in the 1970s but has not been supported empirically since then. Zweimüller (2000) points to increases in inequality in several major OECD countries over the past three decades or so, but with significant variation between countries. According to Deininger and Squire (1998), there is very little support for a Kuznets curve when considering time-series data for most countries of the world.

Channels that have been identified in the literature through which inequality can contribute positively to growth include: the incentivization of work effort and risk-taking; the promotion of innovation; higher savings rates being associated with higher inequality; and concentration of wealth allowing for the large initial investments required for some types of production. Empirical work supporting a positive relationship between inequality and growth includes Forbes (2000) who finds evidence that, in the short and medium term, an increase in a country's level of income inequality has a significant positive effect on subsequent growth.

Conversely, there is extensive theoretical and empirical literature finding that inequality negatively affects growth; see: Alesina and Rodrik (1994), Persson and Tabellini (1994), Clarke (1995), Deininger and Squire (1998) and Aghion et al. (1999). Channels identified for such an effect include: inequality encouraging policies that are not conducive to growth; inequality leading to imperfections in credit, insurance and capital markets with negative effects on investment and growth; inequality leading to weak social capital, instability and conflict; inequality reducing work effort and productivity; and inequality leading to inefficient allocation of education resources with negative effects on human capital.

According to Ferreira (1999), the existing literature and evidence on the effects of inequality on growth suggest that income inequality may not directly affect growth, but that it proxies for wealth inequality, and that wealth inequality does significantly negatively affect growth. The balance of arguments and evidence, especially in the past two decades or so, indicates that inequality does negatively affect growth, with these effects being particularly pronounced for very high levels of inequality.

Bourguignon (2004) emphasizes that distribution matters for poverty reduction, and that comparative international evidence indicates that over the medium-run distributional changes can account for significant increases or decreases in poverty. Highlighting the country specificity of this relationship, he suggests that changing the distribution is likely to be more important than growth for reducing poverty in middle-income and inegalitarian countries.

How high is poverty in South Africa?

AsgiSA does not define exactly what is meant by 'poverty' and hence the precise meaning of the goal of halving poverty. The Minister of Finance announced in his 2005 Budget Speech that a poverty line would be developed for South Africa. A process ensued, led by National Treasury and the national statistical agency, Statistics South Africa, to develop a national poverty line, and the official government targets for halving poverty are then to be framed in terms of that line. The present study therefore uses the proposals contained in the official Statistics South Africa/National Treasury Discussion Document (2007) as a starting point to derive an appropriate line for this study. This is a semi-normative poverty line based on a cost of basic needs approach. Statistics South Africa calculates a food poverty line at R211 per capita per month (in 2000 prices).[1]

It is calculated as the minimum amount needed to buy enough food to meet an average person's basic daily food-energy requirements over a month. The measure is based on the daily energy requirement of 2,261 kilocalories per capita (as recommended by the South African Medical Research Council) without taking into account any differences in nutritional needs by gender or age. Statistics South Africa calculated the cost of meeting this minimum energy requirement, taking into account the types of foods typically available to low-income South Africans.

Statistics South Africa then estimates the non-food component of a poverty line as R111 per capita per month. This is based on the assumption that the non-food items typically purchased by a household that spends about R211 per capita per month on food can be treated as essential in the sense that these households are forgoing necessary food consumption to purchase these non-food items. Statistics South Africa bases the household poverty threshold on a pooling of resources within households, with equal weighting given to all members of the household (without any equivalence scaling).

Drawing on the Statistics South Africa/National Treasury Discussion Document (2007) and consultations with Statistics South Africa officials involved in the process, the study uses as a basis the lower poverty line suggested in the Discussion Document (R322 per capita per month in 2000 prices). This R322 baseline was inflated to March 2006 levels using the consumer price index (CPI) rates for the lowest two quintiles for all areas (Statistics South Africa 2008). (March 2006 is used because this is the month to which the data are calibrated. Further, note that AsgiSA was formally launched in February 2006.) The mean of these CPI rates for the lowest and second-lowest quintiles is used.

The resulting poverty line is R450 per capita per month, which is used as the baseline in the subsequent analysis. This poverty line yields a headcount ratio of 52.45 per cent (using expenditure) and 49.56 per cent (using income) in 2006. So, roughly half of South Africans fall below this poverty line. The aggregate poverty gap comes out at just under R60 billion (R59.65 billion using income and R59.82 billion using expenditure).

The various datasets of the 2005/6 Income and Expenditure Survey (IES) were utilized for this analysis. These are the official national household surveys produced by Statistics South Africa.

A full analysis of poverty would, of course, need to take into account the various monetary and non-monetary dimensions of poverty. These include not only the absolute level of income or expenditure, but also relative poverty, the meeting of basic needs, human dignity, and capabilities. The use of a monetary poverty line in this analysis is not intended to undermine the importance of these aspects. However, the use of a specific line is necessary for empirical analysis of the relationship between growth, distribution and poverty.

What does 'halving poverty' mean?

The poverty headcount ratio measures the incidence of poverty, which is an important dimension of poverty. The simplicity of this measure may make it intuitively appealing from a policy perspective. However, the poverty headcount ratio gives no indication of the intensity of poverty. One suitable measure of the intensity of poverty is the aggregate poverty gap, which is the aggregate sum of the gap between the poverty line and the income or expenditure of everyone falling below the poverty line.

The choice of a poverty measure has significant policy implications, especially when a specific cut in poverty is part of government policy. The purpose of a 'target' is not only to evaluate outcomes but also to inform policy design and implementation. Without the poorest people coming out of poverty, any increase in their incomes or expenditure does not reduce the poverty headcount ratio at all. Measuring poverty reduction only through the poverty headcount ratio could thus implicitly place less emphasis on raising the incomes or expenditure of the poorest. This is particularly important when about one-half of the population falls below the poverty line.

It is thus preferable, both for the analysis here and for government policy, to frame the target of halving poverty not just as halving the poverty headcount ratio, but as halving the poverty gap as well. While this may lose some of the appealing simplicity of using only the poverty headcount ratio, it seems justified by a more comprehensive standard of measure. The analysis that follows uses this dual measure of the 'halving of poverty': halving both the poverty headcount ratio and the aggregate poverty gap.

As both the income and expenditure poverty headcount ratios are in the region of 50 per cent, the target of halving poverty can be defined as reducing the poverty headcount ratio to 25 per cent of the population and reducing the aggregate poverty gap to R30 billion[2] by 2014.

Growing out of poverty?

We begin by investigating whether poverty can be halved through growth alone. AsgiSA sets gross domestic product (GDP) growth targets of at least 4.5 per cent annually between 2005 and 2009, and at least 6 per cent between 2010 and 2014. We consider how poverty would evolve by 2014 with these targeted growth rates and the current distributional structure. These and subsequent results are shown for expenditure; the results for income are very similar.

Neither the poverty gap nor the poverty headcount ratio can be halved with the current distribution of income or expenditure. The poverty headcount ratio would be reduced to 34 per cent (above the target of about 25 per cent) and the poverty gap would be cut to R32 billion (above the target of R30 billion). While these targeted growth rates would considerably reduce poverty, they cannot halve it with the current distributional structure.

We use TIP curves to show the poverty gap and poverty headcount ratio under the current distributions of income and expenditure, the effects on these of the AsgiSA-targeted growth rates and, in the next section, to show what combinations of growth and distributional change would allow for halving the poverty gap and poverty headcount ratio. Derived from Jenkins and Lambert (1997), 'TIP' refers to the 'Three I's of Poverty': the incidence, intensity and inequality of poverty. TIP curves plot the cumulative sum of the poverty gaps per capita (*y*-axis) against the cumulative population share (*x*-axis).

The slope of the TIP curve at any given percentile equals the poverty gap for that percentile. For the subset of the population falling below the poverty line, the TIP curve is an increasing concave function, and, for those above the poverty line, the curve is horizontal (since their poverty gaps are zero). The flattening of curve as it approaches the poverty line shows the decline in the poverty gap as expenditure increases towards the line. The extent of poverty incidence, in terms of the poverty headcount ratio, is shown by the value of cumulative population share (*x*-axis) at the point where the curve flattens out. This is shown by the length of the non-horizontal part of the TIP curve. The intensity of poverty is shown by the overall height of the TIP curve, since the height of the curve is the aggregate poverty gap averaged over the population. The mean poverty gap amongst the population falling below the poverty line is given by the slope of a ray from the origin to the point at which the curve flattens out. The degree of inequality amongst the poor is shown by the degree of concavity of the non-horizontal section of the TIP curve. If all of the poor had equal expenditure then the non-horizontal section of the curve would be a diagonal straight line.

The upper line in Figure 9.1 is the TIP curve for current expenditure (on a household per capita basis, per month). The curve plots over 47 million individual points, the cumulative poverty gaps of every South African (weighted from the original survey data). It can be seen that about one-half of the population currently falls under the poverty line of R450 per capita per month; recall that halving the poverty headcount ratio would mean cutting it to about a quarter (as shown by the dotted vertical line). The mean poverty gap per capita over the whole population is about R105 per capita per month. Halving the poverty gap would mean

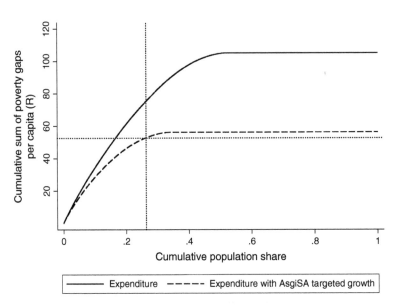

Figure 9.1 TIP curve of expenditure and expenditure with AsgiSA-targeted growth rate

Source: Author's calculations using Income and Expenditure Survey 2005/6 data.

Notes: AsgiSA, accelerated and shared growth initiative – South Africa; TIP, incidence, intensity and inequality of poverty.

bringing it down to about R53 per capita (as shown by the dashed horizontal line). Halving both the poverty gap and the poverty headcount ratio would thus mean bringing the point at which the TIP curve flattens out to the left of the dotted vertical line and below the dashed horizontal line. The lower (dashed) curve in Figure 9.1 shows the projected poverty outcome in 2014 with the AsgiSA-targeted growth rates under the current distributional structure. While poverty is significantly reduced, neither the poverty gap nor the poverty headcount ratio is halved.

It would take annual growth rates of 8.7 per cent per annum from 2006 to 2014 to halve the poverty gap and poverty headcount ratio of both income and expenditure, under the current distribution. GDP in South Africa grew at a real average annualized rate of 4.1 per cent between 2000 and 2006, which was higher than for many years previously, and 2.4 per cent between 2006 and 2009.[3] These rates were reached during the recent commodities boom from which South Africa benefited, and which is unlikely to continue in the near future. The global economic crisis has also depressed growth rates in South Africa and will in all probability result in a decline in growth rates. Realistically, poverty will not be halved by 2014 in the absence of pro-poor distributional change.

With the current distribution, it would take many years of growth to halve poverty (in particular, the poverty headcount ratio). Were GDP to grow at an annual rate of 4 per cent per annum, both measures of poverty would not be halved until the year 2022. With GDP growth of 3 per cent per annum, only by the year 2027 would poverty be halved.

Method for simulating distributional changes

Relying on growth to bring down poverty, without pro-poor distributional change, would mean that poverty would not be halved for a long time to come. It is thus worthwhile analysing what combinations of growth and distributional change could lead to the halving of poverty by 2014.

The methodology used to simulate alternative distributional scenarios is set out below with reference to expenditure for heuristic purposes, but these were undertaken with each of income and expenditure. We begin by ranking the entire South African population from highest to lowest in terms of household per capita expenditure. Let x_i denote the expenditure of person i where the population is ranked from lowest to highest in terms of variable x, for $i = 1,2,...,n$. That is, x_1 is the lowest expenditure and x_n the highest. Here, $n = 47,391,192$.

The simulated distributional changes 'revolve' around a specific point in the distribution. In the simplest case this is the person at the median expenditure; other simulated scenarios use the person at the 66.6[th] percentile (that is, where a third of people have higher expenditure) and the 75th percentile. This 'anchor' point is the only person whose income is unaffected by the distributional change. All those with higher expenditures than this person lose from the distributional change and all those below that person gain. The extent to which an individual loses or gains depends on how far they are from the 'anchor' person: the individual with the highest expenditure loses most, whereas the lowest gains most.

The simulated distributional change is generally rank-preserving because of the small increments spread continuously over a population of over 47 million.

In the simplest case, in which distributional change revolves around the individual with median expenditure, the change is symmetrical around the median. The loss to the individual with the highest expenditure is the exact gain of the lowest; the loss to the individual with the second highest expenditure is the exact gain of the second lowest; and so on. In this case the distributional change is both mean-preserving and median-preserving.

Where the distributional change revolves around the individual at the 66.6th or 75th percentile, the simulated distributional changes are mean-preserving but not median-preserving, and the distributional change is not symmetrical around the 'anchor' individual. If for example the change in the distribution revolves around the 75th percentile, the gain of the three individuals with the lowest expenditure must be matched by the loss of the single individual with the highest expenditure, and so on.

Thus, for a symmetrical distributional change around the median, $\rho = 0.5n$; for a distributional change around the individual at the 75th percentile, $\rho = 0.75n$; and so on, where ρ is the point around which the distributional change revolves.

One parameter of these transformations is the scale or magnitude of the distributional change. The simplest way to think about this is to set by how much the expenditure of the individual with the lowest expenditure increases through the distributional change. In the simulations shown here, expenditure at the bottom increases by amounts between R50 and R300 per month. While this would constitute a very significant increase in expenditure for someone at the lowest end of the distribution, the 'loss' at the top of the distribution is a tiny fraction of expenditure.

For example, in the case of a distributional change in which expenditure at the bottom increases by a maximum of R50 and the distributional change revolves around the median, expenditure at the very top would decline by R50. The expenditure of the individual with the second-lowest expenditure would rise by just under R50 and that of the individual with the second highest expenditure would fall by just under R50, and so on, with the absolute amounts falling uniformly from both sides until converging to zero at the median. In the case of a distributional change of a maximum R50, but revolving around the 75th percentile, the expenditure of the individual with the lowest expenditure rises by R50, while the expenditure of the highest individual with the highest expenditure declines by R150, with the absolute amounts declining from both ends (but in larger increments for the top quarter of the distribution) converging to zero at the 75th percentile.

Formally, let θ_i be the value of the distributional change affecting individual i such that

$$\theta_i > 0 \text{ for } i < \rho, \theta_i < 0 \text{ for } i > \rho, \text{ and } \theta_i = 0 \text{ for } i = \rho.$$

Select ω, the value of the gain to the individual with the lowest expenditure $[i = 1]$. The range of values to be 'redistributed' will be $\omega \leq \theta_i \leq |\phi|$ where ϕ is the maximum loss to the individual with the highest expenditure $[i = n]$ and $\omega > 0$ and $\phi < 0$.

For the special case of distributional change revolving around the median, $(\rho = 0.5n)$, $\omega = -\phi$. For distributional change around points higher than the median (for example, $\rho = 0.75n$), $\omega < |\phi|$. Then for $i < \rho$, the distributional gain will be:

$$\theta_i = \omega - \frac{\omega(i-1)}{\rho-1} = \frac{\omega(\rho-i)}{\rho-1} \tag{9.1}$$

It can be seen that, for the poorest person (that is, with the lowest expenditure), the distributional gain will be the maximum distributional change, ω, while for the person just below the unaffected person (for example, immediately below the median person in the simplest case) the distributional gain will be positive but close to zero.

For $i > \rho$, the distributional loss will be:

$$\theta_i = (\rho-i)\frac{\sum\limits_{i=1}^{\rho-1}\theta_i}{\sum\limits_{i=\rho+1}^{n}(i-\rho)} \tag{9.2}$$

This balances the aggregate loss of all those who lose from the distributional change with the aggregate gain of those who gain from distributional change, irrespective of which point the distributional change revolves around.

The post-distributional-change income of person i will thus be:

$$\tilde{x}_i = x_i + \theta_i \tag{9.3}$$

So,

$$\tilde{x}_i > x_i \forall i < \rho \tag{9.4.1}$$

$$\tilde{x}_i = x_i \ \text{for} \ i = \rho \tag{9.4.2}$$

and

$$\tilde{x}_i < x_i \forall i > \rho \tag{9.4.3}$$

In this presentation of the method, we have selected the maximum gain to the individual with the lowest expenditure $[i = 1]$, ω, and then calculated the gain to the other individuals in subset $i < \rho$; this allowed for the derivation of the loss to the individuals in subset $i < \rho$. One could equally have begun by selecting the loss to the individual with the highest expenditure $[i = n]$, ϕ, and calculating $\theta_i \forall i > \rho$ and hence deriving $\theta_i \forall i < \rho$; the results would be identical.

This method is intended to simulate a generalized outcome of pro-poor distributional change, not to model how distributional changes actually take place in reality or to suggest that policy attempts to produce to exact outcomes simulated here. What is being considered here is not a direct redistribution of income or expenditure through social transfers (although this could certainly be a component of pro-poor distributional change). The analysis is concerned more fundamentally with an overall shift towards more pro-poor growth, where the incomes and expenditure of the poor grow the fastest. The distributional changes simulated here are intended as indicative of the scale of 'redistribution' of incomes and expenditure that could result from a more pro-poor growth path. That would involve, for instance, one in which returns to unskilled labour rose more rapidly than returns to skilled labour, and/or a relative expansion in employment opportunities. Such a shift would not result in the exact distributional changes simulated here; these projections are indicative in nature. Note also that this method is not intended to model the causal relationships between distribution and growth.

An alternative way of modelling distributional changes would have been simply to apply different growth rates to different parts of the distribution spectrum – for instance, that the income or expenditure of the bottom decile grows at 7 per cent, that of the next decile at 6.5 per cent and so on. However, the method developed here is preferable as it avoids an outcome where the income or expenditure of the individual at the top of the bottom decile grows significantly more than that of the person just above them at the bottom of the next decile. In the method employed here, the growth rates vary not by income category (for example, deciles), but by individual, resulting in a much more continuous distributional change across the distributional spectrum.

Note that the 'losers' from the distributional change, at the upper end of the distribution, do not suffer any net loss of income or expenditure in the scenarios set out here, as these simulated distributional changes are combined with various growth scenarios. The income or expenditure at the top still grows considerably in every scenario (and far more than for other people in absolute terms, even with the pro-poor distributional change), but slightly less than it would have in the absence of the equalizing distributional change.

What combinations of growth and pro-poor distributional change could halve poverty?

We simulate the effects on poverty of combining four different 'intensities' of pro-poor distributional change (in which the expenditure of the individual with the lowest expenditure increases by R50, R100, R200 or R300); with distributional change revolving around each of the median, the 66.6[th] percentile and the 75th percentile; and with growth rates of between 1 and 7 per cent per annum through to 2014. This yields 84 alternative combinations of growth and distributional change.

Poverty outcomes under two of these scenarios are shown in Figure 9.2. The solid curve shows the expenditure pattern that would result from 6 per cent GDP mean growth per annum through to 2014, combined with a distributional change in which the poorest South African is just R50 per month better off than they would otherwise have been. The dashed curve shows a scenario in which growth

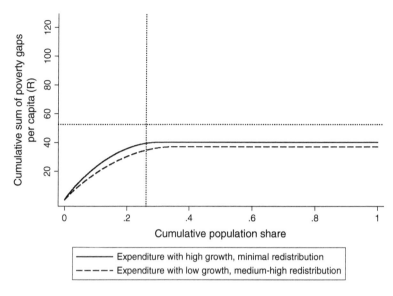

Figure 9.2 TIP curve of expenditure under alternative growth/distribution scenarios

Source: Author's calculations using Income and Expenditure Survey 2005–2006 data.

is fairly low at 2 per cent per annum but there is a more intensive distributional change, with the lowest-expenditure individual gaining an additional R200 per month. The poverty gap is halved in both of these scenarios (both curves lie below the horizontal dotted line). However, while the poverty headcount ratio is reduced, it is not halved (both curves flatten out just to the right of the vertical dotted line).

Figure 9.3 shows two growth–distributional scenarios in which the poverty headcount ratio and the poverty gap are both halved. The solid curve shows GDP growth of 4 per cent per annum combined with distributional change in which the expenditure of the poorest person is R200 per month higher than would otherwise be the case. The dashed curve shows a scenario of GDP growth of 3 per cent per annum with distributional change where the expenditure of the poorest person is raised by R300 per month. The TIP curves for both scenarios fall well below the horizontal dotted line, indicating that the poverty gap is cut by much more than half (in the second scenario the poverty gap is actually cut by almost 80 per cent). Both curves flatten out to the left of the vertical dotted line, showing that the poverty headcount ratio is cut by at least one-half (in the second scenario it falls as far down as low as 12 per cent). In these growth–distribution scenarios the target of halving poverty is thus easily achieved (with both poverty measures).

Tables 9.1–3 show poverty outcomes for the 84 different combinations of growth and distributional change simulated here. These results are shown for expenditure; the results for income are very similar. Table 9.1 shows the results

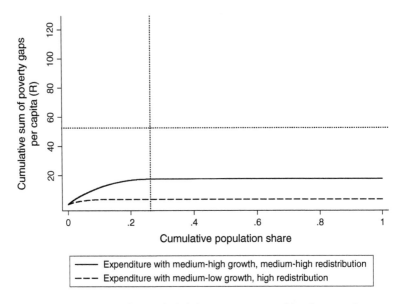

Figure 9.3 TIP curve of scenario halving poverty gap and headcount ratio

Source: Author's calculations using Income and Expenditure Survey 2005/6 data.

Table 9.1 Halving of poverty gap and poverty headcount
ratio under various growth/distribution scenarios:
distributional change around median

Growth (%)	Distribution			
	R300	*R200*	*R100*	*R50*
7	H, G	H, G	H, G	G
6	H, G	G	G	G
5	H, G	G	G	G
4	H, G	G	G	
3	G	G	G	
2	G	G		
1	G	G		

Source: Author's calculations using Income and Expenditure Survey
2005–2006 data.

Notes: 'Growth' refers to the mean growth rate between 2006 and
2014 under the various scenarios. 'Distribution' refers to the distribution scenarios as set out in the text. 'R300': the expenditure of the
individual with the lowest expenditure is R300 per month higher than
it would otherwise have been; similarly for R200, R100, and R50. For
each scenario, H indicates that the poverty headcount ratio is at least
halved and G indicates that the poverty gap is at least halved.

where distributional change revolves around the individual with median expenditure. Tables 9.2 and 9.3 show the results where distributional change revolves around the individuals with expenditure at the 66th and 75th percentiles, respectively. For each scenario an 'H' indicates that the poverty headcount ratio is (at least) halved, while a 'G' indicates that the poverty gap is (at least) halved. The scenarios in which both measures of poverty are halved are shaded in.

Without any distributional change, the poverty headcount ratio cannot be halved, even with growth at 7 per cent (the poverty gap can be halved with growth of 6 per cent or 7 per cent). However, even with low growth rates, both the poverty gap and poverty headcount ratio can be halved where there is distributional change in which the poorest person consumes an additional R300 per month.

For any given growth rate and quantum of distributional change (that is, the net gain to the individual with lowest expenditure), the impact on poverty is higher the higher is the point at which distributional change 'revolves' in the simulations. For instance, Table 9.3 shows distributional change revolving around the 75th percentile; that is, the top quarter is 'losing' (though their expenditure still grows in absolute terms) with the bottom 75 per cent gaining. The impact on poverty here is greater than that shown in Table 9.1, where distributional change revolves around the median. In this case the gains of the bottom half are matched on an individual-to-individual basis by 'losses' of the top half (though the expenditure of individuals in the top half still grows in real terms).

In the final part of the empirical analysis, the reduction in poverty in each of the scenarios is decomposed into the relative contributions of growth and distributional

Table 9.2 Halving of poverty gap and poverty headcount ratio under various growth/distribution scenarios: distributional change around 66th percentile

Growth (%)	Distribution			
	R300	R200	R100	R50
7	H, G	H, G	H, G	G
6	H, G	H, G	G	G
5	H, G	H, G	G	G
4	H, G	G	G	
3	H, G	G	G	
2	H, G	G		
1	G	G		

Source: Author's calculations using Income and Expenditure Survey 2005–2006 data.

Notes: 'Growth' refers to the average annualized growth rate between 2006 and 2014 under the various scenarios. 'Distribution' refers to the distribution scenarios as set out in the text. R300: the expenditure of the individual with the lowest expenditure is R300 per month higher than it would otherwise have been; similarly for R200, R100, and R50. For each scenario, H indicates that the poverty headcount ratio is at least halved and G indicates that the poverty gap is at least halved.

Table 9.3 Halving of poverty gap and poverty headcount ratio under various growth/distribution scenarios: distributional change around 75th percentile

Growth (%)	Distribution			
	R300	R200	R100	R50
7	H, G	H, G	H, G	H, G
6	H, G	H, G	H, G	G
5	H, G	H, G	G	G
4	H, G	H, G	G	
3	H, G	G	G	
2	H, G	G		
1	H, G	G		

Source: Author's calculations using Income and Expenditure Survey 2005/6 data.

Notes: 'Growth' refers to the average annualized growth rate between 2006 and 2014 under the various scenarios. 'Distribution' refers to the distribution scenarios as set out in the text. R300: the expenditure of the individual with the lowest expenditure is R300 per month higher than it would otherwise have been; similarly for R200, R100, and R50. For each scenario, H indicates that the poverty headcount ratio is at least halved and G indicates that the poverty gap is at least halved.

change, following the method of Datt and Ravallion (1992). This decomposition analysis precisely quantifies the relative contributions of growth and distributional change to poverty reduction under each scenario.

Table 9.4 summarizes the results for the poverty headcount ratio and Table 9.5 for the poverty gap. The results shown here are for the scenarios in which distributional change revolves around the 66th percentile; the results are similar for the 50th and 75th percentiles. Recall that the initial poverty headcount ratio was 52.46 per cent, such that halving the headcount ratio would require it to fall below 26.23 per cent. In each of the scenarios, Table 9.4 shows the change in the poverty headcount ratio that would result from that combination of growth and distributional change. For example, in the first cell which combines a 7 per cent growth rate with distributional change in which the poorest person is R300 better off, the headcount ratio would fall by 49.6, with a resultant headcount ratio of under 3 per cent. When the reduction in the headcount ratio is decomposed into its growth and distributional components, it is evident that just over two-thirds of the reduction is accounted for by growth and the remainder by distributional change. By contrast, in the scenario with R300 distributional change but with growth rates of only 1 per cent, almost 70 per cent of the reduction in the poverty headcount ratio is contributed by distributional change (and the absolute reduction in the headcount ratio is less than half that in the afore-mentioned scenario).

Table 9.5 shows the decomposition results for the poverty gap. Halving the initial aggregate poverty gap of R59.82 billion would mean cutting it to below R29.81

Table 9.4 Decomposition of change in poverty headcount ratio under various growth/distribution scenarios

Growth (%)		Distribution				
		R300	R200	R100	R50	None
7	ΔH of which:	−49.6	−39.0	−29.4	−25.7	−22.7
	growth (%)	67.8	75.6	86.4	92.8	100.0
	distribution (%)	32.2	24.4	13.6	7.2	0.0
6	ΔH of which:	−48.7	−35.5	−25.7	−22.3	−19.8
	growth (%)	64.4	73.8	85.9	92.7	100.0
	distribution (%)	35.6	26.2	14.1	7.3	0.0
5	ΔH of which:	−47.0	−31.6	−21.9	−19.2	−16.7
	growth (%)	60.7	71.3	84.8	91.3	100.0
	distribution (%)	39.3	28.7	15.2	8.7	0.0
4	ΔH of which:	−44.0	−26.9	−18.4	−15.4	−13.4
	growth (%)	56.3	67.7	82.5	90.5	100.0
	distribution (%)	43.7	32.3	17.5	9.5	0.0
3	ΔH of which:	−40.3	−21.4	−14.3	−12.1	−10.3
	growth (%)	51.6	63.4	80.4	88.4	100.0
	distribution (%)	48.4	36.6	19.6	11.6	0.0
2	ΔH of which:	−33.7	−16.6	−10.7	−8.9	−7.1
	growth (%)	45.6	56.2	74.9	83.9	100.0
	distribution (%)	54.4	43.8	25.1	16.1	0.0
1	ΔH of which:	−22.6	−11.7	−6.6	−4.9	−3.1
	growth (%)	30.6	39.5	59.0	70.7	100.0
	distribution (%)	69.4	60.5	41.0	29.3	0.0

Source: Author's calculations using Income and Expenditure Survey 2005/6 data.

Notes: In each scenario (growth/distribution combination), ΔH refers to the change in the poverty headcount ratio, from its original level of 52.5. This change is decomposed into components of growth and distributional change. Thus, 'growth (%)' shows the percentage contribution of growth to the reduction in the poverty headcount ratio, while 'distribution (%)' shows the percentage contribution of distributional change to the reduction in the poverty headcount ratio; these components sum to 100 per cent in each scenario.

billion. Taking the example of the scenario combining a 3 per cent growth rate with distributional change in which the poorest person is R100 better off than would otherwise be the case, the aggregate poverty gap falls by R32.5 billion, such that it is cut by a bit more than half, with just over half of this reduction contributed by growth and just under half by distributional change.

The distributional change component plays a more significant role with respect to the poverty gap than with the poverty headcount ratio. The more significant relative contribution of distributional change in the reduction of the poverty gap, as compared to the reduction of the poverty headcount ratio, is related to the fact that the changes in the consumption of those at the bottom, who do not move out of poverty, do not enter into changes in the headcount ratio. However, improvement in the consumption of those at the bottom does significantly affect changes

Table 9.5 Decomposition of change in aggregate poverty gap under alternative growth/distribution scenarios

Growth (%)		Distribution				
		R300	R200	R100	R50	None
7	ΔG of which:	59.3	55.2	46.2	40.4	34.1
	growth (%)	52.5	62.0	75.6	85.7	100.0
	distribution (%)	47.5	38.0	24.4	14.3	0.0
6	ΔG of which:	59.1	53.8	43.4	37.0	30.2
	growth (%)	47.2	57.1	71.7	83.1	100.0
	distribution (%)	52.8	42.9	28.3	16.9	0.0
5	ΔG of which:	58.9	52.1	40.1	33.2	26.0
	growth (%)	41.5	51.7	67.2	79.9	100.0
	distribution (%)	58.5	48.3	32.8	20.1	0.0
4	ΔG of which:	58.5	49.9	36.5	29.1	21.4
	growth (%)	35.2	45.2	61.3	75.4	100.0
	distribution (%)	64.8	54.8	38.7	24.6	0.0
3	ΔG of which:	57.8	47.1	32.5	24.6	16.5
	growth (%)	28.2	37.6	53.5	69.1	100.0
	distribution (%)	71.8	62.4	46.5	30.9	0.0
2	ΔG of which:	56.8	43.8	28.0	19.8	11.4
	growth (%)	20.5	28.2	42.9	59.2	100.0
	distribution (%)	79.5	71.8	57.1	40.8	0.0
1	ΔG of which:	54.9	39.9	23.2	14.6	5.8
	growth (%)	11.3	16.1	26.9	41.5	100.0
	distribution (%)	88.7	83.9	73.1	58.5	0.0

Source: Author's calculations using Income and Expenditure Survey 2005/6 data.

Notes: In each scenario (growth/distribution combination), ΔG shows the change (in R billion) in the aggregate poverty gap, from its original level of R59.8 billion. This change is decomposed into components of growth and distributional change. Thus, 'growth (%) shows the percentage contribution of growth to the reduction in the poverty gap, while 'distribution (%) shows the percentage contribution of distributional change to the reduction in the poverty gap; these components sum to 100 per cent in each scenario.

in the poverty gap. Since the types of distributional changes modelled here affect the consumption of those at the bottom the most, it follows that distributional change affects the poverty gap relatively more than it would the poverty head-count ratio.

Conclusion

Given South Africa's levels of income per capita and status as an upper-middle-income country, the scale of poverty is arguably associated more with distributional patterns than with the total amount of resources available. Poverty in South Africa would be far lower than it is if inequality were to be at anything approaching a typical level of inequality by international standards.[4] While decent rates of growth could make some inroads into poverty, given the scale of poverty, growth alone will fall short.

With the poverty line as defined here, the aggregate poverty gap is only about 3 per cent of GDP. This suggests that poverty in South Africa should not be viewed as an insurmountable problem. In fact, given that one-half of the population falls below that line, 3 per cent of GDP is a surprisingly small amount. Of course the actual cost of eliminating poverty would significantly exceed this amount if considered in terms of direct transfers (given issues of targeting and administration). Nevertheless, that the entire poverty gap is just 3 per cent of GDP suggests that it is economically feasible to significantly reduce poverty in South Africa.

The target of halving poverty by 2014 appears to be achievable under growth rates that are a bit lower than in recent years and with quite mild distributional change. For instance, poverty could be halved with growth rates of 2 per cent combined with distributional change in which the expenditure of the poorest person rises by R300 per month, or alternatively growth of 4 per cent per annum combined with distributional change in which the expenditure of the poorest person rises by R200 more per month. Halving poverty is not impossible. However, it *is* highly virtually impossible to halve poverty by 2014 without pro-poor distributional change. Furthermore, it is unlikely that pro-poor distributional change would materialize without active policy interventions aimed explicitly at this.

The simulations shown here are intended as indicative of the scale of distributional changes needed to halve poverty. The most important dynamics underlying actual distributional changes are likely to be through the labour market, in terms of employment creation (or losses) as well as the distribution of earnings amongst the employed. Social spending certainly has a role to play in ameliorating inequality and poverty, particularly in the short to medium term. However, South Africa's inequality is unlikely to be dramatically and sustainably reduced through social spending, but rather through increased demand for low- and semi-skilled labour and through a closing of wage gaps amongst the employed.[5]

The actual effects of a specific reduction of inequality on growth would of course be contingent on the nature of that reduction and how it came about. The types of policies that could be considered for the reduction of inequality in South Africa might include: land reform and other forms of asset redistribution; a more progressive taxation system; increased expenditure directed at improving the incomes and capabilities of the poor; a more equitable education system; measures to reduce unemployment and in particular to increase employment opportunities for the unskilled and semi-skilled; labour market interventions to narrow the wage gap; and measures to influence the sectoral structure of the economy in favour of sectors from which low-income earners derive a greater share of income. Insofar as the extremely high level of inequality in South Africa has negative effects on sustainable growth, such measures could be considered for the purposes of not only reducing inequality and poverty, but also improving long-term growth performance.

Acknowledgement

Parts of the analysis in this chapter are based on Tregenna (2011b, 2012).

Notes

1 The exchange rate in 2006 (the year of the data) was R6.76/US$.
2 In March 2006 Rands.
3 Calculated from GDP data published by the South African Reserve Bank, downloaded from www.reservebank.co.za (accessed: 2011).
4 See Tregenna and Tsela (2012) for an analysis of inequality in South Africa.
5 See Tregenna (2011a) for an analysis of how unemployment and wage dispersion among the employed contribute to inequality.

References

Adams, R. (2004). 'Economic Growth, Inequality and Poverty: Estimating the Growth Elasticity of Poverty'. *World Development*, 32: 1989–2014.

Aghion, P., E. Caroli and C. Garcia-Penalosa (1999). 'Inequality and Economic Growth: The Perspective of the New Growth Theories'. *Journal of Economic Literature*, 37: 1615–60.

Alesina A. and D. Rodrik (1994). 'Distributive Politics and Economic Growth'. *Quarterly Journal of Economics*, 109: 465–90.

Ardington, C., D. Lam, M. Leibbrandt and M. Welch (2005). 'The Sensitivity of Estimates of Post-apartheid Changes in South African Poverty and Inequality to Key Data Imputations'. Centre for Social Science Research (CSSR) Working Paper 106. Cape Town: CSSR.

Bourguignon, F. (2004). 'The Poverty–Growth–Inequality Triangle'. Indian Council for Research on International Economic Relations, New Delhi Working Paper 125. New Delhi: ICRIER

Bourguignon, F. and C. Morrisson (1998). 'Inequality and Development: the Role of Dualism'. *Journal of Development Economics*, 57: 233–57.

Clarke, R. (1995). 'More Evidence on Income Distribution and Growth'. *Journal of Development Economics*, 47: 403–27.

Datt, G. and M. Ravallion (1992). 'Growth and Redistribution Components of Changes in Poverty: A Decomposition with Applications to Brazil and China in 1980s'. *Journal of Development Economics*, 38: 275–95.

Deininger, K. and L. Squire (1998). 'New Ways of Looking at Old Issues: Inequality and Growth'. *Journal of Development Economics*, 57: 259–87.

Fanta, F. and P.M. Upadhyay (2009). 'Poverty Reduction, Economic Growth and Inequality in Africa'. *Applied Economics Letters*, 16: 1791–94.

Ferreira, H.G. (1999). 'Inequality and Economic Performance: a brief Overview to Theories of Growth and Distribution'. Available at: www.worldbank.org/poverty/inequal/index.htm (accessed: 2011).

Forbes, K. (2000). 'A Reassessment of the Relationship between Inequality and Growth'. *American Economic Review*, 4: 869–87.

Fosu, A. (2008). 'Inequality and the Growth–Poverty Nexus: Specification Empirics using African Data'. *Applied Economics Letters*, 15: 563–66.

Government of the Republic of South Africa (2008). *Towards a Fifteen Year Review*, Pretoria.

Hoogeveen, J.G. and B. Özler (2005). 'Not Separate, Not Equal: Poverty and Inequality in post-Apartheid South Africa'. William Davidson Institute Working Paper 379. Michigan: William Davidson Institute.

Jenkins, S. and P. Lambert (1997). 'Three 'I's of Poverty Curves, with an Analysis of UK Poverty Trends'. *Oxford Economic Papers, New Series* 49: 317–27.

Kuznets, S. (1955). 'Economic Growth and Income Inequality'. *American Economic Review*, 45: 1–28.

Leibbrandt, M., L. Poswell, P. Naidoo, M. Welch and I. Woolard (2004). 'Measuring Recent Changes in South African Inequality and Poverty using 1996 and 2001 Census Data'. Working Paper 84: Centre for Social Science Research. Cape Town: CSSR.

Meth, C. and R. Dias (2004). 'Increases in Poverty in South Africa, 1999–2002'. *Development Southern Africa*, 21(1): 59–85.

Pauw, K. and L. Mncube (2007). 'The Impact of Growth and Redistribution on Poverty and Inequality in South Africa'. IPC Country Study 7, International Poverty Centre and United Nations Development Programme, Brasilia.

Persson, T. and G. Tabellini (1994). 'Is Inequality Harmful for Growth?'. *American Economic Review*, 84: 600–21.

Presidency of the Republic of South Africa (2006). 'Accelerated and Shared Growth Initiative – South Africa (AsgiSA): a Summary'. Available at: www.info.gov.za/asgisa/asgisadoc.pdf (accessed: 2011).

Ravallion, M. (1995). 'Growth and Poverty: Evidence for Developing Countries in the 1980s' *Economics Letters*, 48: 411–17.

Statistics South Africa (2008). Statistical Release P0141: Consumer Price Index (CPI), June 2008, Statistics South Africa, Pretoria.

Statistics South Africa and National Treasury (2007). 'A National Poverty Line for South Africa'. Available at: www.treasury.gov.za/publications/other/povertyline/discussionnote%20povline%20statssa.pdf (accessed: 2011).

Tregenna, F. (2011a). 'Earnings Inequality and Unemployment in South Africa'. *International Review of Applied Economics*, 25(5): 585–98.

Tregenna, F. (2011b). 'What are the Distributional Implications of Halving Poverty in South Africa when Growth Alone is not Enough?'. Economic Research Southern Africa Working Papers, No. 215. Cape Town: Economic Research Southern Africa.

Tregenna, F. (2012). 'What are the Distributional Implications of Halving Poverty in South Africa when Growth alone is not enough?'. *Applied Economics*, 44(20): 2577–96.

Tregenna, F. and M. Tsela (2012). 'Inequality in South Africa: a Study of the Distribution of Income, Expenditure, and Earnings'. *Development Southern Africa*, 29(1): 35–61.

Van der Berg, S., R. Burger, M. Louw and D. Yu (2005). 'Trends in Poverty and Inequality since the Political Transition'. Bureau for Economic Research (BER) Working Papers: 1/2005. Stellenbosch: University of Stellenbosch.

Zweimüller, J. (2000). 'Inequality, Redistribution, and Economic Growth'. *Empirica*, 27: 1–20.

10 Outfits: narrowly tailored laws that harm instead of help

A case study of Liberia's telecommunication laws

Rosalia de la Cruz Gitau

Introduction

Africa has more than one billion inhabitants that have largely been isolated from consumerist culture. To the enterprising ear this translates into one billion new prospective cell phone users, internet surfers and retail bank depositors. The opportunity to make a great deal of money in largely unchartered territory has shown itself too attractive to resist, if recent trends in banking and telecommunications on the continent are any indicators. The telecommunications sector, in particular, presents many exciting prospects to international investors, and many billion-dollar projects are already underway across the continent. The legacy of international involvement in Africa – both politically and economically – has proven overwhelmingly detrimental. Many of the continent's current problems can be traced to the exploitation it has experienced whilst 'doing business' with the foreign entities in the past. As regards telecommunications, there are billions of dollars to be made – or lost. African governments must be vigilant in preventing yet another one of its resources from being taken at a bargain. Half of the sub-Saharan population lives below the poverty line (World Bank 2010a). Creating legal protections can help to prevent another economic pillaging.

This study will present the case of Liberia, and the development of its telecommunications sector, as an opportunity for pillage or profit. I argue that the legal framework of the telecommunications sector – both laws and enforcement – compromise the type of development the government needs to achieve in order to 'develop'. This argument will first require a background discussion of: (a) development and its relationship to the law; (b) the advancement requirements of a country like Liberia to reach a stable level of development; and (c) an overview of how investment operates in Liberia – with an emphasis on the role that international donors play in the process. With this background in place, I will support my argument by demonstrating that current Liberian telecommunications laws offer a competitive advantage to international investors. Collectively, such a legal environment compromises the development requirements of a country like Liberia. This study will rely on reigning literature in law and development, the author's field research, research of major donor agencies and reports of the Liberian telecommunications industry pertinent to the period covered by this study.

Background

Liberia

Liberia is a small West African country with a population of 4.1 million (CIA 2014). The mean life expectancy is 60 years for those who survive the infant stage – Liberia has one of the world's highest infant mortality rates (UNICEF 2011). Over 90 per cent of the population lives on less than US$2 per day, and unemployment is upwards of 80 per cent (IRIN 2007). Liberia did not always have low-income country status and was in fact classified as a middle-income country prior to 1980 (World Bank 2010b). Much of the deterioration is the result of the conflict over the country's vast resources and the subsequent mismanagement of this wealth.

Dubbed the Great War, Liberia's civil conflict spanned more than two decades, from 1979 to 2003 (Levitt 2005), and caused incalculable damage in its wake. Social, political and economic structures in Liberia were left in ruins; between 200,000 and 300,000 people were killed and upwards of one million persons were displaced (Loden 2007). Human rights atrocities of grave depravity were abundant and some studies estimate that as many as 74 per cent of war-affected women in Liberia are survivors of conflict-related sexual violence (Ward and Marsh 2006). Suffice to say, the Great War devastated the social and economic landscape of this otherwise scenic West African state.

Law and development

To understand how Liberia's telecommunications laws are detrimental to the country's development prospects, we must first understand what the relationship is between law and development. To embark on such a complex inquiry first requires that we unpack the terms 'law' and 'development'.

Law

Law represents different things to different people. To understand its substance and force, we have to unpack its meaning by asking four fundamental questions: (a) *Where does the law come from?* (b) *What is the function of law, namely for whom does the law serve?* (c) *What is the force of law?* (d) *Do laws actually affect behaviour?* Answering these questions will enable us to critique the rule of law project in Liberia vis-à-vis the telecommunications sector. From there, I will be better able to support this study's argument, namely, that as currently constructed, the legal framework controlling the telecommunications sector in Liberia may compromise the country's development.

WHERE DOES THE LAW COME FROM?

To understand what a law is, we begin with the vast and ongoing debate about where a law comes from. In general, this debate is split into two camps: legal positivists and natural law theorists. Supporters of natural law argue that laws are manifestations of intrinsic rights of man. In his seminal work Thomas Hobbes (1998) outlines a system of natural laws that govern the order of man. These natural laws are normative, that is, they prescribe what man *should* do in order to avoid a state of war. If such natural laws are followed and enforced by a sovereign, Hobbes argues that this would save man from a destiny that would otherwise prove 'poor, nasty, brutish, and short' (Hobbes 1998: 183).

Legal positivists, however, contend that laws are not representative of inherent rights, but rather are constructed – and that the *real* inquiry should be not in their substance but in their source. John Austin famously articulated that 'the existence of law is one thing; its merit and demerit another' (Austin 1995: 157). The preoccupation with the moral weight of laws is irrelevant to legal positivism. Whether a law is just or unjust, hence, is not a real inquiry. Rather whether a law comes from a legitimate authority will dictate whether it is just or unjust. Kelsen states that a law is:

> an order of human behaviour. An order is a system of rules. Law is not, as it is sometimes said, a rule. It is a set of rules having the kind of unity we understand by the system. It is impossible to grasp the nature of law if we limit our attention to the single isolated rule ... *every rule of law obligates human beings to observe a certain behaviour under certain circumstances.*
>
> (Kelsen 1945: 3)

According to Kelsen, a law is a system of rules dictating how people *should* act in certain situations.

This study will use Kelsen's definition of law for its discussion. The positivist perspective of Kelsen seems most appropriate for the Liberian context. As a former colony experiencing ongoing occupation, Liberian laws are products of exogenous construction. Moreover, whatever natural rights or morality-based laws incorporated in Liberia's current legal order have all been determined in accordance with foreign (often occidental) conceptions of nature and morality in mind. Unlike other countries with arguably more discursive legal origins, Liberia's legal environment is almost entirely constructed from the outside. This is especially the case for those rules governing its economic sector.

WHAT IS THE FUNCTION OF LAW? FOR WHOM DOES THE LAW SERVE?

Following Kelsen's definition of law, as rules that prescribe behaviour, we now look to the objectives of prescribing such behaviour. In the case of Liberia, a small exogenous elite has constructed the legal order to serve their ends. Rousseau (1996, 1755) describes how such elite-serving legal orders originally arose, stating as follows:

> The first person who, having enclosed a plot of land, took it into his head to say this is mine and found people simple enough to believe him, was the true

founder of civil society. What crimes, wars, murders, what miseries and hor-
rors would the human race have been spared, had someone pulled up the
stakes or filled in the ditch and cried out to his fellow men: Do not listen to
this impostor. You are lost if you forget that the fruits of the earth belong to
all and the earth to no one!

(Rousseau 1996, 1755)

This passage demonstrates the power of rule-creation and how those who create
such rules can do so to the detriment of the majority. Indeed, Rousseau's political
construction follows from the premise that laws are created by the few to serve
their interests, and his subsequent political construction involves widening the
sphere of law-making. Nietzsche (2006, 1887) takes an even more drastically
pessimistic view of laws. He goes as far as to say that laws are always created to
serve the minority, in spite of direct democracy efforts advocated by the likes of
Rousseau. Liberian law – from colonialism to the present – was blatantly written
to serve the interest of the foreign elite to the detriment of the indigenous majority population. Subsequent conflicts were fuelled by a keen interest in capturing
the state in order to monopolize and perpetuate such rule-making.

In 1822, Liberia was founded by freed black-American slaves with the support
of the US government. The creation of the Liberian state was conceived in the
halls of the US Congress by a group called the American Colonial Society
(ACS).[1] With funding and institutional support from the Americans, these freed
black slaves arrived in what is now known as Liberia and forced their rule over
the indigenous black population. The black slaves eventually took control of the
government in 1847 upon the election of the colony's first black President, Joseph
Robert Jenkins. The ACS played a pivotal role in the drafting of the Liberian
Constitution, enacted in 1847.[2] This constitution heavily restricted the social,
economic and political liberties of indigenous Liberians. For example, indigenous Liberians were not permitted to vote unless they owned property – a restriction not placed on their American counterparts. Moreover, they were prohibited
from holding public office, and their property ownership was restricted to the
Hinterlands, which were less economically attractive lands located outside of the
capital, port city, Monrovia.

The interests of the elite continued through Liberia's modern history, into the
Taylor and Doe administrations. In an interview for PBS (2002), former Assistant
Secretary of State for African Affairs Herman Cohen (1898–1993) discussed the
savvy with which former President Samuel Doe (1879–1989) exploited the geo-
politics of the Cold War to extract gains from the US government:

Bright: From the 1950s to today, what [changes] have we seen in [the relationships of Western governments to] Africa? Using Liberia as an example …
[have the relationships changed] as a result of the Cold War?

Cohen: The Cold War kept impinging on that policy and made it very difficult to implement, so we were supporting certain governments that were

clearly not going to use their assistance for development but use it for other reasons ... the Cold War tilted us in favor of supporting [him] [President Doe] because we got reciprocal treatment.

(PBS 2002)

Responding to some pressure to loosen the hold of his military regime in 1984, Doe re-established civilian rule and permitted elections to be held. Largely declared fraudulent by international monitors, Doe won the rigged elections; only five parties were legally permitted to run[3] (Global Security Organization 2007). That same year, the country's second constitution was being drafted and circulated; in 1986, it was passed. This new constitution provided that all Liberians were to be treated equally. Restrictions on indigenous voting, for example, were removed.

By amending the constitution and permitting multi-party civilian elections, Doe was able to maintain his power. Demilitarizing the government was appealing to donors; never mind that Doe simply changed hats from military general to civilian president and that the multi-party system was declared un-free and unfair (Massing 2005). Moreover, that equal rights were included in the new constitution assuaged the majority indigenous Liberians that were Doe's principal support-base. This group remained poor during the Doe regime, much as it did under the leadership of the Americo-Liberians. Comprising less than 5 per cent of the population, Americo-Liberians continue to possess over 90 per cent of the country's wealth.[4] Despite constitutional reform efforts and legal mechanisms to devolve away power from Doe, in practice Doe was an authoritarian leader in Liberia until his murder by a Charles Taylor splinter group in 1990.

The legacy of law creation to serve the elite's end was again demonstrated by Taylor. Charles Taylor, the warlord–statesman banked on a disillusioned electorate to usher in his leadership – and won. Garnering 73 per cent of a national vote – deemed free and fair by international monitors – Charles Taylor stole an estimated US$368 million during his short tenure in office.[5] In an effort to best turn the country into 'Charles Taylor Inc.',[6] Taylor passed the Strategic Commodities Act in 2000 making the President the sole person responsible for awarding concessions of the country's abundant natural resources.

The current situation again demonstrates a pattern of the elite creating laws to serve their own interests. The only difference is that the elites have changed somewhat. At the end of the conflict, the international community (led by the WB, IMF and the UN) had largely occupied the role of governing the country. The WB handled the economic policy of the country, the IMF all budgetary and fiscal matters, and the UN ran the day-to-day administrative tasks of governing. Following the election of current President Sirleaf-Johnson, a barrage of legislation, most notably in the economic sector, was drafted and rubber-stamped by the legislature;[7] Liberia's telecommunications policy arose from this period.

At the time of my field research for this study, the capacity of the Liberian judiciary was tantamount to bankruptcy. There was no money to buy paper on which to write the judgements or chairs on which magistrates and parties involved could sit; not even legal texts to create a semblance of continuity in judgements rendered.[8] Dealing with the complexities of competition policy as it relates to interconnectivity, for example, is arguably still beyond the capacity of the Liberian courts.[9] Liberia is largely dependent on foreign aid to function. As a result, the Government of Liberia (GoL) can do little to resist the imposition of laws being created for them by the donors. The telecommunication law in Liberia will be discussed in greater detail later. For now, it is helpful to contextualize this piece of legislation within those laws which were created to serve the ends of the constructors. In addition to the source and objectives of the law, understanding the law requires a brief discussion of the *force* behind laws.

WHAT IS THE FORCE OF LAW?

The force of law relies on an authority. This authority, in turn, punishes or rewards individuals who deviate from, or follow, respectively, these rules. In democratic states, as envisaged by Rousseau, for example, the public elects officials, who in turn represent the public's general will when doling out rewards or punishments. The force of law in such a system is hence the electorate's right to hire or fire their representatives. In the case of Liberia, however, violence has generally been the force behind the laws. Walton (2002) discusses how land disputes in post-colonial Liberia were resolved.[10] Pre-dating the arrival of the Americans, communal property was principally exercised in Liberia. The Americo-Liberians and the US systematized and privatized property upon arrival, thus disrupting the customary legal system. Walton discusses the instability that resulted from this judicialization:

> Violent protest tends to emerge when normal political channels have been blocked or closed off to certain segments of the population. Liberia was no exception and had a built-in foundation for such activities to emerge given its native population ... The Grebos (an aboriginal tribe) had a longstanding dispute over ownership of land at Cape Palmas, dating back to 1857. Since no satisfactory solution had been effected during an eighteen-year period and the Americo-Liberians seemed content to treat the land as their own, the Grebos resolved to take the land back by force. They claimed to have never relinquished said lands (a fact seemingly supported by their custom of treating land as community property). At any rate, in September 1875, there appeared to be an all-out-war being waged by the Grebos.
>
> (Walton 2002: 86)

US Diplomat Turner would later request that the US send a warship to protect US property interests; the *USS Alaska* was subsequently sent and the Grebos were defeated (Walton 2002).

The use of violent force to facilitate obedience persisted through Liberia's leadership; Charles Taylor's rule epitomized this trend. Taylor became the executive of Liberia in the 1997 elections, which largely were declared free and fair by international monitors. Taylor ran on a campaign slogan that said: 'He killed my ma, He killed my pa, I will vote for him' (Left 2003). This statement was read as a threat to Liberians, such that if they did not vote for Taylor, he would resume his attack on the country.

The enforcement of laws remains undemocratic but varies slightly in post-conflict Liberia. At the drafting of the Accra Peace Accord,[11] for example, the parties involved would incite violence in order to gain advantage in the negotiations (Hayner 2007). It is not surprising, therefore, that those most responsible for the conflict have largely gone unpunished. As for the enforcement of laws in contemporary Liberia, Liberian state agencies understand that should they resist passing the laws encouraged by the donor-community, they risk losing the funds that prop up the Liberian economy.[12] The Liberian governing elite continues to skim off the top of even the donor funds. For example, the former interim President (during Liberia's transition from 2003–2006) was charged with embezzlement for allegedly misappropriating US$1 million during his short stint in office; he was subsequently arrested for failing to appear at his hearing (Colombant 2007). The Liberian elite cannot literally or politically afford a donor freeze.

Whilst the theoretical debate about the substance, purpose and force of law remains unsettled, in Liberia a small foreign elite has and continues to construct Liberian laws in order to serve their own interests. This behaviour is largely held responsible for the 14-year conflict and devastating conditions in which the country finds itself (Gitau 2008). When met with possible resistance, law makers have resorted to violence and threats against the public to enforce these laws. This is not new for authoritarian regimes, but it is compelling when the government has and continues to purport itself as a democracy. Democracy creates public expectations as regards the public's involvement in the law-making process. Law-making in contemporary Liberia occurs largely without the consent of the general public. It is especially important to keep in mind what the law is in the Liberian context when probing the laws written to exploit the country's resources.

DO LAWS ACTUALLY AFFECT BEHAVIOUR?

Above, we discussed the power of laws. We discussed how, despite the level of authoritarianism that the various governments exercised, they nevertheless proliferated laws to consolidate their power. One argument for the power of a law is the power to legitimize one's rule – even if entirely rhetorical. Ogowewo (2000) discusses the legitimizing effect of laws. His research looks at *coups d'états* and their relationship with the judiciary. Ogowewo observed that authorities that entered office through *coups* would immediately remove the legislative and executive branches, but leave the judiciaries intact. Ogowewo contends that this was done to legitimize the regime; more surprisingly he found that the judiciary wilfully went along with the legislation, not for fear of corporal punishment, but rather to maintain financial and social benefits. His research indicates, that regardless of how authoritarian a regime may be, they still rely on laws to legitimize and consolidate their power. This is one probable explanation for why in Liberia, despite the monopoly on violence and the willingness to use it to enforce laws, authorities still proliferate laws. The power that laws have stems, in part, from the word 'law' itself, which implies legitimacy in form, even if impetuous in content. The power of laws, in part, underpins the law and development movement and serves as an opportunity for those reformers keen to proliferate laws to help in Liberia's post-conflict development.

Development

Having unpacked the meaning of law, we will similarly deconstruct the notion of development. Like the law, there are competing conceptions of what constitutes development. There is the issue of relativity: what is measured as 'development' in Zimbabwe[13] may not be considered development in Norway. Moreover, there is the issue of what to use as the standard of development; namely, against what standard do we measure whether a country has developed? And furthermore, there is the pragmatic difficulty of measuring development; namely, how do we overcome the problem of evidence-gathering endemic in 'under-developed' and 'developing' countries? Lastly, how do we effectuate development?

THEORIES OF DEVELOPMENT

'Development', as it is commonly used, implies improvement of one's current condition. However, there are various aspects of one's condition that may require improvement – and the pursuit of one improvement may undermine the pursuit of another. For example, increasing workers' productivity may harm social structures such as the family; legislation to attract foreign investment could adversely affect local political participation in the private sector and hence weaken the public's political influence. The decision to prioritize one development objective over another requires tailoring to local needs.

Traditionally, development has been measured by economic factors. A growth in gross national product (GNP), a rise in personal incomes and an increase in national savings rates and personal incomes, are often used to determine whether a country is developing or not (Sen 2001). This process ignores human factors, such as infant mortality, illiteracy rates and life expectancy, which tend to characterize under-developed states. Sen (2001) stresses the use of the latter measures for development. He articulates development as: 'the removal of various types of unfreedoms that leave people with little choice and little opportunity of exercising their real agency' (Sen 2001: 3).

Sen argues that development requires the removal of sources of 'unfreedoms' such as poverty, tyranny, poor economic opportunities and social deprivation. He contends that, though the economic indicators noted above can facilitate the expansion of freedoms, these freedoms depend on other factors such as social and economic arrangements as well as political and civil rights and should not be trickle-down by-products of economic development objectives.

Complementing Sen's definition of development as freedoms, economist William Easterly (2002) describes the process of incorporating more human factors into the development model to achieve overall development. Easterly looks beyond economic indicators to gauge development. His theory of 'complementarities' looks at levels of education, civic culture and politics, and contends that ultimately these factors lead to the creation of certain institutions which beget economic outcomes. Easterly uses his 16 years of experience working for the World Bank to deliver insightful information and amusing anecdotes of how World Bank programmes fell short of achieving development. As principal implementers of the policies derived from the Washington Consensus,[14] the World Bank spent billions of dollars in developing countries trying to realize the economic indicators noted above. Easterly notes how such programmes ignored the significant role of personal incentives and often resulted in wasted resources, where 'capital is spent on useless dams, educated citizens become lobbyists and kids use the condoms as water balloons' (Easterly 2002: 3). What Sen and Easterly both point out, respectively, is that the traditional notion of development is not to be taken as truth, and, furthermore, may not be tenable. Indeed, if we look at the recent research conducted by Zambian economist Dambisa Moyo (2009), she points out that the economic development objectives have largely been failures. Her research focuses on the African continent, where US$1 trillion has been spent on aid and development to little discernible advancements in the economic conditions of the continent, per Washington Consensus economic measures.

In addition to competing technical definitions of what constitutes development, there are also cultural notions to consider when characterizing the term. As previously noted, development implies improvement – indeed, a progression to a better life. What constitutes 'a good life' is loaded with culturally specific undertones. For example, the Washington Consensus indicators, advocated by the Bretton Woods system, loosely equate 'the good life' with the North American life. Whilst there are undoubtedly positive aspects of the American life, it is impossible to decide that it is categorically better than the Senegalese life, for example, and hence that the former should replace the latter.

DEVELOPMENT IN LIBERIA: WHAT IS THE OBJECTIVE?

In our attempt to understand development, it was noted that development has competing claims. There is the traditional position of economic development, where technical economic indicators are measured to gauge progress. Conversely, there are the approaches advocated by Easterly and Sen that expand the notion of development to include social and political life. Furthermore, Gal's (2006) work discusses the distinct development needs of small countries such as Liberia and demonstrates how their needs differ from those of larger countries.

The scope of this study does not attempt to articulate what Liberia's development priorities are. However, there are certain characteristics about the social and political history of Liberia that might not be accounted for in a strictly economic development framework. Specifically, I refer to the marginalization of the vast majority of the Liberian electorate from participating in political and social life as a result of colonialization by Americo-Liberians, and US collaboration with the creation of the colony and its involvement during the Cold War. Moreover, there are the post-conflict concerns that warrant immediate attention, such as employment of ex-combatants and civilians, and access to food, clean water, shelter and basic sanitation amenities. Such pressing concerns may not have the patience to wait for trickling-down fruits born from macroeconomic development plans. To enhance the public participation in government and meet the immediate needs of the majority of Liberians, what constitutes development in Liberia will have to account for the specificities of the country's current conditions. I do not dispute that steps are not currently being taken to tailor development to fit Liberia. However, I do contend that the Liberian Telecommunications Act – as an instance of Liberian law – potentially undermines such development, or at the very least could better support local economic, political and social development in Liberia. The development of an efficient telecommunications sector in Liberia not only stands to profit businesses, but to benefit Liberian people in a more direct way as well. To break away from Liberia's legacy of exogenous law creation and enforcement, it is critical that the interests of the private do not smother the interests of the public in the drafting and enforcement of the Liberian Telecommunications Authority (LTA). Only in so doing will Liberia be better equipped to meet its unique development needs.

The next section provides an overview of the law and development movement. It is important to keep in mind the competing notions of development when analysing the successes and/or failures of the law and development movement. As regards the case of the Liberian telecommunications sector, the telecommunications policy reflects the triumph of its constructors over average Liberians. As such, it imposes a Western conception of development that I contend will realize the same outcome as the ill-fated condom distribution programmes that Easterly describes.

The law and development movement

The law and development movement dates back to the 1960s. Various American institutions such as USAID and the Ford Foundation instigated the movement to attempt to reform the judicial systems and substantive laws of Africa, Asia and Latin America in an effort to spur development in those regions. A principal assumption underpinning this movement was that law could spur development. Note that economic development remained a sought-after development objective. The intellectual foundation of the movement was grounded in Weber's Modernization theory which assumed that 'evolutionary progress would ultimately result in legal ideas and institutions similar to those in the West' (Tamanaha: 473, in Schmidbauer 2006: 3). From this theory, three fundamental assumptions were made:

(1) Law is central to the development process and legal rules could be used as an instrument for changing society and its behaviour towards the Western model.

(2) The state played a central role for controlling and changing a society. As a result, lawyers and judges were seen to be performing the role of social engineers.

(3) Target countries would adopt American legal culture without any complications.

(Schmidbauer 2006: 4)

By the 1970s the movement was declared a failure. As Schmidbauer (2006: 4) states, there were 'many and various' reasons for the failure. He cites three general categories of said reasons. First, the assumption that American legal culture would be easily adopted proved fallacious. America's 'legal liberalism' did not end up fitting into the legal culture of the target countries. For example, the policy-making roles played by lawyers and judges in the US did not generally correspond with the roles of adjudicators in the developing states. The second principal reason for the failure of the law and development programme was an absence of buy-in by local actors. Schmidbauer notes that there was a lack of substantial participation of lawyers and relevant actors in the countries affected by the proposed reforms. The third principal explanation for the failure of the movement is argued to be the lack of a theoretical framework governing the process. As Schmidbauer (2006: 5) notes, the American lawyers involved in implementing the programmes were 'doers not theorists'. This preference for action rather than empirical data is said to have largely accounted for the failure. Despite the failure of the law and development programme, it has nevertheless experienced a resurrection.

The law and development movement alleges to have remedied past errors of research and implementation. Driven largely by economists, proponents of the revival are equipped with economics and econometrics models to assert their theoretical validity; likewise, the approach is alleged to be more bottom-up, in order to account for cultural obstacles to the legal movement. There is a great deal of optimism for the return of the law and development movement. For example, since 1990, the World Bank (the principal actor in the law and development movement) has spent US$2.9 billion on over 300 law reform projects around the world (Trubek 2006). However, the revival is not without its critics. Kevin Davis (2008) cautions us to curb our enthusiasm. He investigates the indicators used to measure the success of law and development programmes proliferated by the movement's economists; specifically, he focuses on the legal data used to measure aspects of the legal system. Davis points out that the research on which current optimism relies suffers from severe methodological flaws. For example, whilst examining the legal data for the World Bank's annual 'Doing Business' report[15] he finds that 'mislabelling' distorts the report's data. For example, as regards the 'Enforcing Contracts' indicator of the report,[16] Davis notes that the label is misleading since it implies a much broader category than the report actually quantifies. While the category seems to broadly include the enforcement of contracts in general, what is actually measured is just the enforcement of one specific type of contract, namely loan contracts (Schmidbauer 2006). It is important to keep in mind that despite their differences in implementation, these two phases of the law and development movement share the intellectual origin of the modernization movement, which identifies development as mimicking life in the Occident. Davis' scrutiny of the data used to support the law and development movement is important and requires serious contemplation. However, scepticism does not appear to have been heeded by many followers in practice. As Davis himself points out, the explosion of rule of law programmes indicates otherwise.

Rule of law

In 1989, Professor Tribe, one of the US' premier scholars of constitution law wrote 'the rule of law… has precious few sophisticated defenders these days' (Tribe 1989 in Ohnesorge 2007: 1). Little did Tribe anticipate that law and development would experience an intellectual revival and one of its instruments, i.e., the rule of law, would become standard practice.

John Ohnesorge (2007: 4) outlines competing notions of the practice and how the practice has developed over time. He concedes that the rule of law has no one-agreed definition, but rather that rule of law programmes 'typically address the formal characteristics of the materials of the legal system, emphasizing the value of rules rather than discretionary standards, and calling for clarity, specificity, and publicity'. Ohnesorge uses Hayek's definition to articulate his description. Hayek defines the rule of law as follows:

> [The rule of law means], stripped of all technicalities, the government in all actions is bound by rules fixed and announced before hand rules which make it possible to foresee with fair certainty how the authority will use its coercive powers in given circumstances and to plan one's individual affairs on the basis of this knowledge.
>
> (Hayek in Ohnesorge 2007: 4)

Thomas Carothers (1998: 95) outlines the rule of law explosion and cautions that political reluctance threatens its success. As Carothers notes: 'One cannot get through a foreign policy debate these days without someone proposing the rule of law as a solution to the world's troubles … the concept is suddenly everywhere – a venerable part of Western political philosophy enjoying a new run as a rising imperative of the era of globalization'.

The ubiquity of these programmes is evident in the amount of spending and the proliferation of the programmes. Over the past two decades, billions of dollars have been used in Latin America, sub-Saharan Africa, Central and Eastern Europe and Asia to institute such programmes (Carothers 1998).

Application of the rule of law in Liberia

Liberia is no exception to the panacea of the rule of law movement. Since the UN intervened in Liberia, the UN and its agencies have administered an extensive rule of law programme across the country. Nearly every international NGO has a rule of law programme buried within its panoply of public health, child-soldier and good governance agendas. Former US President Jimmy Carter's Carter Center plays a major role implementing Liberia's rule of law programme. President Carter (2008) wrote a piece for the Harvard International Review, attributing the Liberian conflict to a breakdown in rule of law, and supporting the merits of instituting such programmes to remedy post-conflict Liberia. Part of the rule of law programmes in Liberia involves re-examining the legal framework of the extractive industry sector.

The cause of the Liberian conflict is largely attributed to a contest to control the state and, more importantly, its resources (Gitau 2008). Liberia is rich in natural resources, such as timber and rubber. However, focusing exclusively on strengthening the rule of law in the extractive industries is unlikely to strengthen the rule of law governing state resources. There is a great deal of money to be made where the government is required to broker deals; indeed, any business deal that requires the interface of government permission and private actors will generate revenue.[17] Rule of law efforts to date are weakened by their narrow focus on regulating, primarily, extractive natural resource industries.

With a population of only 4.1 million, Liberia has enough resources to elevate Liberians to a reasonable standard of life. Though not a natural resource *per se*, Liberia's telecommunication sector is nevertheless capable of turning out huge profits that could enrich the people. Charles Taylor recognized this economic potential; part of his fortune was made from his monopoly of telecommunications services through his company, Lone Star Communications.[18] Moreover, the process that government plays in the telecommunications sector parallels its role in more traditional extractive industries, as this role relates to the distribution of permits, concessions and licences. For example, the government is charged with doling out concessions for the use of the telecommunications spectrum and licences for service provisions. Most importantly, the government accepts bids for the construction of telecommunications infrastructure; this is a significant profit-making aspect of the sector. Rule of law programmes are widely and broadly applied in Liberia and should be further broadened to include the telecommunications sector. The proliferation of legislation since the end of the conflict indicates the popularity of rule of law programmes. However, there are limitations to rule of law programmes – not only in practice, but in theory. The next section explores the critiques of rule of law, asking the question: do rule of law programmes actually work?

Does rule of law actually work?

THEORETICAL CRITIQUES

The rule of law movement functions on an assumption of rationality. Douglass North (1995) advocates for institutional creation as a means of realizing economic development. North begins his discussion with a critique of the traditional neo-classical framework of instrumental rationality. With instrumental rationality, 'institutions are unnecessary; ideas and ideologies do not matter; and efficient markets – both economic and political – characterize economies' (North 1995: 17). North contends that although neo-classicalists may be right in theory, they suffer a fundamental flaw in practice, namely, that transactions are not costless. As a result, carefully crafted institutions must be created to facilitate information flows among actors, thereby reducing transaction costs. 'Institutions …' North declares, 'are the rules of the game'. North's model advocates that governments play a role in the economic development of a country – an outcome distinct from a strict neo-classical school of thought which frowns on government involvement. The role of government in North's case is as a law maker. The laws proliferated in rule of law programmes are the 'rules of the game' to which North famously refers. However, the research done in the school of Behavioural Law and Economics (BLE) has demonstrated that there are behavioural components to humans that frustrate the rational choice model.

The BLE movement looks at certain human actions that deviate consistently from what the rational choice model would otherwise predict. Rather than discount such deviation as irrational (per the rational choice framework) BLE takes a closer look at explaining why certain patterns of deviation arise. In general, BLE has found that misperception and misinformation accounts for a number of common deviations (Bar-Gill 2008).[19] As regards laws, Becker's (1968) Nobel Prize winning work on deterrence has been contested by BLE. Becker assumes that the decision to commit an offence, or not, depends on two factors: (1) the probability of apprehension and (2) the magnitude of the sanction. He argues that in order to achieve optimal deterrence, we should maximize the magnitude of the sanction. BLE contests Becker's finding on empirical grounds – namely that we do not, in practice, see maximum fines imposed for minor offences such as littering, for example. On theoretical grounds, studies have indicated that humans tend to misperceive the risk of apprehension: that is, they tend to underestimate the likelihood of getting caught. North's model takes into account the information gaps inherent in the rational choice framework, but fails to look at the misperception that those affected by laws make in terms of decision-making as to how they should or should not act. That the rule of law movement rests on a precarious theoretical foundation undermines the likelihood that it will deliver the results its proponents promise.

PRACTICAL CRITIQUES

Despite the questionable assumption upon which the rule of law rests, we cannot deny the powers of law, however spurious. Ogowewo's (2000) findings, as previously discussed, demonstrate that contests for power are contests for law creation. Whether or not the subsequent laws *actually* affect behaviour, is questionable, as demonstrated by the theoretical weakness of the rule of law. However, there appears to be a general perception that whoever writes the rules of the games exerts control over the game.

Carothers (1998) goes beyond merely describing the rule of law phenomenon. He discusses factors that rule of law programmes overlook, which, in turn, compromise the success of such programmes. The underlying premise of these development programmes is that creating a legal framework – equipped with clear laws and enforcement authority – will aid in the economic, social and political development of recipient countries.

Carothers distinguishes rule of law from rule *by* law, to demonstrate that the mere institutionalization of a legal order will not necessarily render development. Whereas in rule of law systems, laws apply *equally to everyone*, in rule *by* law programmes, 'the laws exist not to limit the state but to serve its power' (Carothers 1998: 97). In the latter model of legal orders, the government often stands outside of the realm of enforcement and instead enforces the laws against the citizens. Carothers's rule by law category is reminiscent of the Rousseauan and Nietzschean theoretical assertions previously discussed – where the elite create laws to serve their interests and are not subject to them. Carothers stresses rule of law practitioners to be wary of basing the success of a rule of law programme merely on technical aspects (i.e. proliferation of laws and institutions), but to ensure that there is public participation in the process in order to avoid a rule *by* law scenario. As Carothers (1998: 96) notes: 'Citizens must be brought into the process if conceptions of law and justice are to be truly transformed'.

In addition to the practical obstacles that may arise, should practitioners ignore public participation, there are also cultural obstacles to be overcome. North himself admits that culture plays an important role in the successful implementation of rule of law projects. He cautions against exporting boiler plate models of one set of laws modelled for a particular country, to another country. North (1995: 25) states that: 'societies that adopt formal rules of another society … will have very different performance characteristics than the original country because both the informal norms and the enforcement characteristics will be different'.

Moreover, there is an entire literature critiquing development programmes, in general, for failing to account for local buy-in. Chabal and Daloz (1999) propose an alternative methodology to effectuate better buy-in. They propose that rather than adopting the traditional position – where an implementer stands within his own culture and postulates about another culture to determine whether something is amiss – implementers need to immerse themselves in the political life of the target country. Only then will the implementer have a sense of not only the informal but the formal orders as well and be better equipped to prescribe solutions. This more empathetic understanding is implied to render more successful project outcomes.

As regards Liberia's telecommunication sectors, there was little 'immersion' on the part of the law's advocates and implementers to conform to the methodology of Chabal and Daloz. The practical obstacle of cultural dissonance is characterized by the rule of law programme in Liberia as it relates to the telecommunications sector. The next section discusses Liberia's telecommunications sectors. First, I will give an overview of how the Liberian Telecommunications Act was realized; second, I will outline telecommunications' legal framework; third,

I will demonstrate how this framework compromises local Liberian economic development.

The Liberian telecommunications sector

The telecommunications sector in Liberia is governed by the Liberian Telecommunication Act of 2007. An independent regulatory agency, the LTA, was also established in 2007 to oversee the sector and implement the Act. These legal tools were part of a proliferation of laws that were created following Liberia's conflict in order to govern the country's revenue-generating industries.[20] The World Bank played a major role in the creation of the legal framework governing Liberian telecoms. In earlier sections of this chapter the creation of laws in Liberia was discussed, along with how these laws have arguably run counter to the development demands of the majority of Liberians. The laws governing Liberian telecoms are, unfortunately, no different. The new telecommunications laws delegitimize the informal economy and, as a result, directly compromise the development goals of Liberia.[21] Moreover, the laws do not *and cannot* remedy the monopolistic tendencies of the country's telecommunications sector, despite the threat that such a tendency poses to national stability. As such, the legal framework governing telecoms demonstrates, once again, a conscious decision to ignore the articulated interests of the vast majority of Liberians and instead serve the small elite and the outsiders who write the laws to suit their ends.

Overview of the Liberian telecommunications sector

The telecommunications sector in Liberia is limited but has a great deal of potential for growth. The regularly updated CIA Factbook describes the sector as follows:

> *general assessment:* the limited services available are found almost exclusively in the capital Monrovia; coverage extended to a number of other towns and rural areas by four mobile-cellular network operators
>
> *domestic:* fixed line service stagnant and extremely limited; mobile-cellular subscription base growing and teledensity approaching 20 per 100 persons.
>
> CIA Factbook (2009)

Following the conflict, there was genuine concern that, because the telecommunications sector was a significant revenue-generating industry, it posed a threat to Liberia's stability. Historically, conflicts in Liberia have arisen because of contests for control of the state's revenue-generating sector. Charles Taylor's telecommunications monopoly, Lone Star Communications, generated US$38 million per year, of which US$12 million was Taylor's share (Coalition for International Justice 2005). Taylor was able to profit handsomely from the sector, despite the sector's derelict state and the fact that Lone Star only provided one service among the panoply of services available in telecommunications. There is still much room for improvement in the laying of fixed lines to facilitate higher teledensity and increase access to internet services. For the Liberian telecommunications sector to enhance their services, additional fixed lines will have to be installed throughout the country. Such infrastructure projects are the principal money-makers in the telecoms sector. As such, they incentivize conflicts for control of the state.

Profit potential

FINANCIAL GAINS

Despite the tumultuous past of Liberian telecommunications and the increased number of competitors in the sector following the war, there is room to make sizeable profits. Telecommunications is the transmission of signals over a distance for the purpose of communication. Telecommunications is, hence, more than providing services to the national population in the form of mobile phone communication. It involves the sale of spectrum allocation, and infrastructure building of landline and subterranean cables which facilitate the internet. To give an idea about how much is at risk, we can look to telecommunications deals currently being made around Africa. In October 2008, Britain's Vodacom took control of South Africa's leading mobile operator, in a deal worth £1.4 billion (approximately US$2.5 billion at the time); Mubadala, part of the Abu Dhabi sovereign wealth fund, bought a licence to operate mobile, fixed line and broadband services in Nigeria for US$400 million in 2007; and the private equity-funded project SEACOM[22] was contracted for US$700 million and has already listed US$300 million in business returns on the investment – despite not being fully constructed. As Matt Glynn, head of technology, media and communications for emerging markets for DLA Piper stated, as regards African telecommunications: 'Africa is huge for us … whether or not there's a sub-prime crisis in the US has little bearing on whether people need to use their phones over here' (Chellel 2009).

The meeting point of high demand and low supply has created opportunities for wealth creation in the telecommunications industry in Africa.[23] In addition to Glynn's comments, I spoke with a senior executive at France Telecommunication who reported that Africa is similarly the subject of a new strategy plan for one of the world's largest telecommunications operators. As of 2007, the number of mobile phone subscribers tripled in developing countries over the preceding 5 years according to UNCTAD (Information Economy Report 2007). Furthermore, Africa recently reached 250 million unique mobile subscribers,[24] making its market larger than that of North America (Essoungou 2010). In 2007, France Telecommunications was looking to double its revenue in Africa, focusing on accessing rural customers on the continent. This goal of doubling the customer base follows the pursuit of a similar posture in 2007, which resulted in the win of two major bids in Kenya and Ghana – two major urbanizing countries in East and West Africa.[25]

The potential for windfall profits in telecommunications, coupled with the legacy of corruption and conflict in telecommunications, should invite added scrutiny in the drafting of telecommunications law by Liberian policy makers. However, attention to telecommunications law, to date, seems to be largely from the outside. The World Bank, for example, addressed Liberia's telecommunications sector and was instrumental in advising the development of the legal framework for the industry. In theory, the view of the role that the government *should* play in the telecommunications sector is split between whether the government should play a large or a small role, or alternatively, no role at all. In practice, most governments do regulate the sector – albeit to varying degrees. Nevertheless, the World Bank has, and continues to, push for privatization of the income-generating sectors in developing countries (Levy and Spiller 1996), telecommunications in Liberia included. The WB supports the notion that government should play a role – in the short term only and to the extent that it facilitates competition in the sector.[26] In Liberia, the WB has expressly sought as much privatization of the sector as possible (2009). The telecommunications sector has a great deal of potential to profit, not only for companies, but also for Liberian individuals. However, dictating where that profit will go depends on the regulators, whose job is confounded by the inherent proclivity of the organization of the telecommunications sector itself.

The telecommunication sector lends itself to the creation of monopolies. As noted, the Liberian telecommunications framework needs a significant facelift before a resident of Monrovia can chat and e-mail freely with a relative living in the rural areas. Telecommunications infrastructure is a one-time and costly upfront investment; the firm that lays the infrastructure has every incentive to monopolize and block competitors from free-riding on its investment. Pursuant to Michal Gal's (2006) research, small markets such as Liberia may further encourage monopolies or oligarchies given that the country's telecommunications demand (at least in the short term) is limited to 4.1 million people.[27] The profit to be made similarly incentivizes companies to explore illicit means of attaining government bids. Given the potential for profit and perversions inherent to the telecommunications sector, it is important that the GoL safeguard against these risks and play a significant role in curbing such detrimental tendencies. Fully privatizing the industry cannot prevent or thwart anti-competitive behaviour. To the contrary, removing government involvement is likely to exacerbate the problem.

In addition to the anti-competitive incentives inherent to telecoms, additional risks to the profit potential of Liberia are risks to investment. However, it is important to distinguish between perceived risk and actual risk. The international intervention in Liberia has been significant. Not only was there a large peacekeeping contingency deployed in the country, but the day-to-day operations of the state are coordinated in concert with the international community to a great extent – given aid dependence, *inter alia*. The United Missions in Liberia (UNMIL), which is in charge of peace keeping, has a renewed mandate through September 2014. However, even UNMIL aside, the international presence will remain in Liberia for some time. Renewed conflict that would destabilize investment is unlikely as long as there exists such an international presence. Moreover, as previously noted in this chapter, the rule of law programme in Liberia is driven and administered by the international community and is extensive in Liberia. Foreign investors have sympathetic channels through which they can appeal should an investment dispute arise. That said, I contend that the perceived risk of doing business in Liberia is greater than the actual risk. Taking the aforementioned risks into account, suffice to say that the Liberian telecommunications sector has the potential to render large profits. If such profits were reaped in a responsible and accountable manner, the lives of the country's 4.1 million people would be substantially improved.

SOCIAL GAINS

The Liberian telecommunications sector is undoubtedly profitable and will increase the revenue of the Liberian government. Assuming corruption does not skim too much off the top, these added revenues should be helpful to the government in providing the Liberian public with great political, economic and social freedoms, not previously afforded under previous leaderships that co-opted the state. Moreover, in theory, jobs will be created for Liberians who would otherwise not have been employed. This development of the formal economy lends benefits to Liberians, albeit in a trickle-down manner.

The development of telecommunications also lends itself to more populist benefits. Rural inhabitants can better sell their wares and services to market. Phones have the capacity to facilitate banking transaction; in Kenya mobile phones are increasingly equipped with banking capabilities, thus allowing bank transfers in a simple and inexpensive way. Once again, this is helpful to the majority of Liberians living outside of Monrovia. Furthermore, mobile phones enable citizens to mobilize themselves and demand political attention. The overthrow of president Estrada of the Philippines is largely attributed to text messages that were sent out, which, in turn, mobilized thousands of protesters that overthrew the government. The development of the telecommunications sector in Liberia would not only develop Liberians' economic life, but also develop their social and political life.

Accessibility to telecommunications services is an issue that stands between the economic, social and political development of the majority of Liberians. However, although the LTA accounts for universal access, it does not require such a policy. The language of the Act, indeed, is very weak, despite the significant hurdles that rural inhabitants face in terms of becoming involved in the governing of their country.[28] Also, costs of the hardware, such as the mobile phones themselves, can be burdensome to many Liberians, who do not have the capital to purchase a phone. Although this is a commonly known reality, again, there is no provision in the LTA that accounts for subsidization of these costs.[29] The Liberian telecommunications sector is a national resource, not only in the profits it can offer to private businesses, but also in the tools it can provide the average Liberian with, thus facilitating social, economic and/or political empowerment.

Existing legal framework in Liberian telecom

In 2007 the Liberian Telecommunications Act was passed by an act of parliament. Its enforcement agency, the LTA, is an independent government agency[30], staffed by president-appointed commissioners.[31] It is charged with regulating the telecommunications sector and its services[32] and implementing the Telecommunications Act.[33] The LTA is the first point of contact for the initiation of bids.[34]

The LTA is required, *inter alia*, to provide research, devise plans[35] and designs[36] for the functioning of the industry, regulate[37] and monitor[38] compliance of private operators, advise the Ministry of Post and Telecommunications[39], and maintain records of licences[40], as well as publish notices of any changes it makes within its mandate.[41] The LTA has the power to subpoena information,[42] investigate complaints,[43] issue licences,[44] issue binding orders[45] and rules,[46] and amend, modify, suspend and revoke licences.[47] The LTA is also in charge of managing the radio spectrum of the country,[48] resolving disputes among service providers and between service providers and their customers,[49] and preventing anti-competitive practices.[50] Note that the LTA's powers and responsibilities are not confined to the explicit text. Rather the Act provides a catch-all clause which permits the authority to 'take all other actions as are reasonably required to carry out the Telecommunications Act, and all related regulations, rules and orders, and to perform such other responsibilities, functions and powers conferred in the LTA under any other law'.[51] This discretionary clause has fostered various problems to be further discussed.

The objectives of the Act stress privatization and attracting foreign investment on the one hand and affording access to Liberians on the other.[52] In our earlier discussion on development in this chapter, I noted how certain development objectives can undermine others; I used the example of how increasing worker productivity, thereby increasing economic gains, could harm social networks and social development. Deciding which goal will trump the other is the decision of those in charge of government. When a government is captured by narrow interests, it is the majority of people that suffers – as has been the Liberian experience from inception of the state to the present day. Upon a closer inspection of the Liberian Telecommunications Act, certain provisions undermine the realization of development objectives that would improve the lives of the majority of Liberians, but yet confront the interests of foreign investors. The following section discusses three provisions that specifically threaten the interests of the majority of Liberians, and as such, warrant greater scrutiny by the GoL and the international community. If sustained peace is to be realized, the pathology of marginalizing the majority of Liberians must be reconsidered.

Problematic provisions

Liberia's telecommunication law does not demonstrate an understanding of the Liberian context, nor an interest in creating laws that will benefit the average Liberian. First, the telecommunications law delegitimizes the informal economy and, as a result, directly compromises the development goals of Liberia. Second, the laws do not *and cannot* remedy the monopolistic tendencies of the country's telecommunications sector, despite the threat that such an arrangement poses to national stability. Indeed, overall enforcement of the Act by the national government is unlikely, which further obscures Liberians' involvement in their laws. Third, the catch-all provision provides unnecessary discretion that can all too easily be abused, as witnessed by the experience of West Africa Telecommunications (WAT).

Liberia's telecommunication law delegitimizes the informal economy

The Liberian Telecommunications Act delegitimizes the existing telecommunications sector, and, as a result, threatens economic development in Liberia. Hernando de Soto (2000) rose to global prominence by articulating why the occidental world is so wealthy as compared to under-developed states such as Liberia. De Soto begins with the premise that capitalism is a good wealth-generating economic model and that, in order to reap the accordant gains from this model, an individual must have capital. In summation, to gain capital, you have to have capital. And therein lies the problem in most underdeveloped states where capital accumulation is largely in the informal sectors, rather than in more formalized systems such as property ownership. To evidence his claim, de Soto points to the fact that in wealthy occidental states, such as the US, the most abundant source of wealth-generating capital is found in the equity of individuals' homes: 'the single most important source of funds for new businesses in the United States is a mortgage on the entrepreneur's house,' (de Soto 2000: 6).[53] Following de Soto's findings, rule of law programmes focused a great deal on the formalization of the informal economy. What proponents of de Soto's theory arguably did not take into account (or did, and reasoned that the gains would outweigh the costs) was that in formalizing aspects of the economy, parts of the informal economy would either be eliminated or illegalized. Such is the case in Liberia after the creation of the 2007 Telecommunications Act. The Act requires telecommunication licensing for service providers; this licensing scheme formalizes the telecommunications sector, which can, on the one hand be beneficial to the sector, especially for international investors. On the other hand, however, the licensing scheme renders illegitimate existing and indigenous telecommunications services, that are similarly beneficial to the Liberian economy. The Act's licensing provision is as follows:

Act Part IV, Sec. 15: Requirement to hold license

(1) No person shall:

    (a) provide a telecommunications service[54] to the public for direct or indirect compensation;

or

(b) own or operate a telecommunications network used to provide a telecommunications service to the public for direct or indirect compensation, except under and in accordance with a license or an exemption order issued by the LTA.

(2)   For the purposes of this Act, the provision of telecommunications services to the public includes the provision or offering of such a service to any segment of the public, including the resale of telecommunications services obtained from another person, even if only one person is provided or offered such a service.

The Act requires licences for all providers and does not include a *de minimis* threshold beneath which a formal licence is not required. In creating such a scheme, the LTA delegitimizes a major part of the national telecommunications sector and compromises the economic development of the country in two ways: (i) the Act thwarts entrepreneurialism and (ii) the Act creates unemployment amongst a critical demographic.

The following is an instance of a typical small-scale telecommunications service provider, currently working in the Liberian informal economy that is threatened by the Act.

CASE: THE SMALL-SCALE TELECOMMUNICATIONS BUSINESS OWNER

Johnathan S. is a small-scale entrepreneur. When I first met him, he drove a taxi for foreigners, who paid him in US dollars. After generating enough capital, he purchased some second-hand computers, a printer/scanner/fax machine and several mobile phones, and opened an internet café. These small businesses are very popular in Liberia and are peppered throughout the city. They provide the average Liberians affordable access to the internet and telephone services. Among other services offered, Mr S. also offers Skype and other VoIP-like services, which offer free international telephone calls through the internet. Mr S., and other small-scale entrepreneurs like him, does not have a licence from the LTA and is unlikely to get one. Technically, Mr S., and others who own similarly small-scale internet cafes, are in violation of the Liberian Telecommunications Authority.

Earlier in this chapter the competing notions of development were discussed, along with how the types of economic development policies in Liberia run counter to the types of development goals most pressing to the state and its people. Liberia currently has 80 per cent unemployment (BTI 2014)[55], and the brunt of this unemployment is among male youths between the ages of 18 and 35. This is the precise demographic that had been and is recruited to pick up arms for cash and participate in the type of protracted conflicts that Liberians are keen to avoid.[56] Those who are most frequently seen setting up the small communication cafes and peddling mobile phone services on corners throughout the city are precisely these men that fall within this critical demographic. If the Act is enforced, this group may once again find themselves out of work and thus receptive to hire-for-fire type employment.

To be fair, the likelihood of enforcement of the Act is low at the moment. As previously mentioned, the GoL is short of resources; trying to prevent every small-scale entrepreneur from selling services would be a huge cost. However, foreign companies that invest in Liberia and are moving aggressively into African telecoms, might have an interest and the requisite influence to weed out their small-time competitors. Such actors already possess a great deal of bargaining power when negotiating with their government counterparts.[57] In Liberia this disparity is manifold because of the pressure that the GoL receives from the international donors to make deals in order to repay their debts.[58] The telecommunications licensing scheme only further empowers large foreign companies who, in turn, can pressure the governments to enforce the Act and eliminate their small-time competitors. The laws do not and cannot remedy the monopolistic tendencies of the country's telecommunications sector.

In a report tracking Charles Taylor's resources, the Coalition for International Justice noted that Charles Taylor's monopoly over telecommunications allowed him to amass a sizeable fortune which was, in part, spent on protracting his war (Coalition for International Justice 2005). As noted, the telecommunications sector already has a tendency towards anti-competitive behaviour; this tendency is made further likely by Liberia's small market size (Gal 2006). If Liberia's telecommunications law was acutely tailored to the needs of the country, anti-competitive measures would be prioritized. This is not the case.

The telecommunications law prohibits anti-competitive behaviour, to be sure. However, it does not couch it in terms of the conflict nor the resource limits endemic in the post-conflict states. GoL agencies are, in general, starved of resources; the LTA, in particular, is no exception. The administrative investment required to execute is as intricate and complicated a licensing scheme as required by the Act is completely unrealistic; identifying and prosecuting anti-competitive behaviour even more so. Anti-trust violations go unnoticed and unpunished in countries with much more resources at their disposal. Granted, anti-trust violations of telecommunications operators functioning in Liberia may be smaller and hence less expensive to identify and punish. However, given that the court is barely functioning right now, there is unlikely to be judicial enforcement of the Act or even judicial review of the LTA decisions regarding investigations of suspicious telecommunications activity. Courts are famished for resources, making enforcement of the Liberian Telecommunications Act unlikely. A law without enforcement is not a law at all according to Kelsen's (1945) definition, as previously discussed in the chapter. However, that the Liberian Telecommunications Act is not a 'law' is only true for the subjects of it. International private companies doing deals with the GoL in telecommunications have alternative mechanisms of dispute resolution that would not be available to a small Liberian company; such international companies can hence enact the Act to protect their investments. What this means is that the Liberian Telecommunications Act, in effect, is a *rule by law*[59] mechanism vis-à-vis its anti-competition clauses insofar as the companies most likely to violate this provision (large capital-intensive companies) will not necessarily be subject to its enforcement since they have alternative dispute resolution mechanisms to which they can appeal. Conversely, small Liberian companies that seek to invoke the Act's anti-competitive provisions against large, predominantly international companies are unlikely to see the Act enforced, since they are more likely to litigate in national courts. Again, this demonstrates how the Liberian Telecommunications Act thwarts local entrepreneurialism, since its provisions are unenforceable by local companies, which are most likely to seek national judicial relief, but can be enforced against such companies.

The catch-all provision provides unnecessary discretion that can all too easily be abused.

The catch-all provision that permits the Liberian Telecommunications Authority to take all reasonable steps in the fulfilment of its mandate is too broad and has lent itself to disputes. The WB recently sent a team to assess the Liberian telecommunications sector. The team concluded that an 'independent managing audit' of the LTA be undertaken in order to gauge the 'strengths and weaknesses' of the agency (Seeton 2009a). The assessment was conducted in response to allegations of poor management by the LTA over the sector. The following is an anecdote of my experience with Liberia's telecommunication sector.

CASE: WEST AFRICA TELECOMMUNICATIONS

On a visit to the Ministry of Post and Telecommunications in the summer of 2007, a representative of the Ministry voiced his surprise when I informed him that WAT, a French company, had acquired a spectrum licence for US$6 million the week before. That a senior level official at the Ministry was unaware of one of the first and largest bids by a Western investor in Liberia's telecommunications industry demonstrates the informality of the telecommunications bidding process. The establishment of LTA is supposed to clarify bidding procedures. However, WAT's experience since winning their bid in the summer of 2007 again illustrates that this may not be the case in reality.

In July 2007 WAT was granted a spectrum licence. The government is said to have dragged its feet in fulfilling its end of the licensing agreement. By November 2007, a dispute arose between the LTA and WAT, with the latter's licence being revoked by the former. The LTA accused WAT of operating outside of its licence stipulations and WAT accused the government of breach of contract. WAT ultimately took the government to Liberian court. I corresponded with an LTA Commissioner, and, as of 18 April 2008, he insists that WAT went beyond its permitted licence. The matter has been resolved to some extent following a 2009 ruling from the Supreme Court of Liberia (Liberia's highest court) in favour of WAT.

WAT was one of the first major international bids in telecommunications that Liberia had had since the end of the war. That the deal has proceeded so tumultuously signals to other international investors that there are administrative or political misgivings with the GoL and investments should proceed cautiously.

In addition to WAT's allegations of the LTA, allegations of impropriety have plagued the LTA. One Commissioner was noted to be in violation of the Act establishing the LTA: in contravention of Part III, Sec. 10(3) prohibiting conflicts of interests. He owned a telecommunications operator. Moreover, one of the LTA's Commissioners, Albert Bropleh, has come under some serious allegations of corruption.[60] In response to these various problems, the WB team was dispatched to assess the LTA. As mentioned, the team concluded that what was needed was an 'independent management audit' of the LTA. Specifically, this recommendation called for the creation of an external, independent person – that is, not politically appointed – becoming charged with running the day-to-day administrative tasks of the agency (Seeton 2009b). The creation of an independent entity with no public oversight will further remove Liberians from having a say in what happens with their country's resources. This is not the optimal solution to overseeing the industry and ensuring that the gains reaped are adequately redistributed to Liberians in pursuance of their development goals. Rather than create an external and unaccountable institution, the LTA and its partners could, for example, limit the 'catch-all clause' or create an oversight committee within the government. Similarly, it could solicit key Liberian Civil Society groups to act as watchdogs over the industry in particular. Again, I do not contend one solution over a variety of proposals. However, given the conditions specific to Liberia, removing the public from the governing of its telecommunications sector seems unaligned with the development interests of the average Liberian.

Conclusion

Liberians in theory and in fact have distinct desires as to how to manoeuvre the development of their telecommunications sector to serve their distinct development needs. This study has demonstrated that throughout the modern history of the Liberian state, outcomes beneficial to Liberians were compromised to serve the interests of whichever outside force was in power at the time. The process of law creation vis-à-vis the Telecommunications Act betrays institutional biases towards the status quo; the end of conflict presents a unique opportunity to change the status quo. It is important that the parties involved in drafting the country's new laws are aware of this biased legacy and make efforts to preclude recurrence.

Many of the Act's provisions seem to perpetuate the cycle of legal drafting and enforcement that has plagued Liberia since the inception of the state. However, there are various provisions, such as including universal access, that demonstrate a move towards the kind of development that is, arguably, more reflective of Liberian needs. Interest convergence is key: balancing the interests of attracting foreign investment yet not thwarting local entrepreneurialism is ideal and should be further pursued.

The licensing scheme of the Telecommunications Act disengages the public from participating in the telecommunications sector. Small-scale telecommunications providers are on every corner in the capital city, and the agent responsible for drafting the Liberian Telecommunications Act either chose to ignore this substantial demographic or expressly sought to target them – the absence of a *de minimis* threshold demonstrates this. If Liberians are to develop beyond their current conditions, efforts must be made to identify what is lacking and to develop from there. The World Bank can play a fundamental role in such developments. Tailoring the Liberian Telecommunications Law to better outfit what average Liberians lack is a straightforward endeavour that could render significant benefits.

In addition to strengthening the telecommunications law of Liberia to better reflect the needs of the Liberian people, it is similarly important to extract from the Liberian telecommunications example lessons as to how to improve the process of constructing laws and legal orders. The Liberian Telecommunications Law is but one instance within a much broader occurrence of self-perpetuating legal orders. At stake, however – for countries of similarly precarious political, economic and social orders – are security, stability and economic growth for the world's poorest people. As previously discussed, rule of law programmes flail and fail because they operate in a vacuum removed from the local context; among these contexts is the Nietzschean law-generation bias, acute in developing countries, namely, that laws can and often are generated by and for those persons drafting them. Widening the pool of legislative drafters is an additional aim towards which to strive. Technology has made direct democracy cheaper and more feasible, mobile phones having already facilitated various social movements, as previously noted. More persons can participate in the drafting of key laws, especially those that have long-term economic impacts, such as telecommunications. Such an aim should be pursued to the extent possible.

Within the vein of better laws and a better law-making process, the Liberian telecommunications case should similarly highlight that special attention should be paid to all investment laws passed during an interim government period. Several of Liberia's investment laws were passed in the period following the war and preceding the installation of the Sirleaf-Johnson administration. Insofar as laws passed during this transitional period are least likely to reflect the wider interests of the population, interim governments – and the international community that supports them – should refrain from passing such laws, however seemingly innocuous, or, at the very least, limit the duration of their applicability.

Appendix 10A

The objectives of the Liberian Telecommunications Act (see LTA, Part I, Sec. 3a–l) are as follows:

(a) facilitate the development of the telecommunications sector in order to promote social and economic development throughout Liberia

(b) promote the efficient and reliable provision of telecommunications services relying as much as possible on market forces such as competition and private sector investment to achieve this objective

(c) promote affordable telecommunications access in all parts and regions of Liberia, relying on market forces and private sector investment when feasible and Government initiatives where appropriate

(d) ensure the national security policies applicable to both domestic and international activities, are adhered to including through regulations, rules or orders under this Act

(e) establish a fair, objective and transparent regulatory regime for service providers, including the licensing of service providers

(f) establish a framework for the control of anti-competitive conduct in the telecommunication sector, and otherwise protect the interests of subscribers and other customers of telecommunications services

(g) ensure the safety of telecommunications networks and users of telecommunications services, and the privacy and proper use of customer information

(h) promote the use of new and more efficient technologies and efficient management and use of radio spectrum and other scarce resources

(i) encourage sustainable foreign and domestic investment in the telecommunication sector

(j) establish measures to enforce the implementation of this Act and to prohibit certain types of conduct contrary to the orderly development and regulation of the telecommunications sector

(k) encourage participation of Liberians in the ownership, control, and management of communications companies and organizations

(l) promote and safeguard national interests in the development and implementation policies.

Notes

1 Following the American civil war, there were xenophobic concerns over what to do with all the newly freed blacks. Some worried about the political effects that this demographic shift could have; others harboured generally racist reluctance in having blacks integrate into American society. The solution that arose was to send them back. Granted, the slaves who would ultimately make the trans-Atlantic journey had never been to Africa, much less a tiny coast on the western end of the continent. However, the idea garnered support among whites and enterprising blacks alike, with the latter group seeking an opportunity to become landowners (Levitt 2005).

2 The Constitution is reportedly a product of Harvard Professor Simon Greenleaf (University of Liberia 2009 at http://www.universityliberia.org/ul_history.htm).

3 Assistant Secretary of State for African Affairs, Chester Crocker, testified before Congress that the election was imperfect but a step towards democracy (PBS 2002).

4 Ofuatey-Kodjoe (1994) notes that there are 12 Americo-Liberian families that essentially own and control Liberia.

5 UN Security Council Resolution 1760 (2007) permitted investigation into Charles Taylor's 'Hidden Wealth'. Charles Taylor is currently on trial at The Hague and the details of his personal wealth are being increasingly revealed (Global Witness 2009).

6 Liberia was popularly referred to as Charles Taylor, Inc. given Taylor's unabashed private use of public resources, effectively turning the country into a personal fund Polgreen (2006) and the Coalition for International Justice (2005).

7 Economic laws passed during this period were as follows, *inter alia*: Public Procurement and Concessions Act 2005; National Forestry Reform Act 2006; Liberia Telecommunications Act 2007. GEMAP (Governance and Economic Management and Planning) is one of the most intrusive economic laws passed, whereby a foreign official is placed in revenue-generating government ministries to sign-off on every and all actions related to revenues and purchases.

8 As of September 2007, there were two sets of Liberia's legal code, both owned by the American Bar Association, one of which was on loan to the Liberian Bar Association. However, a copy of the Financial Code which addresses all economic crimes was suspiciously missing and not even the Ministry of Finance could find an updated version.

9 This is one of the issues included in the Liberian Telecommunication Act and is a common source of dispute in the telecommunications sector.

10 Walton's archival work tracks the correspondences between US diplomats stationed in Liberia and the State Department.

11 This is the most recent peace agreement, which ended the civil conflict in Liberia.

12 According to the World Bank (2010b), per capita public spending in Liberia is one of the lowest in the world, at US$68 in Fiscal Year 2009/2010, making Liberia highly dependent on foreign aid.

13 The UNDP (2010) placed Norway at the top and Zimbabwe at the bottom of its annual list of human development.

14 Fiscal policy discipline; redirection of public spending from subsidies ('especially indiscriminate subsidies') towards broadbased provision of key pro-growth, pro-poor services like primary education, primary health care and infrastructure investment; tax reform – broadening the tax base and adopting moderate marginal tax rates; interest rates that are market determined and positive (but moderate) in real terms; competitive exchange rates; trade liberalization – liberalization of imports, with particular emphasis on elimination of quantitative restrictions (licensing etc.); any trade protection to be provided by low and relatively uniform tariffs; liberalization of inward foreign direct investment; privatization of state enterprises; deregulation – abolition of regulations that impede market entry or restrict competition, except for those justified on safety, environmental and consumer protection grounds, and prudent oversight of financial institutions; and legal security for property rights.

15 The World Bank's annual 'Doing Business' report is considered an industry standard in measuring the law and development movement.

16 The World Bank's annual 'Doing Business' report ranks countries according to the ease or difficulty it is to do business there. The report uses the various steps usually required to set up a business, such as title to land, judiciary protection and access to credit, and examines how easy or arduous it is to realize these steps. The enforcement of contracts is one step in facilitating business in a given country and as such is used as an indicator in the report.

17 Liberia's principal revenue generating industries are rubber, timber, shipping licensing and telecommunications. Although not natural extractive resources, per se, the issuance of shipping licences and concessions for telecommunications services are major revenue sources.

18 The Coalition for International Justice wrote a forensic accounting report of Charles Taylor's finances. The report estimates that Taylor profited US$1 billion from his company Lone Star Communications (CIJ 2005).

19 Reference to Professor Oren Bar-Gill is of the lectures he delivered in his course on Behavioural Law and Economics at NYU in the spring of 2008.

20 Public Procurement and Concessions Act, 2005; National Forestry Reform Act, 2006; Liberia Telecommunications Act, 2007.
21 Economist Dambisa Moyo calls this process the 'micro–macro paradox', where a 'short-term efficacious intervention may have few discernible, sustainable long-term benefits. Worse still it can intentionally undermine whatever fragile chance for sustainable development may already be in play' (Moyo 2009: 44).
22 SEACOM is a project which will build a high-speed subterranean cable line with landing sites in South Africa, Mozambique, Tanzania and Kenya (www.seacom.mu).
23 Annual International Telecommunications Union report reports that the bottom ten countries in the world as regards telecommunications development are all located in Africa. Conversely, Africa has the highest growth rate in the sector of all emerging markets in the world (ITU Report 2008).
24 There are 520 million mobile subscriptions in Africa, of which 253 million are one-person subscriptions (i.e. one SIM card) (Nyambura-Mwaura 2013).
25 Note that the bid won in Kenya was to acquire 51 per cent of TelKom, the country's incumbent, nationally owned server; this privatization cost France Telecommunications US$390 million (Mullen 2007).
26 The World Bank's (WB) 'Telecommunications Regulation Toolkit' advocates liberalization of the sector that does not preclude regulation in the short term. The WB notes that, in the short term, regulators can facilitate a competitive environment. Deregulation as the ultimate goal is not ruled out (WB Telecommunications Regulation Toolkit 2009).
27 Gal's research looks at competition laws in small countries, and the unique obstacles that said states face in implementing anti-trust regimes that are modelLed on larger countries (Gal 2006).
28 Universal access attained through market forces is promoted in the objectives of the act. 'The objectives of the Act are to ... promote affordable telecommunications access in all parts and regions of Liberia, relying on market forces and private sector investment when feasible and Government initiatives where appropriate', Part I (3). The government is permitted to pursue Universal Access as well, subject to consultation with service providers, Part V (23).
29 The Act does permit the GoL to set up a fund to 'subsidize ... the net costs of providing universal service'. However, it is unclear whether this fund would provide for hardware. Moreover, the fund is subject to the approval of a Universal Access Policy, which, as mentioned, is subject to consultation of service providers. Part V (23)(1).
30 Act. Part III, Sec. 8(2)
31 Act. Part III, Sec. 9(1)
32 Act. Part III Sec.8(2)
33 Act. Part III, Sec.11(1)(b)
34 LTA Correspondence 2007
35 Act. Part III(11)(1)(g): define network termination points, if required; Act. Part III(11)(1)(h) prescribe procedures for the approval of telecommunications equipment for attachment to telecommunications networks in Liberia, using the least onerous method available.
36 Act. Part III(11)(1)(c): design and implement the processes for licences that are issued; Act. Part III(11)(1) (i) establish a radio spectrum plan and manage the radio spectrum allocated to the telecommunications sector;
Act.Part III(11)(1) (k) establish and manage a numbering plan and allocate numbers to service providers.
37 Act. III(11)(1) (j) regulate interconnection between telecommunication networks of different service providers.
38 Act. III(11)(1)(d): monitor and enforce compliance by licencees with the conditions of their licences.

39 Act. Part III, Sec.11(1)(a).
40 Act. Part III, Sec. 11(1)(p).
41 Act. Part III, Sec.11(1)(s).
42 Act. Part III, Sec.11(1)(t); All operator must are required to provide information to the LTA that the Authority reasonably requires.
43 Act. Part III, Sec.11(1) (u); the LTA may investigate complaints on its own initiative.
44 Act. Part III, Sec.11(1)(c).
45 Act. Part III, Sec.11(1)(r).
46 Act, Part III, Sec.11(1)(q); (v) in exercising the LTA's powers and performing its duties under the Telecommunications Act, a regulation, rule, or order determine any question of law or fact, and the LTA's determination on a question of fact is binding and conclusive.
47 Act. Part III(11)(1)(e).
48 Act. Part III, Sec.11(1)(i).
49 Act. Part III, Sec.11(1)(l).
50 Act. Part III, Sec.11(1)(m) institute and maintain appropriate measures for the purpose of preventing service providers from engaging in or continuing anti-competitive practices, including the identification of telecommunication markets, determining dominance and abuse of dominance in identified telecommunication markets and responding to anti-competitive agreement.
51 Act. Part III, Sec.11(1)(w).
52 The objectives of the act are located in Appendix 10A.
53 It is important to note that there are, naturally, limits to de Soto's thesis as evidenced by the housing bubble and the subsequent collapse of global finance. Excessive borrowing against inflated values of home ownership is largely blamed for the Occidental world's current financial dilemma.
54 The Liberian Telecommunications Act defines telecommunications service as: any provision of the voice and data transmission; SIM cards and pre-paid accessories; equipment and facilities to customers; or any form of transmission of signs, signals, text, images or other intelligence by means of a telecommunications network, but does not include a broadcasting service.
55 As previously noted, this figure is probably exaggerated since this statistic was derived using formal sector employment only. As is the case in many developing/underdeveloped countries in the world, employment in the informal sector is often more significant than employment in the formal sector.
56 In January 2009, Secretary General of the UN, Ban Ki-moon noted the connection between conflict and unemployment in Sierra Leone, stating: 'Youth unemployment remains the most acute concern … Urgent action is therefore required to create employment opportunities with a view to reducing the lingering effects of the marginalization of the country's young people, who constitute the largest segment of the population' (IRIN 2009). Liberia and Sierra Leone are indistinguishable in this regard. Both had protracted conflict inspired by enterprising leaders after natural resources; the rank and file that fought the wars were unemployed youth.
57 In 2006, the GoL renegotiated the terms of one particularly grossly inequitable contract for the extraction of steel with Mittal Steel (Global Witness 2006).
58 The GoL qualifies for debt cancellation for the IMF loans accrued by previous governments. However, in order to actualize this debt relief, they have to fulfill a series of conditions. The GoL recently purchased US$1.2 billion of its own debt at a discount.
59 From Carothers' rule of law and rule by law distinction (Carothers 1998).
60 Commissioner Bropleh has been accused of taking money from the LTA's fund for personal use, misreporting job-related expenditures and abusing procurement privileges, among other things.

References

Austin, J. (1995, 1832). *The Province of Jurisprudence Determined*. Ed. W.E. Rumble. Cambridge: Cambridge University Press.

Bar-Gill, O. (2008). Owen Bar-Gill Lectures: Course on Behavioural Law and Economics at NYU.

Becker, G.S. (1968). 'Crime and Punishment: An Economic Approach'. *The Journal of Political Economy*, 76(2): 169–217.

BTI (2014). 'Liberia Country Report'. Available at: www.bti-project.de/uploads/tx_itao_download/BTI_2014_Liberia.pdf (accessed: 2 February 2015).

Carothers, T. (1998). 'The Rule of Law Revival'. *Foreign Affairs*, 77(2). Available at: www.foreignaffairs.com/articles/53809/thomas-carothers/the-rule-of-law-revival (accessed: 17 February 2015).

Carter, J. (2008). 'Reconstructing the Rule of Law: Post-Conflict Liberia'. *Harvard International Review*, 30: 14–18.

Chabal, P. and J. Daloz (1999). *'Africa Works – Disorder as Political Instrument'*. Oxford: James Currey.

Chellel, K. (2009). 'Africa Special Report: The Art of Conversation'. *The Lawyer*, April 2009. Available at: www.thelawyer.com/africa-special-report-the-art-of-conversation/1000338.article (accessed: 2009).

CIA (2009). 'CIA Factbook, Liberia'. Available at: https://www.cia.gov/library/publications/the-world-factbook/geos/li.html (accessed: February 2011).

CIA (2014). 'CIA Factbook, Liberia'. Available at: www.cia.gov/library/publications/the-world-factbook/geos/li.html (accessed: 20 August 2014).

Coalition for International Justice (2005). *Following Taylor's Money: A Path of War and Destruction*. Washington DC: Coalition for International Justice.

Colombant, N. (2007). 'Liberia's former Leader Bryant is Arrested in Corruption Probe'. *VOA*, 7 December 2007. Available at: http://archive.today/FcZbE (accessed: 7 December 2007).

Davis, K. E. and Trebilcock, M. J. (2008). 'The Relationship between Law and Development: Optimists versus Skeptics'. *American Journal of Comparative Law*, 56(4): 895–946.

de Soto, H. (2000). *The Mystery of Capital: Why Capitalism Triumphs in the West and Fails Everywhere Else*. New York: Basic Books.

Easterly, W. (2002). *The Elusive Quest for Growth: Economists' Adventures and Misadventures in the Tropics*. Cambridge: MIT Press.

Essoungou, A.-M. (2010). 'A Social Media Boom Begins in Africa'. *Africa Renewal*, United Nations. Available at: www.un.org/africarenewal/magazine/december-2010/social-media-boom-begins-africa (accessed: February 2011).

Gal, M. (2006). 'The Effects of Smallness and Remoteness on Competition Law – The Case of New Zealand'. New York University Law and Economics Research Paper Series, Working Paper 06-48. New York: New York University.

Gitau, R. (2008). 'God Willing, I Will be Back: Gauging the Truth and Reconciliation Commission's Capacity to Deter Economic Crimes'. *African Security Review*, 17(4): 64–77.

Global Security Organization (2007). 'Liberia Election and Coup Attempt – 1985'. Available at: www.globalsecurity.org/military/world/war/liberia-1985.htm (accessed: 2 February 2015).

Global Witness (2006). 'Heavy Mittal: The State within a State: The Inequitable Mineral Development Agreement between the Government of Liberia and Mittal Steel Holdings'. Available at: https://www.globalwitness.org/sites/default/files/pdfs/mittal_steel_en_oct_2006_low_res.pdf (accessed: 2 February 2015).

Global Witness (2009). 'Undue Diligence: How Banks do Business with Corrupt Regimes'. Available at: www.globalwitness.org/library/undue-diligence-how-banks-do-business-corrupt-regimes (accessed: 2 February 2015).

Hayner, P. (2007). 'Negotiating Peace in Liberia: Preserving the Possibility for Justice'. International Center for Transitional Justice. Available at: https://www.ictj.org/sites/default/files/ICTJ-Liberia-Negotiating-Peace-2007-English_0.pdf (accessed: 2 February 2015).

Hobbes, T. (1998). *The Leviathan*. Buffalo: Prometheus Books.

IRIN (2007). 'Liberia: Government Takes Aim at Unemployment'. UN Office for the Coordination of Humanitarian Affairs. Available at: www.irinnews.org/report/70456/liberia-government-takes-aim-atunemployment (accessed: 2 February 2015).

IRIN (2009). 'Sierra Leone: Could Youth Unemployment Derail Stability?'. UN Office for the Coordination of Humanitarian Affairs. Available at: www.irinnews.org/printreport.aspx?reportid=83278 (accessed: 2 February 2015).

ITU (2008). '*ITU African Telecommunication/ICT Indicators 2008: At a Crossroads*'. 8th edition. Geneva: International Telecommunication Union.

Kelsen, H. (c1945). *A General Theory of Law and State*. Cambridge, MA: Harvard University Press.

Left, S. (2003). 'War in Liberia'. *The Guardian*, 4 August 2003. Available at: www.theguardian.com/world/2003/aug/04/westafrica.qanda (accessed: 2 February 2015).

Levitt, J.I. (2005). *The Evolution of Deadly Conflict in Liberia: From 'Paternaltarianism' to State Collapse*. Durham, NC: Carolina Academic Press.

Levy, B. and T. Spiller (1996). *Regulations, Institutions, and Commitment: Comparative Studies of Telecommunications*. Cambridge, MA: Cambridge University Press.

Loden, A. (2007). 'Civil Society and Security Sector Reform in post-Conflict Liberia: Painting a Moving Train without Brushes'. *The International Journal of Transitional Justice*, 1: 297–307.

Massing, M. (2005). 'How Liberia Held "Free" Elections'. *The Nation*. Available at: www.thenation.com/article/how-liberia-held-free-elections (accessed: 2 February 2015).

Moyo, D. (2009). *Dead Aid: Why Aid Is Not Working and how There Is a Better Way for Africa*. New York: Farrar, Strauss and Giroux.

Mullen, J. (2007). 'France Telecom Looks to Africa for Growth'. *Wall Street Journal*, 26 December 2007. Available at: www.privatizationbarometer.net/news.php?id=13082 (accessed: 2 February 2015).

National Forestry Reform Law (2006). Monrovia: Government of Liberia.

Nietzsche, F. (2006, 1887). *On the Genealogy of Morality*. Ed. K. Ansell-Pearson, trans. C. Diethe. Cambridge: Cambridge University Press.

North, D. (1995). 'The New Institutional Economics and Third World Development'. In J. Harris, C.M. Lewis and J. Hunter (eds), *The New Institutional Economics and Third World Development*: 17–26. London: Routledge.

Nyambura-Mwaura, H. (2013). 'Fewer than One in Three Africans has a Mobile Phone'. *Reuters*, 11 November 2013. Available at: www.reuters.com/article/2013/11/11/africa-telecoms-idUSL5N0IW0HD20131111 (accessed: 2 February 2015).

Ofuatey-Kodjoe, W. (1994). 'Regional Organization and the Resolution of Internal Conflict: The ECOWAS Intervention in Liberia'. *International Peacekeeping*, 11(3): 261–302.

Ogowewo, T. (2000). 'Why the Judicial Annulment of the Constitution of 1999 is Imperative for the Survival of Nigeria's Democracy'. In M. Andenas (ed.), *The Creation and Amendment of Constitutional Norms*. Oxford: British Institute of International and Comparative Law.

Ohnesorge, J. (2007). 'The Rule of Law'. Legal Studies Research Paper 1051, Madison: University of Wisconsin.

Public Procurement and Concessions Act (2005). Monrovia: Ministry of Foreign Affairs.

PBS: Global Connections (2002). 'Liberia and the United States: A Complex Relationship'. Available at: www.pbs.org/wgbh/globalconnections/liberia/essays/uspolicy/ (accessed: 2 February 2015).

Polgreen, L. (2006). 'A Master Plan Drawn in Blood'. *New York Times*, 2 April 2006. Available at: www.nytimes.com/2006/04/02/weekinreview/02polgreen.html? pagewanted=all&_r=0 (accessed: 2 February 2015).

Rousseau, J.J. (1996, 1755). 'Discourse on the Origins of Inequality'. In D. Wootton (ed.), *Modern Political Thought: Readings from Machiavelli to Nietzsche*. Indianapolis: Hackett Publishing.

Telecommunications Act (2007). Monrovia: Government of Liberia.

Sen, A. (2001). *Development as Freedom*. Oxford: Oxford University Press.

Schmidbauer, R. (2006). '*Law and Development: Dawn of a New Era?*'. Manchester: University of Manchester.

Seeton, T. (2009a). 'World Bank: "Management Audit" Needed at Liberia's Telecom Authority'. *The Daily IIJ* weblog. Available at: http://inwent-iij-lab.org/Weblog/2009/ 02/23/world-bank-management-audit-needed-at-liberias-telecom-authority/ (accessed: 2 February 2015).

Seeton, T. (2009b). 'Liberia: President Sirleaf Uncovers Excess Spending at LTA'. *The Daily IIJ* weblog. Available at: http://inwent-iij-lab.org/Weblog/2009/03/03/liberia-pres-sirleaf-uncovers-excess-spending-at-lta/ (accessed: 2 February 2015).

Trubek, D. (2006). 'The "Rule of Law" in Development Assistance: Past, Present, and Future'. In David Trubek and Alvaro Santos (eds), *The New Law and Economic Development: A Critical Appraisal*: 74–94. Cambridge: Cambridge University Press.

UNCTAD (2007). 'Information Economy Report 2007–2008'. Geneva: United Nations.

UNDP (2010). 'Human Development Report'. Available at: http://hdr.undp.org/en/ statistics/ (accessed: 2 February 2015).

UNICEF (2011). 'Liberia at a Glance'. Available at: www.unicef.org/infobycountry/ liberia_statistics.html (accessed: 2 February 2015).

University of Liberia (2009). Available at: www.universityliberia.org/ul_history.htm (accessed: 2 February 2015)

Walton, H. (2002). Liberian Politics: The Portrait by African American diplomat J. Milton Turner. Lanham, MD: Lexington Books.

Ward, J. and M. Marsh (2006). 'Sexual Violence against Women and Girls in War and Its Aftermath: Realities, Responses and Required Resources'. UNFPA Briefing Paper. Brussels: UNFPA.

World Bank (2009) 'Telecommunications Regulation Toolkit'. Washington, DC: World Bank.

World Bank (2010a). 'Beyond Economic Growth'. Available at: www.worldbank.org/ depweb/english/beyond/global/chapter6.html (accessed: 2 February 2015)

World Bank (2010b). 'Liberia: Country Results Profile'. Available at: http://web. worldbank.org/WBSITE/EXTERNAL/COUNTRIES/AFRICAEXT/0,,contentMDK:2 3294184~pagePK:146736~piPK:226340~theSitePK:258644,00.html (accessed: 2 February 2015)

11 Does foreign aid support democracy development?

Aid, democracy and instability from trade

Thierry Kangoye

Introduction

The positive role of institutions in development has been widely assessed and confirmed; fundamentally, institutions cause economic growth and development (North 1990; Hall and Jones 1999; Acemoglu *et al.* 2001; Rodrik *et al.* 2004). The obvious next question for some scholars has naturally been to know how countries acquire good institutions. Rodrik (2000) explained that countries face two strategies to optimize their institutions: copying well-functioning institutions from advanced countries (with a risk of failure, since the effectiveness of institutions is highly specific to local conditions), or taking advantage of local knowledge and engaging in an experimentation process of institutional designs.

However, from another policy point of view, one can propose another formulation of strategies: still following Rodrik (2000), a first strategy could be that countries invest their resources directly in institutional improvement (through experimentation or copying from abroad – which can be costly for their current economic performance); while a second strategy could be that instead of focusing directly on institutions, countries give preference to an indirect way of institutional building. They can do so by investing their resources in the determinants of good institutions, such as economic performance.

As we will discuss in the next section, growth stability matters for institutional building and external assistance can be given a role, which is the subject of this chapter. Recent studies on aid effectiveness have highlighted macroeconomic instability as a factor for promoting aid. Guillaumont and Chauvet (2001), Collier and Dehn (2001), Chauvet and Guillaumont (2004, 2009), and Collier and Goderis (2007) have shown that aid, by protecting growth against the negative effects of shocks, is more effective in vulnerable countries. The core assumption of this chapter is based upon these findings and can be formulated as follows: if one accepts that stable growth is good for institutional building and that aid can make growth more stable by protecting it against shocks, a positive effect of aid on institutions in countries exposed to these shocks can therefore be expected. The question this chapter attempts to answer is important, since reducing the adverse effects of macroeconomic instability has become a great challenge for developing countries.

We focus on democracy, as measured by synthetic indexes. Democracy is considered as a 'meta-institution' which helps to build better institutions and helps societies to select good economic institutions from the available menu, and to deliver higher-quality growth (more stable, better redistributed, more predictable) (Rodrik 1997, 2000). Democracy has also gained importance with the worldwide diffusion of its ideology, which has induced a great deal of pressure for the underdeveloped world to adopt democratic forms of governments. We also focus in this chapter on terms-of-trade (TOT) instability as a source of instability, since most of developing countries rely on the export sector of primary products and are dependent on world markets, making them particularly sensitive to TOT fluctuations. Moreover, the exogenous character of TOT fluctuations provides some technical benefits in the econometric estimations.[1]

We empirically test the hypothesis that TOT instability is a source of income instability, which has negative effects on democracy, and that aid has a positive effect on the quality of democracy conditional on this instability. We explain that this outcome is probably due to the 'growth-stabilizing' effect of aid shown in previous studies. We use panel data from 70 developing and emerging countries[2] over the period 1980–2003 (pooled in two 12-year periods) and find evidence that aid mitigates the adverse effects of TOT instability on democracy. The effect of aid on institutions conditional on instability is assessed through an interaction of aid and TOT instability. We also use instrumental variables to isolate the exogenous variation in aid flows. Our results contribute to the existing literature; to the best of our knowledge, this research is the first to empirically test a conditional impact of aid on institutions.

The remainder of the chapter proceeds as follows: first, we review the determinants of democracy and the relationships between the instability of economic performance and democracy. Next we focus on the relationships between aid and democracy and on how aid may have a positive impact on democracy conditional on TOT instability. The section Empirical evidence provides the empirical evaluation of the theoretical arguments, and we finish with the Conclusion.

The determinants of democracy

Non-economic determinants of democracy

Theoretical and empirical models in the literature have identified and discussed a number of non-economic determinants of democracy, the most prominent being colonial heritage, cultural factors (religious affiliation) and social fractionalization.

Colonial heritage

Colonial heritage could be an important determinant of democracy. British colonial heritage is quite widely evidenced as good for democracy (Weiner 1987; Lipset 1996; Mainwaring and Shugart 1997). According to some authors, British colonists handed down traditions of law (lowering the control of local landed elites over the colonial state), parliamentarianism and civil-service professionalism that left their former colonies in a better position to sustain open rule than the former colonies of other European powers. Lipset *et al.* (1993) also argue that British rule provided a crucial learning experience for subsequent democracy. Przeworski *et al.* (2000) support this view by arguing that transitions to democracy are more likely in former British colonies, where citizens had historical positive experience with democratic practice.

However, the empirical evidence of that argument is not clear. When testing the effect of colonial history on democracy, La Porta *et al.* (1999) find a positive relationship between British colonial heritage and democracy, while Barro (1999) only succeeds in identifying an indirect effect through economic development factors (standard of living and education). Barro (1996) argues that the former possessions of Britain and Spain are substantially more democratic than are those of France, Portugal and other European countries. However, he concludes that the breakdown among different colonizers is irrelevant and colonial history is insignificant for democracy when measures of the standard of living (such as schooling and infant mortality) are held constant.

Ethnic diversity

Many academic writings on the determinants of democracy assume or aver that social heterogeneity lowers democracy's prospects. A number of eminent political scientists have seen diverse societies disadvantaged when it comes to democratization (Dahl 1971; Rabushka and Shepsle 1972; Lijphart 1977; Welsh 1993). Accordingly, ethnic differences divide society and make compromise and consensus difficult. Heterogeneity also potentially undermines open politics by increasing the risk of intercommunal violence. When political parties and other organizations are formed more readily around ethnic than other identities, political entrepreneurs have an incentive to play on such divisions and to neglect efforts to mobilize citizens around civil rights and class concerns (Horowitz 1985). Fish and Brooks (2004) also explain that more ethnically diverse countries are less likely to sustain democracy, because ethnic diversity, by contributing to inequality, can reduce democratic tendencies. The 2001 Freedom House survey provided support for these points by showing that democracy has been significantly more successful in mono-ethnic societies than in ethnically divided and multi-ethnic societies (Karatnycky 2002). Barro (1999), in his empirical investigation of the determinants of democracy, also highlighted that the population degree of heterogeneity with respect to ethnicity, language and culture also matter for democracy, the common idea being that more heterogeneous societies are less able to sustain democracy.

Economic performance and democracy

Although the focus is on the determinants of democracy in this chapter, the extent to which democracy itself leads to economic development outcomes such as economic growth[3] and high level of income remain a matter of interest.

The question has been the subject of much interest in the field of political economy. Competing theoretical and empirical studies have yielded few robust conclusions supporting each of the following possibilities: 'democracy facilitates development', 'democracy hinders development', and 'there is no independent relationship between democracy and development outcomes'. Using indexes of democracy (political openness, political regimes, civil liberties), a huge empirical literature has examined the question by looking at the causal effects of democracy on economic growth and has reached inconclusive findings. Helliwell (1994) finds that while democracy (measured by index of political rights and civil liberties) affects education and investment positively, it has a negative and insignificant impact on growth once these factors are controlled for, concluding that democracy has no significant effect on economic growth. Barro (1996) highlights a non-linear relationship between democracy and growth. His results explain that, at low levels of democracy, growth increases with democracy and, at higher levels of democracy, growth decreases with democracy. Monali (1997) finds a positive association between the degree of non-elite participation in politics and economic growth. Tavares and Wacziarg (2001) find that the positive effect of democracy on growth works through the channels of education, reduced inequality and lower government consumption. Rodrik (1997) investigates the effect of democracy (as measured by indexes of civil liberties and political rights) on economic performance and shows that as compared with autocracies, democracies yield higher and more predictable growth rates. Tavares and Wacziarg (2001) provide empirical evidence that after taking into account the positive and negative indirect effects of democracy on growth (negative effect through the physical capital accumulation and the government consumption, and positive effect through the accumulation of human capital and the lowering of income inequality), the overall effect of democracy on economic growth is moderately negative. Barro (1999) explains that the net effect of democracy on growth is uncertain. While an expansion of political freedom provides a check on governmental power and thereby limits the potential of public officials to amass personal wealth and to carry out unpopular policies, this may also encourage rich-to-poor redistributions of income and thus enhance the power of interest groups. Using a measure of democracy based upon the number of years that a country can be regarded as a democracy. De Haan and Siermann (1996) conclude that there is no robust relationship between democracy and economic growth. Persson and Tabellini (2006) found that the relationship between democracy and economic growth depends on the details of democratic regimes such as electoral rules, forms of government, stability and persistence of democratic institutions. More recently, using panel data for African countries and an index of electoral competitiveness as a measure of democracy, Fosu (2008) finds a U-shape relationship between democracy and economic growth. Summing up, what comes out from the number of studies that have investigated the causal relationships from democracy to economic development and growth is that there are no robust findings.

However, beside and inside the huge analytical literature about the beneficial effects of democracy on economic performance and development, a number of studies have also addressed the other-way linkage between democracy and economic development outcomes; that is, the effect of income on democracy.

The modernization theory articulated by Lipset (1959) claims that countries should become more democratic as they become richer. This seminal work of Lipset (1959) discusses a broad category of economic development as a determinant of democracy, including indices of wealth (per capita income), urbanization and industrialization. The key element of this hypothesis is that richer countries are more willing to promote democratic values and receptivity to democratic political tolerance norms.

Many studies have followed up this theory insofar as they recognize that the level of income is an important background condition for democracy (Lipset 1960; Dahl 1971; Bollen 1979; Lipset 1994), although the exact form of the relationship is still a matter of debate. However, this theory has received mixed empirical support. While Helliwell (1994) and Barro (1999) find that improvements in the standard of living (or income level) favour democracy (as measured by a subjective indicator of electoral rights, political rights and civil liberties), Acemoglu *et al.* (2005a), using post-war data, find that when the factors simultaneously affecting income and democracy are controlled for in regressions, the strong cross-country correlation between democracy and income no longer holds.

Recent studies of democratization do, however, point out that other factors can play a causal role in the emergence of democracy. Sachs and Warner (2001) and Ross (2001) highlight natural resource endowments of countries as a strong determinant, arguing that greater reliance on mineral exports leads to concentrated power and then reduces the probability that dictatorships will become democratic. The work of Lipset (1959) predicts that a better educated population favours democracy and democratic practices because education provides individuals with a higher value of staying politically involved. While a number of empirical studies provide support for this view (Barro 1999; Przeworski *et al.* 2000; Glaeser *et al.* 2004), Acemoglu *et al.* (2005b) find that, when considering *within*-country variation, there is no evidence that countries that increase their education are more likely to become democratic.

Instability of economic performance and democracy: causation and reverse causation

Few academic works deal explicitly with issues about causal relationships between macroeconomic instability (or its determinants) and the quality of institutions. One aim of this chapter is to explain how macroeconomic instability, more precisely TOT instability, can affect the quality of democracy. However, the well-known papers in the literature about macroeconomic instability and institutions have been interested in the reverse causation, which is about the institutional causes of instability. Rodrik (1997) has explained that countries with weak institutions of conflict management, and in which latent social conflicts exist, are more likely to experience severe external shocks. The core idea of his argument is that by reducing the level of wealth to be redistributed shocks, or more precisely negative TOT shocks, tend to weaken growth stability because of redistribution conflicts when there are no rules to manage them. Thus, good institutions of conflict management (democratic institutions, rule of law, good social insurance system and so on) can mitigate the impact of shocks on growth. Acemoglu *et al.* (2003) have also explained that macroeconomic volatility is deeply determined by weak institutions rather than distortionary macroeconomic policies. Countries characterized by weak institutions are more likely to experience macroeconomic instability because of weak constraints on the executive, lack of entrepreneurs' confidence and weak security of contracts. Democratic institutions have also proved to have direct effects on macroeconomic stability, meaning that countries led by democratic regimes experience greater macroeconomic stability than non-democratic countries (Weede 1996; Rodrik 1997; Quinn and Woolley 2001; Almeida and Ferreira 2002; Mobarak 2005). Satyanath and Subramanian (2004) showed that democratic political institutions have a strong and statistically significant causal impact on macroeconomic stability. Yang (2008) has also examined the causal relationship between democracy and growth volatility, and has shown that democratic institutions lower the volatility of real GDP per capita growth in ethnically divided countries.

However, the idea that institutions can be affected by instability also has important policy implications and is relevant for our research. In this chapter we are interested in knowing how TOT instability can affect the quality of democracy. Our main theoretical reasoning is that TOT instability affects democracy negatively by generating income instability (Easterly and Kraay 2000) and in turn, by lowering growth (Mobarak 2005), which has been found to be unfavourable to democratic processes. Studies on the economic determinants of democracy have highlighted the level of development as one of the main determinants (Lipset 1959; Helliwell 1994). Nonetheless, while most of them have established a positive effect of the level of growth on democracy, very few of them have discussed the quality of growth and, more specifically, its stability (although both can be closely related).

We support the view that TOT instability causes growth instability which, in turn, weakens democracy. Growth instability can have an effect on the quality of democracy through (income) growth volatility in various ways. The first argument is that macroeconomic volatility is costly for growth and development, which are important determinants of democracy. Indeed, development which is favourable to the emergence of good political institutions requires sustained increases in income. The influential work of Ramey and Ramey (1995),[4] based on a sample of 92 countries, has shown that countries with higher volatility have lower growth rates. However, and more interestingly, Mendoza (1997) has shown that volatility associated with TOT fluctuations could lead to slower growth (depending on the degree of risk aversion). Democratic institutions tend to evolve slowly while their establishment and reinforcement require considerable financial resources: for organizing democratic elections, supporting the effectiveness of civil society, and for the establishment of an efficient parliament and independent judiciary and so on. Such resources of course have opportunity costs in terms of reducing other growth-enhancing factors, or income volatility that may diminish the quality of democracy.

Instability from trade, proxied in this chapter by TOT instability, per se can also be harmful to democracy. High trade dependency, (which increases countries' exposure to external shocks, has been found to be unfavourable for the installation and consolidation of democratic regimes. Indeed, TOT instability which can be seen as one of the symptoms of economic dependence and weak diversification is a source of high exposure to fluctuations in world markets and economic instability, which in turn penalizes the stabilization and legitimation of democratic regimes (Huber *et al.* 1993). In this regard, Djankov *et al.* (2008) have argued that negative shocks bring pressure on governments to reduce the levels of democracy and checks and balances.

Income volatility, arising from TOT instability, can also have a negative effect on democratic institutions, by generating uncertainty and risks associated with resources to be redistributed in an economy. Income instability may create uncertainty in the politico-economic environment, which can in turn have a direct negative effect on the democratic process by changing the way of assuming power. Further, this uncertainty may incite elites in power to exclude other competing political groups in order to maximize their rent capture in the present given the increased level of uncertainty. Hence, elites are likely to engage in rent-seeking activities in 'good times' (when income is high[5]), in order to smooth their private consumption across time. As a consequence, there would be weak political competition and therefore poor quality of democracy.

Does foreign aid promote democracy?

Aid and democracy

Many papers have examined the potential direct impact of aid on institutional development, but with mixed results. Several of them have focused on legal institutions (rule of law, corruption, bureaucracy, contracts, property rights) and others on economic and political institutions. They find that aid can have negative as well as positive effects on these institutions (see Svensson 2000; Goldsmith 2001; Knack 2001; Alesina and Weder 2002; McNab and Everhart 2002; Hoffman 2003; Tavares 2003; Brautigam and Knack 2004; Knack and Rahman 2004; FMI 2005; Coviello and Islam 2006).

Regarding the specific effect of aid on democracy, however, the empirical findings in the literature seem to be less debated. The general view of the relationship between foreign aid and democracy is that aid is intended in part to promote democracy in the developing world. With the exception of the work of Djankov *et al.* (2008) which finds that aid has a negative effect on democracy, most empirical papers conclude either positive effects or simply to no effects. Djankov *et al.* (2008) explain their findings of a negative effect of aid by the observation that foreign aid could lead politicians in power to engage in rent-seeking activities in order to appropriate aid resources and to exclude other groups from the political process.

The democracy-building efforts of aid donors potentially contribute to improving democratization by enhancing the learning of electoral processes (through technical assistance and conditionalities) and by improving the quality of human resources and income levels (Knack 2004). This point is supported by Kalyvitis and Vlachaki (2005), who find strong evidence that, when directed at democratization, political aid[6] in the form of electoral and technical assistance positively influences democratic transitions in recipient countries, though aggregate aid-flows may not.

While most empirical studies on aid and democratization have concluded that aid has no effect on democracy (Hoffman 2003; Knack 2004; Kalyvitis and Vlachaki 2005), several studies find that aid could lead to better civil liberties, political competition and participation. Goldsmith (2001) supports this view, arguing that aid could improve health and literacy, making people better informed and aware of public politics, which in turn enhances the quality of democracy. Dunning (2004) also demonstrates that foreign aid has a (small) positive effect on democracy in the post-Cold War period.

Summing up, the main empirical studies about the direct effect of aid on democratic institutions conclude that aid has no effect on them, or at most has a positive effect on democracy. But what impacts of aid on institutions could be expected in some exogenous circumstances?

Aid and growth: the stabilizing nature of aid

The aid-effectiveness literature, focusing on macroeconomic instability and economic vulnerability of recipient countries, provides us with the general intuition of the research underlying this chapter. If one accepts the point that aid has proved to be more effective in vulnerable countries by protecting growth against external shocks (more precisely by making it more stable), then it could have an indirect positive effect on institutions in these countries through this channel, since institutional development requires some stability in the economic environment.

Guillaumont and Chauvet (2001) and Chauvet and Guillaumont (2004, 2009) have shown that negative TOT shocks have adverse effects on growth and that aid is more effective in vulnerable countries by making growth more stable in the medium term. Chauvet and Guillaumont (2009) have discussed the stabilizing nature of aid for exports and, more interestingly for the present chapter, for growth volatility. They explain that more than aid cyclicality (pro or counter), it is the relative trend level of aid and its relative volatility compared with the flow of the variable of interest (exports, national revenues and so on), that contribute to explaining its dampening character. They conclude that the level of aid tends to dampen income volatility. In cases where shocks occur, aid smoothes public expenditures and limits the risk of fiscal deficits (Guillaumont and Chauvet 2001; Chauvet and Guillaumont 2004, 2009). In recipient countries, national income and fiscal revenues are indeed likely to be influenced by aid disbursements, with the level of aid likely to cushion the negative effects of external shocks on economic growth.[7] Collier and Goderis (2009) have pursued this idea and have shown that the level of aid lowers the negative effects of commodity export price shocks on growth, because aid finances precautionary expenditure, which reduces vulnerability to shocks. Elsewhere, Collier and Dehn (2001) have focused on export price shocks to explain aid effectiveness and have shown that, while positive shocks have insignificant effects on the growth process, negative shocks reduce growth but the interaction between the negative shocks and aid is significantly positive, suggesting that aid mitigates the negative effects of TOT deterioration on growth.

Easterly and Kraay (2000) have shown for small states that, because of their greater openness, TOT shocks volatility is a source of growth instability. We can generalize this point to the underdeveloped countries because of their high dependence on trade and their specialized exports, making their growth performance fragile in cases of trade shocks. In the previous sections in this chapter, we have argued that growth instability is not good for institutions partly because a stable growth allows quality institutions to emerge. So, if aid reduces growth volatility, it could also protect institutions in a situation of instability. Thus our main theoretical prediction is that, by mitigating the adverse effects of shocks on growth, aid could have a positive conditional effect on democracy. The next section provides an empirical evaluation of this prediction.

Empirical evidence

The data

We use data over the period 1980–2003 for 70 developing countries, 28 of which are African (see Table 11C.1). Aid data are from the World Development Indicators (World Bank 2005b) and the Global Development Finance (World Bank 2005a; originally taken from OECD/DAC). Data on exports and imports of goods and services, gross development product (measured in 2000 constant US$ and in purchasing power parity) and population are also from the same source. The Global Development Network Growth Database collected by William Easterly provides us with data on legal origin, ethnolinguistic fractionalization, geography and infant mortality. We focus in this chapter on political institutions and more precisely on democratic institutions. So, we use two synthetic democratic indicators from the Polity IV project database and the Freedom House database (See Appendix 11A for a complete description of these indicators). Data on TOT are from the United Nations Conference on Trade and Development (UNCTAD) statistics (UNCTAD 2009).

The measure of term-of-trade instability

Our TOT instability variable measures the gap between TOT and an estimated trend of TOT. Instability is indeed always measured over a reference, which is often an estimated trend. This requires making some assumptions about the nature of this trend. Estimations can give wrong results if a deterministic trend is estimated with a non-stationary variable. Because most economic variables include a trend which is not purely stochastic, we assume the trend in TOT to be mixed (both deterministic and stochastic). Then, we get the predicted value of TOT by running the following regression (Equation 11.1) on 12-year periods[8] (*i* refers to countries, *t* refers to years. *X* is the TOT variable and ε is the idiosyncratic error term):

$$X_{it} = \alpha + \beta X_{i(t-1)} + \gamma t + \varepsilon_{it} \tag{11.1}$$

Then, we compute for each period t an instability index by using the following formula of the quadratic mean:

$$Instab_{it} = 100 \sqrt{\frac{1}{T} \Sigma_{i=t_1}^{t_2} \left(\frac{\widehat{X}_I - \widehat{X}_I}{\widehat{X}_I} \right)^2} \tag{11.2}$$

where $T = (t_2 - t_1)$ is the length of the period, X_i and $\widehat{X}_I$ are the observed and predicted values of TOT, respectively.

Some stylized facts

Our theoretical arguments predict a negative effect of instability on the quality of institutions (democracy). Sorting countries by deciles on TOT instability[9] supports this view: the more TOT-unstable countries have weaker democratic institutions. This negative correlation evidence is displayed in Figure 11.1.

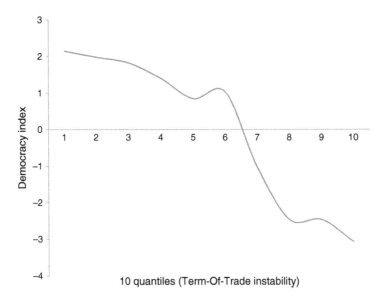

Figure 11.1 Quality of democracy (Polity2) compared with deciles of term-of-trade instability

Source: Author's elaboration.

Table 11E.1, which reports the correlation matrix, further shows a negative correlation between TOT instability and the level of democracy as measured by Polity 2 or by the Freedom House democratic index. Though a correlation does not necessarily imply causality, we infer a causal effect of instability on democracy here, since one can reasonably assume exogeneity of TOT instability. Most developing countries rely on their primary sectors' exports and are price-takers on the world markets. So, by using TOT instability in the present analysis, we minimize the likelihood of reverse causal relationship from institutions to instability.

Identification of causal effects

Our econometric model includes, as main controls[10], net aggregate official development assistance, TOT instability and an interaction term involving these two variables. The interaction variable allows us to test for the dampening effect of aid. We write the baseline model as follows:

$$Democ_{it} = \beta I_{it} + \gamma A_{it} + \kappa A_{it} \times I_{it} + \omega X_{it} + \upsilon_{it} \tag{11.3}$$

where $Democ_{it}$ is an index of democracy, A_{it} is the aid variable, I_{it} is TOT instability and $A_{it} \times I_{it}$ is the interaction term. X_{it} is a vector of controls including geography, education, ethnolinguistic fractionalization, initial conditions, estimated settler mortality rate, life expectancy and an African dummy variable;[11] *i* and *t*, respectively, stand for countries and time indexes. Since we are interested in estimating the effects of time-invariant variables such as geography, ethnolinguistic fractionalization, initial income and settler mortality, we do not include country-fixed effects in our baseline estimations. However, we included them for robustness checks but the main results remained unchanged; these results are not shown for space-constraint reasons.

Democracy is indeed a function of many factors. Ethnic diversity, measured by ethnolinguistic fractionalization, is often assumed to have an effect on political freedom and political competition; democracy is less likely to prevail in countries which are socially divided and which lack cultural and linguistic coherence (Lijphart 1977; Horowitz 1993). Socio-economic development, proxied by income per capita and education, has long been believed to be conducive to the emergence or survival of democracy. Democracy can also be explained by geographical characteristics, which are a good control for climatic conditions and contagion effects and which may predict political regime classification. Initial economic conditions, represented by the initial level of per capita income, also matter for democracy, since they are assumed to determine the initial quality of democracy. So, we anticipate positive coefficients for the interaction term, geography[12] and education, and negative coefficients for instability and fractionalization. Since we focus on long-run effects of aid and instability, and because democratization is a long-term process, we average our variables over 12-year periods (1980–91 and 1992–2003).

Dealing with endogeneity issues

It is often argued that aid and democracy are endogenously related, since countries that make progress in their democratization process are able to attract more aid ('conditionality' argument), as some donors tend to reward recipients showing better democratic performance with more aid. As demonstrated by Wooldridge (2006), ordinary least squares (OLS) estimation of such a model produces biased and inconsistent estimators. Although in principle, the endogeneity problem can be avoided by applying instrumental variable techniques, the fundamental problem is that there are no ideal instruments available. A good instrument in this case would be a variable which is highly correlated with aid but not with the error term in the regression. Nevertheless, following Brun *et al.* (2006), we create an instrumental variable for aid *à la* Tavares (2003), which should be correlated with the level of foreign aid received by a country while being presumably exogenous to the level of democracy in the country. The instrument is the amount of official development assistance and grants of the five main donors (identified each year), weighted by the inverse of the geographical distance between the donor and the recipient.[13]

Findings

The main results are presented in Table 11.1.[14] In columns 1, 2 and 3 the dependent variable is the quality of democracy, measured by the *polity2* combined index of democracy and autocracy. All of our estimations include country-fixed effects intended to take into account country-specific heterogeneity. The aid variable is aid per capita in the three specifications. Column 1 is the baseline specification and includes as controls: geography, education, ethnolinguistic fractionalization and initial income.

Unsurprisingly, Table 11.1 shows that an increase in TOT instability is associated with a significant decline in democracy, which confirms our theoretical expectations. But since both the coefficients of TOT instability and the multiplicative variables are significant, the marginal effect of TOT instability on democracy must be interpreted with caution. As demonstrated by Wooldridge (2006), this marginal effect depends on aid values and equals:

$$\frac{\partial Democ}{\partial Instab} = \alpha + \beta Aid$$

where α is the estimated coefficient of TOT instability and β the one of the interaction variable. From our main findings:

$$\frac{\partial Democ}{\partial Instab} = -0.51 + 0.005 Aid$$

This means that, at the sample mean value of aid per capita, which is 54.82, the marginal effect of TOT instability on the quality of democracy is negative and is estimated as $-0.51 + 0.005(54.82) = -0.235$. More interestingly, however, we find

Table 11.1 The impact of aid and TOT instability on democracy, panel instrumental variable (IV) regressions, 1980–2003, 12-year periods

	Dependent variable: democracy (polity2)		
	(1)	*(2)*	*(3)*
Aid (per capita)	−.07(−1.31)	−.0718(−1.31)	−.07(−1.32)
Terms-of-trade instability	−.51[a](−2.54)	−.512[a](−2.54)	−.51[b](−2.44)
Aid X instability	.005[b](2.00)	.005[b](2.00)	.005[b](1.99)
Geography	−.02(−0.48)	.13(1.28)	.348[a](3.27)
Education	.25[a](3.23)	.25[a](3.23)	.25[a](3.13)
Eth. fractionalization	.12[a](6.16)	.08[c](1.77)	−.07[b](−2.46)
Initial income	1.10(0.30)	1.77(0.50)	2.49(0.68)
Settler mortality		.24(0.17)	4.03[c](1.88)
Life expectancy			−.0002(−0.00)
Africa			−13.8[a](−4.45)
Country Fixed Effects	*Yes*	*Yes*	*Yes*
Adj. R^2	0.86	0.86	0.87
Obs	88	88	88
Groups	44	44	44
Overidentification test for aid instruments			
Hansen J stat.(*p*-value)	2.34(0.12)	0.36(0.54)	1.82(0.17)

Source: Author's compilation.

Notes:
a significance at 1%;
b significance at 5%;
c significance at 10%. Heteroscedasticity robust *t*-statistics in parentheses. All variables are defined, and data sources provided, in Appendix 11B.

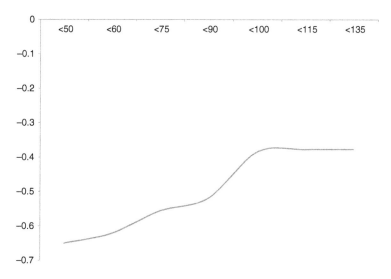

Figure 11.2 Evolution of regression coefficient of the TOT instability variable according to countries' levels of aid dependency (aid per capita)

Source: Author's calculations.

that aid dampens the effect of instability on democracy. This effect is shown by the positive and significant coefficient of the interactive variable (see Figure 11.2). Figure 11.2 shows that the effect of TOT instability on democracy becomes less negative as countries receive more aid.

Among the control variables (see the fully specified model in column 3, Table 11.1), education and geography appear to be the most powerful positive predictors of democracy, while 'Africa' is the most significant and dominant adverse predictor. The ethnolinguistic fractionalization variable displays a significantly negative coefficient[15], suggesting that a higher level of ethnic division may lead to greater difficulty in democratization. However, the positive effect of 'settler mortality' is unexpected, as larger values of this variable should worsen the quality of institutions (Acemoglu *et al.*, 2001).

We now test the robustness of our main results by using another democracy index (the Freedom House index of democracy), another measure of aid intensity (net official development assistance as a proportion of GDP) and different temporal periods (8-year periods). The results, which are summarized in Table 11E.2, are similar to our main results reported in Table 11.1. TOT instability remains detrimental to the quality of democracy and aid remains stabilizing while having no direct effect on democracy.[16]

Conclusions and policy implications

Aid neither promotes nor undermines directly democratic processes, but has an indirect positive effect on democracy in the long-term by dampening the adverse effects of TOT instability. While the debate about how external assistance could improve political institutions is still ongoing, the present study finds that aggregate aid inflows mitigate instability from trade and protect democracy. This finding is probably due to the likelihood that aid makes growth more stable, as shown by some recent studies (Collier and Dehn 2001; Guillaumont and Chauvet 2001; Chauvet and Guillaumont 2004, 2009; Collier and Goderis 2009).

Thus foreign aid can be useful in promoting democratic institutions. However, in the context of a debate about how to significantly increase aid in developing countries to reach the Millennium Development Goals by 2015, the findings from this study must not be interpreted as calling for a big push of aid. Other types of institutions (legal and economic institutions) also matter for growth and development, and several studies have shown that the quality of these institutions can be severely damaged by large amounts of aid.

Nonetheless, our empirical findings suggest some important policy recommendations regarding selectivity in aid allocation. In line with some recent research which has emphasized macroeconomic vulnerability, the present results suggest that allocating aid to the more vulnerable countries could have some positive impacts in terms of long-term institutional building. The findings also give credit to the view that on top of increasing the importance of economic vulnerability as a criterion for aid allocation, donors' strategies might indeed give greater priority to the long-term reduction of developing countries' economic vulnerability.

Appendix 11A: The Freedom House and Polity IV indicators of democracy

The Freedom House democracy index

The Freedom House index focuses on two aspects of democracy: political rights and civil liberties. The methodology of assessing democracy consists of ranking each country regarding these two aspects, from 7 (worst democratic situation) to 1 (best democratic situation), according to the Freedom House classification. (Note, however, that these numbers have been reversed in the current analysis, in order to ensure that a larger value indicates a higher level of democracy.) Evaluations are made on the basis of the answers to a questionnaire submitted to respondents from civil society, the political world and the media, which are mostly non-governmental organizations or the press. Next, the synthetic index is computed by averaging the index of political rights (proxied through the election mode of the chief of executive and the existence of an electoral framework) and the index of civil liberties (proxied through the freedom of opinion, the freedom of beliefs, the freedom of association, the legitimate state and human rights, the autonomy of people and the economic rights). The questionnaire consists of 8 questions about political rights and 14 questions about civil liberties; the scale of each question goes from 1 to 4, with a higher score being associated with a lower quality of civil liberties. Finally, depending on the total score, the two indexes are given a value between 1 and 7, with 1 being the most democratic and 7 the least democratic (www.freedomhouse.org).

The Polity IV democracy index

The Polity IV project from the University of Maryland provides a database about several indicators of democracy (executive constraints, political partici-pation, openness in recruitment and so on). The polity2 index is computed by summing an index of democracy (DEMOC) which is positively scaled from 0 to 10 and an index of autocracy (AUTOC) which is positively scaled from −10 to 0. The (DEMOC) index of democracy assesses democracy on the basis of four criteria: competition in political participation, competition and open-ness in the executive recruitment and institutional constraints on the executive power. For instance, to assess openness in executive recruitment, assessors will ask whether all people have access to the power if elections are free, or whether the power is hereditary. Similarly, in order to assess executive con-straints, assessors will be interested in the existence of a legislative power or constitutional strength. These data are used to compute a ranking for each variable. The total score based on the different components of democracy is the score for the DEMOC index. The AUTOC index of autocracy, which assesses political competition and respect for political liberties, is computed similarly. The AUTOC index ranges from −10 to 0, with −10 as the most auto-cratic, while the DEMOC index ranges form 0 to 10, with 10 as the most dem-ocratic. Finally, the polity2 synthetic variable is obtained by summing the two indexes, with appropriate normalization between the two indexes by the assessors (see Marshall *et al.* 2009).

Appendix B

Table 11B.1 Variables definitions and data descriptions

Variable	Definition	Source
Aid per capita	Net aggregate official development assistance transfers (2004 US$ millions) per capita	Author's calculations from Development Assistance Committee (DAC) online database and World Development Indicators (World Bank 2005b)
Aid/GDP	Net aggregate official development assistance transfers (2004 US$ millions) as share of gross domestic product	
Polity2 index	Combined democracy and autocracy score, ranged from −10(full autocracy) to +10(full democracy)	Polity IV project
Freedom House index	Democracy index, ranged from 1(best democratic situation) to +7(worse situation)	Freedom House
Terms-of-trade instability	Net barter terms-of-trade instability (see section 4.2 for the calculation method)	Author's calculations
Income instability	Instability of GDP per capita (2000 US$), computed with the calculation method described in section 4.2	Author's calculations
Geography	Distance from equator of capital city measured as abs (latitude)/90	World Bank (2002)
Education	Literacy rate, adult total (% of people 15+)	World Development Indicators (World Bank 2005b)
Ethnolinguistic fractionalization	Probability that two persons randomly selected in the population do not belong to the same ethnic group	Atlas Narodov Mira (https://ideas.repec.org/a/ebl/ecbull/eb-08j10005.html)
Settler mortality	Natural logarithm of estimated European settlers' mortality rate	Acemoglu *et al.* (2001)
Life expectancy	Life expectancy at birth, for total population (years)	World Development Indicators (World Bank 2005b)
Africa	Dummy variable taking value 1 if a country belongs to Africa, 0 otherwise	Author's calculations
Initial income	Natural logarithm of GDP per capita in 1980 (2000 US$ and PPP)	World Development Indicators (World Bank 2005b)
Income growth	Natural logarithm of GDP per capita growth (2000 US$ and PPP)	World Development Indicators (World Bank 2005b)

Source: Author's compilation.

Appendix C

Table 11C.1 Base sample countries

Number	Country	Number	Country
1.	Algeria*	36.	Lesotho*
2.	Argentina	37.	Liberia*
3.	Bahrain	38.	Malawi*
4.	Bangladesh	39.	Malaysia
5.	Benin*	40.	Mali*
6.	Bolivia	41.	Mauritania*
7.	Botswana*	42.	Mexico
8.	Brazil	43.	Morocco*
9.	Burkina Faso*	44.	Mozambique*
10.	Burundi*	45.	Nepal
11.	Cameroon*	46.	Nicaragua
12.	Central African Rep.*	47.	Niger*
13.	Chad*	48.	Nigeria*
14.	Colombia	49.	Oman
15.	Congo (Rep.)*	50.	Pakistan
16.	Costa Rica	51.	Panama
17.	Ivory Coast*	52.	Paraguay
18.	Cyprus	53.	Peru
19.	Dominican Rep.	54.	Philippines
20.	Ecuador	55.	Rwanda*
21.	Egypt*	56.	Saudi Arabia
22.	El Salvador	57.	Senegal*
23.	Fiji	58.	Singapore
24.	Ghana*	59.	Sri Lanka
25.	Guatemala	60.	Sudan*
26.	Honduras	61.	Syrian Arab Republic
27.	India	62.	Thailand
28.	Indonesia	63.	Togo*
29.	Iran, Islamic Rep.	64.	Trinidad and Tobago
30.	Israel	65.	Tunisia*
31.	Jamaica	66.	Turkey
32.	Jordan	67.	United Arab Emirates
33.	Kenya*	68.	Uruguay
34.	Kuwait	69.	Venezuela
35.	Lao PDR	70.	Zimbabwe*

Source: Author's compilation.

Note: *African countries.

Appendix D

Table 11D.1 Descriptive statistics

	Obs	Mean	Std. Dev.	Min.	Max.
A. Aid variables					
Net ODA per capita (US $)	204	54.82	71.29	−2.40	485.52
Net ODA as prop. of GDP	198	.106	.139	−.0002	.89
B. Institutional measures					
Polity2 index	203	−.86	6.41	−10	10
Freedom House index	204	4.61	1.59	7	1
C. Terms-of-trade					
Net barter terms-of-trade	150	113.37	42.39	26.25	397.54
Terms-of-trade instability (12-years trend)	150	9.53	9.33	7.63	90.22
D. Country characterstics					
Geography	204	16.84	10.92	0	39
Education	168	66.04	22.46	9.81	97.87
Eth. fractionalization	166	47.62	29.10	0	93
Settler mortality	138	4.90	1.06	2.43	7.98
Life expectancy	203	59.11	11.21	35.80	77.95
Africa	204	0.45	0.49	0	1
Initial income	174	2677.96	5898.56	126.35	46473.4
Income growth	193	0.88	0.65	−0.93	3.37

Source: Author's compilation.

Appendix E

Table 11E.1 Pair–wise correlation matrix

	Aid per cap.	Aid%GDP	Polity2	Fr. House	TOT ins.*	Income ins.*
Aid per cap.	1.00					
Aid%GDP	0.41[b]	1.00				
Polity2	−0.07	−0.22[b]	1.00			
Fr. House	0.02	−0.27[b]	0.88[b]	1.00		
TOT ins.*	−0.07	0.06	−0.13	−0.17[b]	1.00	
Income ins.*	0.09	0.13	−0.18[b]	−0.19[b]	0.19[b]	1.00

Source: Author's compilation.

Notes: [b]Significance at 5%. *Terms-of-trade instability and income instability are computed with 12-year trends.

Table 11E.2 Robustness checks, panel IV regressions, 1980–2003

	Dependent variable: democracy		
	Freedom house (12–year periods)	*Aid%GDP (12–year periods)*	*8–year periods*
Aid/GDP	−0.027(−1.56)	−0.099(−1.50)	−0.061(−1.42)
Terms–of–trade instab.	−0.18[a](−2.97)	−0.184[a](−3.39)	−0.054[a](−2.74)
Aid×instability	0.0016[a](2.38)	0.007[a](2.90)	0.003[c](1.86)
Geography	0.062[c](1.86)	0.028[b](2.18)	0.068[a](2.34)
Education	0.02(0.99)	0.027(1.37)	0.024(1.48)
Eth. fractionalization	0.003(0.33)	−0.013(−1.12)	0.012(1.43)
Initial income	0.84(0.94)	0.94(1.02)	10.45[b](2.09)
Settler mortality	0.41(0.72)	0.77[b](2.43)	0.74[b](2.04)
Life expectancy	−0.05(−0.85)	−0.09(−1.43)	−0.01(−0.37)
Africa	−1.94[b](−2.12)	−2.12[a](−3.20)	−0.63(−0.92)
Countries fixed effects	Yes	Yes	Yes
Adj. R^2	0.85	0.85	0.82
Obs	88	88	131
Overidentification test for aid instruments			
Hansen J stat.$_{(p\text{-value})}$	0.397$_{(0.52)}$	0.57$_{(0.44)}$	0.56$_{(0.45)}$

Source: Author's compilation.

Notes:
a significance at 1%;
b significance at 5%;
c significance at 10%. Heteroscedasticity robust *t*–statistics in parentheses.

Notes

1 We discuss this argument in the section 'Some stylized facts'.
2 See the complete list in Appendix 11C.
3 For a complete survey of economic theories on the link between democracy and growth, see Przeworski and Limongi (1993) and Przeworski *et al.* (2000).
4 Followed by many other studies.
5 Since instability can be viewed as an alternation of positive and/or negative shocks.
6 The data they used is government and civil society aid, provided by OECD.
7 In Guillaumont and Chauvet (2001), the indicator of vulnerability takes into account the size of population, the instability of exports agricultural production, while in Chauvet and Guillaumont (2004), it only takes into account exports instability and the negative trend of TOT. Since (exogenous) TOT instability is also a source of vulnerability (which causes a risk on growth), the growth-stabilization effect of aid can also be valid for this type of instability.
8 We also considerer 12-year trends.
9 See previous section for the calculation method of instability and Appendix 11C for the sample countries.
10 See Appendix 11B for a more detailed description and definition of the data.
11 Appendix 11B gives a precise description of all of these variables.
12 Proxied here as the distance from equator of capital city (see Appendix 11B).
13 For each recipient country and each year, the five main aid donors are identified. The total amount of aid is then weighted by the geographical proximity (proxied by the inverse of bilateral distance) of the recipient country with Washington (for Canadian and US aid), Brussels (for European Union aid), Tokyo (for Japanese aid), and Canberra

(for Australian and New Zealand aid). As explained by Tavares (2003), the reasoning is that, when a donor country increases its total aid outflows, recipient countries that are closer to that donor experience an exogenous increase in aid inflows. We also use, as an instrument for the interactive variable, the instrumented aid variable times TOT instability, in order to obtain the exogenous variation of this variable. As argued earlier in the chapter, we assume TOT instability to be exogenous. Indeed, over-identification tests confirm the quality of these two variables as instruments. The use of the distance between capital cities in the recipient and the donor country assumes that new donors are more likely to give aid to countries that are closer to them; Harmer and Cotterrell (2005) for example has found that humanitarian aid by non-DAC donors is concentrated in neighboring countries.

14 Regarding the number of countries we basically consider, the number of observations seems to be somewhat small; this is due to gaps in some important variables we control for in regressions.

15 In columns 2 and 3, ethnolinguistic fractionalization enter the regressions with a counter-intuitive sign.

16 We also ran all of our regressions using a sample only of African countries. Similar results were obtained. The TOT instability negatively and significantly affected African countries' democratic institutions. More importantly, the coefficient of the TOT instability and aid ineteactive variable was positive and significant, suggesting that aid mitigates the negative impact of TOT instability. However, we have chosen to report here those results based on the larger sample of developing countries.

References

Acemoglu, D., S. Johnson and J. Robinson (2001). 'The Colonial Origins of Comparative Development: An Empirical Investigation'. *American Economic Review*, 91(5): 1369–401.

Acemoglu, D., S. Johnson, J. Robinson and Y. Thaicharoen (2003). 'Institutional Causes, Macroeconomic Symptoms: Volatility, Crises and Growth'. *Journal of Monetary Economics*, 50(1): 49–123.

Acemoglu, D., S. Johnson, J. Robinson and P. Yared (2005a). 'Income and Democracy'. Discussion Paper 5273, CEPR. London: Centre for Economic Policy Research.

Acemoglu, D., S. Johnson, J. A. Robinson and P. Yared (2005b). 'From Education to Democracy?' *American Economic Association, Papers and Proceedings*, 95(2): 44–49.

Alesina, A. and B. Weder (2002). 'Do Corrupt Governments Receive less Foreign Aid?'. *American Economic Review*, 92(4): 1126–37.

Almeida, H. and D. Ferreira (2002). 'Democracy and the Variability of Economic Performance.' *Economics and Politics*, 14(3): 225–57.

Barro, R. (1996). 'Democracy and Growth'. *Journal of Economic Growth*, 1(1): 1–27.

Barro, R. (1999). 'Determinants of Democracy'. *Journal of Political Economy*, 107(6): 158–83.

Bollen, K. (1979). 'Political Democracy and the Timing of Development'. *American Sociological Review*, 44: 572–87.

Brautigam, D. and S. Knack (2004). 'Foreign Aid, Institutions, and Governance in Sub-Saharan Africa'. *Economic Development and Cultural Change*, 52: 255–85.

Brun, J.F., G. Chambas and S. Guerineau (2006). 'Aide et Mobilisation Fiscale dans les Pays en Développement'. AFD Programme RCH Aide et Politique Budgétaire 065-2006: AFD.

Chauvet, L. and P. Guillaumont (2004). 'Aid and Growth Revisited: Policy, Economic Vulnerability and Political Instability'. In B. Tungodden, N. Stern and I. Kolstad (eds), Toward Pro-Poor Policies – Aid, Institutions and Globalization. Washington, DC: World Bank/Oxford University Press.

Chauvet, L. and P. Guillaumont (2009). 'Aid, Volatility and Growth again: When Aid Volatility Matters and When it Does Not'. *Review of Development Economics*, 13(3): 452–63.

Collier, P. and J. Dehn (2001). 'Aid, Shocks and Growth'. Policy Research Working Paper 2688. Washington DC: World Bank.

Collier, P. and B. Goderis (2007). 'Does Aid Mitigate External Shocks?' CSAE WPS 2007-18. Oxford: Centre for the Study of African Economies.

Coviello, D. and R. Islam (2006). 'Does Aid Help Improve Economic Institutions?'. Policy Research Working Paper Series 3990. Washington DC: World Bank.

Dahl, R. (1971). *Polyarchy: Participation and Opposition*. New Haven: Yale University Press.

De Haan, J. and C. Siermann (1996). 'New Evidence on the Relationship between Democracy and Economic Growth'. *Public Choice*, 86(1–2): 175–98.

Djankov, S., J. Montalvo and M. Reynal-Querol (2008). The Curse of Aid. *Journal of Economic Growth*, 13(3): 169–94.

Dunning, T. (2004). 'Conditioning the Effects of Aid: Cold War Politics, Donor Credibility, and Democracy in Africa'. *International Organization*, 58: 409–23.

Easterly, W. and A. Kraay (2000). 'Small States, Small Problems? Income, Growth and Volatility in Small States'. *World Development*, 28(11): 2013–27.

Fish, S. and R. Brooks (2004). 'Does Diversity Hurt Democracy?' *Journal of Democracy*, 15: 154–71.

FMI (2005). Perspectives de l'Economie Mondiale. Développement Institutionnel. Département des Etudes Economiques et Financières.

Fosu, A. (2008). 'Democracy and Growth in Africa: Implications of Increasing Electoral Competitiveness', *Economics Letters*, 100 (September): 442–44.

Glaeser, E., R. La Porta, L. de Silanes Florencio and A. Shleifer (2004). 'Do Institutions Cause Growth?' NBER Working Paper 10568. Cambridge, MA: National Bureau for Economic Research.

Goldsmith, A. (2001). 'Foreign Aid and Statehood in Africa'. *International Organization*, 55(1): 123–48.

Guillaumont, P. and L. Chauvet (2001). 'Aid and Performance: A Re-assessment'. *The Journal of Development Studies*, 37(6): 66–92.

Hall, R. and C. Jones (1999). 'Why do some Countries Produce so much more Output per Worker than Others?'. *Quarterly Journal of Economics*, 1(114): 83–116.

Harmer, A. and L. Cotterrell (2005). Diversity in Donorship. The Changing Landscape of Official Humanitarian Aid. Humanitarian Policy Group Research Report 20. London: Overseas Development Institute.

Helliwell, J. (1994). 'Empirical Linkages between Democracy and Economic Growth'. *British Journal of Political Science*, 24(2): 225–48.

Hoffman, B. (2003). *Development Despots: Foreign Aid, Domestic Policies, and the Quality of Governance*. San Diego: University of California.

Horowitz, D. (1985). *Ethnic Groups in Conflict*. Berkeley: University of California Press.

Horowitz, D. (1993). 'Democracy in Divided Societies'. *Journal of Democracy*, 4: 18–38.

Huber, E., D. Rueschemeyer and J. Stephens (1993). 'The Impact of Economic Development on Democracy'. *The Journal of Economic Perspectives*, 7(3): 71–86.

Kalyvitis, S. and I. Vlachaki (2005). *Foreign Aid and Democratization: Evidence from a Multinomial Logit Model*. Athens: University of Economics and Business.

Karatnycky, A. (2002). 'The 2001 Freedom House Survey: Muslim Countries and the Democracy Gap'. *Journal of Democracy*, 15(1): 154–71.

Knack, S. (2001). 'Aid Dependence and the Quality of Governance: a Cross Country Empirical Test'. *Southern Economic Journal*, 68(2): 310–29.

Knack, S. (2004). 'Does Foreign Aid Promote Democracy?'. *International Studies Quarterly*, 48: 251–56.

Knack, S. and A. Rahman (2004). 'Donor Fragmentation and Bureaucratic Quality in Aid Recipients'. The World Bank Policy Research Working Paper Series 3186. Washington DC: World Bank.

La Porta, R., F. Lopez-De-Silanes, A. Shleifer and R. Vishny (1999). 'The Quality of Government'. *Journal of Law, Economics, and Organization*, 1(15): 222–79.

Lijphart, A. (1977). *Democracy in Plural Societies: A Comparative Exploration*. New Haven: Yale University Press.

Lipset, S. (1959). 'Some Social Requisites of Democracy: Economic Development and Political Legitimacy'. *The American Political Science Review*, 53(1): 69–105.

Lipset, S. (1960). *Political Man: The Social Basis of Modern Politics*. New York: Doubleday.

Lipset, S. (1994). 'The Social Requisites of Democracy Revisited'. *American Sociological Review*, 59: 1–22.

Lipset, S. (1996). 'The Centrality of Culture'. In L. Diamond and M. Plattner (ed.), *The Global Resurgence of Democracy*. Baltimore: Johns Hopkins University Press.

Lipset, S., K.R. Seong and J.C. Torres (1993). 'A Comparative Analysis of the Social Requisites of Democracy'. *International Social Science Journal*, 45: 155–75.

Mainwaring, S. and M. Shugart (1997). 'Juan Linz, Presidentialism and Democracy: A Critical Appraisal'. *Comparative Politics*, 29(4): 449–71.

Marshall, M., T. Gurr and K. Jaggers (2009). 'Political Regime Characteristics and Transitions, 1800–2009. Dataset User's Manual'. Discussion paper, Polity IV Project.

McNab, R. and S. Everhart (2002). 'Aid, Governance, and Growth'. In S. Rashid (ed.), *Rotting from the Head: Donors and LDC Corruption*. Dhaka: Bangladesh University Press.

Mendoza, E. (1997). 'TOT Uncertainty and Economic Growth'. *Journal of Development Economics*, 54(2): 323–56.

Mobarak, A.M. (2005). 'Democracy, Volatility and Economic Development'. *The Review of Economics and Statistics*, 87(2): 348–61.

Monali, C.A. (1997). 'Political Openness and Economic Performance'. University of Minnesota, unpublished paper.

North, D. (1990). *Institutions, Institutional Change, and Economic Performance*. Cambridge: Cambridge University Press.

Persson, T. and G. Tabellini (2006). 'Democracy and Development: The Devil in the Details'. *American Economic Review Papers and Proceedings*, 96: 319–24.

Przeworski, A., M. Alvarez, J. Cheibub and F. Limongi (2000). *Democracy and Development: Political Institutions and Well-Being in the World, 1950–1990*. Cambridge: Cambridge University Press.

Przeworski, A. and F. Limongi (1993). 'Political regimes and economic growth'. *Journal of Economic Perspectives*, 7(3):51–69.

Quinn, D. and J. Woolley (2001). 'Democracy and National Economic Performance: the Preference for Stability'. *American Journal of Political Science*, 45(3): 634–57.

Rabushka, A. and K. Shepsle (1972). *Politics in Plural Societies*. Columbus, OH: Merrill.

Ramey, G. and V. Ramey (1995). 'Cross-Country Evidence on the Link between Volatility and Growth'. *The American Economic Review*, 85(5): 1138–51.

Rodrik, D. (1997). 'Democracy and Economic Performance'. Available at: http://ksghome. harvard.edu/.drodrik.academic.ksg/demoecon.PDF (accessed:).

Rodrik, D. (2000). 'Institutions for High-Quality Growth: What they are and how to Acquire them'. NBER Working Paper 7540. Cambridge, MA: National Bureau of Economic Research.

Rodrik, D., A. Subramanian and F. Trebbi (2004). 'Institutions Rule: The Primacy of Institutions over Geography and Integration in Economic Development'. *Journal of Economic Growth*, 9(2): 131–65.

Ross, M. (2001). 'Does Oil Hinder Democracy?'. *World Politics*, 53: 325–61.

Sachs, J. and A. Warner (2001). 'The Curse of Natural Resources'. *European Economic Review*, 45: 827–38.

Satyanath, S. and A. Subramanian (2004). 'What Determines Long-run Macroeconomic Stability?. Democratic Institutions'. Working Paper WP/04/215, IMF.

Svensson, J. (2000). 'Foreign Aid and Rent-Seeking'. *Journal of International Economics*, 51(2): 437–61.

Tavares, J. (2003). 'Does Foreign Aid Corrupt?'. *Economics Letters*, 79(1): 99–106.

Tavares, J. and R. Wacziarg (2001). 'How Democracy affects Growth'. *European Economic Review*, 45(8):1341–78.

UNCTAD (2009). UNCTAD stat. Available at: http://unctadstat.unctad.org/ (accessed: March 2008).

Weede, E. (1996). 'Political Regime Type and Variation in Economic Growth Rates'. *Constitutional Political Economy*, 7(3): 167–76.

Weiner, M. (1987). 'Empirical Democratic Theory'. In M. Weiner and E. Ozbudun (ed.), *Competitive Elections in Developing Countries*. Durham, NC.: Duke University Press.

Welsh, D. (1993). 'Domestic Politics and Ethnic Conflict'. In M.E. Brown (ed.), *Ethnic Conflict and International Security*. Princeton: Princeton University Press.

Wooldridge, J. (2006). *Introductory Econometrics,* 3rd edition. Mason, OH: Thomson South-Western.

World Bank (2005a). Global Development Finance (CD- ROM).

World Bank (2005b). World Development Indicators (CD- ROM).

Yang, B. (2008). 'Does Democracy lower Growth Volatility? A Dynamic Panel Analysis'. *Journal of Macroeconomics*, 30: 562–74.

12 Who is the alien?

Xenophobia in post-apartheid South Africa

Marguerite Duponchel

Introduction[1]

On 11 May 2008, Alexandra township witnessed the start of violent attacks against outsiders who some perceived were not South African enough. The extreme violence quickly spread to other provinces and eventually lasted until the end of that month. Those events are remembered as the May 2008 xenophobic riots. Hundreds of homes and shops were looted and burnt. Sixty-two people died across the country, 21 of whom were South African citizens. Many were injured. An estimated 100,000 fled their homes and found refuge wherever they could.

A colleague at the United Nations Development Programme (UNDP) recalled her story. When the xenophobic violence erupted in May 2008 and started to spread around the country, she got worried that Mike, her Mozambican gardener, might be in danger. Mike, who had previously stayed in Pretoria, had moved to Thembisa[2] three years before to live with his South African girlfriend. As the violence quickly reached the township, she phoned to make sure that he was alright. Mike confirmed that there had been violent attacks against migrants around the neighbourhood. When he was asked if he was safe his answer was: 'Yes, they would not attack me'. Mike's story raised questions. Why, in the same communities, were some foreigners attacked and some were not? What made some residents South African enough in the eyes of the community when some became aliens that needed to be chased away at any cost? What made someone a likely target? The violence might not have been as randomly conducted as it seemed after all. Yet, to my knowledge, these questions had not been investigated at the start of this research – for a good reason: the absence of data. Nevertheless, finding answers is essential for the design of policies and programmes targeting the reintegration of victims in the short term and the issue of xenophobia in the longer run. The South African Red Cross (SARC) underwent a data collection exercise on vulnerabilities in February 2009. Some minor additions to the questionnaire enabled them to capture experiences of violence at the household level. While I believe that quantitative analysis has the potential to reveal important features and draw new lines of research, qualitative research should not been ignored. Xenophobia is a multi-dimensional, complex phenomenon, and pluridisciplinary analysis is necessary for a wider understanding of xenophobia in South Africa, its roots, its consequences and the way forward.

The following section recounts the xenophobic attacks of May 2008, the origins and aftermath, and presents a short literature review of the subsequent analysis on the causes of the events. The data section describes the database, the econometric model and the explanatory variables. The last two sections are the results and conclusion.

Xenophobia in South Africa: facts and analysis

South Africa, and more particularly the Gauteng province hosting Johannesburg and Pretoria, has become today's economic centre of sub-Saharan Africa. Its success has attracted a wide range of domestic and international migrants seeking economic opportunities or refuge from oppression as well as a better life. Expected to be large, the exact number of immigrants is unknown, with a significant number of them crossing the border illegally. Gindrey and Landau (2008) estimate an annual net gain of approximately 78,000 migrants per year in the province. Their results also show that the Gauteng province hosts 46 per cent of the country's total foreign population. 11 May 2008 will be remembered by all of them. Violent attacks on people considered as outsiders started in Alexandra township, on the outskirts of Johannesburg. The levels of violence observed during this month of attacks shattered Mandela's dream of a rainbow nation.

Facts and figures

The events of May 2008 cannot be analysed without understanding the global post-apartheid context of xenophobia. Xenophobic violence can be traced to as early as a few months after the first democratic elections in April 1994. In December 1994, in Alexandra, 'armed youth gangs destroy foreign-owned property and demand that foreigners be removed from the area' (Misago *et al.* 2009). Evictions, looting of property and even killings were reported elsewhere in the country. The frequency of such events gradually increased, with an unprecedented level of violence reached in May 2008.[3] In the months leading to the May 2008 riots, at least 13 foreigners were killed, a large number of shops burnt down, and many people made homeless. Violence was reported in the Eastern Cape, in the Western Cape, in Gauteng, in Kwazulu-Natal and in the Free State.

On 11 May, an armed mob attacked foreigners in Alexandra, Gauteng. Two people were killed and two women raped; 60 people were injured. Shops and homes were looted and self-appropriated by the perpetrators. Violence in Alexandra continued for several days. Hundreds of people fled their homes and found refuge at the police station. Meanwhile, the violence spread across the province, reaching several townships including Diepsloot, Thembisa and Soweto. By 16 May, attacks reached Cape Town, where one Somali shopkeeper was killed. On 17 May, violence gripped Jeppestown in downtown Johannesburg and the following day, the inner city neighbourhood of Hillbrow. Violence and forced evictions continued in most places. Durban was shaken on 17 May. Attacks were reported in Maukasi, Dukhatole, Zandspruit, Ramaphosa, Primrose, Reiger

Park, Kya Sands, Jerusalem, Zamimplio, Joe Slovo informal settlement and Mayfair among other places. On 21 May, clashes were again reported in Durban, Mpumalanga, the Free State and the North West province. On the same day, President Mbeki brought in the military to stop the violence. Violence in Gauteng gradually scaled down, but incidents were still reported in the other provinces. Meanwhile, thousands marched against xenophobia in different parts of the country.[4] By 26 May, the violence was declared under control: 1,384 suspects had been arrested, 342 shops looted and 213 burnt down. Hundreds had been wounded. Sixty-two lost their lives, 21 of whom were South Africans. Thousands were made homeless, forced to seek shelter with friends, in the government administered camps or in churches. The last official shelters closed in October, five months after the riots started.

Among those displaced, some victims were reintegrated into their communities, with assurance from the residents that they would be safe. In some neighbourhoods, return was impossible. Those victims either resettled elsewhere in South Africa or simply decided to return to their countries of origin. For some, however, going home was just not an option. Unfortunately, these post-crisis movements were not extensively monitored. One year after the event, it had become hard to locate the victims of the attacks. Foreign nationals living in South Africa stayed as quiet and invisible as possible, fearing more violence. As the data collection shows, outsiders are still harassed. Xenophobic violent acts did not cease on 26 May 2008. In September 2008, a Somali mother was murdered with her three children in her shop in Queenstown, Eastern Cape. In Alexandra, shacks inhabited by foreigners were burnt down around Christmas. In May 2009, two Somalis were found burnt in their shops. In late November 2009, 3,000 Zimbabwean farm workers were forcibly chased from a farm in the Western Cape, marking the first event of this kind in a rural setting.

Literature review on xenophobia and ethnic violence

Xenophobia is a complex phenomenon, widely under-researched. Nevertheless, in the aftermath of the violence that shook South Africa in May 2008, sociologists, anthropologists and political scientists produced a variety of research materials trying to explain the outburst of violence at different levels of analysis. Two types of explanations can be identified: political and socio-economic, which most certainly worked alongside.

Sociologist Neocosmos (2008) links the outbreak of violence to a widespread xenophobic feeling among South Africans, a sentiment widely fed by the South African elite, which wants to protect its interests and wealth by pointing a finger at the 'other' (also in Sharp 2008). This strategy to retain power can also be identified in other nations. Tadjo (2008) draws the comparison between the xenophobic violence in South Africa and the rise of the concept of 'Ivoirité' in Côte d'Ivoire. The author points out that 'Ivoirité' was re-conceptualized from colonialism by the Ivorian elite in order to define national legitimacy by stigmatizing foreigners. In the recent history of Côte d'Ivoire, the concept of identity has been manipulated to refer to local territory in contrast to national territory. Outsiders became those who did not come from the locality. A clear parallel can be drawn in the South African context, where outsiders are not only foreign-born, but also migrants coming from the poorer north. Xenophobic violence can be seen as a competition between the richest and the poorest. The poorest are manipulated by the elite to turn against outsiders, the elite itself created, so that the richest can retain power and wealth. Uvin (1999) also underlines the role of the elite in deepening the Hutu-Tutsi ethnic divisions in Rwandan post-colonial history. The author states that, when threatened, the elite fuelled ethnic divisions to impede democratization and power sharing. In 1991–92, the Hutu regime was under threat from all sides and the most radical factions used the revival of ethnicity as a strategy. Anti-Tutsi propaganda incited mass murder, verbal attacks, listings of Tutsis and threats against those having relations with Tutsis. In Yugoslavia, Gagnon (1994) states that threats of economic crisis and strong demand for reforms led the coalition of leaders to provoke violent ethnic confrontation.

Illustrating a national phenomenon using the Alexandra context, South African historian Nieftagodien (2008) recalls that the distinction between insiders and outsiders has long been defined by politics. The laws of apartheid were purposely designed to create division between groups, and rural migrants were considered as outsiders. Yet the freedom struggle helped create a sense of community. The common enemy now defeated, the threat of outsiders has re-emerged since the end of the apartheid regime. Along the same lines underlying the cultural determinants of xenophobia, anthropologist Banton (1996) draws a parallel between xenophobia in France and Britain and explains xenophobic attitudes by differentialism. Where brothers have been raised with the presumption of equality, xenophobia will be less widespread. Indeed, children learn unconsciously whether brothers are equal and then project this. In South Africa, the institutionalization of differentialism by the apartheid system could only have exacerbated the organization of society around values of inequalities, at the extreme, resulting in violence against 'others'.

Misago *et al.* (2009) attempt to identify the causes of violence while comparing seven sites: five where xenophobic violence was reported and two where the presence of foreigners did not lead to attacks. Through qualitative interviews with a wide range of respondents, the study identifies four factors that triggered the violence: (1) the presence of 'institutionalized practices that exclude foreigners from political participation and justice'; (2) the absence of conflict resolution mechanisms; (3) the presence of 'political vacuums or competition in community leadership that encourages the emergence of unofficial, illegitimate and often violent forms of local leadership'; and (4) a culture of impunity, particularly with regard to xenophobic violence. The latter point is also highlighted in Rwanda, where the culture of impunity vis-à-vis violence towards Tutsis allowed killings without fear (Uvin 1999).

The complexity of the phenomenon is titanic and cannot be clearly separated from the broader reality of inequality and poverty in South Africa. Sociologist

Pillay (2008) suggests that huge socio-economic inequalities between the poorest and the richest of the population lie at the root of the violence. South Africa's Gini coefficient has kept on rising since 1994 (Central Intelligence Agency (CIA) 2008). Victims of this 'market violence' as the author refers, are unable to recognize or reach the real perpetrators, that is, the richest that hold power. As a consequence, violence is directed towards those living the closest, that is, outsiders, whether they are foreign nationals or coming from the northern provinces (Pillay 2008). Neocosmos (2008) and Allport (1954) confirm that it is a common phenomenon for the powerless to regularly take out their frustrations on the weakest.

Gelb (2008) explains the xenophobic attacks as a manifestation of hostility towards those perceived to be better off – whether true or not. This sentiment translated into the interviews of South Africans in the aftermath of the crisis (HSRC 2008; Misago *et al.* 2009). Unequal job opportunities, among others, were regularly cited as a reason for the attacks. According to Pillay (2008), the violence was mainly directed at foreign nationals who owned houses and had jobs or small businesses. Yet this needs to be scientifically proven. At this stage, there is no evidence that better-off foreigners were the principal targets.

Similarly, a few years before the outbreak of violence, Dodson and Oelofse (2000), in a study of the causes of xenophobia in Cape Town, find that, in a context of extreme poverty and very high unemployment, competition for jobs, mainly in the local fishing industry, was the main factor driving the division among the communities between indigenes and foreigners. Misago *et al.* (2009) also identify necessary, but not sufficient, pre-conditions for the violence, among which are high unemployment and poor service delivery. Confirming the theory of relative deprivation, psychologists Sherif *et al.* (1961) suggest that competition for access to limited resources results in a conflict between groups. Competition for limited resources between groups leads to prejudices against the out-group, whose members are viewed by the in-group as a source of competition, such as jobs being given to the members of the out-group.

In addition, one of the explanations for the outbreak of violence was that the influx of Zimbabweans exacerbated tensions between communities as competition for services tightened. In North America, Esses *et al.* (2001) found that 'large scale migration can result in a feeling of threat for the host community either because of perceptions of economic strain or as a result of cultural dissimilarity'. Yet Misago *et al.* (2009) conclude that inadequate border control and the supposedly mass influx of Zimbabweans were not valid explanations for the xenophobic riots in South Africa. The results indeed underlined that outsiders who were attacked had been living there for years and the places where the violence occurred were not necessarily the ones with the highest proportion of foreign nationals. If the mass influx of migrants into South African cities increased the competition for already scarce resources, testing whether Zimbabweans are more at risk than other foreigners, would invalidate the assumption that the recent influx of Zimbabwean migrants was not a direct cause of the outbreak of violence.

In the only existing quantitative analysis on the subject, Wa Kwabe-Segatti and Fauvelle-Aymar (2012) attempt to identify all factors potentially at the root of the May 2008 xenophobic violence. Using a database covering 839 wards[5] in 21 municipalities, they compared the characteristics of the wards where xenophobic violence was reported during the xenophobic episode of May 2008. The results show that the ratio of black men under 60 has a positive and significant impact on the occurrence of violence at the ward level. Similarly, they identify a significant effect of the diversity of groups among foreign nationals. The quality of housing in the ward also seems to significantly impact on whether or not violence erupted in a ward. In contrast to what this analysis suggests, they found no significant impact of the level of unemployment.

This study opts for a different approach, which aims at portraying the outsiders and focuses at the household level. It attempts to identify the characteristics that played a significant role in defining the victims of May 2008.

Data

The data was collected in February 2009. Two places were chosen in the Gauteng province where the violence started: Alexandra township and the Johannesburg inner city. But before going into the data description, it is essential to give some historical background about these two surveyed sites. The apartheid era has undoubtedly left deep scars both in the minds of South Africans and in the geography of the territory. Not taking into account history in post-apartheid South Africa will certainly lower the accuracy of the analysis. Because Alexandra and the Johannesburg city centre are so particular, results, at this stage, cannot be generalized to the whole country. More data is needed and townships in Kwa Zulu-Natal, Eastern Cape and Western Cape provinces, in particular, need ideally to be surveyed.

'Alexandra is, and has always been, a special place'[6]

A reminder of the apartheid regime and also one of the strongholds of the struggle for freedom during the war years, Alexandra is a striking illustration of urban poverty and inequalities in the new South Africa. Established in 1904, the overcrowded ghetto spreads over 2 km^2 of houses and shacks, north east of Johannesburg. On the horizon, one can stare at the shining towers of the wealthy Sandton neighbourhood only a few blocks away, where billions of rand trade daily. Back in its early days, its location, along with the ease with which new arrivals could secure a pass to work in the city, often made it the first stop for rural black people seeking jobs in the semi-industrial suburbs.

Its tumultuous history has left its traces. The township struggled to survive apartheid, going from intense threats of removals to numerous failures of upgrading plans, mainly as a result of a clear lack of interest on the side of the government. More recently, the Alexandra Renewal Plan, launched by President Mbeki in 2001, has improved the neighbourhood despite a very difficult first period of implementation. The R1.3 billion seven-year development plan brought new infrastructure and housing, road upgrades and other improvements to Alexandrians' daily lives. But the highly cosmopolitan and ethno-fractionalized township is still gravely overcrowded. Alexandra, once constructed to host 30,000 black workers, has reached a population estimated at half a million. Since the end of apartheid, the number of its residents has nearly quintupled, exacerbating the intense pressure for already scarce service delivery. Poverty is striking,[7] and the level of criminality remains tremendously high.[8]

Meanwhile, Alexandra has always been a place whose people have been strongly politically engaged, leading the fight for freedom from its very early days through multiple ways, such as infamous bus-boycotts and demonstrations. Alongside the Soweto students, the residents played a central role in 1976 in the fight against the Bantu Education Act, which required black students to be taught through the medium of Afrikaans. Alexandra has always been on the front-line of social movements. It is by no means a surprise that it stands at the epicentre of the xenophobic events that broke out on 11 May 2008.

Johannesburg inner city

When arriving in Johannesburg, one can distinguish the city centre from a distance. Wherever one comes from, by land or by air, there is a view of the famous television tower and the 53-floor Ponte Tower from far away. At the time of its construction, the Ponte Tower was the highest building in Africa. The price of a square metre was unaffordable to most South Africans. By the 1990s it had become a symbol of crime, drugs and decay. The story of this once highly coveted building is a perfect illustration of Johannesburg inner city.

In 1955, the Native Amendment Act urged the removal of black residents from the city centre. The inner city was declared a 'Whites Only Area', and the government removed illegal tenants, mainly coloured and Indian families. It was the economic and cultural centre of Johannesburg, hosting many firms' headquarters. Its skyscrapers were the pride of South Africa. Between 1978 and 1982, the grand apartheid project started to erode, and a large influx of coloureds and Indians was recorded moving back into the neighbourhood. The main reason for this was the shortage of flats in some areas and the oversupply in Hillbrow (Morris 1994). Black people also started to illegally penetrate the forbidden area. White families who could afford it started to migrate to the wealthy suburbs of the north. By the end of the apartheid era, Hillbrow and Joubert Park had switched from an essentially white population of all classes to an 'overcrowded crime-ridden black ghetto' (Olufemi 1998), hosting among its residents notorious gangs and drug dealers.

With the upcoming 2010 FIFA World Cup, the City of Johannesburg launched a R171 million uplift programme for the inner city in 2008. The place has gradually been cleared, but remains one of Johannesburg's most feared areas. Its population is essentially black and includes migrants who were not attracted by township life, creating an intensely cosmopolitan place.

The data collection

The sampling strategy was designed to gather a sample with 50 per cent of foreign nationals. Among the national population, targets were set to 50 per cent of South Africans who had lived in the location of interview for at least ten years (i.e. long-term residents), and 50 per cent of recent migrants who had arrived in the location less than ten years ago. As constraints prevented a proper listing exercise from being conducted, interviewers were assigned enumeration areas randomly, chosen from the Statistics South Africa framework, and knocked on every fourth door. Respondents were restricted to adults over the age of 18, with the exception of those over the age of 16 only if they were heads of households.

In total, 2,028 people were interviewed over the course of a month. In Alexandra, the sampling strategy was switched to snowballing, as the quota of foreign nationals proved impossible to reach. First, foreign nationals constitute a minority of Alexandra's residents.[9] Second, foreign nationals refuse to answer or try to mask their identity, underlying the accuracy of the assumption that the situation of foreign nationals was still tense at the time of enumeration. Using snowballing methods, 277 foreign nationals were interviewed in Alexandra, constituting 28 per cent of the location's total sample; 385 interviewees were long-term residents and 326 were recent internal migrants. In the Johannesburg inner city, three neighbourhoods were surveyed: Hillbrow, Berea and Yeoville. There, the 50 per cent target of foreign nationals was met without issues, which confirmed the initial intuition that the location was hosting a large proportion of foreigners. Using the 'every fourth door' sampling strategy, 548 foreign nationals were interviewed along with 470 South Africans. Of the latter, 160 were long-term residents[10] and 310 recent migrants. Overall, the data was composed of 59 per cent of South Africans, 25 per cent of Zimbabweans, 6 per cent of Mozambicans, 3 per cent of Congolese (DRC) the rest being other, less represented foreign nationals, including Malawians, Nigerians and Zambians.

Information was collected on a wide range of issues: demographics, migration patterns, livelihoods, access to health and education services, social participation and also on violence linked to the May attacks. Respondents were asked whether they had been threatened or attacked because of their ethnic/tribal/national identity before May, during May/June 2008 and after the xenophobic events. Further enquiries were made about the length of displacement, the relocation site and so on. Respondents were also asked whether they returned to the place from which they had been chased away, and the reason for this decision. Table 12.1 shows the patterns of xenophobic violence observed in the sample, by area, as well as by country of birth.

As mentioned earlier, the survey covered two particular places. Consequently the data is not representative of the country. Table 12A.1 compares the descriptive statistics of the sample to some key variables of the most recent Census (2001). Although the 2001 Census data is outdated, it is useful to benchmark the data used in this chapter to some national and provincial household data. The key statistics show no striking difference between our data and the Gauteng

Table 12.1 Patterns of violence: 'Have you, or has someone from your household, ever been a victim of threat because of your nationality, ethnicity or tribe?'

Alexandra	National-born and long-term resident	6%
	National-born and recent migrant (less than 10 years)	8%
	Foreign born	47%
Johannesburg inner-city	National-born and long term resident	4%
	National-born and recent migrant (less than 10 years)	5%
	Foreign born	15%
Country of birth,	South Africa	6%
Percentage of population threatened	Zimbabwe	21%
	Mozambique	49%
	DRC	26%
	Malawi	32%

Source: Author's calculations.

province data. Yet living conditions (type of dwelling, access to flush or chemical toilet) appear slightly worse than in the 2001 provincial data, while the percentage of respondents who completed secondary school is much higher in our sample than in the 2001 Census (63.4 per cent compared with 28 per cent in Gauteng in 2001). This could be partly explained by the eight years' gap between the two exercises of data collection. In terms of unemployment, however, almost 60 per cent of the persons interviewed report to be unemployed, about twice as much as in the 2001 Census data. Clearly the locations surveyed count among the places the most affected by unemployment in the country.[11]

The econometric model

Potential selection biases

The data suffers from two potential selection biases. First, people who fled their homes and never came back are completely absent from our sample. Very little is known about the victims who decided to leave, as there was no adequate monitoring.

The United Nations High Commissioner for Refugees (UNHCR) assisted the displaced refugees, but very few went home. Quickly, the agency decided that resettlements would not be awarded on the basis of xenophobic violence. Meanwhile, the United Nations Children's Fund (UNICEF) gave grants to support movements home. The International Organization for Migration (IOM) also assisted vulnerable individuals who expressed the desire to return to their country of origin. In two successive phases, IOM assisted 578 individuals who resigned themselves to going back home, mostly originating from the Great Lakes Region.[12] The Mozambican government provided its citizens with a bus ticket to Maputo. A majority returned home by their own means, which makes it even more difficult to track movements.

What is even less sure is how many of these people who first left came back when the storm had settled; probably a majority. Numerous stories from the camps suggested that some individuals used the repatriation process to go home and then came back. The border-crossing statistics from the Department of Home Affairs give a vague idea on movements out and back to the country. Figure 12A.1 shows the different trends of arrivals (of African nationals) and departures (by road)[13] between 2007 and 2008. The cycles correspond to South African holidays. With the exception of Zimbabweans, trends should be following approximately the same path from one year to the other; the only difference should be in scale. Figure 12A.1a shows very few differences between the two years, apart from a decline in both arrivals and departures in August/September 2008. Looking at the breakdown in arrivals by nationalities (Figure 12A.1b and c), the only main difference is an increase, relative to the preceding year, in the rate of arrivals of Mozambicans, Namibians and Zimbabweans in July 2008. Possibly, it can be explained by those who were returning to South Africa after the violence. This is yet just a hypothesis but the proximity of those countries would have made it easy to leave and return. Out of a large number of displaced persons, we can assume that the ones who decided to leave South Africa for good constitute a clear minority. IOM, which assisted many of them, seems to believe that the foreigners who left were the ones who had lost everything and greatly feared for their lives. Meanwhile, most of the interviews carried out with humanitarian staff present in the camps at the time of the crisis revealed the same observation: when it was announced that resettlement would not occur, people started to leave and return to their communities. While it is important to keep in mind that we do not observe the characteristics of individuals who left, it can be assumed that this will not result in a significant bias in the analysis.

Another potential and more problematic source of selection bias resides in the fact that Alexandra was where it all started, and people who could afford not to come back might have preferred to resettle somewhere else. The main reason mentioned for returning to Alexandra was 'we had no choice', suggesting that if targeted respondents had had the means to do so, they would not have come back. If indeed only the poorest victims came back, the results, at least on the Alexandra sub-sample, would overestimate the poverty factor.

Overall, these two selection biases could affect the results. Precise information on the characteristics of those who fled during the violence and never came back is needed: whether they resettled in their home countries or in other neighbourhoods of South Africa. Yet this information does not exist and one can only speculate. In the data, only 16 individuals were displaced during the violence and did not go back to their neighbourhood, which is too small a sub-sample to even conclude on descriptive statistics. Potentially, there is more than one profile of foreigners who did not return: (1) those who had less to lose relocated, including the newly arrived as well as those whose property was burnt and looted; (2) those who could afford to move somewhere else; that is, those who either had money or family elsewhere in South Africa (in both cases we can assume that those individuals were well-established as they had either jobs or strong social networks); (3) the more vulnerable who stayed at shelters might have received help from

UNHCR and IOM to resettle or go home, in which case the effect of poverty on the probability of being attacked would be underestimated; and (4) refugees who could not afford to go back to their homeland, although they could have received particular assistance from UNHCR to resettle. As a result of this variety of profiles of the missing population, coefficients of both the poverty variables and the length of stay could be under- or overestimated and interpretation should remain careful.

The analysis also suffers from potential reporting errors resulting from the way the data was collected. Indeed, by asking the respondents whether they, or a household member, were attacked on xenophobic grounds during the May 2008 events, there was an opportunity, in particular for foreigners, to classify any crime as xenophobic. However, the high levels of crime observed in the survey area justify differentiating between the types of crime.[14] In order to reduce misreporting to a minimum, the questionnaire was designed for detailed questions on general crime to be asked before questions on xenophobic crime. Twenty-seven per cent of those in the sample (or a household member) reported that they had been a victim of crime since moving to the location of survey. A lower number – 15 per cent – reported xenophobic crimes. The two variables are correlated at 47 per cent. Only 10 per cent of the sample, and 20 per cent of foreigners interviewed, reported to have been attacked or threatened on xeno-phobic grounds during May/June 2008. Looking at the extent of the violence, even if over-reporting cannot be completely ruled out, it does not seem unlikely that one out of five foreigners was victimized. Confirming this hypothesis, two-thirds of the victims of xenophobia live in Alexandra, which was more affected during the attack than the city centre.

Model

The dependent variable is constructed using the answer to the question 'Were you, or anyone in your household, threatened or attacked because of your ethnic group, your tribe or your nationality during May/June 2008?'[15] A probit model was chosen to deal with the binary character of the dependent variable. The following equation is estimated:

$$Violence^*_{ij} = \alpha' + \beta'X_i + \theta'W_j + \varepsilon_{ij} \tag{12.1}$$

where

$$Violence = \begin{cases} 1 \text{ if } Violence^* > 0 \\ 0 \text{ if } Violence^* \le 0 \end{cases}$$

where X_i is a vector of characteristics for the household i and W_j control for characteristics of the ward j. The analysis is clustered by enumeration area to allow correlation of covariance within locations. When ward level characteristics are introduced as controls, the standard errors are corrected for a potential Moulton bias (1990) while clustering at the ward level.

The variables

Table 12.2 reports the key descriptive statistics and the differences between sub-samples.

Demographic and migration history variables

The size of the household describes the number of persons, including children, sharing the same shelter and budget. Single migrants, especially young men, can potentially be perceived as outsiders in the sense that they come to work and do not struggle for their families – at least present with them – like most in the community.

A dummy variable is used whether the respondent was born in South Africa. For an in-depth analysis of the characteristics of foreigners in relation to victimization, the data can be broken down by country of origin. Foreigners are expected to face a higher chance of threat.

A binary variable is used to capture whether the household is composed of both South Africans and foreigners. On the one hand, it can be assumed that foreigners living with South Africans would be assimilated to insiders. For instance, it is assumed that these foreigners would have easier access to community life through their partners. On the other hand, foreigners who have South African partners can be perceived as competitors. In the aftermath of the violence, interviews with South Africans in the zones affected by violence revealed that foreigners were blamed for stealing women. In this case, mixed households would be more at risk than non-mixed households. A priori, the effect is unknown.

A binary variable captures whether the respondent speaks IsiZulu. This stands as a proxy for the household. Speaking IsiZulu, the dominant African street language, is expected to decrease the probability of being attacked or threatened for being an outsider. Potentially speaking the language facilitates integration and reduces recognizability.

The time since arrival in South Africa/in the location provides information on the level of integration. Long-term migrants should be more integrated in their host communities than new arrivals that have less time to settle and be involved in community activities. The former should therefore face a lower risk of being attacked. If the hypothesis were verified, it would corroborate the hypothesis that the recent influx of migrants could have been a major cause of the May 2008 attacks. Yet the length of time since arrival, particularly in Alexandra, could be correlated to the level of poverty of the household. The poorer the household, the longer it takes to afford moving to a safer neighbourhood (Richards et al. 2007). Meanwhile, we control for the different aspects of poverty. Both durations are de facto highly correlated. Therefore the time in the current location is preferred for the analysis. The impact of the time spent in South Africa is also considered for foreigners.

A binary variable is used to identify rural migrants. Under apartheid rules, rural migrants were perceived as 'outsiders' in Alexandra (Nieftagodien 2008).

Table 12.2 Descriptive statistics: differences between sub-samples

	Total	Foreign vs native	Alexandra vs inner-city
Household size	3.99	−1.60 (0.22)***	5.25 (0.21)***
Mixed household	0.23		0.18 (0.02)***
Speak IsiZulu	0.72	0.05 (0.02)**	0.04 (0.02)**
Length in current location	10.49	2.64 (0.18)***	−2.28 (0.18)***
Length in South Africa/Gauteng	11.69	3.03 (0.16)***	−1.64 (0.17)***
Rural background	0.46	0.15 (0.02)***	−0.29 (0.02)***
Secondary school education	0.63	−0.02 (0.02)	0.24 (0.02)***
Wealth index	50.48	−9.50 (1.35)***	28.09 (1.17)***
Relative poverty dummy	0.35	0.04 (0.02)**	−0.31 (0.02)***
Criminal record	0.03	0.03 (0.01)***	−0.02 (0.01)*

Source: Author's calculations.

Notes: Standard errors reported. *, **, ***: differences significant at 1%, 5%, and 10%.

The regime purposely created preferences towards residents. Migrants from rural areas in the country were consistently stigmatized into an out-group. Moreover, rural migrants are expected to have more difficulties in adapting to a new urban environment than migrants coming from urban centres, whether they originate from cities in South Africa, or elsewhere in Africa.

The data also captures the main purposes of migration, with economic reasons, educational reasons, escaping conflict or political oppression, and familial reunion being the most often cited. We can expect that different types of migrants face different degrees of vulnerability and victimization.

Socio-economic variables

The level of education of the respondents serves as a proxy for the level of education of the head of household. In the case of a validation of the relative deprivation theory, the level of education should be positively correlated to the probability of victimization.

The wealth index is created using a (PCA) analysis (see 12B for details). It computes different aspects of poverty such as access to water, electricity and schooling as well as the employment status of the respondents. If victims were systematically richer, then the May 2008 xenophobic violence was a struggle of classes: perpetrators chasing those whom they regarded as privileged. If on the other hand, the poorest were more likely to be victims, the hypothesis under which people lashed out their frustration on the more vulnerable, those competing for the same scarce resources, would be validated.

A dummy capturing the perceived level of relative poverty equals 1 if the respondent affirms to poorer than average compared with others in the area where he/she lives, which is the case for 35 per cent of respondents who consider their household poorer than average, 50 per cent about average and 15 per cent richer than average. The assumption is the same as for the relationship between the level of absolute probability and the risk of being victimized.

Legal variables

Criminal activity is estimated using the respondent self-reported record of arrest by the police, either as part of a criminal investigation or related to participation in criminal activity. Although the information is not collected at the household level it constitutes a proxy and most likely an underestimation. In the data, only 3 per cent of respondents report a criminal record. Yet for those who reported a criminal record, it surely shattered the image of the whole household, which then is associated with criminal activities. Crush and Ramachandran (2009) report that a common belief is that migrants are the cause of the increased level of crime. Following this assumption, households whose members have criminal records should be more at risk of violence than others. If this is not the case, it will confirm that those perceptions are divorced from reality.

The dummy for whether or not the respondents have legal documentation takes the value of 1 if a foreign respondent reports to possess neither an asylum seeker nor a refugee permit, nor a valid visa to be in South Africa. Defined as such, 453 respondents are classified as illegal. Again, this infdividual information is a proxy for the status of other household members. We observe little difference between residents of Alexandra and the inner city. Crush and Ramachandran (2009) identify that irregular migrants are much more prone to victimization than others. If this is true, the coefficient should be positive and significant.

Location controls

The ward variables allow controlling for the characteristics of the location of survey and are constructed using the 2001 Statistics South Africa Census (Statistics South Africa 2004).[16]

We control for the proportion of black males aged 15 to 60. Assuming that women are equally represented across age and ethnicity, the variable is constructed by multiplying the proportion of black inhabitants by the proportion of males and by the proportion of people aged between 15 and 60. It varies between 37 and 44 per cent. We expect that the higher the proportion of black males, the higher the chance of being victimized *ceteris paribus*. Indeed, Wa Kwabe-Segatti and Fauvelle-Aymar's (2012) results suggest a positive impact on the risk of violence at the ward level. However, as our data was collected in areas where the proportion of black people exceeds 90 per cent, the introduction of this variable is for control rather than explanation purposes.

In addition we control for the percentage of foreigners in the ward. A large percentage of foreigners in the location can create a safer environment for foreigners. Conversely, numbers can exacerbate the resentment of the adoptive community.

The diversity index of the foreign population is constructed the same way as the ethno-linguistic fractionalization index (ELF) (Bossert *et al.* 2011). The ELF is a decreasing transformation of the Herfindhal concentration index. For a ward composed $N \geq 2$ nationalities (excluding South Africans) and p_n indicates the share of the group of nationality n in the foreign population, the diversity index is given by $1 - \sum_{n=1}^{N} p_n^2$.

The diversity index of the foreign population in a given ward varies from 60 to 77. Overall the foreign population is heterogeneous. Again no systematic differentiation between Alexandra and the inner city is observable. Wa Kwabe-Segatti and Fauvelle-Aymar (2012) find that the more heterogeneous the foreign population, the lower the probability of violence in the ward.

Due to high correlation between these last two variables, it was preferred to introduce an interactive term between the percentage of foreigners and the diversity of the foreign population. The expected combined impact on the probability of victimization is negative.

The rate of unemployment is constructed as the percentage of the population who reported either to be unemployed or seasonal workers but not working at the time of interview, or who answered that they could not find a job. In the surveyed wards, the unemployment rate varies between 26.5 per cent and 38.5 per cent. The effect of the rate of unemployment in the ward on the probability of being a victim of xenophobia cannot be identified *ex ante*. It is expected to positively impact the probability of victimization. Nevertheless, Wa Kwabe-Segatti and Fauvelle-Aymar (2012) find no significant impact of the location unemployment rate on the probability that a given ward experienced violence in May 2008.

Results

Step 1: Which characteristics influence the probability of being victimized?

The results are reported in the first three columns of Table 12.3.

The main result is that foreigners face a higher probability of being victims of attacks than South Africans. In reality, their chances of victimization are 20 per cent higher than the rest of the population, everything else being held constant. This is particularly high compared with the mean predicted probability of 11 per cent. Not surprisingly, foreigners were the primary target of the May 2008 aggressors. The results of columns 2 and 3 show a striking difference between

Table 12.3 Characteristics of the victims, probit (marginal effects)

	(1)	(2)	(3)	(1)	(2)	(3)	(4)	(5)
Demographics								
Household size	-0.008	-0.015	-0.004	-0.015	-0.008	-0.008	-0.008	-0.015
	(0.003)**	(0.006)**	(0.003)	(0.007)**	(0.003)**	(0.003)**	(0.003)**	(0.008)**
Mixed household = 1	0.003	0.011	-0.004	-0.016	0.003	0.003	0.006	-0.023
	(0.014)	(0.030)	(0.016)	(0.015)	(0.014)	(0.014)	(0.014)	(0.011)**
Speak IsiZulu = 1	0.010	0.036	-0.015	0.009	0.021	0.011	0.020	0.017
	(0.012)	(0.019)*	(0.018)	(0.028)	(0.007)***	(0.012)	(0.007)***	(0.021)
Poverty								
Secondary school = 1	-0.009	-0.009	-0.002	-0.014	-0.007	-0.006	-0.011	-0.023
	(0.009)	(0.019)	(0.019)	(0.035)	(0.008)	(0.009)	(0.009)	(0.036)
Absolute poverty index	0.001	0.001	0.000	0.002	0.001	0.001	0.001	0.001
	(0.000)***	(0.000)**	(0.000)	(0.000)***	(0.000)***	(0.000)***	(0.000)***	(0.000)***
Relative poverty index	0.034	0.042	0.038	0.064	0.034	0.034	0.033	0.052
	(0.006)***	(0.020)**	(0.024)	(0.034)*	(0.006)***	(0.006)***	(0.006)***	(0.033)
Migration history								
Length in current location	0.044	0.048	0.039	0.099	0.043	0.044	0.043	0.097
	(0.018)**	(0.018)***	(0.012)***	(0.046)**	(0.018)**	(0.018)**	(0.019)**	(0.048)**
Length in current location, squared	-0.002	-0.002	-0.002	-0.005	-0.002	-0.002	-0.002	-0.005
	(0.001)**	(0.001)***	(0.001)***	(0.002)**	(0.001)**	(0.001)**	(0.001)**	(0.002)**

(Continued)

Table 12.3 (Continued)

	(1)	(2)	(3)	(1)	(2)	(3)	(4)	(5)
Rural origin = 1	-0.003 (0.016)	0.019 (0.019)	-0.022 (0.015)	-0.067 (0.031)**	-0.005 (0.016)	-0.005 (0.016)	-0.001 (0.015)	-0.066 (0.029)**
Foreign born = 1	0.203 (0.025)***	0.322 (0.036)***	0.091 (0.016)***					
Economic migrant								-0.042 (0.060)
Education migrant								0.042 (0.058)
Conflict migrant								0.040 (0.024)*
Familial reunion migrant								-0.050 (0.028)*
Legal characteristics								
Criminal record = 1	0.000 (0.042)	0.015 (0.066)	-0.009 (0.052)		0.002 (0.042)	0.001 (0.043)	0.002 (0.041)	
Illegal status = 1				0.023 (0.035)				0.030 (0.033)
Nationality								
SA		-0.235 (0.022)***			-0.235 (0.022)***	-0.191 (0.030)***	-0.197 (0.026)***	
ZIM		-0.038 (0.019)**						

(Continued)

Table 12.3 (Continued)

	(1)	(2)	(3)	(1)	(2)	(3)	(4)	(5)
MOZ						0.032 (0.039)		
DRC							0.101 (0.020)***	
Ward characteristics								
Percentage of black males (15–60)	-0.997 (0.181)***			-3.759 (1.041)***	-0.848 (0.213)***	-0.958 (0.174)***	-0.881 (0.178)***	-3.568 (0.990)***
Percentage of unemployed	0.605 (0.233)***			2.645 (0.877)***	0.510 (0.221)**	0.590 (0.210)***	0.543 (0.230)**	2.558 (0.787)***
Percentage of foreigners × Diversity of foreigners' population	-0.293 (0.138)**			-0.305 (0.523)	-0.342 (0.138)**	-0.260 (0.151)*	-0.380 (0.133)***	-0.421 (0.524)
Pseudo R^2	0.187	0.242	0.112	0.123	0.192	0.188	0.191	0.133
ll	-485.5	-277.9	-220.5	-316.9	-482.4	-484.7	-483.0	-317.8
Predicted p at × bar	0.071	0.089	0.056	0.181	0.183	0.071	0.069	0.180
Observations	1715	902	898	696	1715	1715	1715	704

Source: Author's calculations.

Note: Robust standard errors in parentheses. Significant at *10%, at **5%, at ***1%.

Alexandra and the inner city: foreigners living in Alexandra face a 32 per cent higher chance of having been attacked or threatened, while it is only 9 per cent higher in the city centre.

Looking at the demographic variables, only the coefficient of the size of the household is significant. Although its effect is relatively small, it confirms the hypothesis that larger households are perceived more as insiders than as competitors. A single person household is more at risk than a family of five whose members would face a 4 per cent less chance of being victimized on the grounds of xenophobic hatred. This effect is magnified by the fact that the analysis investigates the probability of someone from the household being attacked or threatened. Mathematically, more people can be at risk in a larger household, yet single households appear to face a higher probability of victimization. Against the odds, mixed households are not significantly more or less at risk than others. Similarly speaking, IsiZulu does not seem to matter.

The coefficients of the migration variables give some complementary answers on the characteristics of the victims. First of all, the impact of the time spent in the current location of survey is positive, following a U-inverted pattern. The probability of attacks or threats rises to reach a maximum at the end of the first decade living in the location. The results are robust when introducing the time since arrival in South Africa for foreigners, and in Gauteng, for local migrants. The results are reported in Table 12.4 column (2). This can be interpreted as contradicting the hypothesis that the recent influx of migrants from Zimbabwe fleeing the political and economic crisis is one of the underlying causes of the May 2008 attacks. Indeed, if the growing number of migrants exacerbated resentment and competition for resources in the host community, the ones who were most at risk would have been the newly-arrived, not the long-time neighbours. An alternative explanation is that the xenophobic attacks were more an explosion of a long lasting resentment. For many years, inhabitants lived with and competed with those perceived as outsiders and collective frustrations would have arisen against those frustrating agents. Knowing who they were, they became an easy target once the violence started. By contrast, the newcomers were harder to identify and locate. However, as mentioned earlier, results should be taken with caution as the selection bias might result in an overestimation of the effect of the length of stay in the location, as newcomers might have been less likely to come back to the neighbourhood once peace was restored.

The poverty indicators are significant, but their coefficients appear contradictory. Indeed, absolute wealth, as calculated using the PCA, has a positive impact on the risk of attack. The possibility of a non-linear relationship is ruled out. The richest 1 per cent in the sample face a 10 per cent higher risk of attacks than the poorest percentile. Households at the median face a 5 per cent higher risk. This tends to validate the hypothesis that, everything else constant, richer households were the primary target. Nevertheless, the result is not robust when using a wealth index constructed with only two components. Table 12.4 column 4 reports a positive but not significant effect of the alternative absolute poverty measure. On the contrary, the coefficient of the relative poverty variable suggests that households who perceived themselves as 'on average poorer' face a

Table 12.4 Characteristics of the victims: robustness checks, probit (marginal effects)

	(1)	(2)	(3)	(4)	(5)
Demographics					
Household size	-0.009	-0.009	-0.013	-0.008	-0.015
	(0.003)***	(0.003)***	(0.002)***	(0.002)***	(0.001)***
Mixed household = 1	0.005	0.000	-0.025	0.003	-0.019
	(0.014)	(0.013)	(0.005)***	(0.014)	(0.005)***
Speak IsiZulu = 1	0.015	0.012	0.010	0.013	0.012
	(0.012)	(0.010)	(0.008)	(0.013)	(0.011)
Poverty					
Secondary school = 1	-0.006	-0.011	-0.015	-0.009	-0.013
	(0.009)	(0.009)	(0.009)	(0.008)	(0.011)
Absolute poverty index	0.001	0.001	0.001		
	(0.000)***	(0.000)***	(0.000)***		
Absolute poverty index (PCA 2 comp)				0.000	0.001
				(0.000)	(0.000)***
Relative poverty index	0.042	0.042	0.062	0.030	0.043
	(0.006)***	(0.006)***	(0.013)***	(0.004)***	(0.011)***
Migration history					
Length in current location				0.051	0.091
				(0.019)***	(0.014)***
Length in current location^2				-0.002	-0.004
				(0.001)***	(0.001)***
Ln length in current location	0.032				
	(0.011)***				
Length in GP/SA		0.056	0.102		
		(0.023)**	(0.017)***		
Length in GP/SA, sq		-0.003	-0.005		
		(0.001)**	(0.001)***		

(Continued)

Table 12.4 (Continued)

	(1)	(2)	(3)	(4)	(5)
Rural origin = 1	-0.003	-0.004	-0.060	-0.004	-0.058
	(0.014)	(0.014)	(0.009)***	(0.014)	(0.008)***
Foreign born = 1	0.321	0.309		0.314	
	(0.034)***	(0.031)***		(0.033)***	
Legal characteristics					
Criminal record = 1	0.006	0.003		0.005	
	(0.038)	(0.040)		(0.042)	
Illegal status = 1			0.015		0.018
			(0.010)		(0.011)*
Ward characteristics					
% of black males (15–60)	-1.121	-1.096	-3.386	-1.099	-3.746
	(0.151)***	(0.207)***	(0.371)***	(0.188)***	(0.368)***
% of unemployed	0.646	0.687	2.360	0.659	2.565
	(0.223)***	(0.231)***	(0.283)***	(0.216)***	(0.304)***
% of foreigners × diversity of the foreign population	-0.274	-0.322	-0.345	-0.356	-0.442
	(0.123)**	(0.133)**	(0.170)**	(0.135)***	(0.184)**
Pseudo R^2	0.17	0.18	0.12	0.18	0.12
ll	-493.142	-490.144	-320.993	-488.600	-321.649
Predicted p at × bar	0.073	0.073	0.182	0.072	0.183
Observations	1715	1708	707	1715	706

Source: Author's calculations.

Note: Robust standard errors in parentheses. Significant at *10%, at **5%, at ***1%.

higher risk of being attacked. In fact, half of those who responded to be on average poorer are situated in the 30 per cent poorer group of the sample. Columns 2 and 3 show that relative poverty is mainly a factor of victimization in Alexandra. Indeed the coefficient loses significance when the regression is run on the inner city sub-sample. Yet it is acknowledged that relative poverty could be endogenous to xenophobic victimization, as victims might enter this parameter in their self-evaluation of relative poverty. In order to correct for this possible bias in the coefficients, the relative poverty binary variable is instrumented using the level of education (and has no effect on the probability of being threatened or attacked) and whether the respondent states to have nowhere to go to borrow 500 ZAR[17] if in need. Contrary to expectations, it seems that, when corrected for endogeneity, the relative poverty variable has a largely positive effect on the probability of victimization. Relatively poorer households face a 50 per cent higher chance of victimization than other residents of the community, everything else held constant. Results are reported in Table 12A.2. Column 1 presents the results of the full sample and column 2 presents the results of the sample restricted to foreigners only.

The absolute impact of each poverty dimension suggests that perpetrators of the attacks turned against the most vulnerable in the community rather than the richest. If this result is not dependent on the selection bias of the sample, then it can rightly be assumed that more than a fight built up on frustrations against wealthier outsiders, the May 2008 violence was a violent reaction against a failing service delivery system. Unable to attack the source of poverty and frustrations, desperate people turned against the easiest target they could reach – the most vulnerable individuals.

Whether the respondent reports having a criminal record in the country does not impact the probability of being attacked. This suggests that the May 2008 attacks were not orchestrated against criminals, or if they were, there was a clear misperception of whom to evict.

The core regression controls for some of the characteristics of the ward: the percentage of black males between 15 and 60; the unemployment rate; and the percentage of foreigners interacted with the heterogeneity of the foreign population. All coefficients are significant. The results suggest that a percentage point higher in the proportion of black males decreases the probability of attacks by one percentage point. Similarly, the sign of the interacted term suggests that the higher the proportion of foreigners and the more heterogeneous the foreign population in the location of the survey, the lower the chances of attack for the respondent household. This finding confirms that of Wa Kwabe-Segatti and Fauvelle-Aymar (2012), that the heterogeneity of the foreign group negatively impacts the probability of violence in the ward.

The rate of unemployment in the location seems to increase the probability of victimization. The coefficient of the ward unemployment rate is positive and significant at a 1 per cent threshold in all regressions. This result is all the more important as very little variation is observed among wards (min: 26.5 per cent; max: 38.5 per cent). This can potentially be an explanation for the observed higher probability of victimization in Alexandra. Indeed, 68 per cent of respondents reported to be unemployed compared with 52 per cent in inner city Johannesburg. Similarly, twice as many report to be employed full-time in the inner city compared with in Alexandra (26 per cent compared with 13 per cent). This result contradicts the findings of Wa Kwabe-Segatti and Fauvelle-Aymar (2012) that conclude for a non-significant impact of the employment rate on the likelihood of violence at the ward level. There could be two distinct explanations for the observed difference between the two analyses. First, the result could be the direct consequence of a likely high correlation rate between the unemployment variable and the very low level of income used as another explanatory factor for the occurrence of violence. Consequently, both coefficients would be biased. Alternatively, one can assume that if employment conditions do not determine the places where the violence erupted in May 2008, a higher unemployment rate implies higher probabilities of victimization at the household level. In other words, unemployment conditions in the areas affected by attacks result in a larger scale of violence. If unemployment is not a trigger it certainly is an aggravating factor. Inhabitants of more deprived areas are more at risk of attacks or threats.

All the above results are robust to the inclusion of ward-fixed effects. The results are reported in Table 12A.3

Step 2: What characteristics make a foreigner an outsider?

Column 1 of Step 2 is similar to column 1 of Step 1, the difference being that the sample is reduced to foreign nationals only. The legal status of the responding migrant is introduced as an explanatory variable. It is expected that undocumented migrants will face higher levels of resentment linked to their illegal status in the country; but the community members might not necessarily know the exact legal status of foreign neighbours. The variable capturing criminal record is dropped, as no foreigners in the sample report having been arrested for criminal activities. The predicted probability of victimization rises to 0.18.

The demographic and migration history variables follow the same pattern as previously observed. Household size has a negative and significant effect. The probability of being victimized increases with the length of stay in the location, following a U-inverted shape. This calls for cautious interpretation as the coefficients might be upward biased as a result of the sample selection. Absolute poverty has a positive impact on the probability of attack, while relative poverty has the inverse effect. The result is robust to the use of an alternative measure of absolute poverty based on two components only (Table 12.4, column 5). Once corrected for potential endogeneity using education level, the relative poverty effect is large and significant, suggesting that poorer foreigners were more at risk than relatively richer ones. A few differences can nevertheless be observed in Step 2. Foreigners with urban backgrounds are more at risk than those coming from rural areas; a highly unexpected result as one could assume that rural migrants would have more trouble integrating into Johannesburg life.

Columns 2 and 3 of Step 1 illustrate that Alexandrians are significantly less safe than inhabitants of the inner city, suggesting that township environments lead to more resentment towards foreigners. The descriptive statistics of the population which has been victimized confirms a striking difference between Alexandra and Johannesburg inner city. In the township, 38 per cent of foreign nationals reported having been victims of violence in May/June 2008, as opposed to only 12 per cent in the inner city. One reason could be that foreign-born constitute a minority of township inhabitants (about 2–3 per cent according to the estimation of the latest Alexandra Renewal Project's study). Hence, as a small proportion, they become an easy target.

A major assumption to verify, once controlling for demographics, wealth, migration and location characteristics, is whether all nationalities face the same probability of threats or whether some are more at risk than others. In order to do so, binary variables for the main foreign nationalities in the sample were introduced to the core regression, while controlling for South Africans, that is, Zimbabweans (62 per cent of the total foreign population in the sample), Mozambicans (16 per cent) and Congolese-DRC (8 per cent). The results are reported in columns 2, 3 and 4 and suggest that Zimbabweans are less at risk of xenophobic violence than others. Once again this tends to confirm the findings of Misago *et al.* (2009) that the influx of Zimbabweans was not one of the reasons for the eruption of violence in May 2008. Indeed, if it was the case, we would expect Zimbabweans to face higher probabilities of threats. On the contrary, Zimbabweans are relatively less victimized in our sample. Congolese, on the other hand, face a 10 per cent higher probability of victimization. There could be many explanations for this phenomenon. Not coming from neighbouring countries, they might have more problems integrating into South African society. It could also be a language barrier. It could simply be that they are more recognizable among the population. There is also a possibility that they associate aggression with xenophobia more easily.

Finally, migrants do move to South Africa for different reasons. Some escape political oppression or conflict in their home countries. Some migrate for economic opportunities, hoping that the receiving country will give them a better life. Some reunite with family members already living in the host country. Some come to South Africa from all over the continent to study (South Africa has a wide range of educational institutions of high quality). Some migrate for a combination of those reasons and others. Integration in the new community can prove more or less successful depending on why one left home in the first place. To verify this, binary variables capturing the reasons for migrating[18] are introduced in the core regression. Results are reported in column 5. Migration reasons do not seem to influence the probability of being a target of violence, with the exception of migrants who came to South Africa for familial reunion who face a 5 per cent lower chance of having been attacked during the xenophobic violence. A simple explanation can be that existing family networks facilitate integration into the host society.

The results of the analysis confirm that the violence was not purely conducted at random. Mike's story was not the exception. Some foreigners were and are more at risk of being threatened or attacked. So who, in our sample, faces the highest chance of being attacked or threatened? Who is the 'alien'? According to the results of Table 12.1, the 'perfect outsider' is a single migrant who has lived in South Africa for about a decade. He/she comes from an urban environment in the DRC and is relatively poorer than his/her neighbours. Finally, he/she lives in a place with high unemployment and few foreigners.

Conclusion

The present results are based on specific settings in South Africa. Hence, to be generalizable, more data need to be collected from different areas across the country. These results, nonetheless, provide interesting insights into what makes people more likely to be victims of xenophobia.

During the May 2008 xenophobic attacks, not every migrant was attacked. This was the observation at the root of this analysis. Who is the alien? Is it possible to identify what makes some individuals the targets? Or was violence directed at random? Using household data collected from the Alexandra township and Johannesburg inner city, the results show that particular characteristics of the household significantly affect the probability of victimization on the grounds of xenophobia.

First and not surprisingly, foreign nationals are more at risk. Second, nationality does matter. Third, the alien is not newly arrived; it is someone who has been living in the location of the survey for about a decade. However, the quality of the data does not rule out the potential bias resulting from a specific sample selection. It is indeed likely that those who fled from their neighbourhood were the least established individuals. Fourth, relative poverty has a positive effect on the probability of victimization and this is particularly true for the Alexandra residents. It confirms that the violent attacks were targeted towards the more vulnerable and in closer proximity.

Frustrations do not seem to emanate from the fact that foreigners do better. More likely, xenophobic violence is the outcome of the rising inequalities between the poorest and the richest classes of society. Violence is then targeted at the ones the frustrated can harm, although they might not be the intrinsic source of frustrations. Confirming this result, Alexandra appears more dangerous than the inner city, in particular for foreigners. Similarly, households living in areas with high unemployment face a higher probability of xenophobic violence. If a high unemployment rate does not trigger violence, it increases the scale of violence, with residents of those areas of high unemployment facing higher chances of xenophobic attacks. In this context, South Africa's tensions cannot be solved without tackling poverty and inequality.

Appendix 12A

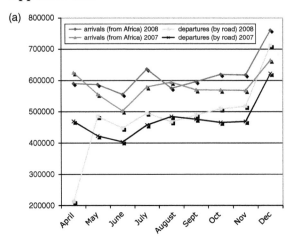

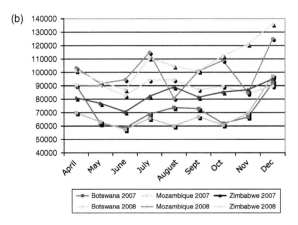

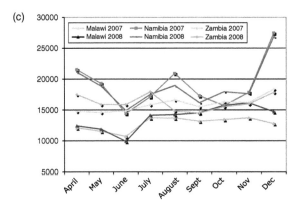

Figure 12A.1 a–c Arrivals of African nationals and departures, by road, between 2007 and 2008: (a) border crossings; (b, c) country of origin

Table 12A.1 Benchmarking sample compared with census data

Variable	2009 Data	Census 2001 (National)	Census 2001 (Gauteng only)
Living in informal dwelling	39.9	20.4% of black population	32.2% of black population
Access to electricity	79.9	62.0% of black population	74.3% of black population
Flush or chemical toilets	69.0	41.9% of black population	77.2% of black population
Unemployed (15–65 years old)	59.8	28.1% of black population	32.2% of black population
Some secondary school		30.8	34.3
Completed grade 12	63.4	20.4	28.0
Sample size	2,028	44,819,778	8,837,178

Source: Author's calculations.

Notes: Standard errors. *, **, ***: differences significant at 1%, 5%, and 10%.

Table 12A.2 Instrumentation of the relative poverty index

	(1)	(2)
	IV- all sample	IV- foreigners only
Demographics		
Household size	−0.066	−0.065
	(0.024)***	(0.028)**
Mixed household = 1	0.015	−0.070
	(0.104)	(0.062)
Speack IsiZulu = 1	0.092	0.057
	(0.089)	(0.106)
Poverty		
Absolute poverty index	0.006	0.007
	(0.002)***	(0.002)***
Relative poverty index	0.559	0.733
	(0.242)**	(0.284)***
Migration history		
Length in current location	0.311	0.333
	(0.140)**	(0.179)*
Length in current location²	−0.015	(0.009)*
	(0.007)**	***
		−0.016
Rural origin = 1	−0.020	−0.275
	(0.118)	(0.099)
Foreign born = 1	1.218	
	(0.149)***	
Legal characteristics		
Criminal record = 1	0.024	
	(0.310)	
Ward characteristics		
% of black males (15–60)	−6.429	−12.563
	(1.235)***	(4.575)***
% of unemployed	4.078	9.495
	(1.792)**	(3.780)**
% of foreigners x diversity of the foreign population	−1.835	−0.491
	(0.998)*	(2.294)
First stage instrumentation: relative poverty		
First stage Secondary school = 1	−0.061	−0.039
	(0.024)***	(0.038)
No where to borrow 500R = 1	0.189	0.191
	(0.028)***	(0.029)***
athrho	−0.145	−0.217
	(0.104)	(0.126)*
insingma	−0.852	−0.924
	(0.051)***	(0.062)***
ll	−457.806	−661.183
Observations	1715	696

Source: Author's calculations.

Notes: Robust standard errors in parentheses. Significant at *10%, at **5%, at ***1%.

Table 12A.3 Characteristics of the victims, robustness checks: ward-fixed effects, probit

	(1)	(2)	(3)	(1)	(2)	(3)	(4)	(5)
Demographics								
Household size	−0.010	−0.019	−0.004	−0.015	−0.009	−0.009	−0.010	−0.014
	(0.003)***	(0.006)***	(0.003)	(0.003)***	(0.003)**	(0.003)***	(0.003)***	(0.003)***
Mixed household = 1	0.007	0.018	−0.006	−0.006	0.007	0.007	0.011	−0.013
	(0.014)	(0.030)	(0.015)	(0.004)	(0.014)	(0.014)	(0.014)	(0.003)***
Speak IsiZulu = 1	0.014	0.046	−0.017	0.007	0.024	0.014	0.025	0.014
	(0.013)	(0.023)*	(0.015)	(0.010)	(0.009)***	(0.013)	(0.008)***	(0.008)
Poverty								
Secondary school = 1	−0.009	−0.016	−0.001	−0.014	−0.008	−0.008	−0.012	−0.023
	(0.008)	(0.019)	(0.017)	(0.012)	(0.008)	(0.009)	(0.008)	(0.012)*
Absolute poverty index	0.001	0.002	0.000	0.002	0.001	0.001	0.001	0.001
	(0.000)***	(0.000)***	(0.000)	(0.000)***	(0.000)***	(0.000)***	(0.000)***	(0.000)***
Relative poverty index	0.038	0.052	0.032	0.066	0.037	0.038	0.037	0.054
	(0.007)***	(0.022)**	(0.022)	(0.013)***	(0.007)***	(0.007)***	(0.007)***	(0.013)***
Migration history								
Length in current location	0.051	0.052	0.043	0.095	0.049	0.050	0.050	0.093
	(0.019)***	(0.017)***	(0.013)***	(0.015)***	(0.018)***	(0.019)***	(0.020)***	(0.015)***
Length in current location, sq	−0.002	−0.003	−0.002	−0.005	−0.002	−0.002	−0.002	−0.005
	(0.001)***	(0.001)***	(0.001)***	(0.001)***	(0.001)***	(0.001)***	(0.001)***	(0.001)***
Rural origin = 1	−0.005	0.015	−0.025	−0.057	−0.006	−0.006	−0.003	−0.056
	(0.014)	(0.021)	(0.012)**	(0.009)***	(0.014)	(0.015)	(0.014)	(0.008)***
Foreign born = 1	0.276	0.338	0.160					
	(0.028)***	(0.036)***	(0.037)***					

(Continued)

Table 12A.3 (Continued)

	(1)	(2)	(3)	(1)	(2)	(3)	(4)	(5)
Economic migrant								−0.039
								(0.018)*
Education migrant								0.034
								(0.020)
Conflict migrant								0.033
								(0.008)***
Familial reunion migrant								−0.051
								(0.008)***
Legal characteristics								
Criminal record = 1	−0.003	0.012	−0.009		−0.001	−0.003	−0.002	
	(0.040)	(0.060)	(0.050)		(0.039)	(0.041)	(0.039)	
Illegal status = 1				0.019				0.025
				(0.012)				(0.012)**
Nationality								
SA					−0.099	−0.094	−0.094	
					(0.003)***	(0.005)***	(0.004)***	
ZIM					−0.038			
					(0.017)**			
MOZ						0.019		
						(0.029)		
DRC							0.109	
							(0.016)***	
Ward-fixed effects	x	x	x	x	x	x	x	x
Pseudo R^2	0.193	0.253	0.112	0.139	0.198	0.194	0.198	0.141
ll	−481.6	−258.6	−215.8	−313.4	−479.1	−481.3	−478.8	−314.8
Predicted p at x̄	0.071	0.086	0.058	0.182	0.071	0.071	0.070	0.178
Observations	1715	851	864	696	1715	1715	1715	706

Source: Author's calculations.

Note: Robust standard errors in parentheses. Significant at *10%, at **5%, at ***1%

Appendix 12B

Creating an indicator of wealth

The PCA method identifies important poverty indicators and calculates the weight related to each variable suspected to have an impact on poverty. It isolates and measures the poverty component embedded in the various poverty indicators, and creates a household specific poverty index that can be then introduced in the core analysis as a dependent variable. The PCA technique slices information contained in the set of indicators into several components. Each component is constructed as a unique index, based on the values of all the indicators. The main idea is to formulate a new variable that is the linear combination of the original indicators, such that it accounts for the maximum of the total variance in the original indicators. In order to choose the number of components to retain, two techniques can be used. The first is to keep the components with an eigenvalue superior to 1 (Kaiser criterion). In this case, the first six components are used to create the aggregate value of poverty. Table 12B.1 presents the eigenvalues for the six components and Table 12B.2, the eigenvectors. The second method is to observe the slope of the eigenvalues. The number of components to retain, corresponds to the change in the slope (scree test). Using this method, only two components are retained. The first method is preferred as it gives a more precise estimation of poverty, while the second method serves as a robustness check. The indicator is then constructed as the sum of the component. It has a zero mean and a standard deviation equal to 1. In this analysis, the indicator is then rescaled by quintile. The poverty index thus defined then varies from 0 to 1 depending on the value of the indicator.

Table 12B.1 Principal component analysis

	Eigenvalue	Difference	Proportion	Cumulative
Comp1	6.4347	4.72803	0.2925	0.2925
Comp2	1.70667	0.211419	0.0776	0.3701
Comp3	1.49525	0.257404	0.0680	0.4380
Comp4	1.23785	0.147286	0.0563	0.4943
Comp5	1.09056	0.0656347	0.0496	0.5439
Comp6	1.02493	0.0417156	0.0466	0.5905

Source: Author's calculations.

Note: Kaiser–Meyer–Oklin (sampling adequacy) = 0.9170.

Table 12B.2 Principal component analysis: eigenvectors

	Comp1	Comp2	Comp3	Comp4	Comp5	Comp6
Household size	0.1512	0.5231	−0.0796	0.1553	−0.1661	0.0969
Ratio of children	0.0655	0.4022	0.3310	0.0914	0.0752	−0.1018
Decent accommodation	0.3245	0.0699	−0.3256	0.0347	0.0103	−0.0518
No of rooms	−0.0271	0.5728	0.2249	0.0966	−0.2183	0.2088
Rent	0.2789	0.0444	−0.2820	0.0505	−0.0312	−0.0508
Electricity in the dwelling	0.2673	0.0050	0.0574	−0.2376	0.0103	0.1053
Running water in the dwelling	0.3234	0.0677	−0.3178	0.0571	0.0220	−0.0592
Hot water	0.3046	0.0207	−0.2615	0.1124	−0.0185	−0.1061
Toilets in the dwelling	0.3091	0.0455	−0.1694	−0.0891	0.0282	0.0554
Difficulty to access to health	−0.0084	0.1020	0.0009	−0.1860	0.5261	−0.2888
Difficulty to access to schooling	0.0110	0.2871	0.0064	−0.0675	0.5336	−0.1403
Malnutrition	−0.1253	0.0887	−0.0567	−0.2021	0.1536	−0.3027
Owns a radio	0.2105	−0.1206	0.2708	−0.1645	0.0482	0.0023
Owns a refrigerator	0.2811	−0.0706	0.2764	−0.1308	−0.0415	−0.0747
Owns a television	0.2938	−0.0461	0.2649	−0.1991	−0.0052	0.0434
Owns a cellphone	0.1749	−0.0491	0.2542	−0.1263	0.0821	0.2373
Owns a dvd player	0.2909	−0.0604	0.2444	−0.1130	−0.0052	0.0315
Owns a Microwave	0.2406	−0.1389	0.1352	0.1599	−0.0372	−0.1548
Owns a bicycle	0.0680	−0.1186	0.1793	0.5715	0.0533	−0.1039
Owns a car	0.1314	−0.1650	0.1998	0.4727	0.0391	−0.3182
Works	0.0643	−0.1797	−0.0922	0.0943	0.2470	0.6220
Has other sources of income	−0.0020	0.0353	0.0146	0.3117	0.5035	0.3466

Source: Author's calculations.

Notes

1 The author thanks UNDP South Africa, UNOCHA-ROSA, the South African Red Cross and the Forced Migration Studies Programme at Wits University as well, as Lopa Barjenee, Laura Brown, Veronique Gindrey, Pete Manfield, J.P. Misago, Loren Landau, Pinky Vilakazi, Hein Zeelie and all the volunteers of the Red Cross. The author is also grateful to Jean-Claude Berthelemy, Paul Collier, Fabrizio Coricelli, Patrick Guillaumont and Eliana La Ferrara for useful comments on earlier drafts.
2 Thembisa is located in the Gauteng province. It is one of the townships most affected during the riots.
3 See Misago *et al.* (2009) for details on the violent incidents recorded since the end of the apartheid era and during the May/June 2008 episode.
4 These facts are gathered from different sources including BBC News, *Mail* and *Guardian*, and UNOCHA.
5 Wards constitute demarcation area delimited by the Demarcation Board after consulting the Electoral Commission. Each has approximately the same number of voters. The number of registered voters in each ward may not vary by more than 15 per cent from the norm, where the norm is determined by dividing the total number of registered voters on the municipality's segment of the national common voters roll by the number of wards in the municipality. The delimitation also takes into account the need to avoid, as far as possible, the fragmentation of communities.
6 Bonner and Nieftagodien (2008).

7 In our sample, 87 per cent of the respondents in Alexandra report not having access to running water in their dwelling; 4 out of 10 households interviewed do not have electricity in their dwelling.
8 SAPS reports an average of four murders per month.
9 No more than 3 per cent according to the Alexandra Renewal Project survey.
10 The inner city happens to be mainly a place of transit.
11 The dynamism of the Gauteng province attracts a lot of migrants seeking work in Johannesburg. Alexandra and the inner city are both places where those migrants would settle while looking for employment. As a result, it is not surprising that the unemployment rate is relatively higher there than elsewhere.
12 Phase 1: 170 Burundians, 137 Congolese (DRC), 44 Tanzanians, 15 Somalis (who went back to Ethiopia), five Kenyans, one Congolese, one Sudanese and one Rwandese. Such details are not available for phase 2.
13 For departures Home Affairs only gives a breakdown by means of transport and not by nationalities (see Figure 12A.1). Presumably, most victims would have returned home by road. However, those statistics also include departures of tourists travelling in the region.
14 Alexandra and Hillbrow's reputation make them rank amongst the most dangerous places in South Africa. Theft and mugging are a daily routine there.
15 We decide to focus on the May 2008 attacks as opposed to a larger period of coverage, mainly because the responses are believed to be more accurate: it is possible that attacks before or after May are remembered as xenophobic when they were not.
16 Overall, the core sample covers eight distinct wards. Enumeration Areas (EAs) were arbitrarily attached to the adjacent wards in case they originally belonged to another large ward which did not allow us to capture the living conditions in the EA. In particular, due to Alexandra's proximity to the wealthy Sandton suburbs, some EAs in Alexandra originally belonging to Sandton wards are reattached to adjacent wards capturing the living conditions in the area.
17 About US$60 at the time of the survey.
18 Respondents were asked to give the two main reasons for coming to Gauteng/South Africa.

References

Allport, G. (1954). *The Nature of Prejudice*. Cambridge, MA: Addison-Wesley.

Banton, M. (1996). 'The Cultural Determinants of Xenophobia'. *Anthropology Today*, 12(2): 8–12.

Bonner, P. and Nieftagodien, N. (2008). *Alexandra: A History*. Johannesburg: Witwatersrand University Press.

Bossert, W., C. D'Ambrosio and E.L. Ferrara (2011). 'A Generalized Index of Ethno-Linguistic Fractionalization'. *Economica*, 78(312): 723–50.

Central Intelligence Agency (CIA) (2008). The World Fact Book: Distribution of Family Income, Gini Index.

Crush, J. and S. Ramachandran (2009). 'Xenophobia, International Migration and Human Development'. Research Paper 2009/47. New York: United Nations Development Programme.

Dodson, B. and C. Oelofse (2000). 'Shades of Xenophobia: In-migrants and Immigrants in Mizamoyethu, Cape Town'. *Canadian Journal of African Studies*, Special Issue: Transnationalism, African Immigration, and New Migrant Spaces in South Africa, 34(1): 125–48.

Esses, V.M., J.F. Dovidio, L.M. Jackson and T.L. Armstron (2001). 'The Immigration Dilemma: The Role of Perceived Group Competition, Ethnic Prejudice, and National Identity'. *Journal of Social Issues*, 57(3): 389–412.

Gelb, S. (2008). 'Behind Xenophobia in South Africa – Poverty or Inequality?'. In S. Hassim, T. Kupe, and E. Worby (eds), *Go Home or Die Here: Violence, Xenophobia and the Reinvention of Differences in South Africa*. Johannesburg: Wits University Press.

Gindrey, V. and L. Landau (2008). 'Migration and Population Trends in Gauteng Province 1996–2055'. Working Paper 42. Johannesburg: African Centre for Migration and Society.

Gagnon V. P. (1994). 'Ethnic Nationalism and International Conflict: the Case of Serbia'. *International Security*, 19(3): 130–66.

Human Sciences Research Council (2008). 'Violence and Xenophobia in South Africa: Developing Concensus, Moving to Action'. Pretoria: Human Sciences Research Council.

Misago, J. P., L. Landau and T. Monson (2009). 'Towards Tolerance, Law and Dignity: Addressing Violence against Foreign Nationals in South Africa'. Arcadia: IOM, Regional Office for Southern Africa.

Morris, A. (1994). 'The Desegregation of Hillbrow, Johannesburg, 1978–82'. *Urban Studies*, 31(6): 821–34.

Moulton, B. R. (1990). 'An Illustration of a Pitfall in Estimating the Effects of Aggregate Variables on Micro Units'. *The Review of Economics and Statistics*, 72 (2): 334–38.

Neocosmos, M. (2008). 'The Politics of Fear and the Fear of Politics: Reflections on Xenophobic Violence in South Africa'. *Journal of Asian and African Studies*, 43(6): 586–94.

Nieftagodien, N. (2008). 'Xenophobia in Alexandra'. In S. Hassim, T. Kupe and E. Worby (eds), *Go Home or Die Here: Violence, Xenophobia and the Reinvention of Differences in South Africa*. Johannesburg: Wits University Press.

Olufemi, O. (1998). 'Street Homelessness in Johannesburg Inner-City: A Preliminary Survey'. *Environment and Urbanization*, 10(2): 223–34.

Pillay, D. (2008). 'Relative Deprivation, Social Instability and Cultures of Entitlements'. In S. Hassim, T. Kupe and E. Worby (eds), *Go Home or Die Here: Violence, Xenophobia and the Reinvention of Differences in South Africa*. Johannesburg: Wits University Press.

Richards, R., B. O'Leary and K. Mutsonziwa (2007). 'Measuring the Quality of Life in Informal Settlements in South Africa'. *Social Indicators Research*, 81: 375–88.

Sharp, J. (2008). 'Fortress SA: Xenophobic Violence in South Africa'. *Anthropology Today*, 24(4): 1–3.

Sherif, M., O.J. Harvey, B.J. White, W.R. Hood and C.W. Sherif (1961). *Intergroup Cooperation and Competition: The Robbers Cave Experiment*. Norman, OK: University Book Exchange.

Statistics South Africa (2004). 'Primary Tables South Africa: Census '96 and 2001 Compared'. Pretoria: Statistics South Africa.

Tadjo, V. (2008). 'Constructing the other Learning from the Ivorian Example' In S. Hassim, T. Kupe and E. Worby (eds), *Go Home or Die Here: Violence, Xenophobia and the Reinvention of Differences in South Africa*. Johannesburg: Wits University Press.

Uvin, P. (1999). 'Ethnicity and Power in Burundi and Rwanda: Different Paths to Mass Violence'. *Comparative Politics* 31 (3): 253–71.

Wa Kwabe-Segatti, A. and C. Fauvelle-Aymar (2012). 'People, Space and Politics: An Exploration of Factors Explaining the 2008 Anti-foreigner Violence in South Africa'. In L. B. Landau (ed.), *Exorcising the Demons Within, Xenophobia, Violence and Statecraft in Contemporary South Africa*. Johannesburg: Wits University Press.

13 How does colonial origin matter for economic performance in Sub-Saharan Africa?

Julius A. Agbor

Introduction

Over the past decades, a substantial volume of literature has dwelt on the subject of colonization and economic performance of former colonies.[1] Economists became interested in colonial legacies in their search for the reasons why some countries have grown relatively slower than others. Notably, recent cross-country empirical evidence suggests that the identity of the colonizing power (or colonial origin) might help explain the observed growth differential amongst former colonies around the world.[2] In particular, it is claimed that, on average, former British colonies have grown faster than former French colonies, although much controversy still surrounds the probable mechanisms of transmission of any such colonial legacy.

For instance, using a sample of 49 former colonies around the world during 1960–2003, Klerman *et al.* (2008) found that differences in educational policies are the main reason why former British colonies have grown faster than former French colonies. In addition, they showed that colonial origin does not matter after geographical factors are controlled for, which lends support to the initial endowments hypothesis[3] that differences in the initial conditions of pre-colonization, rather than in colonial policy (legal, educational, or other), are the best explanation for different growth rates amongst former colonies. However, these results, as the authors themselves admit, are inconclusive due to their high sensitivity to regional considerations and to the choice of sample.[4]

Like Klerman *et al.* (2008), Rostowski and Stacescu (2006, 2008) find that colonial origin matters more than legal origin, and education is the probable channel through which colonial origin affects growth. Like Klerman *et al.*, they do not probe into the different mechanisms through which colonial origin affects growth.[5] Furthermore, their analyses are limited to the initial conditions at independence. They suggest, however, that 'examining the channels through which colonial origin could affect growth is therefore the first priority for future research' (Rostowski and Stacescu 2006: 17).

This chapter further investigates the channels through which colonial origin affects economic growth performance, focusing only on sub-Saharan African (SSA) countries. Besides limiting the sample of study to a set of countries which do not appear to display significant differences in the initial geographical conditions, this chapter goes beyond the previous studies by distinguishing between the direct and indirect effects of colonial legacies, that is, by separating the initial conditions at the time of independence from the changes that were subsequently introduced by independent African states themselves.

The sample comprises 36 SSA countries over the period 1960–2000. The Hausman–Taylor (HT) estimation technique is applied to annualized panel data. We investigate two probable transmission channels between colonial origin and growth, namely, education and trade.

The results suggest that the indirect influences of colonial educational policies matter more for post-colonial growth than the direct influences emanating from colonization. They suggest further that former British SSA colonies have grown marginally faster than former French colonies during 1960–2000, and this is attributable to the favourable contribution of the indirect influence of the legacy of British colonization in education. I do not find any evidence in support of the trade transmission mechanism. The finding that post-independence education matters more than the initial conditions at the time of independence seems to contradict the findings of previous studies which suggest that it is the initial condition at independence that mattered for the post-colonial growth path.

The rest of the chapter is organized as follows. First, there is a brief historical overview of the probable transmission mechanisms at work between colonial origins and growth, then the next section presents the methodology of the study. This is followed by a discussion of the key findings and checks for their robustness, also a comparison of the results with those in the literature. The final section is the Conclusion.

Historical overview of the probable mechanisms of transmission between colonial origins and growth

Historical sources claim that, as of the late nineteenth century, Britain was the only imperial power that was committed to free trade, whilst the other European powers, notably France, were still building up their rival industries through protectionism.[6] Correspondingly, whilst British colonial economies were not under the obligation to export only to Britain, French colonial economies were compelled to trade mainly with France.[7] As such, it can be argued that one of the important legacies of British colonization on its former colonies has been a long exposure to world competition through trade openness,[8] which might possibly explain why former British SSA colonies adjusted more rapidly to structural adjustment programmes implemented in the late 1980s in comparison with their French counterparts.[9]

Another important legacy of colonization, which has found much less expression in the cross-country empirical growth literature, is the distortionary impact of different colonial taxation systems on private investment incentives.[10] Historical sources[11] claim that the dual system of administration of their colonies, characterized by punitive taxation and forced labour on the general population, was a distinctive feature of French colonial rule in SSA.[12] The implication of this unique approach to local administration is to be found in the colonial legacy of taxation pursued in the post-colonial era. By contrast, Maddison (1971) has argued that one of the important legacies of British colonization is that its former colonies inherited relatively lower levels of taxation, because indirect rule is cheaper to administer than direct rule, which was characteristic of French colonial rule. Austin (2008) also argues that, until very late in the colonial period, there was no direct taxation in southern Ghana and Nigeria – two of the relatively successful British colonies in tropical Africa. If this is true, then it could imply that former British colonies are associated with relatively lower degrees of distortions of economic activity through taxation, which could in turn imply greater private investment incentives or more free trade on the domestic scale.

Furthermore, it is well documented that educational policy was potentially the area of greatest distinction between different imperial colonial administrations. It is generally claimed that Britain pursued more enlightened educational policies in its colonies than did France, whose educational objective aimed essentially at training personnel for the colonial bureaucracy. For instance, Gann and Duignan (1970: 354), argue that

> Mission teachers in British Africa not only taught their pupils how to read and write, but also taught them how to try their hands at many different jobs because the teachers themselves, besides giving lessons, were also engaged in such diverse activities as constructing their own buildings, cultivating their own crops, experimenting in agriculture and building roads.

In addition, it is widely held that primary instruction in former British colonies was administered through village schools using native teachers and the local vernacular languages of the people, whilst in former French colonies, pupils were generally boarded from their homes to far away schools where they were taught in French by French teachers, using French textbooks. This is suggestive of a different approach to educational provision with different repercussions on post-independence human capital accumulation and development.

Finally, an important colonial legacy that also merits further attention in the empirical literature is the impact of the Franc CFA[13] currency board which links France to most of its former SSA colonies. Julan (2010) has recently shown that being part of the Franc CFA currency board increases the likelihood of currency crisis, which might impede economic performance. The Franc CFA currency board, it is also argued, has been instrumental in lowering inflation and the black market exchange premium while enhancing the contribution of imports to GDP growth. However, as the evidence suggests, the impact of the currency board on economic performance could go the other way.[14] Thus, a major distinction between the former British and French SSA colonies has been the fact that almost all former British SSA colonies have floating exchange regimes; whereas almost all former French SSA colonies operate under a fixed exchange regime.

In summary, this chapter will focus primarily on two probable channels of transmission between colonial origins and growth:

- *The education or human capital channel*, which will be proxied by two variables, namely, secondary enrolment rates during 1960–2000 (SEC), and the average years of schooling in the population aged 15 and above during 1960–2000 (AYS).
- *The trade channel*, which will be proxied by the export share in GDP during 1960–2000 (EXP) and openness to international trade during 1960–2000 (OPEN).

Methodology

Empirical model

The questions this chapter seeks to answer are: whether colonial origin really matters for post-independence economic growth in SSA, and if yes, what are its channels of transmission?

To answer these questions, I specify the regression model as follows:

$$GROW_{it} = \alpha + \beta COLO_i + \gamma TRANSM_{it} + \eta INTERACT_{it}$$
$$+ \delta CONTROLS_{it} + \mu_i + \varepsilon_{it} \qquad (13.1)$$

Where:

- $GROW_{it}$ is the per capita GDP growth of country i in year t.
- β, γ, η, *and* δ are vectors of coefficients, while μ_i is a vector of individual country effects reflecting unobservable country heterogeneity and ε_{it} is the remainder (non-systematic) disturbance term.
- $COLO_i$ is a matrix of colonial origin dummies comprising BCORG (which takes the value 1 for British colonial origin and zero otherwise), FCORG (which takes the value 1 for French colonial origin and zero otherwise) and PCORG (which takes the value 1 for Portuguese former colonies and zero otherwise) and BECORG (which takes the value 1 for Belgian former colonies and zero otherwise).[15]
- $TRANSM_{it}$ is a matrix of variables that serve as probable transmission channels between colonial origin and growth.
- $INTERACT_{it}$ is a matrix of interaction terms linking colonial origin dummies ($COLO_i$) with the transmission mechanisms ($TRANSM_{it}$). A model with interaction terms can be presented in a simplified form as:

$$Y = a + bX_1 + cX_2 + dX_1X_2 + \mu_i$$

where X_1 and X_2 represent the matrix of transmission channels and the vector of colonial origin dummies respectively. Thus,

$$\frac{\partial Y}{\partial X_1} = b + dX_2$$

tells us whether the impact of a specific transmission channel is significantly different across colonial origins.

- *CONTROLS$_{it}$* is a matrix of control variables that are standard in the growth literature, in addition to controls for the duration of colonization.

Choice of estimator

I estimate Equation 13.1, using a core dataset of 36 SSA countries over 1960–2000. A key consideration in choosing a suitable estimator for the model is how well the estimator handles the problem of endogeneity resulting from the likelihood that some of the explanatory variables might be correlated with the unobserved country effects. As Baltagi (2001) argues, the fixed effects (within) estimator assumes that all the explanatory variables are related to the individual effects and the within-estimator is a best linear unbiased estimator (BLUE) once the individual effects are modelled as a linear function of all the explanatory variables. Using the within-transformation (henceforth FE) in estimating Equation 13.1 above should result in the elimination of the μ_i term and, hence, the bias as well. However, the FE eliminates the time-invariant regressors and may be inefficient, while it also fails to deal with potential endogeneity of the remaining regressors.

The random-effects (RE) model, on the other hand, assumes no correlation between the explanatory variables and the individual effects. Thus in the presence of endogeneity RE will yield biased estimates. Hence, inferences from the RE model are likely to be misleading. This is equally true for the OLS estimator, which also assumes exogeneity of all regressors.

Against these two contrasting worlds, Jerry Hausman and William Taylor (see Baltagi *et al.* 2003) proposed a model where some of the regressors, but not all, are correlated with the individual effects. According to Baltagi *et al.* (2003), the Hausman–Taylor (HT) model is preferable whenever the specification requires some of the regressors, but not all, to be correlated with the individual effects.

The HT model can be written as

$$y_{it} = \beta X_{it} + \varphi Z_i + \alpha_i + \mu_{it} \tag{13.2}$$

where $i = 1, 2, \ldots . N$ and $t = 1, 2, \ldots . T$, while μ_{it} is *IID* $(0, \sigma_\mu^2)$.
Both α_i and μ_{it} are independent of each other and among themselves, while α_i, like Z_i, are individual time-invariant variables.

Hausman and Taylor split $X = [X_1, X_2]$ and $Z = [Z_1, Z_2]$ into two sets of variables such that X_1 is $n \times k_1$, X_2 is $n \times k_2$, Z_1 is $n \times g_1$, Z_2 is $n \times g_2$ and $n = NT$.

X_1 and Z_1 are assumed exogenous and not correlated with α_i or μ_{it}, while X_2 and Z_2 are endogenous due to their correlation with α_i but not with μ_{it}.

Under Equation 13.2, OLS will yield biased and inconsistent estimates, while the FE (or within-transformation) estimator gives consistent estimates. The FE controls for α_i and removes the bias, but, in the process, it also eliminates the time-invariant variables, Z_i. Hence it cannot yield estimates of φ. The RE estimator, which is a generalized least square estimation of Equation 13.2, ignores the endogeneity due to the presence of the α_i term and will therefore yield biased though consistent estimates.

To get around the shortcomings of the within-estimator in estimating the time-invariant regressors, Hausman and Taylor suggest an instrumental variable estimator which pre-multiplies Equation 13.2 by $\Omega^{-\frac{1}{2}}$ where Ω is the variance-covariance term of the error component $\alpha_i + \mu_{it}$ and then performs two-stage least squares (2SLS), using as instruments $[Q, X_1, Z_1]$. Q is the within-transformation matrix with $\tilde{y} = Qy$ having a typical element $\tilde{y}_{it} = y_{it} - \bar{y}_i$, where $\bar{y}_i$ is the individual mean. As Baltagi *et al.* (2003) show, this turns out to be equivalent to running 2SLS with $[\tilde{X}, \bar{X}_1, Z_1]$ as the set of instruments.[16]

It is important to emphasize that the order of identification $k_1 \geq g_2$ must hold for Equation 13.2 to be non-singular. In other words, the number of time-varying exogenous regressors X_1 must be at least as large as the number of individual time-invariant endogenous regressors Z_2. Specifically, the model is said to be just-identified, when $k_1 = g_2$ and, in this case, the HT estimates of φ are equivalent to estimates obtained from 2SLS estimation. The model is said to be over-identified when $k_1 > g_2$ and, in this case, the HT estimates of φ are more efficient than estimates obtained from the FE estimator. Finally, the model is under-identified when $k_1 < g_2$ and, in this case, the HT model cannot provide estimates of φ.

Estimation strategy

In order to answer the question whether colonial origin matters for economic growth in SSA, I first specify a simple growth model in which the only explanatory variables are the various colonial origin dummies (BCORG, FCORG, PCORG and BECORG). This is easily achieved using OLS with robust standard errors.

To determine which transmission mechanisms are at work, I then include variables that capture the different transmission channels, alongside their corresponding interaction terms with colonial origin dummies. To distinguish the direct effects of colonization (that is, impacts of colonial legacies measured in the year of independence) from the indirect effects (that is, the impacts of the additional changes brought in by the independent African states), I include for each transmission channel considered, the time-invariant values measured in the year of independence and the time-variant values measured throughout the period of analysis. I also include control variables that are standard in the growth literature in addition to control for the duration of colonization. I test for robustness of the results by using alternative proxies for the transmission channels and alternative estimation techniques, as well as different time intervals (5-year and 10-year period means). The dependent variable in all model specifications is the annual growth rate of per capita GDP during 1960–2000.

Thus, the principal explanatory variables in each model specification are the time-invariant educational and trade variables measured in the year of independence of each country included in the sample, the corresponding time-variant educational and trade variables, alongside their corresponding interaction terms with colonial origin dummies. A statistically significant sign on the time-invariant educational and trade variables measured in the year of independence would suggest a direct influence of the transmission channels on post-colonial growth, while a statistically significant sign on the time-variant educational and trade variables would suggest an indirect influence of the transmission mechanism.

Irrespective of the nature of the influence of the channel (direct or indirect), it would be important to know whether the impact of the channel is identical across the board for all colonial origins or whether it matters disparately across colonial origins – which is the role of the interaction terms between the transmission variables and colonial origin dummies in the regression models.

Variables and data

The dependent variable in all model specifications is the per capita GDP growth during 1960–2000 (GROW). Amongst the explanatory variables are the colonial origin dummies. I classify the SSA countries in the sample into four broad colonial origin families: (i) British colonial origin (BCORG), for colonies that acquired their independence from Britain; (ii) French colonial origin (FCORG), for countries that acquired independence from France; (iii) Portuguese colonial origin (PCORG), for countries that acquired their independence from Portugal; and (iv) Belgian colonial origin (BECORG), for countries that acquired their independence from Belgium. By basing colonial origin on the identity of the colonizer through which independence was acquired, I am assuming, in line with the tradition in the literature, that it is the colonial power that significantly shaped the country's post-colonial future.[17] Countries that witnessed a relatively short period of colonization (for example Ethiopia) or which were never colonized (for example Liberia) are excluded from the sample. Furthermore, countries that had multiple appreciable colonization experiences (for example South Africa) are also excluded. I also exclude Cape Verde and the Comoros Islands, for lack of consistent data. See Price (2003: 481–2) for a classification of the countries in the dataset together with their dates of colonization and independence.

Besides the colonial origin dummies, the other choice explanatory variables are a set of variables that capture the two transmission mechanisms between colonial origin and growth. These are:

*   *The gross secondary enrolment rates during 1960–2000 (SEC) to capture the education or human capital transmission channel.* The conventional growth literature suggests that human capital enhancement is good for growth either because it raises the overall productivity of the economy or because it favours the development of pro-growth institutions.[18] However, this evidence is inconclusive as other empirical studies, notably by

Pritchett (2001), suggest that growth in human capital could be detrimental for per capita GDP growth. The interaction terms of colonial origin with secondary enrolment rates during 1960–2000 are: SEC_BRI, SEC_FRE, SEC_POR and SEC_BEL, for British, French, Portuguese and Belgian colonial origins respectively. I also include the time-invariant secondary enrolment rates measured in the year of independence of each country included in the sample (SEC_IND). For robustness, I use an alternative measure of education, namely, the average schooling years in the population aged 15 years and above. Hence, the measure for average schooling years at the time of independence is AYS_IND, while the respective post-colonial interactive measures are given by: AYS_BRI, AYS_FRE, AYS_POR and AYS_BEL.

- *The average share of exports in GDP during 1960–2000 (EXP) to capture the trade transmission mechanism.* The literature suggests that SSA countries that were more open to trade have indeed grown faster than those that were not.[19] Rodrik (2002), however, holds a dissenting view. Thus, the sign on exports in the regressions can go either way. The interaction terms of colonial origin with exports during 1960–2000 are EXP_BRI, EXP_FRE, EXP_POR and EXP_BEL, for British, French, Portuguese and Belgian colonial origins respectively. Similarly, the export measure in the year of independence of the country is represented by EXP_IND. Where necessary, I use openness to international markets as an alternative proxy for the trade channel.

Furthermore, I introduce another set of six control variables that are standard in the growth literature. These are:

- The natural logarithm of initial real per capita GDP in 1960 (LOGPCGDP60) to capture convergence effects. Quah (1993) argues that due to the problem of reversion to the mean, the sign on initial per capita income can either be positive or negative depending on the sample.
- The growth rate of population during 1960–2000 (GPO) to control for the effect of demographic factors on growth. I follow the endogenous growth literature, notably by Kremer (1993) in suggesting a possible correlation between labour force growth (proxied by population growth) and income growth and the two are expected to be positively correlated, Solow (1956) and Swan (1956) suggest the opposite.
- The inflation rate during 1960–2000 (INFL) to capture the negative effects of price instability on growth. According to Grier (1999: 322), Friedrich Hayek and Milton Friedman both claim that inflation uncertainty increases price variability, thus harming economic growth.
- The average share of real investment[20] in GDP purchasing power parity during 1960–2000 (INV) to account for the contribution of physical capital accumulation to GDP growth. The standard neoclassical growth literature suggests that investment in physical capital is good for growth during transitional

dynamics, although this might not be the case at steady states. The expected sign on INV in the regressions should therefore be positive.

- An annual index of the black market exchange rate premium during 1960–2000 (BMP) to capture the effects of market distortion that might be detrimental to growth. Easterly and Levine (1997) find a strong negative association between black market premium and growth.
- Finally, a measure of the ethno-linguistic fractionalization (ETHNIC). The expected sign of ETHNIC in the growth regression is negative, according to the evidence from Mauro (1995) and Easterly and Levine (1997).

In addition to this set of control variables, I introduce a variable, DUREE, to capture the duration of colonial rule. DUREE is obtained by subtracting the respective country independence year from the year that the country was first colonized.[21] Table 13.1 summarizes the definition of variables and data sources.

Finally, I indicate the a priori classification of these variables into the various HT categories. The HT model requires classification of variables into the following four categories: time-variant exogenous variables, time-invariant exogenous variables, time-variant endogenous variables and time-invariant endogenous variables. However, the last category need not be included for the model to be correctly specified.

Based on economic theory, I classify the variables into the HT model as exogenous due to their supposed non-correlation with both the unobserved individual effects (α_i) and with the error term μ_{it}. Similarly, I classify some variables as endogenous in the model because of their supposed correlation with α_i but not with μ_{it}. I thus regroup the variables into the following four HT categories viz.:

- *Time variant exogenous variables*: the black market exchange rate premium during 1960–2000 (BMP). Following Easterly and Levine (1997), I classify black market exchange premium as exogenous in the HT model, because it tends to capture growth-inhibiting institutional imperfections that might not necessarily be correlated with the individual country effects.
- *Time-variant endogenous variables*: secondary enrolment rates during 1960–2000 (SEC), average years of schooling during 1960–2000 (AYS), export share in GDP during 1960–2000 (EXP), investment during 1960–2000 (INV), inflation during 1960–2000 (INFL) and population growth during 1960–2000 (GPO). Accordingly, all the interaction terms for education and trade enter in this category. Following the tradition in the empirical growth literature, we classify these variables as endogenous in the HT model.[22]
- *Time invariant endogenous variables*: secondary enrolment rates at independence (SEC_IND), average schooling years at independence (AYS_IND), and export share in GDP at independence (EXP_IND).
- *Time-invariant exogenous variables*: all colonial origin dummies[23] (BCORG, FCORG, PCORG and BECORG), the duration of colonial rule (DUREE), the natural logarithm of initial per capita GDP in 1960 (LOGPCGDP60) and ETHNIC.

Table 13.1 Variables definition and sources

Variable	Description	Source
BCORG	British Colonial Origin Dummy	Author's Construction
FCORG	French Colonial Origin Dummy	Author's Construction
PCORG	Portuguese Colonial Origin Dummy	Author's Construction
BECORG	Belgian Colonial Origin Dummy	Author's Construction
SEC	Postcolonial Secondary Enrolment Rates (1960–2000)	WDI & GDF (World Bank)
SEC_IND	Independence Secondary Enrolment Rate	WDI & GDF (World Bank)
SEC_BRI	Postcolonial Secondary Enrolment Rates for former British Origin	WDI & GDF (World Bank)
SEC_FRE	Postcolonial Secondary Enrolment Rates for former French Origin	WDI & GDF (World Bank)
SEC_POR	Postcolonial Secondary Enrolment Rates for former Portuguese Origin	WDI & GDF (World Bank)
SEC_BEL	Postcolonial Secondary Enrolment Rates for former Belgian Origin	WDI & GDF (World Bank)
EXP	Postcolonial Export Share in GDP (1960–2000)	WDI (World Bank)
EXP_IND	Independence Export Share in GDP	WDI (World Bank)
AYS	Postcolonial Average Schooling Years in Population 15+ (1960–2000)	Barro & Lee (2010)
AYS_IND	Independence Average Schooling Years in Population 15+	Barro & Lee (2010)
AYS_BRI	Postcolonial Average Schooling Years in Population 15+ for former British Origin	Barro & Lee (2010)
AYS_FRE	Postcolonial Average Schooling Years in Population 15+ for former french Origin	Barro & Lee (2010)
AYS_POR	Postcolonial Average Schooling Years in Population 15+ for former Portuguese Origin	Barro & Lee (2010)
AYS_BEL	Postcolonial Average Schooling Years in Population 15+ for Former Belgian Origin	Barro & Lee (2010)
GROW	Postcolonial Per Capita GDP Growth (1960–2000)	WDI (World Bank)
GPO	Postcolonial Population Growth Rate	WDI & GDF (World Bank)
LOGPCGDP60	Per Capita GDP level in 1960	WDI (World Bank)
DUREE	Duration of Colonization	Author's Construction
BMP	Black Market Exchange Premium	Africa Research Program Dataset, Harvard
ETHNIC	Ethno-linguistic fractionalization	Africa Research Program Dataset, Harvard
INFL	Inflation Rate (1960–2000)	WDI (World Bank)

Source: Author's compilation.

Table 13.2 provides summary descriptive statistics of variables included in the sample, while Table 13.3 provides the partial correlation coefficients. Most of my data come from the Global Development Finance and the World Development Indicators. The partial correlation results suggest that the duration of colonization is strongly positively correlated with the education and trade variables, and the education measures at independence (SEC_IND and AYS_IND) are also strongly positively correlated with the post-independence education variables (SEC and AYS, respectively), which suggests a strong persistence of colonial educational practices in the post-colonial era. This is also true for the independence trade (EXP_IND) and post-independence trade (EXP) variables.

Discussion of results

The discussion of the results follows the two-stage empirical strategy. Accordingly, I first analyse stage-one results based on simple OLS estimation and then proceed to stage two results based on the HT estimator.

Table 13.2 Summary descriptive statistics

Variable	Obs	Mean	Std. dev.	Min.	Max.
GROW	1238	6.034893	9.458898	−33.33333	92.2078
GPO	1360	2.611742	.7187012	−.6744879	4.66606
LOGPCGDP60	1271	7.023608	.5592167	6.045005	8.093157
ETHNIC	1271	65.67742	22.47371	0	90
BMP	1094	59.93946	282.1426	−89.16118	4806.89
INV	1350	10.35901	8.975847	−2.809372	69.91588
INFL	884	54.90318	817.2855	.0123	23773.13
DUREE	1394	70.97059	15.23022	55	111
SEC_IND	1394	5.321176	7.070332	1	32.12
SEC	1379	16.71777	15.32025	1	93.117
SEC_BRI	1379	9.566787	15.49098	0	93.117
SEC_FRE	1379	6.153485	11.44275	0	79
SEC_POR	1379	.4136563	1.981223	0	21.6
SEC_BEL	1379	.581665	3.092819	0	25.7
AYS_IND	1025	1.22084	.891196	.17	3.172
AYS	985	1.955401	1.320378	.16	5.73
AYS_BRI	985	1.313589	1.603382	0	5.73
AYS_FRE	985	.4967868	.8953029	0	4.68
AYS_POR	985	.0256853	.1355198	0	1.19
AYS_BEL	985	.1193401	.4368924	0	3.18
EXP_IND	1353	24.38445	17.15794	4.861965	75.61404
EXP	1271	27.44242	16.84334	2.524708	84.11205

Source: Author's compilation.

Table 13.3 Matrix of correlation coefficients

	GROW	GPO	LOGPCGDP60	ETHNIC	BMP	INV	INFL	DUREE	SEC_IND	SEC	AYS_IND	AYS	EXP_IND	EXP
GROW	1.000													
GPO	0.113	1.000												
LOGPCGDP60	-0.119	-0.235	1.000											
ETHNIC	-0.035	0.331	0.313	1.000										
BMP	-0.023	-0.026	-0.024	0.025	1.000									
INV	0.026	-0.132	0.038	-0.263	0.071	1.000								
INFL	-0.001	0.057	-0.028	0.087	0.031	-0.087	1.000							
DUREE	0.052	-0.134	-0.157	-0.233	0.109	0.454	-0.035	1.000						
SEC_IND	-0.049	-0.389	0.465	-0.08	0.003	0.273	-0.018	0.46	1.000					
SEC	-0.137	-0.261	0.209	-0.002	0.037	0.227	0.018	0.367	0.632	1.000				
AYS_IND	-0.039	-0.393	0.121	-0.429	-0.045	0.467	-0.051	0.541	0.656	0.444	1.000			
AYS	-0.178	-0.356	0.057	-0.153	-0.015	0.338	0.036	0.532	0.601	0.788	0.728	1.000		
EXP_IND	-0.08	-0.061	0.206	0.300	-0.004	0.067	-0.006	0.287	0.530	0.493	0.174	0.491	1.000	
EXP	-0.061	0.007	0.248	0.014	-0.154	0.253	-0.074	0.126	0.424	0.506	0.203	0.352	0.565	1.000

Source: Author's Compilation.

Stage one results based on simple OLS

Table 13.4 presents the results from three model specifications of Equation (13.1). Model 1 includes only colonial origin dummies as explanatory variables for growth and tests the hypothesis that colonial origin matters for growth in SSA. The results suggest that, indeed, colonial origin matters and former British SSA colonies have grown on average roughly 1 percentage point faster than former

Table 13.4 Preliminary results based on OLS estimation

	Model 1	Model 2	Model 3
BCORG	1.007**	0.090	3.383
	(0.553)	(2.203)	(3.026)
PCORG	−1.045	7.760**	7.822**
	(1.883)	(3.321)	(4.171)
BECORG	0.106	1.839	2.018
	(1.194)	(1.591)	(1.511)
BMP		−0.001	−0.001**
		(0.001)	(0.000)
EXP		0.031	0.016
		(0.035)	(0.034)
EXP_IND		−0.032	0.028
		(0.048)	(0.054)
SEC		−0.125***	
		(0.038)	
SEC_IND		0.293	
		(0.189)	
AYS			−3.144***
			(0.549)
AYS_IND			2.758**
			(1.061)
GPO		1.849**	0.659
		(0.864)	(1.012)
LOGPCGDP60		−2.447	−2.032
		(1.447)	(1.409)
INV		0.187***	0.063
		(0.064)	(0.088)
ETHNIC		0.013	0.018
		(0.025)	(0.029)
INFL		−0.000	0.001*
		(0.000)	(0.000)
DUREE		−0.006	−0.015
		(0.079)	(0.106)
CONSTANT	5.621***	16.274	17.570
	(0.371)	(10.521)	(13.358)
No. OBS.	1238	620	448

Source: Author's compilation.

Notes: Dependent variable: per capita GDP growth (GROW). Robust standard errors are presented in parentheses. *** significant at 1% level, ** significant at 5% level and * significant at 10%. The omitted category is French Colonial Dummy (FCORG).

French colonies. However, there seems to be no significant difference in growth between the former French, Portuguese, or Belgian SSA colonies.

Model 2 includes, in addition to the colonial origin dummies, the transmission mechanisms investigated (trade measured by EXP and EXP_IND and education measured by SEC and SEC_IND), controls for the duration of colonization and other standard controls. The former British colonial origin dummy (BCORG) now loses all of its statistical significance and also diminishes in magnitude while the former Portuguese colonial origin dummy (PCORG) gains statistical as well as economic significance. This result suggests that former Portuguese colonies have grown on average 7 percentage points faster than former French colonies.

Of the two transmission mechanisms tested, only the education channel appears to matter while the trade channel is insignificant. Of the two education channel variables, only SEC is statistically significant (at 1 per cent level), although negative, suggesting that the indirect influence of colonial educational policies matters more than the direct influence. This result also suggests that the contribution of human capital development to SSA growth during 1960–2000 has generally been detrimental, which is Pritchett-consistent.

Model 3 tests the robustness of the results in Model 2 by using an alternative measure of the education channel, namely, the average schooling years in the population aged 15 and above (AYS and AYS_IND). The results in Model 3 basically uphold the results of Model 2 with the only difference that both the direct and indirect effects of colonial educational policies matter for post-independence growth performance. However, the direct effects of the legacy of colonial education have had a positive repercussion while the indirect effects have had a negative repercussion. In other words, the legacy of colonial education practices per se, has had positive repercussions on post-independence growth while the additional changes brought in by the independent African states have had a negative effect on growth.

The findings from these different model specifications give an idea of the possible transmission channel between colonial origin and growth in SSA. However, because of the potential bias and inconsistency of OLS estimation, this evidence is inconclusive and requires further investigation using alternative techniques and measurement.

Stage two results based on HT estimation

Table 13.5 presents the results from four model specifications of Equation (13.1). Model 1 includes, in addition to the colonial origin dummies, the transmission channel variables (trade measured by EXP[24] and education measured by SEC and SEC_IND), controls for the duration of colonization and other standard controls. The results suggest that only the education channel matters and of the two education channel variables analysed, only SEC is statistically significant (at 1 per cent level), although negative, suggesting that the post-independence educational policies of the former colonies are largely responsible for the observed growth differences amongst these countries. In other words, the indirect influence of colonial educational policies matters more than the direct influence. The lack of statistical significance on the independence education variable (SEC_IND)[25] suggests that the initial education conditions of SSA countries at independence cannot explain growth differences amongst former SSA colonies during 1960–2000. These results seem at variance with those of previous studies, notably, the works of Grier (1999), Bertocchi and Canova (2002), Rostowski and Stacescu (2006, 2008) and Klerman *et al.* (2008), who find that education conditions at independence are the main determinants of the post-colonial growth path.

Table 13.5 Main results using Hausman-Taylor estimator

	Model 1	*Model 2*	*Model 3*	*Model 4*
Time variant exogenous variables				
BMP	−0.001	−0.001	−0.002	−0.001
	(0.001)	(0.001)	(0.001)	(0.002)
Time variant endogenous variables				
INF	−0.000	0.001	0.001	0.004
	(0.002)	(0.002)	(0.002)	(0.003)
GPO	1.087	1.136	0.119	0.318
	(0.087)	(0.879)	(0.982)	(1.009)
INV	0.116	0.133	−0.088	−0.049
	(0.088)	(0.088)	(0.111)	(0.112)
EXP	0.018	−0.007	−0.005	−0.029
	(0.056)	(0.057)	(0.071)	(0.072)
SEC	−0.137***	−0.251***		
	(0.043)	(0.085)		
SEC_BRI		0.173*		
		(0.098)		
SEC_POR		0.813		
		(1.865)		
SEC_BEL		−0.299		
		(0.258)		
AYS			−4.394***	−6.974***
			(0.804)	(1.648)
AYS_BRI				3.758**
				(1.906)
AYS_POR				13.298
				(19.823)
AYS_BEL				−3.631
				(4.391)
Time invariant exogenous variables				
BCORG	−3.764	−9.661	5.240	−3.615
	(20.834)	(26.451)	(4.906)	(7.063)
PCORG	1.682	−6.272	6.378	−4.460
	(9.914)	(21.242)	(10.232)	(22.460)

(Continued)

Table 13.5 (Continued)

	Model 1	Model 2	Model 3	Model 4
BECORG	3.363	4.466	2.076	5.736
	(6.995)	(9.079)	(4.022)	(7.767)
DUREE	0.132	0.139	−0.012	−0.062
	(0.239)	(0.335)	(0.168)	(0.187)
LOGPCGDP60	−1.204	−4.147	−1.354	−4.209
	(16.476)	(19.686)	(3.056)	(3.659)
ETHNIC	0.057	0.093	0.037	0.103
	(0.175)	(0.225)	(0.155)	(0.183)
Time invariant endogenous variables				
SEC_IND	0.607	0.886		
	(2.576)	(3.195)		
AYS_IND			4.576	7.155
			(7.559)	(8.737)
CONSTANT	−2.550	17.345	14.989	35.111
	(97.323)	(114.947)	(20.666)	(27.841)
No. OBS.	620	620	448	488
No. GROUPS	28	28	22	22
Prob > Chi-square	0.09	0.07	0.00	0.00

Source: Author's compilation.

Notes: Dependent variable: per capita GDP growth (GROW). Robust standard errors are presented in parentheses. *** significant at 1% level, ** significant at 5% level and * significant at 10%. The omitted categories are French Colonial Dummy (FCORG, SEC_FRE, and AYS_FRE).

The results in Model 2 which controls for possible differences in post-independence educational policies across colonial origins reveal a positive and highly statistically significant (at 1 per cent) sign on the British colonial origin post-independence education interaction term (SEC_BRI). This result suggests that, in comparison with former French colonies, the post-independence education conditions in former British SSA colonies have been more favourable to growth. In other words, the reason why former British SSA colonies appear to do better than former French colonies is because the indirect influence of British colonial education legacy is more likely to produce growth than the indirect influence of French colonial education legacy.

The results in Models 3 and 4 test the robustness of the results in Models 1 and 2 respectively, by using an alternative measure of the education channel, namely, the average schooling years in the population aged 15 and above (AYS and AYS_IND). The results in Model 3 basically uphold the results of Model 1 while the results of Model 4 uphold those of Model 2. In other words, the indirect influence of colonial educational policies matters more for growth than does the direct influence and former British colonies do comparatively better than former French colonies, presumably because of a superior legacy of education inherited from Britain.[26]

Conclusion

This chapter sought to investigate whether colonial origin really matters for post-colonial economic growth in SSA and, if it does, what its probable transmission mechanisms are. Two probable channels of transmission, education and trade, were investigated. The methodology applied in this study is slightly different from that of previous works, where only initial conditions at independence were held to influence the subsequent growth path. In contrast, this study attempts to distinguish between the direct and indirect influences of colonization by combining both the initial conditions at independence and the subsequent post-independence changes.

The results suggest that the indirect influences of colonial educational policies matter more for post-colonial growth than the direct influences. The results further suggest that former British SSA colonies have grown marginally faster than former French colonies during the 1960–2000 sample period, and that this is attributable to the favourable contribution of the indirect influence of the legacy of British colonization in education. In other words, education has a more favourable impact on growth in former British colonies, in comparison to former French colonies. These findings suggest that the choices made by European colonizers during the colonization of Africa, notably, in educational policies, continue to matter today. I do not, however, find any evidence in support of the trade transmission mechanism.

Notes

1 The impact of colonialism on current developmental trajectories continues to be debated by economists; see recent studies by Heldring and Robinson (2012) and Agbor *et al.* (2014).
2 See, for instance, the works by Grier (1999), Bertocchi and Canova (2002), Price (2003), Rostowski and Stacescu (2006, 2008), and Klerman *et al.* (2008).
3 Pioneered in the works of Engerman and Sokoloff (2002).
4 For instance, Klerman *et al.* (2008) admit that their results controlling for geographical factors are highly dependent on their definition of the regional dummies for Latin America and SSA and on which set of countries is analysed.
5 A concurrent strand of literature pioneered by La Porta *et al.* (1997, 1998, 1999) and La Porta *et al.* (2008) suggests that countries that followed the English Common Law legal tradition, by colonization or conquest, have on average grown faster than countries that followed the Civil Law tradition, specifically the French Civil Law countries. Mahoney (2001), Levine *et al.* (2000), and Levine *et al.* (2002) also arrive at a similar conclusion. However, other evidence, as shown in the works of Acemoglu and Johnson (2005) and Klerman *et al.* (2008), suggests that the effect of legal origin on economic growth is weak. Indeed, Roe and Siegel (2009) have presented a range of conceptual and factual evidence in support of why the legal origins explanations may be flawed.
6 Grier (1999) reports that Britain had had a free trade policy from 1830 and, as from 1846, British colonies were no longer forced to give British goods preferential treatment. Hence these colonies have had a long history of free trade, while the French enforced mercantilist and protectionist measures throughout the colonial period. For additional evidence, see also, Gann and Duignan (1970), Maddison (1971) and Bolton (1973).
7 See Fieldhouse (1966).

8   During the inter-war period, Nigeria alone exported five times as much as all the French colonies in West Africa (Rostowski and Stacescu 2006).
9   The evidence also points to the fact that former British SSA colonies grew much faster than French SSA colonies after structural adjustment.
10 The few existing works are single-country studies, notably, Banerjee and Iyer (2005) on India, and Berger (2009) on Nigeria.
11 See for instance, Crowder (1968) and Asiwaju (2000).
12 Crowder (1968) argues that the '*code d'indigénat*', which was instituted in French SSA aimed at achieving the employment of native labour through the imposition of relatively high taxes on blacks and in default of payment they would incur a sentence of forced labour.
13 The Franc CFA stands for Franc de la Communauté Financiere en Afrique, meaning Financial Community of Africa Franc.
14 For instance, one of the main arguments for devaluing the Franc CFA by 50 per cent in January 1994, was because of its excessively distortionary effects on the economies of those countries. See Collier and Gunning (1999).
15 Of course, only three of the colonial origin dummies enter the regression at a time, while the fourth dummy serves as base.
16 Baltagi *et al.* (2003) also argue that the HT estimator is based on an instrumental variable estimator which uses both the between and within variation of the strictly exogenous variables as instruments. More specifically, the individual means of the strictly exogenous regressors are used as instruments for the time-invariant regressors that are correlated with the individual effects, as in Baltagi (2001).
17 This might be a significant limitation, especially for those countries that had more than one European colonial experience. This is especially true for Cameroon and all the former German colonies (Togo, Tanzania and Namibia). One way to get around this limitation is to add another set of dummy variables capturing 'prior colonizers'. However, this option leaves me with another problem – that of a small sample – as a result of the reduced degrees of freedom. Furthermore, this detail adds less to the analysis. Admittedly, including the 'prior colonizers' would add substantially to the results only where the first colonizer stayed for a significant period. This is perhaps true only for South Africa, which had a long Dutch tenure followed by extended British rule, but I have excluded this case from the sample.
18 For instance, Easterly and Levine (1997) and Glaeser *et al.* (2004) find a positive contribution of human capital to GDP growth in their regressions.
19 See, for instance, Sachs and Warner (1997).
20 The variable includes both private and public investment.
21 It would have been consistent to take into account only the year that the last colonizer arrived (for those countries that had multiple colonization experiences), but this detail would not add much to the present analysis.
22 For instance, Glaeser *et al.* (2004) treat human capital as endogenous, while Rostowski and Stacescu (2006) treat both human capital and openness as endogenous in their regressions.
23 The intuition for placing colonial origin dummies in this category is mainly because of selection effects.
24 Based on the preliminary results of the OLS estimation presented above, only the education transmission channel merits further detailed empirical investigation. An additional reason for dropping the independence trade variable (EXP_IND) is to enable comparability of my results to those of previous studies.
25 In addition, interaction terms of SEC_IND (and AYS_IND) with colonial origin were also included in the regressions, but they lacked statistical significance for most of the variables and are therefore not reported here.
26 It may be worth noting that I repeated the empirical strategy employed in this study using a 5-year and then a 10-year panel; similar results were obtained in both cases.

References

Acemoglu, D. and S. Johnson (2005). 'Unbundling Institutions'. *Journal of Political Economy*, 113(5): 949–95.

Agbor, J.A., J.W. Fedderke and V. Nicola (2014). 'How Colonial Educational Practices Helped Shape the Pattern of Decolonization in West Africa'. *International Journal of Development and Conflict*, 3(2) (December): 1–23.

Asiwaju, A.I. (ed.) (2000). *West African Transformations: Comparative Impact of French and British Colonialism*. Ikeja: Malthouse Press.

Austin, G. (2008). 'The "Reversal of Fortune" Thesis and the Compression of History: Perspectives from African and Comparative Economic History'. *Journal of International Development*, 20: 996–1027.

Baltagi, B.H. (2001). *Econometric Analysis of Panel Data*. Chichester: Wiley.

Baltagi, B.H., G. Bresson and A. Pirotte (2003). 'Fixed Effects, Random Effects or Hausman–Taylor? A Pretest Estimator'. *Economic Letters*, 79: 361–9.

Banerjee, A. and L. Iyer (2005). 'History, Institutions and Economic Performance: The Legacy of Colonial Land Tenure Systems in India'. *The American Economic Review*, 95(4): 1190–213.

Berger, D. (2009). 'Taxes, Institutions and Local Governance: Evidence from a National Experiment in Colonial Nigeria'. PhD Dissertation. New York: New York University. Available at: homepages.nyu.edu/~db1299/Nigeria.pdf (accessed 31 March 2011).

Bertocchi, G. and F. Canova (2002). 'Did Colonisation Matter for Growth? An Empirical Exploration into the Historical Causes of Africa's Underdevelopment'. *European Economic Review*, 46: 1851–71.

Bolton, G.C. (1973). *Britain's Legacy Overseas*. Oxford: Oxford University Press.

Collier, P. and J.W. Gunning (1999). 'Explaining African Economic Performance'. *Journal of Economic Literature*, 64–111.

Crowder, M. (1968). *West Africa under Colonial Rule*. London: Hutchinson & Co Publishers Ltd.

Easterly, W. and R. Levine (1997). 'Africa's Growth Tragedy: Policies and Ethnic Divisions'. *Quarterly Journal of Economics*, 112(4): 1203–50.

Engerman, S.L. and K.L. Sokoloff (2002). 'Factor Endowments, Inequality, and Paths of Development among New World Economies'. *Economia*, 3(1): 41–109.

Fieldhouse, D.K. (1966). *The Colonial Empires from the 18th Century*. New York: Dell Publishing.

Gann, L.H. and P. Duignan (1970). *Colonialism in Africa, 1870–1960*. Cambridge: Cambridge University Press.

Glaeser, L.P., R. Lopez-de-Silanes and A. Shleifer (2004). 'Do Institutions Cause Growth?'. NBER Working Paper 10568. Cambridge, MA: NBER.

Grier, R. (1999). 'Colonial Legacies and Economic Growth'. *Public Choice*, 98: 317–35.

Heldring, L. and J.A. Robinson (2012). 'Colonialism and Economic Development in Africa'. NBER Working Paper 18566. Cambridge, MA: NBER.

Julan, D. (2010). 'Institutional Quality and Economic Crisis: Legal Origin Theory Versus Colonial Strategy Theory'. *The Review of Economics and Statistics*, 92(1): 173–9.

Klerman, D., P. Mahoney, H. Spamann and M. Weinstein (2008). 'Legal Origin and Economic Growth'. Unpublished Manuscript. Available at: http://www.law.ucla.edu/docs/klerman_paper.pdf.

Kremer, M. (1993). 'Population Growth and Technological Change: One Million B.C. to 1990'. *Quarterly Journal of Economics*, 108(3): 681–716.

La Porta, R., F. Lopez-de-Silanes, A. Shleifer and R.W. Vishny (1997). 'Legal Determinants of External Finance'. *The Journal of Finance*, LII(3): 1131–50.

La Porta, R., F. Lopez-de-Silanes, A. Shleifer and R.W. Vishny (1998). 'Law and Finance'. *Journal of Political Economy*, 106(6): 1113–155.

La Porta, R., F. Lopez-de-Silanes, A. Shleifer and R.W. Vishny (1999). 'The Quality of Government'. *Journal of Law Economics and Organizations*, 15: 222–79.

La Porta, R., F. Lopez-de-Silanes and A. Shleifer (2008). 'The Economic Consequences of Legal Origins'. *Journal of Economic Literature*, 46(2): 285–332.

Levine, R., N. Loayza and T. Beck (2000). 'Financial Intermediation and Growth: Causality and Causes'. *Journal of Monetary Economics*, 46(1): 31–77.

Levine, R., T. Beck, A. Demirgüç-Kunt (2002). 'Why Does Legal Origin Matter?'. Policy Research Working Paper 2904. Washington, DC: World Bank.

Maddison, A. (1971). *Class Structure and Economic Growth*. London: George Allen and Unwin.

Mahoney, P.G. (2001). 'The Common Law and Economic Growth: Hayek Might be Right'. *Journal of Legal Studies*, 30(2): 503–25.

Mauro, P. (1995). 'Corruption and Growth'. *Quarterly Journal of Economics*, 110(3): 681–712.

Price, G.N. (2003). 'Economic Growth in a Cross-section of Nonindustrial Countries: Does Colonial Heritage Matter for Africa?'. *Review of Development Economics*, 7(3): 478–95.

Pritchett, L. (2001). 'Where Has All the Education Gone?'. *World Bank Economic Review*, 15(3): 367–91.

Quah, D. (1993). 'Galton's Fallacy and Tests of the Convergence Hypothesis'. *Scandinavian Journal of Economics*, 95(4): 427–43.

Rodrik, D. (2002). 'Trade Strategy, Investment and Exports: Another Look at East Asia'. *Pacific Economic Review*, 2(1): 1–24.

Roe, M.J. and J.I. Siegel (2009). 'Finance and Politics: A Review Essay based on Kenneth Dam's Analysis of Legal Traditions in the Law-Growth Nexus'. *Journal of Economic Literature*, 47(3): 781–800.

Rostowski, J. and B. Stacescu (2006). 'The Wig and the Pith Helmet–the Impact of "Legal School" versus Colonial Institutions on Economic Performance'. (Second version). CASE Network Studies and Analyses 0300. Warsaw: Center for Social and Economic Research.

Rostowski, J. and B. Stacescu (2008). 'Impact of "Legal School" versus Recent Colonial Origin on Economic Growth'. In A. Aslund and M. Dabrowski (eds), *The Challenges of Globalization*. Washington, DC: Peterson Institute.

Sachs, J.D. and A. Warner (1997). 'Sources of Slow Growth in African Economies'. *Journal of African Economies*, 6: 335–73.

Solow, R.M. (1956). 'A Contribution to the Theory of Economic Growth'. *Quarterly Journal of Economics*, 70(1): 65–94.

Swan, T.W. (1956). 'Economic Growth and Capital Accumulation'. *Economic Record*, 32: 334–61.

14 Institutional reforms, private sector and economic growth in Africa

Mawussé K.N. Okey

Introduction

The relationship between institutional reforms and economic performance is now the subject of several studies that analyse empirically (Djankov *et al.* 2006) or theoretically (Antunes *et al.* 2008) the impact of reforms on the indicators of economic performance of countries, especially on their private sector. Often defined as all private enterprises, whose capital is majority-owned by private individuals or private companies, the private sector is a powerful driver of economic growth. It is also understood through indicators such as the share of private sector investment in gross domestic product (GDP), changes in foreign direct investment (FDI), manufacturing exports and the evolution of domestic credit to private sector (Ruhashyankiko and Yehoue 2006). Other studies incorporate into the private sector analysis, entrepreneurship, the creation of small- and medium-sized enterprises (SMEs) and the informal sector.

Therefore, institutional constraints to these indicators of dynamism of the private sector can seriously damage a country's economic performance. Through the Doing Business programme, the World Bank provides a quantification assessment of regulations that apply to SMEs in various fields, notably regulations for starting a business, dealing with construction permits, employing workers, registering property, arranging credit, protecting investors, paying taxes, trading across borders, enforcing contracts and closing a business. These indicators, constructed to measure the reform of the institutions, have become fundamental to a successful development and have significant effects on the economic performance of the countries. Moreover, according to North (1990), institutions can be defined as the rules of society, the combination of constraints that shape human interaction between people.

Following North (1990), several studies, notably those of Acemoglu *et al.* (2001), Djankov *et al.* (2006) and Antunes *et al.* (2008), have explored the concepts of institutions and institutional reforms, and their relationship with economic performance. Most of these studies generally tested the hypothesis that differences in capital accumulation, productivity and the level of income per capita are basically due to differences in social infrastructure across countries. Social infrastructure means the political institutions and governments that determine the economic environment in which individuals accumulate knowledge, and where firms accumulate capital and produce output. Indeed, social infrastructure favourable to high levels of output provides a good economic environment, promotes capital accumulation, acquisition of knowledge, invention and technology transfer. But some reforms through regulations and laws are often the main driver of diversion in economics (Mylène and Kirsten 2001).

Carlin and Seabright (2008) have shown that the literature on the importance of business climate for economic development is too wide and often contradictory. Moreover, the relative importance of constraints in the business climate varies from one country or group of countries to another. For example in South and East Asia, access to finance is less of a problem than many other constraints are; in Latin and Central America, the tax administration is less problematic than many other constraints, and in the OECD countries, policy uncertainty is a less frequent problem than other constraints. The enterprises in South Asian countries do not classify the anti-dumping practices as problematic, but these practices are raised as a major problem in African countries. Analysis of Nabli *et al.* (2008) helps to understand the progress in reforms and private sector development in the Middle East and North Africa. It shows the critical role played by relations between the public and the private sector in determining progress in reforms and their impact on private sector development.

The 2007 and 2008 editions of *Doing Business* provide some results according to which the heaviness and slowness of the formalities creating an enterprise in some African countries, as well as expenses to which those that try to create an individual enterprise are exposed, constitute obstacles to the development of the private sector. According to the 2009 edition, African countries have adopted more positive reforms in 2007–2008 than in any previous year covered by Doing Business and three of the top ten reformers in the world are in Africa: Senegal, Burkina Faso and Botswana. Reforms are also increasing in countries emerging from conflict: Liberia, Rwanda, Sierra Leone and Mauritius. Note that these reforms take place in an institutional environment that is not at all favourable. According to the report by Transparency International (2009), among 180 countries, the sub-Saharan Africa countries and the Middle East are among the most corrupt. For example, the USA, perceived as not corrupt, is at 18th place, while Zimbabwe is 166th, Nigeria 121st, Kenya, 147th, Ethiopia 126th and Cameroon 141st. This report mentions notable advances in some African countries, such as Rwanda (102nd).

We note, however, that even if the business climate indicators are clearly defined and vary considerably from one African country to another, many questions remain about their relevance in explaining differences in economic performance between countries and differences in the size of the private sector. Thus we can ask whether differences between countries in indicators of business climate are a source of differences in economic performance of African countries. If yes, what are the indicators that explain the differences in the more dynamic private sector? This chapter aims to determine the impact of positive changes in business environment indicators of the Doing Business programme and the *Index of Economic Freedom* of the Heritage Foundation on the private sector development indicators and economic performance of African countries.

The rest of the chapter is organized as follows: in the next section, we evaluate the progress in economic reforms and the status of recent economic performance in African countries. Following that, we review the economic literature on the relationship between institutions and private sector growth. The section entitled Methodological approach is followed by the results of econometric estimates of the effects of some institutional indicators on the private sector and the growth rate. In the last section, we draw some conclusions and remark on future prospects for reform.

Reforms, business environment and economic performance of African countries

The Doing Business project, launched in 2002, is studying the situation of SMEs of countries and the regulations that apply to them during their life cycle. Doing Business is also currently one of the standard tools used to measure the impact of national regulations on business activity. The project uses information provided by governments, universities, specialists and evaluation panels. The fundamental objective is to gather the information needed to assess the regulation of business and improve it. This project provides information on almost every African country, of which some characteristics are described in the paragraphs below.

Institutional reform efforts

The report of 2009, for instance, covers ten types of indicators in 181 countries. In 2009 at least one African country (Mauritius) appears on the list of top 25 countries for ease of doing business. Four countries are among the top 10 reformers in the period 2007–2008 (Senegal, Burkina Faso, Botswana and Egypt). The reformers are also relevant in the formal sector through the creation of businesses and jobs, one of the best ways to reduce poverty. However, it is noted that certain countries like Rwanda have made great efforts in institutional reforms. In contrast we note that during the period some reforms have actually made business activities more difficult. The most striking case is the set of reforms in Zimbabwe in recent years. As noted in Table 14.1, the facilitation of business creation and cost reduction of import and export are the areas where most African countries have undertaken reforms. In contrast, fewer reforms were undertaken in the field of business closures. In sum, the implementation of reforms clearly shows the commitment of governments creating strong institutions and adopting sound policies, thus helping to attract investors.

But there is room to do more. African firms still face greater regulatory and administrative burdens, and less protection of property and investor rights, than firms in any other region. Many African countries are on the bottom of the list of rankings on the ease of doing business; thus, nine countries in recent years are among the last ten on the list: Niger, Eritrea, Chad, Sao Tome and Principe,

Table 14.1 Number of African countries that have made positive reforms during the period 2003–2008 in fields covered by Doing Business

Period	Starting a business	Obtaining licenses	Employing workers	Property registration	Getting credit	Protecting investors	Paying taxes	International trade	Enforcement contracts	Closing a business
2003–04	1	0	0	1	2	1	2	2	2	0
2005–06	11	3	0	13	2	2	11	5	5	1
2006–07	12	6	1	12	5	1	7	9	5	1
2007–08	16	8	2	10	12	3	8	14	2	1
Total	40	17	3	36	21	7	27	30	14	3

Source: Author's computations based on the Doing Business data base (World Bank 2004 2005, 2006a, 2006b, 2008).

Burundi, Congo, Guinea-Bissau, Central African Republic and the Democratic Republic of Congo.

A strong preponderance of the informal sector

Table 14.2 presents, in order of importance, the weight of the informal sector in national income for 24 countries in Africa. In Zimbabwe, Tanzania and Nigeria the informal sector contributes over 50 per cent of national income. The rationale behind such dominance is complex. However, when the regulation guiding the creation and the exploitation of a firm is complex, the entrepreneurs give up operating in the formal sector and pursue their activities in the informal sector. In contrast, in countries like South Africa, Cameroon and Botswana, the informal sector is less dominant.

A relatively high number of private companies

According to Esfahani (2000) many developing countries, particularly those with poor institutions, maintained for a long time large and inefficient public sectors during the 1980s and 1990s, with the share of state corporations in GDP remaining around 14 per cent in low-income economies; it oscillated between 8 per cent and 10 per cent in middle-income countries, but declined from 9 per cent to 7 per cent in industrialized economies. During the 1990s, the number of private companies in most African countries was around 75 and 98 per cent of the total number of enterprises. This shows the importance of the private sector in African economies during this period, which coincided with the period of privatization.

Table 14.2 Classification of countries according to the weight of the informal sector in national income

Countries	Weight of the informal sector (% of the national income)	Countries	Weight of the informal sector (% of the national income)
Zimbabwe	59.4	Côte d'Ivoire	39.9
Tanzania	58.3	Madagascar	39.6
Nigeria	57.9	Burkina Faso	38.4
Zambia	48.9	Ghana	38.4
Benin	45.2	Tunisia	38.4
Senegal	43.2	Morocco	36.4
Uganda	43.1	Egypt	35.1
Niger	41.9	Kenya	34.3
Mali	41.0	Algeria	34.1
Ethiopia	40.3	Botswana	33.4
Malawi	40.3	Cameroon	32.8
Mozambique	40.3	South Africa	28.4

Source: author's computations based on World Bank (2004).

Literature review

Institutions, private sector and growth

Traditional analyses of public policy on entrepreneurship focus on the effects of taxation, subsidies and governmental services such as entrepreneurial training and provision of social insurance, risk taking and occupational choice (Hyytinen and Takalo 2003).

Recent studies address roles of institutions and improvement of the business climate through the reforms and regimentations that constitute a major interest of the Doing Business programme. For Chemin (2009), for instance, a less developed legal system constitutes an obstacle to entrepreneurship; the weakness of the legal system reduces the incentive to start an activity because it limits the security of property rights, thus diminishing the possibilities to access credit. The improvement of the legal system is therefore fundamental for economic growth.

The judiciary may affect entrepreneurship through two mechanisms. First, efficient judiciaries that swiftly punish law violations may improve entrepreneurs' confidence in their property rights. Johnson *et al.* (2000) show in a theoretical model that an improvement of the level of laws attracts more businesses towards the formal economy – this process can later be reinforced by a larger fiscal base. Second, the legal institutions can affect entrepreneurship through the credit markets. According to Bianco *et al.* (2005), a key function of courts in credit relationships is to force solvent borrowers to repay when they fail to do so spontaneously. The study explains that poor judicial enforcement increases opportunistic behaviour in borrowers. Anticipating that creditors will not be able to recover their loans easily and cheaply via courts, borrowers are more tempted to default. Creditors respond to this strategic behaviour by reducing credit availability.

The indicators of institutional reforms

Since 2004, Doing Business has been tracking reforms aimed at simplifying business regulations, strengthening property rights, opening up access to credit and enforcing contracts by measuring their impact on ten indicator sets. According to Doing Business (2009), a few years of Doing Business data have enabled a growing body of research on how performance on Doing Business indicators (and reforms relevant to those indicators) relate to desired social and economic outcomes. Among the findings are:

- Lower barriers to start-up are associated with a smaller informal sector;
- Lower costs of entry can encourage entrepreneurship and reduce corruption;
- Simpler start-up can translate into greater employment opportunities.

Investor protection

Castro *et al.* (2004) seek to answer the question of whether investor protection promotes economic growth. They show through a theoretical model that investor protection has two opposing effects on economic growth. First, the demand effect that improved investor protection leads to better risk-sharing, which promotes a strong demand for capital. This effect implies a positive relationship between investor protection and economic growth. Second, the effect of supply works in the opposite direction – better investor protection implies a higher interest rate due to changes in demand forecasts, which in turn reduces the income of entrepreneurs.

Empirically La Porta *et al.* (1998) show that the effect of supply is lower than the demand effect in countries with lower restrictions on capital flows. If investors are not protected, the financial markets fail to grow and banks become the only sources of funding. Therefore, companies fail to reach the size they would need to be competitive because of inadequate funding, which hampers economic growth. The existence of legal and regulatory instruments to protect investors account for more investment decisions than the characteristics of the business (World Bank 2008).

Other studies, such as that of Haidar (2009), confirm that the level of investor protection determines the differences in GDP growth between countries, countries with better protection for investors growing faster than those with low protection. Economies that rank among the best in the index of investor protection impose strict conditions for disclosure of information to shareholders and give general access to information, both before and during court proceedings, so determine the liability of directors.

Using a cross-sectional analysis, Perotti and Volpin (2006) show that the rate of entry of new firms and the total number of procedures are positively correlated with investor protection in areas that are financially dependent. Then countries with greater credibility of political institutions have better investor protection and a low entry cost. The results show also that investor protection depends on both the quality of legal rules and their performance; it is influenced by politicians and bureaucrats. Weak contract enforcement reduces access to finance and creates an effective barrier to entry for poor entrepreneurs.

Contract enforcement

In the absence of efficient courts, firms invest less and reduce their business operations; they prefer to move within a small group of people they know and with whom they have worked together. Antunes and Cavalcanti (2007) examine how differences in the levels of informal sector and per capita income between countries can be explained by costs related to regulations and the degree of enforcement of financial contracts with a general equilibrium model (GEM) with heterogeneous agents and credit constraints. The results show that: (1) costs related to regulations and the level of contract performance do not explain the differences in the informal sector observed in the USA and Europe; (2) for developing countries like Peru, enforcing contracts and costs are important in explaining the size of the informal sector; and (3) costs and contract enforcement are not important in explaining income differences observed between countries. Still using a GEM with heterogeneous agents, Antunes *et al.* (2008)

show that differences across countries in intermediation costs and enforcement generate differences in occupational choice, firm size, credit, output and in income inequality.

Reforms in other areas, such as creditors' rights, help to increase the number of bank loans only if contracts can be enforced in the courts (Safavian and Sharma 2007). A study conducted on 41 developing countries shows that every 10 per cent improvement in resolving commercial disputes will reduce the informal sector share of the national economy by 2.3 per cent (Dabla-Norris *et al.* 2008; World Bank 2008).

Starting a business

The ease of starting a business can be analysed by examining the procedures, time, cost and minimum capital required. Simplification of entry procedures in the formal sector encourages the creation of new businesses. Globally, facilitating entry into the formal sector has led to an increase of about 4 per cent of new businesses (World Bank 2008). There is also a positive correlation between the simplification of procedures for business creation and increased productivity of existing enterprises. An analysis of 97 countries shows that reducing entry costs in an amount equivalent to 80 per cent of income per capita has increased the total factor productivity (TFP) of about 22 per cent (World Bank 2008). An analysis of 157 countries also finds that the same reduction in entry costs results in an increase of about 29 per cent of output per employee (Berseghyan 2008). And, according to the World Bank (2008), competition from new entrants leads to lower prices by 1 per cent in Mexico, reducing corporate income by 3.5 per cent in a fiscal year.

Paying taxes

Economic theory exhibits controversy about the effect of tax on entrepreneurship (Fossen and Steiner 2009). On the one hand, high taxes are a barrier to private sector activity, reducing income after taxes for entrepreneurs, thus discouraging risky projects (Gentry and Hubbard 2000). On the other hand, governments can encourage entrepreneurship by sharing risk through the use of revenues from high taxation to subsidize highly risky ventures.

Henrekson (2007) argues that it is difficult to establish empirically a negative relationship between tax level and entrepreneurship, because high taxes can stimulate self-employment, but reduce the productive entrepreneurship. Djankov *et al.* (2008) reveal that higher effective corporate income taxes are associated with lower investment in manufacturing and a larger unofficial economy. The analysis indicates, for example, that an increase of 10 per cent effective tax rate on corporate profits reduces the ratio of investment to GDP by 2 per cent. In countries where taxes are high and gains seem low, many companies simply prefer to remain informal.

Trading across borders

The Doing Business project measures the procedural requirements, including the number of necessary documents and the associated time and cost (excluding trade tariffs) for exporting and importing. The more time consuming the export or import process is, the less likely that a trader will be able to reach markets in a timely fashion. This affects the ability of business development and job creation. A study of 126 countries evaluated the possible loss from export trade by 1 per cent for each additional day. For perishable agricultural products, the cost amounts to nearly 3 per cent of the volume of transactions for each additional day. Some non-agricultural products are also subject to timing, such as fashion accessories and consumer electronics. Another study found that each additional signature that an exporter must obtain reduces trading volume by 4.2 per cent. For high-end exports, the reduction is about 5 per cent (Sadikov 2007).

Methodological approach

The analytical approach is crucial in determining reliable estimates of the effect of reforms on economic performance. According to Carlin and Seabright (2008), the ability of cross-sectional regressions to reveal which agencies or elements of the business environment really matter for long-term development is severely limited by: (1) the correlation between the approximations that are used to char-acterize them; (2) the problems in measuring the variables characterizing the business environment – the persistence of institutions over time; (3) the limited number of countries; and (4) the lack of credible instruments to deal with the problem of reverse causality, as the measurement errors and omitted variables may be correlated.

In this study, to determine the effects of positive changes in indicators of business climate on private sector development, we proceed first by presenting a theoretical model based on endogenous growth models. Second, we consider empirical equations in which the private sector indicators are explained by indi-cators of institutional reform.

The model

Econometric models for analysing the role of institutions and institutional reforms on economic performance are often derived from endogenous growth models.

Let us consider the Cobb – Douglas production function:

$$Y_{it} = A_{it} K_{it}^{\alpha} L_{it}^{\beta} \tag{14.1}$$

where Y is the level of output, A the level of productivity, K the stock of capital, L the stock of labour; i and t stand for country and time, respectively.

Assuming that the production function exhibits constant returns to scale with respect to physical inputs, it can be written in per capita terms as

$$y_{it} = A_{it} k_{it}^{\alpha} \tag{14.2}$$

where, lower case letters refer to per capita units.

The traditional approach in the empirical literature on growth and institutions is to include a measure of institutional quality in a linearly additive term to a conventional growth regression

$$g = B_Z Z + B_I I + \eta \tag{14.3}$$

where I is a measure of institutional quality and Z is a set of control variables (following from the theory, Z typically includes, at minimum, initial income, physical capital investment and human capital investment). This approach can be theoretically justified by assuming that A is a linear function of institutional quality.

However, the literature on institutions suggests a more complex relationship between institutions and growth. For example, North (1990) shows that institutions affect not only the production efficiency but also the technology employed. This suggests the possibility of some type of threshold levels of institutional quality that must be met before different technology can be employed. Specifically, it suggests the possibility that institutions should be viewed as a variable that indexes the aggregate production function.

$$Y_i = A_i K_i^{\alpha_0} L_i^{\beta_0} \text{ if } I_t < I_0,$$

and

$$Y_i = A_i K_i^{\alpha_1} L_i^{\beta_1} \text{ if } I_t \geq I_0 \tag{14.4}$$

where the coefficients α_i and β_i vary with the underlying institutional state I_t. The quality I_0 is the threshold level of institutional quality that must be achieved in order to be able to exploit the new level of technology (Bernard and Jones 1996).

The treatment of institutions as indexing the aggregate production function in the empirical analysis of growth is important, as it implies the presence of multiple growth regimes and thus parameter heterogeneity (Minier 2007).

Jalilian et al. (2007) assume a simple Keynesian capital accumulation rule according to the following specification

$$dk / dt = sy - (n + \delta)k \tag{14.5}$$

where dk/dt is the rate of change of the per capita capital stock assumed to be equal to the flow of savings (or investment) minus capital depreciation and the growth of the labour force. In this equation, s is the share of gross saving in output per capita, δ is the depreciation of capital, and n is the rate of growth of population as a proxy for the growth of the labour force.

Setting (5) equal to zero, leads us to the solution of the steady state capital stock per capita $k = sy/(n + \delta)$.

Tacking the logarithm of both sides of Equation 14.2 and replacing the solution of the steady-state solution of k into (2) gives the solution of the steady-state solution for output per capita which is as follows

$$\ln(y_{it}^*) = [1/(1-\alpha)][\ln A_{it} + a\ln(s_{it}/(n_{it} + \delta_{it}))] \tag{14.6}$$

where (*) means the value at steady state.

We adopt the assumption of Mankiw *et al.* (1992) that economies tend to their steady state according to the following approximation:

$$\ln y_{it} - \ln y_{i0} = \lambda(\ln y_{it}^* - \ln y_{i0}) \tag{14.7}$$

where y_0 represents the initial level of income per capita and $\lambda = (1 - e^{-nt})$ the dynamic adjustment to the steady state, η is the speed of convergence. From Equation 14.5 we can drive growth in output per capita as follows

$$g_{it} = (\lambda/t)(\ln y_{it}^* - \ln y_{i0}) \tag{14.8}$$

If we $(\ln y_{it}^*)$ replace by the equivalent of Equation 14.4 that gives us a relationship of growth of output per capita

$$g_{it} = (\lambda/t(1-\alpha))[\ln A_{it} + \alpha\ln(s_{it}/(n_{it} + \delta))] - (\lambda/t)\ln y_{i0} \tag{14.9}$$

TFP plays an important role in growth; we assume that it takes the following form:

$$A_{it} = A_{i0}e^{\gamma_i^t} \tag{14.10}$$

where A_{i0} specifies the initial level of productivity and γ its rate of efficiency growth per period. Substituting A from Equation 14.10 into Equation 14.9, the growth rate of output per capita is represented by the following relationship

$$g = \phi_1 \ln A_{i0} + \phi_2 \ln \gamma_i + \phi_3 \ln(s_{it}/(n_{it} + \delta_{it})) - \phi_4 \ln y_{i0} \tag{14.11}$$

where $\phi_1 = \lambda/t(1-\alpha)$, $\phi_2 = \lambda/(1-\alpha)$, $\phi_3 = \lambda\alpha/t(1-\alpha)$ and $\phi_4 = \lambda/t$.

Adding some control variables and qualitative variables and a stochastic term to Equation 14.11 we obtain an econometric model to assess the role of institutional reforms in economic performance.

This specification is similar to that of Temple and Johnson (1995). To take account of regulation, we adopt the Jalilian *et al.* (2007) assumption that the rate of efficiency growth γ varies directly with the quality of regulatory institutions in developing countries.

In this chapter we focus on one component of growth: the contribution of the private sector. Dalamagas (1998) shows that per capita output growth can be decomposed into the rates of growth of the public and private sectors. These in turn depend on the per capita growth rates of private capital and public capital approximated, respectively, by the annual shares of private and public investment in production. That is:

$$g = \theta g^{pub} + (1-\theta)g^{priv} \qquad (14.12)$$

where g is the per capita growth rate, and g^{pri} and g^{pub} respectively denote the growth rates of the private and public sector sizes, respectively; θ is the share of the growth in the size of the public sector in the per capita output growth.

The interest here is to isolate the growth rate in the private sector, with

$$g^{priv} = [1/(1-\theta)]g - [\theta/(1-\theta)]g^{pub} \qquad (14.13)$$

Empirical equations

We empirically analyse the effects of institutional and economic reforms on differences in economic performance particularly in terms of indicators of the dynamism of the private sector through an econometric estimation for a panel of African countries. To do this, following the theoretical analysis above, we use the following econometric model inspired by Djankov *et al.* (2006) studying the effect of regulation on growth:

$$SP_{it} = \rho_0 + \rho_1 RI_{it} + \varphi X_{it} + \varepsilon_{it} \qquad (14.14)$$

where, SP_{it}, RI, X and ε denote the indicator of the private sector development of country i in the period (year) t, the indicator of institutional reforms, the vector of other control variables and the error term respectively. ρ_0, ρ_1 and φ represent the constant term, the effect of institutional reforms on private sector and the vector of coefficients associated with the vector of control variables respectively.

SP, the dependent variable (private sector development), is decomposed into several indicators, taking into account the various aspects of the private sector. We estimate three equations, capturing the private sector by indicators such as the gross fixed capital formation of the private sector (*linvest*), domestic credit to private sector (*lcredit*) and Foreign Direct Investments (*lfdi*).

In this chapter, institutional reforms are measured by annual changes in indicators of the business environment as measured by the Doing Business data of the World Bank, and also of the *Index of Economic Freedom* of the Heritage Foundation. The indicator of institutional reforms, RI, is here proxied by three measures: the first is a binary variable that takes the value 1 if the country adopted the reform for at least one year (*dbreform*); the second is the number of areas, defined by Doing Business, in which the reforms were implemented during one year (*dbnumber*); and the third is the Economic Freedom Index (*EFI*). As a measure of economic reform, Pitlik and Wirth (2003) use indices of economic freedom produced by the Fraser Institute. According to Dreher and Rupprecht (2007), recent studies suggest using changes in the Economic Freedom Index to measure the liberalization reforms (Heinemann 2004). As alternative measures, Amin and Djankov (2009a, 2009b) adopt two indices of the Doing Business reforms. The first is the information encoded as a binary variable that equals 1 if a country implements a positive reform during the year and 0 otherwise; the second is a measure that is equal to (log of 1 plus) the number of indicators on which the reforms have increased during the year. The Doing Business data have the advantage of covering a specific set of policy reforms. The hypothesis tested is $\rho_1 > 0$, implying that institutional reforms lead to private sector development and higher economic growth. X, the set of control variables, includes inflation, public investment (*lpubinvest*), GDP growth rate (*gdp_growth*), corruption and primary school enrolment (*lschool*).

The data and econometric strategy

In this study we use indicators of the business environment of the World Bank available in the Doing Business database over the period 2003–2008 (World Bank 2004, 2005, 2006a, 2006b) to measure institutional reforms. Data on gross fixed capital formation private sector, domestic credit to the private sector, and FDI come from the African Development Indicators statistical yearbooks, and the pocketbook of the African Development Bank (AfDB 2009a, 2009b), and data on institutions and institutional reform come from the database of Doing Business (various editions from 2003 to 2008) and the Heritage Foundation (*Index of Economic Freedom*) over the period 1995–2008. The corruption perception index is from the Transparency International data. Data sources are presented in Table 14A.1. Descriptive statistics of data variables are presented in Table 14A.2. Certain countries, such as Libya and Somalia, are not included in the analysis due to unavailability of data.

Private sector and institutional reforms indicators may be potentially endogenous. Thus the estimators of ordinary least squares (OLSs) are not robust. We use system GMM estimators developed by Arellano and Bover (1995) and Blundell and Bond (1998). This estimation method is suitable for the study because it deals with endogeneity problems and takes into account the dynamic specification. We use lagged variables as instruments. The regressions include the small sample correction proposed by Windmeijer (2005) in order to obtain robust two-step standard errors.

Results and interpretations of the econometric analysis

The results of our estimates are contained in Appendix 14A (Tables 14A.3, 14A.4, 14A.5 and 14A.6). According to these results, the institutional reforms significantly affect the private sector and the differences in economic performance of African countries. AR tests and the Hansen tests suggest that our instruments are valid. Furthermore, all the lagged dependent variables have positive and statistically significant coefficients, highlighting not only the dynamism of the private sector in Africa, but also the suitability of the dynamic GMM approach used for estimating our equations.

Private investment

Table 14A.3 in Appendix 14A presents estimation results of the private investment equation. According to the results, the coefficient of *dbreform* is statistically positive (column 3.1). The result shows that, on average, countries that have adopted reforms in at least one of the areas defined by the Doing Business project experience higher private investment compared with countries that have not implemented any reform. If we consider the estimation using the number of reforms (*dbnumber*) as the reform indicator, the coefficient is also significantly positive (column 3.2).

Other institutional factors also significantly explain private investment. Corruption appears to be negatively associated with private investment (column 3.3), while democracy tends to promote private investment (column 3.2). Our third indicator of reforms (*EFI*) has a positive and statistically significant coefficient (column 3.2). Reforms that allow more economic freedom promote private investment. Thus these findings provide support for the hypothesis that institutional reforms matter favourably for private sector development in African countries. Results also show private investment to be negatively affected by public investment (crowding-out effect) and by inflation, while promoted by FDI.

Bank credit to private sector

The results of the estimation of the equation involving bank credit to the private sector are reported in Table 14A.4. These results show that in Africa, the Doing Business programme and reforms for economic freedom positively explain the expansion of bank credits to the private sector. When a country implements reforms in at least one of the fields covered by the Doing Business programme, the credit to the private sector increased (column 4.1). Similarly, a larger number of reforms increase the credit to the private sector (column 4.2). These results then confirm the hypothesis that Doing Business reforms are relevant in explaining the development of credit to private sector. Other institutional factors are also relevant in explaining the credit to the private sector. For example, democracy positively affects private sector credit. However, economic freedom reforms, as measured by an increase in the overall score of Economic Freedom Index, do not seem to matter for private sector credit.

Furthermore, such inflation appears to negatively affect credit to the private sector, while the effect of Foreign Direct Investment is positive.

Foreign direct investment

The results in Table 14A.5 show that reforms create situations that attract foreign investors. In the FDI equation, the coefficient of *dbreform* is positive and statistically significant (column 5.1). This result suggests that on average, countries that have adopted reforms in at least one of the areas defined by the Doing Business project experience higher FDI inflows compared with countries that have not implemented any reform. Similarly, the number of reforms and economic freedom each has a positive impact on FDI (5.2 and 5.3, respectively).

One of the objectives for the Doing Business reforms is the protection of (foreign) investors. Indeed, these reforms are designed to particularly attract FDI from multinational firms that are sensitive to protecting minority shareholders against the private use of corporate assets by directors and creating conditions that guarantee the protection of the profits of the shareholder.

The growth rate

In order to examine how institutional reforms may directly affect economic growth, we estimate an equation in which the GDP growth rate (*gdp_growth*) is the dependent variable. These results of estimating the GDP growth equation which incorporates indicators of institutional reforms and private sector indicators are contained in Table 14A.6. They show both a direct effect that the reforms may have on growth and an indirect effect through the indicators of private sector development.

The coefficient of *dbreform* is positive and statistically significant (column 6.1). This shows that, on average, countries that have adopted reforms in at least one of the areas covered by the Doing Business project experience higher GDP growth compared with countries that have not implemented any reform. Similarly, the number of reforms positively affects GDP growth (column 6.2) and so does economic freedom (column 6.3). We conclude, then, that apart from their indirect effects through private investment, bank credit to private sector and FDI inflows, institutional reforms directly affect economic growth. These results are in line with Djankov *et al.* (2006) and confirm the hypothesis that institutional reforms and better business regulations have positive effects of on economic growth.

For the indirect effects, we note that private investment positively affects GDP growth, while FDI exhibits a negative effect. The latter finding is surprising, since one could expect FDI to exert a positive influence on GDP growth. Meanwhile, public investment and education have positive effects, while democracy and corruption exhibit negative effects.

Conclusion

This chapter aims to determine the effect of institutional reforms on private sector development and economic growth. These reforms were captured particularly by changes in indicators of the business climate from the Doing Business programme and the Economic Freedom Index. Our results based on econometric panel data estimation show that the reforms have positively influenced private investment, FDI, domestic credit to private sector and the growth rate of GDP. Thus a key to sustaining the recent economic growth of African economies may lie in continued improvements in these reforms. As recommendations, therefore, we propose more refined studies for each African country in order to identify the areas of reforms that might be most helpful in enhancing private sector development and economic growth.

Appendix 14A

Table 14A.1 Description of variables and data sources

Variables	Description	Source
linvest	Private investment: gross fixed capital formation of private sector (as a percentage of GDP) in logarithm	Africa Development Indicators (2009)
lpubinvest	Gross fixed capital formation in the public sector (as a percentage of GDP) in logarithm	Africa Development Indicators (2009)
Inflation	Inflation rate in percentage (using consumer price index)	Africa Development Indicators (2009)
lfdi	Foreign Direct Investment net inflows (as a percentage of GDP) in logarithm	Africa Development Indicators (2009)
gdp_growth	Real GDP growth rate in percentage	Africa Development Indicators (2009)
lcredit	Bank credit to private sector in logarithm	Africa Development Indicators (2009)
democracy	Polity2 that is a combined index of democracy and autocracy of POLITY IV project, ranged from −10 (strongly autocratic) to +10 (strongly democratic)	PolityIV
corruption	Mean score of the Corruption Perception Index on a scale from 0 (most corrupt) to 10 (least corrupt)	Transparency International
dbreform	Binary variable that takes the value 1 if the country adopted the reform at least one year and 0 otherwise	Doing Business database, various editions, 2003–2008: World Bank (2004, 2005, 2006a; 2006b, 2008)
dbnumber	Number of areas defined by Doing Business, in which the reforms were implemented during one year	Doing Business database, various editions, 2003–2008: World Bank (2004, 2005, 2006a; 2006b, 2008)
EFI	Overall score of Economic Freedom Index in logarithm	Heritage Foundation
lschool	Gross school enrollment, primary (percentage) in logarithm	World Development Indicators

Table 14A.2 Descriptive statistics

Variables	Obs	Mean	Std. Dev.	Min	Max
linvest	686	2.34	0.76	−1.30	4.72
lpubinvest	672	1.83	0.68	−2.30	3.41
Inflation	616	25.07	203.17	−14.55	415
lfdi	662	0.47	1.87	−11.49	4.98
gdp_growth	700	4.81	7.58	−31.3	71
lcredit	700	2.46	1.24	−4.13	5.08
democracy	687	0.61	5.31	−9	10
corruption	411	3.04	1.10	0.7	6.4
dbreform	300	0.47	0.50	0	1
dbnumber	300	0.94	1.35	0	7
EFI	644	3.96	0.18	3.16	4.28
lschool	686	4.39	0.39	3.08	5.04

Source: Author's estimations. All the variables definitions and data sources are provided in Table 14A.1.

Table 14A.3 Private investment

	3.1	3.2	3.3
L.linvest	0.721	0.350	0.487
	(11.10)***	(2.43)**	(2.87)***
dbreform	0.025		
	(2.19)**		
dbnumber		0.133	
		(2.10)**	
EFI			1.507
			(2.11)**
Inflation	−0.005	−0.012	−0.005
	(2.54)**	(2.70)***	(0.83)
lfdi	0.064	0.446	0.352
	(2.42)**	(2.38)**	(2.22)**
gdp_growth	−0.013	−0.016	−0.075
	(2.96)***	(1.75)*	(2.10)**
lpubinvest	−0.068	−0.234	−0.081
	(1.76)*	(1.32)	(0.61)
lcredit	0.007	0.181	0.089
	(0.21)	(1.54)	(1.39)
democracy	0.010	0.024	0.006
	(1.17)	(2.30)**	(0.40)
corruption	−0.007	−0.122	−0.149
	(0.14)	(1.33)	(1.97)**
constant	0.883	1.672	−4.131
	(3.60)***	(3.67)***	(1.63)

(Continued)

Table 14A.3 (Continued)

	3.1	3.2	3.3
N	236	236	326
Countries	41	41	41
Instruments	18	40	35
AR(1) (*p*-value)	0.179	0.095	0.030
AR(2) (*p*-value)	0.306	0.412	0.564
Hansen (*p*-value)	0.749	0.428	0.641

Note: The estimation method is two-step system GMM with Windmeijer (2005) small sample robust correction. *L.linvest* is the lagged dependent variable. The values in parentheses are absolute value of *z*-statistics. The null hypothesis of the AR tests is that the errors exhibit no second-order serial correlation. ***, ** and * denote statistical significance at the 1 per cent, 5 per cent and 10 per cent levels, respectively. All the variables definitions and data sources are provided in Table 14A.1.

Table 14A.4 Credit to private sector

	4.1	4.2	4.3
L.lcredit	0.967	0.970	1.000
	(65.19)***	(64.23)***	(11.24)***
dbreform	0.055		
	(2.18)**		
dbnumber		0.023	
		(2.77)***	
EFI			−1.162
			(0.90)
gdp_growth	−0.005	−0.005	−0.007
	(1.75)*	(2.14)**	(1.90)*
linvest	−0.047	−0.044	0.094
	(1.33)	(1.27)	(1.66)*
Inflation	−0.000	−0.000	−0.025
	(0.01)	(0.17)	(2.21)**
lfdi	0.030	0.033	0.073
	(2.56)**	(2.61)***	(2.08)**
democracy	0.005	0.006	0.080
	(1.95)*	(2.27)**	(4.01)***
constant	0.219	0.211	4.494
	(2.32)**	(2.16)**	(0.90)
N	229	229	229
Countries	41	41	41
Instruments	28	27	36
AR(1) (*p*-value)	0.264	0.153	0.077
AR(2) (*p*-value)	0.093	0.255	0.592
Hansen (*p*-value)	0.186	0.260	0.482

Note: The estimation method is two-step system GMM with Windmeijer (2005) small sample robust correction. *L.lcredit* is the lagged dependent variable. The values in parentheses are absolute value of *z*-statistics. The null hypothesis of the AR tests is that the errors exhibit no second-order serial correlation. ***, ** and * denote statistical significance at the 1 per cent, 5 per cent and 10 per cent levels, respectively. All the variables definitions and data sources are provided in Table 14A.1.

Table 14A.5 Foreign direct investment (as a percentage of GDP) in logarithm

	5.1	5.2	5.3
L.lfdi	0.581	0.580	0.484
	(8.49)***	(8.60)***	(7.98)***
dbreform	0.140		
	(1.99)**		
dbnumber		0.080	
		(2.00)**	
EFI			4.060
			(1.99)**
linvest	0.298	0.306	0.157
	(1.89)*	(1.84)*	(0.70)
gdp_growth	0.002	0.001	0.006
	(0.25)	(0.20)	(0.47)
Inflation	0.014	0.014	0.029
	(2.75)***	(2.52)**	(2.53)**
lcredit	−0.124	−0.130	−0.332
	(2.22)**	(2.31)**	(2.21)**
democracy	−0.022	−0.025	−0.036
	(1.21)	(1.32)	(1.94)*
corruption	0.051	0.048	−0.012
	(0.47)	(0.43)	(0.09)
constant	−0.345	−0.354	−15.562
	(0.72)	(0.69)	(2.01)**
N	228	228	316
Countries	41	41	38
Instruments	32	31	26
AR(1) (p-value)	0.026	0.029	0.004
AR(2) (p-value)	0.165	0.130	0.061
Hansen (p-value)	0.484	0.334	0.255

Notes: The estimation method is two-step system GMM with Windmeijer (2005) small sample robust correction. L.lfdi is the lagged dependent variable. The values in parentheses are absolute value of z-statistics. The null hypothesis of the AR tests is that the errors exhibit no second-order serial correlation. ***, ** and * denote statistical significance at the 1 per cent, 5 per cent and 10 per cent levels, respectively. All the variables definitions and data sources are provided in Table 14A.1.

Table 14A.6 GDP growth rate

	6.1	6.2	6.3
L.gdp_growth	0.133	0.107	0.071
	(7.52)***	(6.72)***	(3.43)***
dbreform	1.045		
	(3.58)***		
dbnumber		0.750	
		(4.52)***	

(Continued)

Table 14A.6 (Continued)

	6.1	6.2	6.3
EFI			5.125
			(2.59)***
linvest	1.433	1.506	1.905
	(6.87)***	(6.43)***	(6.53)***
lpubinvest	7.742	7.203	8.033
	(12.52)***	(11.41)***	(9.45)***
lfdi	−0.127	−0.156	−0.037
	(2.29)**	(2.01)**	(0.44)
lcredit	0.363	−0.338	−0.274
	(1.04)	(0.88)	(1.04)
lschool	1.428	0.852	1.140
	(3.03)***	(1.33)	(1.77)*
democracy	−0.130	−0.106	−0.062
	(3.60)***	(3.71)***	(1.25)
corruption	−1.612	−1.728	−1.328
	(7.88)***	(7.69)***	(7.91)***
constant	−16.718	−11.472	−35.911
	(7.41)***	(3.63)***	(4.42)***
N	234	234	326
Countries	45	45	43
Instruments	44	44	42
AR(1) (*p*-value)	0.046	0.044	0.011
AR(2) (*p*-value)	0.297	0.295	0.118
Hansen (*p*-value)	0.558	0.708	0.767

Note: The estimation method is two-step system. *L.gdp_growth* is the lagged dependent variable. The values in parentheses are absolute value of *z*-statistics. The null hypothesis of the AR tests is that the errors exhibit no second-order serial correlation. ***, ** and * denote statistical significance at the 1 per cent, 5 per cent, and 10 per cent levels, respectively. All the variables definitions and data sources are provided in Table 14A.1.

References

Acemoglu, D., S. Johnson and J.A. Robinson (2001). 'The Colonial Origins of Comparative Development: An Empirical Investigation'. *American Economic Review*, 91(5): 1369–401.

African Development Bank (AfDB) (2009a). *Livre de Poche des Statistiques de la BAD Volume XI* 2009. Tunisia: AfDB.

African Development Bank (2009b). *Annuaire Statistique pour l'Afrique 2009*. Tunisia: AfDB.

Amin, M. and S. Djankov (2009a). 'Democracy and Reforms'. Policy Research Working Paper 4835. Washington, DC: World Bank.

Amin, M. and S. Djankov (2009b). 'Natural Resources and Reforms'. Policy Research Working Paper 4882. Washington, DC: World Bank.

Antunes, A. and T. Cavalcanti (2007). 'Start Up Costs, Limited Enforcement, and the Hidden Economy'. *European Economic Review*, 51: 203–24.

Antunes, A., T. Cavalcant and A. Villamil (2008). 'The Effect of Financial Repression and Enforcement on Entrepreneurship and Economic Development'. *Journal of Monetary Economics*, 55: 278–97.

Arellano, M. and O. Bover (1995). 'Another Look at the Instrumental Variable Estimation of Error-Components Models'. *Journal of Econometrics*, 68(1): 29–51.

Bernard, A.B. and C.I. Jones (1996). 'Technology and Convergence'. *Economic Journal*, 106(437): 1037–44.

Berseghyan, L. (2008). 'Entry Costs and Cross-Country Differences in Productivity and Output'. *Journal of Economic Growth*, 13(2): 145–67.

Bianco, M., T. Jappelli and M. Pagano (2005). 'Courts and Banks: Effects of Judicial Enforcement on Credit Markets'. *The Journal of Money, Credit and Banking*, 37(2): 223–44.

Blundell, R. and S. Bond (1998). 'Initial Conditions and Moment Restrictions in Dynamic Panel Data Models'. *Journal of Econometrics*, 87(1): 115–43.

Carlin, W. and P. Seabright (2008). 'Apportez-Moi un Rayon de Soleil: Quelles Parties du Climat des Affaires les Politiques Publiques Devraient-Elles Essayer de Corriger?'. *Revue d'Économie du Développement*, 4(22): 31–87.

Castro, R., G.L. Clement and G. MacDonald (2004). 'Investor Protection, Optimal Incentives, and Economic Growth'. *Quarterly Journal of Economics*, 119(3): 1131–175.

Chemin, M. (2009). 'The Impact of the Judiciary on Entrepreneurship: Evaluation of Pakistan's Access to Justice Programme'. *Journal of Public Economics*, 93: 114–25.

Dabla-Norris, E., G. Mark and I. Gabriela (2008). 'What Causes Firms to Hide Output? The Determinants of Informality'. *Journal of Development Economics*, 85(1): 1–27.

Dalamagas, B. (1998). 'Fiscal Deficits and the Productivity of Public Capital'. *Revue Économique*, 49(5): 1241–268.

Djankov, S., C. McLiesh and R.M. Ramalho (2006). 'Regulation and Growth'. *Economics Letters*, 92: 395–401.

Djankov, S., C. McLiesh and A. Shleifer (2008). 'The Effect of Corporate Taxes on Investment and Entrepreneurship'. Working Paper 13756. Cambridge, MA: National Bureau of Economic Research.

Dreher, A. and S.M. Rupprecht (2007). 'IMF Programs and Reforms: Inhibition or Encouragement?'. *Economics Letters*, 95: 320–6.

Esfahani, H.S. (2000). 'Institutions and Government Controls'. *Journal of Development Economics*, 63: 197–229.

Fossen, F.M. and V. Steiner (2009). 'Income Taxes and Entrepreneurial Choice: Empirical Evidence from Two German Natural Experiments'. *Empirical Economics*, 36: 487–513.

Gentry, W.M. and R.G. Hubbard (2000). 'Tax Policy and Entrepreneurial Entry'. *The American Economic Review*, 90(2): 283–87.

Heinemann, F. (2004). 'Explaining Reform Deadlocks'. *Applied Economics Quarterly*, 55: 9–26.

Henrekson, M. (2007). 'Entrepreneurship and Institutions'. *Comparative Labor Law & Policy Journal*, 28: 717–42.

Heritage Foundation/Wall Street Journal (various years). *Index of Economic Freedom*. Washington, DC: Heritage Foundation/Wall Street Journal.

Hyytinen, A. and T. Takalo (2003). 'Investor Protection and Business Creation'. Discussion Paper 17/2003. Helsinki: Bank of Finland.

La Porta, R., L. Florencio, S. Andrei and V. Robert (1998). 'Law and Finance'. *Journal of Political Economy*, 106: 1113–155.

Perotti, E. and P. Volpin (2006). 'Investor Protection and Entry'. Discussion Paper TI 2007–006/2. Amsterdam/Rotterdam: Tinbergen Institute.

Haidar, J.I. (2009). 'Investor Protections and Economic Growth'. *Economics Letters*, 103(1), 1–4.

Jalilian, H., C. Kirkpatrick and D. Parker (2007). 'The Impact of Regulation on Economic Growth in Developing Countries: A Cross-Country Analysis'. *World Development*, 35(1): 87–103.

Johnson, S., D. Kaufmann, J. McMillan and C. Woodruff (2000). 'Why do Firms Hide? Bribes and Unofficial Activity after Communism'. *Journal of Public Economics*, 76(3): 495–520.

Mankiw, N.D., P. Romer and D. Weil (1992). 'A Contribution to the Empirics of Economic Growth'. *Quarterly Journal of Economics*, 107: 407–37.

Mylène, K. and J. Kirsten (2001), 'The New institutional Economics: Applications for Agricultural Policy Research in Developing Countries' MSSD Discussion Paper No. 41. International Food Policy Research Institute (IFPRI). Washington DC: IFPRI.

Minier, J. (2007). 'Institutions and Parameter Heterogeneity'. *Journal of Macroeconomics*, 29: 595–611.

Nabli, M., C. Silva-Jáuregui and A. Aysan (2008). 'Autoritarisme Politique, Crédibilité des Réformes et Développement du Secteur Privé au Moyen-Orient et en Afrique du Nord'. *Revue d'Économie du Développement*, 3(22): 49–85.

North, D. (1990). *Institutions, Institutional Change and Economic Performance*. Cambridge: Cambridge University Press.

Pitlik, H. and S. Wirth (2003). 'Do Crises Promote the Extent of Economic Liberalization? An Empirical Test', *European Journal of Political Economy*. 19: 565–81.

Ruhashyankiko, J.-F. and E.B. Yehoue (2006). 'Corruption and Technology-Induced Private Sector Development'. Working Paper 06/198. Washington, DC: International Monetary Fund.

Sadikov, A. (2007). 'Border and Behind the Border Trade Barriers and Country Exports'. Working Paper 7/292. Washington, DC: International Monetary Fund.

Safavian, M. and S. Sharma (2007). 'When Do Creditor Rights Work?'. *Journal of Comparative Economics*, 35(3): 484–508.

Temple, J. and P.A. Johnson (1995). 'Social Capabilities and Economic Growth'. *Quarterly Journal of Economics*: 110: 965–90.

Transparency International (2009). *Rapport Mondial sur la Corruption 2009: La Corruption et le Secteur Privé*. Paris: Nouveau Monde Editions.

Windmeijer, F. (2005). 'A Finite Sample Correction for the Variance of Linear Efficient Two-Step GMM Estimators'. *Journal of Econometrics*: 126: 25–51.

World Bank (2004). *Doing Business in 2004: Understanding Regulation*. Washington, DC: World Bank.

World Bank (2005). *Doing Business in 2005: Removing Obstacles to Growth*. Washington, DC: World Bank Group.

World Bank (2006a). *Doing Business in 2006: Creating Jobs*. Washington, DC: World Bank.

World Bank (2006b). *Doing Business in 2007: How to Reform*. Washington, DC: World Bank.

World Bank (2008). *Doing Business in 2009*. Washington, DC: World Bank.

15 Women's labour supply and household insurance in Africa

Sonia Bhalotra and
Marcela Umaña-Aponte

Introduction[1]

A vast literature discusses risk and informal insurance in poor countries in general and in Africa in particular (Dercon 2004). Incomes are low and uncertain, and most households have limited access to credit (Morduch 1995) or to formal insurance mechanisms such as unemployment benefits (van Ours and Vodopivec 2006). As a result, even if income shocks are transitory, they often have irreversible consequences.

Previous work shows how households attempt to cope with idiosyncratic shocks through asset decumulation or reliance upon informal insurance networks (Morduch 1995; Skoufias 2003). However, many households have no assets to sell, and risk-pooling arrangements are challenged by aggregate shocks that impose covariant risks on members (Townsend 1995). Households may therefore need to fall back on the one asset they have, which is their labour. We focus upon women's labour supply, investigating its response in economic downturns and upturns.

Women's labour supply in richer countries is procyclical, rising in upturns when the offered wage is more likely to exceed the opportunity cost of women's time; for example, see Joshi (1981) for the UK, Killingsworth and Heckman (1987) for the USA and Darby *et al.* (2001) for other OECD countries. There are no stylized facts regarding the cyclicality of women's work in poorer countries.

We use a micro-dataset of unprecedented scope in this literature that contains comparable information on 0.4 million ever-married women (and a further 0.05 million never-married women), from sub-Saharan Africa, of age 20–49 at the date of survey. The data include 75 survey rounds conducted in 30 countries across 20 years, 1987–2006. The micro-data are merged by country and year of interview with cross-country panel data on income (gross domestic product, GDP) and other relevant macroeconomic variables.

The macro-panel is exploited to create country–year specific indicators of the state of the business cycle. In line with a wider literature (Ruhm 2000), we use the words 'recession' and 'cycle' to refer to deviations of GDP from a country-specific trend. The micro-data are exploited to investigate heterogeneity in the response parameters predicted by theory; for example, with respect to wealth and the stage of the life cycle (Gruber and Cullen 1996; Attanasio *et al.* 2005). We report a range of specifications designed to explore robustness of the estimates to controls for trended unobservables and country–year varying shocks.

Our main finding is that economic fluctuations are mirrored in significant fluctuations in women's work. Our estimates predict that a one-standard-deviation change in GDP (3.84 per cent) in the estimation sample results in a 0.27 per cent change in women's employment. There is thus no evidence that women are able to insure household earnings. Although there is variation across countries in Africa, the average tendency is for African women to fall out of paid employment in recessions, to the more vulnerable position of being self-employed or unemployed. This contrasts with Asia and Latin America (Bhalotra and Umaña-Aponte 2010). Amongst possible explanations for this difference are that African couples are likely to pool their earnings (Udry 1996), that opportunities for paid employment are more limited and that aggregate income variation is more closely tied to rainfall variation, with the implication that income shocks strike the sector where women most naturally seek employment.

Studies of the effects of macroeconomic crises on poverty in poorer countries have paid limited attention to the mediating influence of labour market dynamics (Fallon and Lucas 2002; Skoufias 2003; Conceição *et al.* 2009). This is topical given the ongoing world recession, thought to be the worst since the Great Depression. Growth in developing countries was 1.2 per cent in 2009, compared with 5.6 per cent in 2008 (World Bank 2010).[2] It has wider relevance given that developing countries are routinely ravaged by crises stimulated by natural disasters, wars, debt, commodity price shocks, financial collapse and the spread of HIV/AIDS. This study is therefore more broadly relevant to growing interest in the effects of income volatility in poor countries (Koren and Tenreyro 2007). The literature on household insurance mechanisms in developing countries has considered child labour as an insurance mechanism (Jacoby and Skoufias 1997; Skoufias 2003), but it contains relatively limited investigation of the role of changes in women's labour supply.

Background

The motivating hypothesis is rooted in a literature on the added worker effect (AWE) that originated around the Great Depression (see Humphrey 1940; Woytinsky 1940) and that casts married women as secondary workers who temporarily increase labour supply when their husbands suffer unemployment. In Africa, where most people have no access to unemployment insurance and limited access to credit, we may expect that subsistence constraints are more likely to bind following job loss and to stimulate an increase in women's labour supply. In fact recessions will make it hard for women to find jobs but, relative to richer countries, poor country labour markets are characterized by a large informal sector in which entry (and exit) barriers and search costs are low (Basu *et al.* 2000).

Data and descriptive statistics

Data

The micro-data are assimilated from 75 demographic and health surveys (DHS 2012) conducted using a similar questionnaire in 30 African countries between 1986 and 2006. The data contain repeated cross-sections that are exploited to analyse within-country variation in women's work as a function of GDP. The micro-data are merged by country and year of interview with country panel data on GDP per capita in constant prices. Definitions and sources of all variables are in Appendix 15B.

The surveys were not designed to study labour market behaviour, but they query employment, providing unique cross-country micro-data on employment. The potential sample contains 590,495 observations at the woman–year level.[3] Countries and survey years in the sample are in Table 15.1, where it is clear that six countries have only a single survey round. These countries do not contribute to the main results, which are estimated on deviations from country-means across multiple survey rounds.

The surveys interview all women of reproductive age, which is set at 15–49 years in most of the surveys. To allow for the possibility that women are not in the labour force because they have remained in education, we excluded women younger than 20 at the time of the survey. There are no data on hours of work or wages. Information on years of education is used to construct dummy variables indicating whether the individual is uneducated (none), has some education, but less than secondary (some), or has completed secondary or higher education (high). A household wealth index is constructed using data on ownership of assets for each country and this is used to create indicators for the quartile of the wealth distribution that the household falls into (see Appendix 15B).

Descriptive statistics

This section profiles women's employment in Africa (see Table 15.2). On average, 64.4 per cent of women work compared with about 98.6 per cent of men. As many as 50 per cent of all African women are self-employed, and just 11.6 per cent are in paid employment. Agricultural employment, at 39 per cent, dominates non-agricultural employment, which occupies 32 per cent of women. The employment rate of unmarried women is about 7 percentage points higher than that of married women and about 3.4 percentage points lower if there is at least one child under the age of five in the household. Employment rates are increasing in age, possibly reflecting the fact that younger women are more likely to have young children at home. Employment is increasing in women's education and, in contrast to the case in Asia and Latin America, is also increasing in their partner's education and largely invariant with respect to household wealth. The pooled and the between-country relationships between women's work and GDP in Africa are negative, but a slightly larger percentage of women are employed in booms (65 per cent) as opposed to recessions (61 per cent). Overall, there is no

Table 15.1 African countries by region and subregion, observations, rounds and years of interview

Country / region	Acronym	Total obs.	Percentage obs.	No. of surveys	ln(GDP)*	Years of interview
West Africa						
Benin	BJ	29,504	1.7	3	12.6	1996, 2001, 2006
Burkina Faso	BF	25,276	1.4	3	12.23	1992/93, 1998/99, 2003
Côte d'Ivoire	CI	11,139	0.6	2	13.34	1994, 1998/99
Ghana	GH	19,584	1.1	4	12.36	1988, 1993, 1998, 2003
Guinea	GN	14,707	0.8	2	12.8	1999, 2005
Mali	ML	40,336	2.3	4	12.36	1987, 1995/96, 2001, 2006
Niger	NI	23,303	1.3	3	12.08	1992, 1998, 2006
Nigeria	NG	26,211	1.5	3	12.82	1990, 1999, 2003
Senegal	SN	33,920	1.9	4	13.02	1986, 1992/93, 1997, 2005
Togo	TG	11,929	0.7	2	12.43	1988, 1998
Central Africa						
CAR	CF	5,884	0.3	1	12.42	1994/95
Cameroon	CM	20,028	1.1	3	13.42	1991, 1998, 2004
Chad	TD	13,539	0.8	2	12.15	1996/97, 2004
Congo	CG	7,051	0.4	1	13.89	2005
Gabon	GA	6,183	0.3	1	15.32	2000
East Africa						
Burundi	BU	3,970	0.2	1	11.72	1987
Comoros	KM	3,050	0.2	1	12.88	1996
Ethiopia	ET	29,437	1.7	2	11.68	2000, 2005
Kenya	KE	30,766	1.7	4	12.95	1989, 1993, 1998, 2003
Madagascar	MD	21,269	1.2	3	12.39	1992, 1997, 2003/2004
Malawi	MW	29,767	1.7	3	11.84	1992, 2000, 2004
Mozambique	MZ	21,197	1.2	2	12.28	1997, 2003
Rwanda	RW	28,293	1.6	3	12.38	1992, 2000, 2005
Tanzania	TZ	27,687	1.6	3	12.51	1992, 1996, 2004
Uganda	UG	27,577	1.6	4	12.24	1988, 1995, 2000/01, 2006
Zambia	ZM	22,739	1.3	3	12.75	1992, 1996, 2001/02
Zimbabwe	ZW	25,143	1.4	4	13.28	1988, 1994, 1999, 2005/2006
Southern Africa						
Lesotho	LS	7,095	0.4	1	12.95	2004
Namibia	NM	12,176	0.7	2	14.4	1992, 2000
South Africa	ZA	11,735	0.7	1	14.95	1998
Total	30	590,495	33.2	75	12.79	

Source: Demographic and Health Surveys, DHS (raw data). Authors' calculations.

Note: *Mean ln(GDP), 1986–2006.

Table 15.2 Employment status and individual characteristics of African women in the sample

	All women	Employment status	
		Not working	Working
Occupation			
Not working	29.1		
Agriculture	39.2		
Non-agriculture	31.8		
Type of work			
Not working	38.3		
Self-employed	50.1		
Paid employee	11.6		
Total	100	35.6	64.4
Age			
20–24	20.5	44	56
25–35	46	35.6	64.5
36 +	33.6	30.6	69.4
Education			
None	52.2	36.4	63.6
Some	44.2	35.3	64.7
Complete	3.6	28.3	71.7
Partners' education			
None	43.4	37	63
Some	48	34.8	65.2
Complete	8.6	33.5	66.5
Wealth quartiles			
1	38.2	36.9	63.1
2	21.4	33.7	66.3
3	20.9	35	65
4	19.5	35.9	64.1
Area			
Urban	26.4	37.7	62.3
Rural	73.6	34.9	65.1
Marital status			
Not married	11	29.7	70.3
Married	89	36.3	63.7
Children under 5 in HH			
No	22.7	33	67
Yes	77.3	36.4	63.6
log(GDP p.c.) quintile			
1	51	35.7	64.3
2	24.8	24.6	75.4
3	19.4	46	54
4	1.1	29.3	70.7
5	3.8	55.2	44.8
Asymmetry			
Booms (dlgdp>0)	78.2	34.6	65.4
Recessions (dlgdp>0)	21.8	39.2	60.8

Source: Demographic and Health Surveys, DHS (raw data). Authors' calculations.

Notes: Sample of women 20–49 years old at interview. Marital status is recorded at the time of survey. 'Some' education is greater than zero but less than secondary. dlgdp is the change in logs.

clear evidence in the descriptive statistics to suggest that women's workforce participation is stimulated by poverty or unemployment shocks.

Model specification and results

Studies of the AWE have tended to model women's work participation as a function of the labour market status of their husbands (Lundberg 1985; Stephens 2002), but this encounters endogeneity and selection problems (Gruber and Cullen 1996). We avoid these by modelling women's employment as a function of the business cycle. However, this does mean that we do not directly estimate AWEs (because we do not model the husband's employment status) but, rather, we characterize cyclicality in women's employment, which will involve both supply and demand factors.

The dependent variable in the analysis is an indicator for whether the woman reports working in the week of the survey.[4] Since employment in developing countries exhibits considerable seasonal variability, the pattern of which may differ across space and time, we control in all specifications for the quarter of interview of the individual woman. We also adjust annual GDP data by the month of interview of the woman so that, for every woman, GDP refers to GDP in the 12 months preceding her month of interview.

The data are micro-data 'nested' within a short country panel. The baseline model incorporates country-fixed effects and trends, and consistently allows heterogeneity in the income effect by education (see Baseline specification). So as to evaluate the labour supply behaviour of women who have relatively limited alternative sources of insurance, we exploit availability of individual data to model interactions of aggregate income with proxies for the wealth and the consumption commitments of women (see Gradients of the relationship). We then investigate cyclical employment transitions across sectors (see Employment transitions). The results are subject to a range of robustness checks (see Specification checks). The findings are woven into the discussion of methods that follows.

Baseline specification

Individual employment is regressed upon country-specific log income (Y_{ct}), controlling for individual characteristics, country-fixed effects and country-specific trends:

$$L_{ict} = \alpha + \beta Y_{ct} + X_{ict}\gamma + Z_{ct}\theta + \eta_c + \delta_{1c}t + \varepsilon_{ict}, \tag{15.1}$$

L_{ict} is an indicator for whether woman i from country c reports employment when interviewed in year t. Country dummies comprehensively capture persistent institutional and cultural determinants of women's work, so that time-invariant omitted variables will not bias the estimates even if they are correlated with the explanatory variables. The country-level panel is unbalanced and contains irregular time intervals between observations once it is matched into the micro-data because the number of surveys and the spacing between surveys varies across countries. The within-groups estimator is robust to this (unlike the first difference estimator) as it simply translates each observation into deviations from the country mean. The distance between observations (typically quinquennial) diminishes serial correlation in the errors. Country trends control for trended unobservables, including trends in GDP. Therefore, our variable of interest Y_{ct} captures the effect of deviations of GDP from its trend (that is, the cycle).

Controls, X and Z, for individual heterogeneity include dummy variables for the woman's age cohort (20–24, 25–35, 36+), her education (none, some, high), her current marital status, her partner's education if she is currently married, whether she is the household head, the season of her interview, her rural/urban location, the wealth quartile of her household and the number of children in the household under the age of five. Z includes the share of women of working age in the population and the inverse of the urbanization rate. These are not displayed in Equation 15.1), but we also include interactions of income with the index woman's education.

We estimate linear probability models (LPM) and adjust the standard errors for heteroscedasticity. The LPM is expected to behave well, as the mean of the dependent variable is close to 0.5. We nevertheless checked that there were few (1.2 per cent) predictions outside the 0–1 range, and that the marginal effect from a probit (0.067) is almost identical to the LPM coefficient. A number of alternative specifications are investigated below. The estimation sample pools data from the 23 African countries with at least two survey rounds. It contains 352,893 women (n), 23 countries (N), and between two and four survey rounds (T).

Results are presented in Table 15.3. We find that women's employment is significantly procyclical (0.07). A recession involving a 10 per cent drop in GDP is associated with a 0.70 per cent point decrease in women's employment. A 1-standard-deviation change in GDP in this sample is 3.84 per cent, and our estimates predict that this would result in a 0.27 percentage change in women's employment. This effect is increasing in the level of women's education. Coefficients on covariates other than income are in Table 15A.1.

Country-specific equations

As the model is linear, the pooled coefficient in Equation 15.1) provides the average treatment effect. To investigate heterogeneity in the income coefficient across countries, we estimate the following country-specific equation for the six countries for which $T \geq 4$:

$$L_{it} = \breve{\alpha} + \breve{\beta} Y_t + X_{it} \breve{\gamma} + Z_t \breve{\theta} + \breve{\delta}_1 t + \breve{\varepsilon}_{it}, \tag{15.2}$$

To benchmark the country-specific results, we present panel estimates of Equation 15.1) using the (smaller) sample of countries for which $T \geq 4$ ($n = 0.110$m, $N = 6$), see panel B, Table 15.3. In this sub-sample, in contrast to the full sample,

Table 15.3 Income effects on women's employment by education, country-fixed effects

	N	Country-fixed effects			
		Women's level of education			
		Total effect (1)	None (2)	Some (3)	Higher (4)
A. The 30 countries with two or more surveys					
lgdp	352,893	0.070*	0.064*	0.075*	0.099*
SE (robust)		[0.023]	[0.023]	[0.023]	[0.024]
Percentage each category (mean)		100	54	42.9	3.1
B. The six countries with 4 or more surveys: restricted sample					
lgdp	110,422	−0.466*	−0.500*	−0.445*	−0.245*
SE (robust)		[0.035]	[0.036]	[0.035]	[0.041]
Percentage each category (mean)		100	48.7	47.9	3.4

Source: Data from DHS on 30 African countries 1986–2006. Estimates are authors' calculations.

Notes: Robust standard errors (SE) in brackets. *significant at 5 per cent. The dependent variable is a dummy for women's employment (mean 0.49). The estimator is OLS. The model includes country-fixed effects and trends, the woman's age cohort, her level of education, her current marital status, whether she is household head, her partner's level of education, number of children under 5 years in household, rural/urban location, number of adult members in household, wealth quartile of her household, the share of women of working age in the population, the inverse of the urbanization rate and seasonal controls; see Equation 15.1. ln(GDP) is interacted with the level of education of the index woman.

the income coefficient is negative, the average coefficient being −0.47. The country-specific estimations in Table 15.4 show that the negative coefficient is driven by two of the six countries, namely Kenya and Senegal. The income coefficient is insignificant in Mali and Uganda, and significantly positive in Ghana and Zimbabwe. The heterogeneity revealed by the country-specific results implies that the sign of the pooled coefficient for Africa will be sensitive to the country composition of the sample and to the strength of controls for regional heterogeneity (as we shall see in the section Specification checks).[5] This is likely to be the case in most cross-country regression studies, whether using micro or aggregate data, but country-specific parameters are seldom explored in cross-country studies.

Gradients of the relationship

We investigated sensitivity of the income coefficient to indicators of alternative sources of insurance (*W*). The baseline equation is augmented to include interactions of income with marital status, partner's education, household wealth, land ownership, rural location and the presence of at least one child under the age of five.

Table 15.4 Income effects on women's employment by country for six countries

	Sub-Saharan Africa					
	Ghana	Kenya	Mali	Senegal	Uganda	Zimbabwe
log(gdp)	10.609	−7.871	0.140	−11.692	0.573	0.449
	[1.598]*	[0.296]*	[0.205]	[2.344]*	[0.335]	[0.086]*
Elasticity	13.230	−15.687	0.236	−24.425	0.856	0.914
Mean(working)	0.802	0.502	0.592	0.479	0.669	0.492
ln(GDP)	12.35	12.96	12.37	13.01	12.26	13.26
Observations	12,393	19,685	29,843	15,306	18,390	14,805
R^2	0.13	0.22	0.06	0.06	0.33	0.07

Source: Data from DHS on 30 African countries 1986–2006. Estimates are authors' calculations.

Notes: Robust standard errors in brackets. *Significant at 5%. See notes to Table 15.3. These are estimates from country-specific time series, Equation 15.2, for the six countries with T ≥ 4.

Table 15.5 Income effects by marital status and partners' education

	N	Marital status			Partner level of education			
		Total effect	Not married	Currently married	Total effect	None	Some	Higher
Sub-Saharan Africa								
lgdp	352,893	0.072*	0.061*	0.073*	0.067*	0.055*	0.078*	0.074*
SE (robust)		[0.023]	[0.023]	[0.023]	[0.023]	[0.023]	[0.023]	[0.023]
Percentage of category (mean)		*100*	*10.7*	*89.4*	*100*	*44.8*	*47.4*	*7.9*

Source: Data from DHS on 30 African countries 1986–2006. Estimates are authors' calculations.

Notes: Robust standard errors (SE) in brackets. *Significant at 5%. See notes to Table 15.3. The specification estimated corresponds to Equation 15.3. ln(GDP) is interacted with either the marital status of the index woman or her partner's level of education.

$$L_{ict} = \hat{\alpha} + \hat{\beta}Y_{ct} + \varphi(Y_{ct} \times W_{ict}) + \omega W_{ict} + X_{ict}\hat{\gamma} + Z_{ct}\hat{\theta} + \hat{\eta}_c + \hat{\delta}_{1c}t + \hat{\varepsilon}_{ict}, \quad (15.3)$$

The striking finding is that the employment of women who own agricultural land is immune to the business cycle. The mean procyclicality identified on the full sample reflects the behaviour of women in landless households. In line with this, the point estimate is larger for urban than for rural households. It is also larger for women without young children and for women in the top quartile of the household wealth distribution, but these differences fall short of being statistically significant. Marital status and partner's education exert no impact on the cyclicality of women's employment (Tables 15.5–15.8).

Table 15.6 Income effects by household wealth quartiles and agricultural land ownership

	N	Household wealth quartiles					N	Owns agricultural land		
		Total effect	First	Second	Third	Fourth		Total effect	No	Yes
Sub-Saharan Africa										
lgdp	352,893	0.075*	0.063*	0.065*	0.072*	0.110*	344,442	0.066*	0.094*	0.027
SE (robust)		[0.023]	[0.023]	[0.023]	[0.023]	[0.023]		[0.022]	[0.022]	[0.022]
Percentage of category (mean)		100	38.4	21.3	21.0	19.4		100	56.4	43.6

Source: Data from DHS on 30 African countries 1986–2006. Estimates are authors' calculations.

Notes: Robust standard errors (SE) in brackets. *Significant at 5%. See notes to Table 15.3. The specification estimated corresponds to Equation 15.3. ln(GDP) is interacted with either the wealth quartile of household or the family's land ownership.

Table 15.7 Income effects by location and fertility

	N	Zone			Children under 5 in household		
		Total effect	Urban	Rural	Total effect	No	Yes
Sub-Saharan Africa							
lgdp	352,893	0.072*	0.098*	0.063*	0.070*	0.088*	0.065*
SE (robust)		[0.023]	[0.023]	[0.023]	[0.023]	[0.023]	[0.023]
Percentage each category (mean)		*100*	*25.1*	*74.9*	*100*	*22.0*	*78.0*

Source: Data from DHS on 30 African countries 1986–2006. Estimates are authors' calculations.

Notes: *significant at 5%. Robust standard errors (SE) in brackets. *Significant at 5%. See notes to Table 15.3. The specification estimated corresponds to Equation 15.3. ln(GDP) is interacted with either rural/urban location or whether there are children under five in household.

Table 15.8 Employment transitions, probit estimations of individual employment status and sector

	N	Marginal effects		
Employment status		*Paid employee*	*Self-employed*	*Not working*
log(GDP)	306,175	0.253*	−0.339*	−0.090*
		[0.013]	[0.027]	[0.025]
Mean		38.3	50.1	11.6
Sector		*Agriculture*	*Non-agriculture*	*Not working*
log(GDP)	320,403	0.166*	−0.112*	0.190*
		[0.028]	[0.027]	[0.024]
Mean		29.1	39.2	31.8

Source: Data from DHS on 30 African countries 1986–2006. Estimates are authors' calculations.

Notes: Robust standard errors in brackets. *Significant at 5%. See notes to Table 15.3. The specification estimated corresponds to Equation 15.1 in text.

Employment transitions

We estimated three individual probit models by employment status or sector. First, we defined the dependent variable to indicate whether the woman is self-employed (50 per cent of women), not employed (38 per cent) or a paid employee (12 per cent). Definitions of these categories of work are in Appendix 15B. The sample and the specification of the independent variables are the same as in the baseline Equation 15.1). On average, recessions are associated with a large increase in self-employment, a smaller increase in non-employment and a decline in paid employment. The average result of procyclicality implies that the decline in paid employment dominates the increase in self-employment.

We also cut the data by agriculture (29 per cent), non-agriculture (39 per cent) and unemployment (32 per cent). We find that recessions are associated with increases in non-agricultural employment relative to agricultural employment and non-employment. Overall, it appears that recessions induce women to shift towards non-agricultural self-employment (Table 15.8).

Aggregate income variation in Africa is closely tied to rainfall variation, and the main sector in which women work is agriculture. We ran a regression of ln(GDP) on rainfall shocks, country and year dummies, country-specific trends and demographic controls. The coefficient on rain shocks was −0.048 in Africa, in contrast to 0.007 in Asia and 0.021 in Latin America, significant at the 1 per cent level in each case.

Specification checks

Sub-region and region-fixed effects

While including country-fixed effects contributes to identification of causal effects by removing correlated unobserved heterogeneity, this reduction in bias is gained alongside an exacerbation of measurement error and a loss of efficiency. For these reasons, Barro (1997), Temple (1999), Pritchett (2000) and Wacziarg (2002) argue that country-fixed effects in cross-country models need to be used with caution; see Durlauf *et al.* (2005). The increase in the noise-to-signal ratio generated by taking differences or deviations from means is greater the more persistent the variable, and income (GDP) is a highly persistent variable (Griliches and Hausman 1986). If measurement error bias were to dominate our estimates, we would underestimate the GDP coefficient. This is pertinent given that GDP in developing countries is often measured with error. For example, it is estimated that GDP data provided in the Penn World Tables for sub-Saharan African countries have margins of error of 30–40 per cent; Johnson *et al.* (2009) show that successive versions of the Penn World Tables produce radically different rankings of African countries by rates of growth between the same years.[6]

For these reasons we re-estimated Equation 15.1), replacing country-fixed effects (c) with subregion-fixed effects (r), using the four subregions of Africa (West, Central, East and South) indicated in Table 15.1.[7] As the time series within-region is longer once countries within-region are pooled, these equations include quadratic subregion trends and year-fixed effects.[8]

$$L_{ict} = \ddot{\alpha} + \ddot{\beta} Y_{crt} + X_{icrt}\ddot{\gamma} + Z_{crt}\ddot{\theta} + \eta_r + \ddot{\lambda}_t + \ddot{\delta}_{1r}t + \ddot{\delta}_{2r}t^2 + \ddot{\varepsilon}_{icrt}, \qquad (15.4)$$

It is useful to consider the potential omitted-variables bias that may contaminate the estimates in this specification, which effectively pools cross-country variation within-region with within-country variation. The omitted variables that will tend to bias estimates of the relationship between women's employment and income are labour market or family institutions; for example, the extent of state-provided unemployment insurance or conventions regarding income pooling. However, in Africa in particular, the country may not be the natural level at which these institutions vary; for example, family norms may vary across ethnic groups that cut across countries. The African regions provide a fair representation of a stable division of people with a distinct history and culture, while country borders within the regions are, in many cases, arbitrary.[9]

Our finding that women's work in Africa is procyclical is robust to replacing country with region-fixed effects (Table 15.9). It is also robust to incorporating in the sample countries with just one survey round which are necessarily excluded when the specification includes country-fixed effects (panel B).

Other specification checks

Our main specification adjusts the annual GDP measure for the month of interview of the index woman; here we investigate how much difference this makes by using unadjusted GDP. The coefficient is now almost four times as large. See Table 15.10.

If families do not anticipate aggregate income variation or there are job-search lags, women's employment may respond with a lag. To allow for this we included lagged GDP in the model together with its current value. The results show that the action is in the first lag and that the long-run effect (the sum of the coefficients on current and lagged income) is the same as in the baseline model (column 4). If we retain only lagged income in the model (not shown), its coefficient and standard error are almost identical to those on current income. This ratifies the estimates from the baseline model.[10]

Table 15.9 Income effects on women's employment by women's education and region. (subregion fixed effects)

	N	Subregion fixed effects			
		Total	Women's level of education		
		effect (1)	None (2)	Some (3)	Higher (4)
(A) 23 Countries (T ≥ 2)					
lgdp	352,893	0.152*	0.186*	0.109*	0.146*
SE		[0.003]	[0.004]	[0.004]	[0.008]
Percentage of each category (mean)		100	54.0	42.9	3.1
(B) All 30 countries (T ≥ 1)					
lgdp	378,145	0.068*	0.111*	0.016*	0.078*
SE		[0.003]	[0.003]	[0.003]	[0.005]
Percentage of each category (mean)		100	52.2	44.2	3.6

Source: Data from DHS on 30 African countries 1986–2006. Estimates are authors' calculations.

Notes: Robust standard errors (SE) in brackets. *Significant at 5%. See notes to Table 15.3. The specification estimated corresponds to Equation 15.4 in text.

Table 15.10 Specification checks

	Unadjusted GDP (1)	Lagged GDP (2)	Quadratic GDP (3)
log(GDP)		−0.115 [0.062]	3.854* [0.513]
log(real GDP pc)	0.215* [0.022]		
log(GDP)$_{t-1}$		0.179* [0.056]	
[log(GDP)]^2			−0.149* [0.020]

Source: Data from DHS on 30 African countries 1986–2006. Estimates are authors' calculations.

Notes: Robust standard errors in brackets. *Significant at 5%. Column 2 shows the baseline model (Equation 15.1 in text); column 3 is run using the specification in column 2.

We next included a quadratic in Y, so as to allow larger income shocks to have different impacts. The results show that procyclicality in women's employment is weaker for larger shocks, possibly because women are more likely to be compelled into distress work at such times.

Discussion

Our main finding is that women's labour supply in Africa is, on average, procyclical. This is, as far as we know, the first investigation of the impact of income shocks on women's employment in Africa. The results suggest that women are not secondary workers in Africa, whose labour supply is primarily motivated by the need to insure household income. Whether or not added worker effects are apparent will depend, amongst other things, upon labour markets and marriage institutions. The common assumption that spouses pool their incomes (Lundberg 1985) has been questioned in Africa (Jones 1986; Udry 1996; Schultz 1999), and, to the extent that men and women have independent financial spheres, we would expect women to behave as primary workers.

We find that the tendency for women's overall employment to rise in upturns and fall in downturns is driven by their employment in paid jobs. We find, consistent with an insurance motive, that women's self-employment rises in recessions, but only amongst landless households. Almost 40 per cent of working women are employed in agriculture, and their employment in this sector is not sensitive to the business cycle (or aggregate income variation in general).

Conclusions

The between-country relationship of women's employment and aggregate income is negative in Africa, but the within-subregion and the within-country relationships are, we find, on average, positive. So, in general, African women increase their labour supply when GDP is above trend and withdraw it when it is below trend. Our estimates indicate that this is driven by recessions inducing women to move from paid employment to self-employment, predominantly in non-agriculture. While the average characterization is useful, country-specific estimates for selected countries indicate considerable heterogeneity in income responses within the continent.

A striking finding in the present chapter is that the employment of women who own agricultural land is immune to the business cycle. This suggests that agricultural landownership by women may play a role in mitigating the effects of income volatility and, in this way, it supports the case for improving women's (agricultural) land ownership in Africa.

Future work might conduct more experimental studies of specific cases and analyse more carefully the role of institutions. A fine extension of the analysis would be to model fertility timing jointly with the timing of women's employment. Further research is also needed on the impact of exogenous changes in the employment of mothers on current and later life outcomes of young children.

Appendix 15A

Table 15A.1 Covariates in the baseline model

	Country-fixed effects and trends
log(gdp)	0.072*
	[0.023]
Woman is 25–35 years	0.091*
	[0.002]
Woman is 36 years or older	0.150*
	[0.003]
Woman – some educ	0.038*
	[0.002]
Woman – higher educ	0.133*
	[0.005]
Partner – some educ	0.035*
	[0.002]
Partner – higher educ	0.016*
	[0.004]
No. children under 5 years	−0.004*
	[0.001]
Married or living together	−0.042*
	[0.003]
Rural	0.062*
	[0.002]
Woman is HH head	0.062*
	[0.002]
No. adult members in HH	0.002*
	[0.000]

(Continued)

Table 15A.1 (Continued)

	Country-fixed effects and trends
HH wealth – quartile 2	0.012*
	[0.002]
HH wealth – quartile 3	0.008*
	[0.002]
HH wealth – quartile 4	0.002
	[0.002]
Percentage of women working age	196.452*
	[13.276]
Rural (% of total) pop.	−9.821*
	[0.717]
Interview was in 2nd quarter	0.006*
	[0.002]
Interview was in 3rd quarter	−0.005
	[0.003]
Interview was in 4th quarter	0.019*
	[0.003]
Constant	6.319*
	[0.744]
Observations	352,893
R^2	0.15

Source: Data from DHS on 30 African countries1986–2006. Estimates are authors' calculations.

Notes: Robust standard errors in brackets. *Significant at 5%. Results are from the baseline model (Equation 15.1 in text). HH, household. See Notes to Table 15.3.

Appendix 15B

Data

This section presents further information on the sources and definitions of the variables used in the analysis. The demographic and health surveys are available at www.measuredhs.com, where information on survey design and sampling strategy is available.

• **The Julian and Nepali calendars**: The year of interview was adjusted for two countries. The Julian calendar is 7 years and 8 months behind the Gregorian calendar. The cut-off date for asking health questions is normally in Meskerem which roughly corresponds to September. See Chapter 8 of the 2000 (Central Statistical Authority (Ethiopia) and ORC Macro 2001) and 2005 (Central Statistical Agency (Ethiopia) and ORC Macro 2006) DHS reports for Ethiopia). The Nepali calendar is 56 years and 9 months ahead of the Gregorian calendar. The cut-off date for asking health questions is normally in Baisakh, which corresponds to April. See Chapter 8 of the 2001 (Ministry of Health (Nepal) 2002) and 2006 (MOHP (Nepal) 2007) DHS reports for Nepal).

- **Employment**: Source: DHS. Women are asked the following question: 'As you know, some women take up jobs for which they are paid in cash or kind. Others sell things, have a small business or work on the family farm or in the family business. Are you currently [/in the last 7 days] doing any of these things or any other work? (y/n)'. We define employment as a positive response to this question. In addition, women who work were classified into two categories, paid employee and self-employed using three DHS variables. Every woman was asked (i) whether she worked for a family member, for someone else or was self-employed (v719) and (ii) whether she received cash for this work (v720)[11], or (iii) whether she received cash for her work, or was paid in kind, or in cash and kind, or not paid (v741).[12] As a check on the DHS data, we obtained employment rates as country-level means and showed that they compare well with labour force participation rates for the 15+ population recorded in the World Development Indicators of the World Bank (see our companion study, Bhalotra and Umaña Aponte 2010). The labour force participation rate is defined as the proportion of the population (ages 15+) that is economically active, that is, who supply labour for the production of goods and services.

- **GDP**: Per capita GDP in constant prices, namely year US$2,000 from the World Development Indicators (WDI) of the World Bank (2014). We adjust GDP for month of interview. For example, if a woman is interviewed in December 1992, then she is matched to GDP for the calendar year January to December 1992. If she is interviewed January 1993 then she is matched to GDP constructed as 1/12(GDP in 1993) +11/12(GDP in 1992) and so on.

- **Education**: Source: DHS. We identified cut-off points for the number of years of education needed to complete primary and secondary school by (sub) regions and created the variables accordingly. People complete secondary school when they have 12 years of education in sub-Saharan Africa. For women who do not have a partner at the time of the survey (that is, who are not 'currently married') the indicators for partner's education are set to zero and an indicator for current marital status is included in the model.

- **Wealth index**: Source: DHS. The index is calculated as the first principal component using DHS information on the household's ownership of radio, fridge, bike, motorbike, car, television set, the type of toilet (flush, pit, none) and whether the household has electricity, for each country. Agricultural land was not included in the index as only women who reported working in agriculture were asked about land ownership.

- **Rural population as per cent of total population**: Source: World Bank, World Development Indicators (World Bank 2014).

- **Rainfall**: Rainfall data are obtained from the Food and Agriculture Organization of the United Nations (2012) (http://geonetwork3.fao.org/climpag/agroclimdben.php). We constructed rainfall shocks as deviations from the mean of country rainfall across 1985–2005 excluding the year of interview.

Notes

1 This study has benefited from presentation at the CSAE Oxford conference (March 2009), the IZA/World Bank Employment and Development conference (Bonn, May 2009), the Gender and Development Department of the World Bank (Washington DC, June 2009), the European Society of Population Economics conference (June 2009), the Regulating for Decent Work conference at the ILO (Geneva, July 2009) and CMPO (Bristol, July 2009). We are grateful to Alex Barr for excellent assistance with setting up the data and to David Newhouse, Frank Windmeijer and Jon Temple for helpful comments.

2 Uncertainty concerning the likely impact on women's labour market status is evident in the media, not only for developing countries but also in, for example, the UK and the USA.

3 See www.measuredhs.com, where the data, documentation and reports are available by country. We have harmonized the data across countries and survey years. For example, we have adjusted the dates in the Ethiopia and Nepal surveys for the fact that they follow the Julian and the Nepali calendar (Vikram Samwat), respectively. Details are in Appendix 15B.

4 Current employment is likely to be reported by women with little error. In contrast, labour-force participation and unemployment are notoriously difficult concepts in developing countries where unemployment insurance is scarce and job search is largely informal. The exact definition of our dependent variable is in Appendix 15B.

5 The countries in Africa which show positive $\ln(GDP)$ coefficients (even if it is not significant) tend to have low GDP (Table 15.4) and a high rate of female employment (60 per cent to 80 per cent). This is consistent with our argument that African women are relatively likely to be primary workers (see Discussion).

6 If the measurement error is fixed at the country level then the country-fixed effects model is at an advantage. However, this may be too restrictive a characterization of measurement error.

7 This sort of strategy is not uncommon. For example, Besley and Kudamatsu (2006) use region (continent) rather than country-fixed effects in their baseline model, and Acemoglu et al. (2001), amongst others, include no controls for unobserved heterogeneity in their baseline specification, exploring region-fixed effects in a variant. In the micro-panel literature, there are thousands of individual firms or households that, unlike countries, have no particular identity of interest, and the accepted strategy is to purge firm effects. In the growth literature, on the other hand, including country-fixed effects often absorbs a lot of the variation of interest, especially when the variation is limited, whether because the variable is naturally sluggish or because T is small. The latter is the case in our baseline model.

8 The income coefficient is stronger if instead we use region–year-fixed effects.

9 This literature cuts across history, political science and anthropology. Amongst them the following studies more than make the point. All of the chapters in Cohen (1995) are relevant; but see Aderanti Adepoju's contribution to Section 6. Baud and van Schendel (1997) and Parker (2006) provide an accessible overview. The Centre for International Borders Research (2014) at www.qub.ac.uk/cibr/ provides links to a wealth of material for each subregion; for example, www.qub.ac.uk/cibr/BordersBiblioAfrica.htm. Howard French (2005) provides useful detail for Africa. Multiple authors document subregion-specific cases in a book series, *Arbitrary Borders: Political Boundaries in World History Set, 17 Volumes*, published by Chelsea House (Matray 2007).

10 Recall that the DHS sample contains irregular intervals between years. However, we have annual GDP data and so we use the genuine first lag. A simple regression of income (GDP) on its first lag yields a coefficient of 1 and has an R^2 of 0.996.

11 Available from 1990–1999.

12 Available from 2000–2006. Payment in kind or in kind and cash is considered paid work.

References

Acemoglu, D., S. Johnson and J. Robinson (2001). 'The Colonial Origins of Comparative Development: An Empirical Investigation'. *The American Economic Review*, 91(5): 1369–401.

Attanasio, O., H. Low and V. Sánchez-Marcos (2005). 'Female Labor Supply as Insurance Against Idiosyncratic Risk'. *Journal of the European Economic Association*, 3(2–3): 755–64.

Barro, R. (1997). *Determinants of Economic Growth: A Cross-Country Empirical Study*. Cambridge, MA: MIT Press.

Basu, K., G. Genicot and J. Stiglitz (2000). 'Unemployment and Wage Rigidity When Labor Supply Is a Household Decision'. Economics Working Paper 00-01-11. Irvine: University of California.

Baud, M. and W. van Schendel (1997). 'Toward a Comparative History of Borderlands'. *Journal of World History*, 8(2): 211–42.

Besley, T. and M. Kudamatsu (2006). 'Health and Democracy'. *American Economic Review*, 96(2): 313–18.

Bhalotra, S. and M. Umaña-Aponte (2010). 'The Dynamics of Women's Labour Supply in Developing Countries'. Discussion Paper 4879. Bonn: Institute for the Study of Labor.

Central Statistical Authority (Ethiopia) and ORC Macro (2001). *Ethiopia Demographic and Health Survey 2000*. Addis Ababa, Ethiopia and Calverton, MD, USA: Central Statistical Authority and ORC Macro.

Central Statistical Agency (Ethiopia) and ORC Macro (2006). *Ethiopia Demographic and Health Survey 2005*. Addis Ababa, Ethiopia and Calverton, MD, USA: Central Statistical Agency and ORC Macro.

Centre for International Borders Research (2014). Available at: http://www.qub.ac.uk/research-centres/CentreforInternationalBordersResearch/ (accessed: January 2012).

Cohen, R. (1995). *The Cambridge Survey of World Migration*. Cambridge: Cambridge University Press.

Conceição, P., N. Kim and Y. Zhang (2009). 'Economic and Human Development Impact of the Economic Crisis on Developing Countries'. Working Paper. New York: UNDP/ODS.

Darby, J., R. Hart and M. Vecchi (2001). 'Labour Force Participation and the Business Cycle: A Comparative Analysis of France, Japan, Sweden and the United States'. *Japan and The World Economy*, 13(2): 113–33.

Demographic and Health Surveys (2012). Available at: http://dhsprogram.com/ (accessed: 2012).

Dercon, S. (ed.) (2004). *Insurance against Poverty*. Oxford: Oxford University Press.

Durlauf, S., P. Johnson and J. Temple (2005). 'Growth Econometrics'. In L.E. Jones and R. Manuelli (eds), *Handbook of Economic Growth*, 1 (Part 1): 555–677. Amsterdam: Elsevier.

Fallon, P. and R. Lucas (2002). 'The Impact of Financial Crises on Labor Markets, Household Incomes, and Poverty: A Review of Evidence'. *The World Bank Research Observer*, 17(1): 21–45.

Food and Agriculture Organization of the United Nations (2012). *Rainfall Data*. Available at: http://geonetwork3.fao.org/climpag/agroclimdben.php (accessed: 2012).

French, H. (2005). *A Continent for the Taking: The Tragedy and Hope of Africa*. New York: Alfred A. Knopf.

Griliches, Z. and J. Hausman (1986). 'Errors in Variables in Panel Data'. *Journal of Econometrics,* 31(1): 93–118.

Gruber, J. and J. Cullen (1996). 'Spousal Labor supply as Insurance: Does Unemployment Insurance Crowd out the Added Worker Effect?'. Working Paper 5608. Cambridge, MA: NBER.

Humphrey, D. (1940). 'Alleged "Additional Workers" in the Measurement of Unemployment'. *Journal of Political Economy,* 48(3): 412.

Jacoby, H. and E. Skoufias (1997). 'Risk, Financial Markets, and Human Capital in a Developing Country'. *The Review of Economic Studies,* 64(3): 311–35.

Johnson, S., W. Larson, C. Papageorgiou and A. Subramanian (2009). 'Is Newer Better? The Penn World Table Revisions and the Cross-Country Growth Literature'. Working Paper 15455. Cambridge, MA: NBER.

Jones, C. (1986). 'Intra-household Bargaining in Response to the Introduction of New Crops: A Case Study from North Cameroon'. In J. Lewinger Moock (ed.) *Understanding Africa's Rural Households and Farming Systems.* Boulder, CO: Westview Press.

Joshi, H. (1981). 'Secondary Workers in the Employment Cycle: Great Britain, 1961–1974'. *Economica,* 48(189): 29–44.

Killingsworth, M. and J. Heckman (1987). 'Female Labor Supply: A Survey'. In O.C. Ashenfelter and R. Layard (eds), *Handbook of Labor Economics,* 1: 103–204. Amsterdam: Elsevier.

Koren, M. and S. Tenreyro (2007). 'Volatility and Development'. *The Quarterly Journal of Economics,* 122(1): 243–87.

Lundberg, S. (1985). 'The Added Worker Effect'. *Journal of Labor Economics,* 11–37.

Matray, Senator J. (2007). *Arbitrary Borders Series: Political Boundaries in World History.* Broomhall PA: Chelsea House.

Ministry of Health (Nepal), New ERA and ORC Macro (2002). *Nepal Demographic and Health Survey 2001.* Calverton, MD: Family Health Division, Ministry of Health, New ERA and ORC Macro.

Ministry of Health and Population (MOHP) (Nepal), New ERA, and Macro International (2007). *Nepal Demographic and Health Survey 2006.* Kathmandu, Nepal: Ministry of Health and Population, New ERA, and Macro International.

Morduch, J. (1995). 'Income Smoothing and Consumption Smoothing'. *Journal of Economic Perspectives,* 9(3): 103–14.

Parker, B.J. (2006). 'Toward an Understanding of Borderland Processes'. *American Antiquity,* 71(1): 77–100.

Pritchett, L. (2000). 'Understanding Patterns of Economic Growth: Searching for Hills among Plateaus, Mountains, and Plains'. *The World Bank Economic Review,* 14(2): 221.

Ruhm, C. (2000). 'Are Recessions Good for Your Health?'. *The Quarterly Journal of Economics*, 115(2): 617–50.

Schultz, T. (1999). 'Women's Roles in the Agricultural Household: Bargaining and Human Capital Investments'. In B.L. Gardner and G.C. Rausser (eds), *Handbook of Agricultural Economics* 1. Amsterdam: Elsevier.

Skoufias, E. (2003). 'Economic Crises and Natural Disasters: Coping Strategies and Policy Implications'. *World Development,* 31(7): 1087–102.

Stephens, Jr. M. (2002). 'Worker Displacement and the Added Worker Effect'. *Journal of Labor Economics,* 20(3): 504–37.

Temple, J. (1999). 'The New Growth Evidence'. *Journal of Economic Literature,* 112–56.

Townsend, R. (1995). 'Consumption Insurance: An Evaluation of Risk-Bearing Systems in Low Income Economies'. *Journal of Economic Perspectives,* 9(3): 83–102.

Udry, C. (1996). 'Gender, Agricultural Production, and the Theory of the Household'. *Journal of Political Economy,* 104(5): 1010–46.

van Ours, J. and M. Vodopivec (2006). 'How Shortening the Potential Duration of Unemployment Benefits Affects the Duration of Unemployment: Evidence From a Natural Experiment'. *Journal of Labor Economics,* 24(2): 351–78.

Wacziarg, R. (2002). 'Review of Easterly's "The Elusive Quest for Growth"'. *Journal of Economic Literature,* 40(3): 907–18.

World Bank (2010). *The Global Outlook in Summary, 2007–2011, Global Economic Prospects 2010.* Washington, DC: World Bank.

World Bank (2014). *World Bank Indicators.* Available at: http://data.worldbank.org/ indicator (accessed: 2014).

Woytinsky, W. (1940). *Additional Workers and the Volume of Unemployment in the Depression.* Washington, DC: Committee on Social Security, Social Science Research Council.

Index

For Product Safety Concerns and Information please contact our EU
representative GPSR@taylorandfrancis.com
Taylor & Francis Verlag GmbH, Kaufingerstraße 24, 80331 München, Germany

www.ingramcontent.com/pod-product-compliance
Ingram Content Group UK Ltd.
Pitfield, Milton Keynes, MK11 3LW, UK
UKHW021623240425
457818UK00018B/710